ANGER
AND AFTER

JOHN RUSSELL TAYLOR

Anger and After

**A GUIDE TO THE
NEW BRITISH DRAMA**

METHUEN & CO LTD
11 NEW FETTER LANE LONDON EC4

First published 1962
Reprinted 1963
Copyright © 1962 John Russell Taylor
First paperback edition, Penguin 1963
Second hardback edition, revised, 1969
First published in University Paperback 1969
Reprinted 1971
Reprinted 1974
Printed in Great Britain
by T. & A. Constable Ltd,
Hopetoun Street, Edinburgh
SBN 416 12780 0 *Hardback*
     416 27820 5 *Paperback*

Contents

Illustrations

Introduction

> The novel . . . in England at least has been the
> natural prose form for a creative mind to adopt
> since the time of Richardson.

So, at any rate, said Robert Liddell in his *Treatise on the Novel*,
first published in 1947, and then probably no one would have
disagreed with him. But now one would have to add a vital
coda: until John Osborne. The whole picture of writing in this
country has undergone a transformation in the last six years or
so, and the event which marks 'then' off decisively from 'now'
is the first performance of *Look Back in Anger* on 8 May 1956.
Not that this event was startlingly novel in itself. John Osborne
was twenty-six at the time, which is young but not extraordinarily so; Noel Coward made a similar impact at an even earlier
age with *The Vortex*. What is important about it is the success
the play enjoyed and the consequences this had for a whole
generation of writers; writers who fifty, fifteen, or even five
years before would probably have adopted the novel as their
chosen form but now, all of a sudden, were moved to try their
hand at drama and, even more surprisingly, found companies
to stage their works and audiences to appreciate them.

For *Look Back in Anger* had a *succès d'estime*, a *succès de scandale*,
and finally just a *succès*, It was constantly revived at the Royal
Court, went on tour, was staged all over the world, made into a
film, and in the end even turned up in a novelized version as the
book of the film of the play. It was not just another play by
another young writer, staged in a fit of enterprise by a provincial
rep and then forgotten; it was something much more, something
suspiciously like big business, and for the first time the idea
got around that there might be money in young dramatists
and young drama. Rather in the same way that French film
producers began to feel differently about young directors after
Et Dieu créa la femme, theatres began to feel differently about

young writers, and with a new willingness to consider staging new plays by new and unknown writers came, not surprisingly, the new and unknown writers to supply the plays.

What sort of young writers came, and what sort of plays they wrote, is the principal subject of this book. It has, ideally, more to do with art than commerce, since what matters finally is the plays that get written and staged, not the way that this came about. But commerce, of course, has a great deal to do with art, especially an art, like the theatre (or the cinema, or television), in which a large amount of money has to be spent, and a large number of people employed, to bring to fruition a work which began in one man's brain. Idealists there are now in the theatre, as there always have been, and some of them – George Devine, Joan Littlewood, and others – play a large part in these pages, because they have played a large part in making the British drama as we know it today possible. But even they could not do what they have done without an audience to back them up, a shrewd ability to pay for the failure of some plays with the success of others, and a clear grasp of the theatre as a commercial venture.

So we should not overlook the commercial side of things. The success of *Look Back in Anger* started the movement off, and the success of other, later plays – *A Taste of Honey, The Hostage, The Caretaker, Chips with Everything* – has kept it going. Without these successes it would rapidly founder, but while they continue the hope of finding another success of the sort will induce people to put money into new plays, even if the financial results of doing so are often disappointing. It will serve as an additional inducement to the young writer to look to the stage as an advantageous way of putting his talents to work; where the ultimate success was not so long ago a best-selling novel, now it is a hit play. For writers are only human. Ivy Compton-Burnett once remarked: 'I would write for a few dozen people; and it sometimes seems that I do so; but I would not write for no one.' If there were little likelihood of anything one wrote in dramatic form ever reaching production at all, then most writers would turn to other fields of activity: they want an audience, and, reasonably enough, they want some return for their labours. But if successful production is at least a fair possibility, as during these last few years it has been for young dramatists, then anyone with the slightest desire to try his hand at a play will do so. And this is just what has happened. Not all the plays which have emerged have been good, of course, or even interesting, and the mere fact that a playwright is under forty can hardly be regarded by even the most optimistic as a guarantee of quality. But there is a hard core of exciting new writing in the theatre, almost entirely from writers under forty, and quite often from writers under thirty. They have, moreover, two further distinguishing features: their tremendous variety and patent unwillingness to fall neatly behind any one standard or one leader; and the fact that the great majority of them have working-class origins. The first quality is striking enough: with the great commercial success of *Look Back in Anger* one would have expected a host of imitations to follow, but, in fact, there has never been any 'School of Osborne', and Anger in his special sense has on the whole been conspicuous by its absence. Nor is there any clear overriding influence from any other source, native or foreign. N. F. Simpson's rigidly logical brand of linguistic fantasy may owe something to his admiration of the Rumanian–French Ionesco's fantastic elaborations on phrasebook formulas in *The Bald Prima Donna*, but owes quite as much to *The Goon Show*. Harold Pinter's admiration for the Beckett of *Waiting for Godot* may be appreciable in *The Caretaker*, but only as one thread in an intricate fabric of wholly personal creation. The admiration of Clive Exton for Strindberg or of John Arden for Brecht seems to betoken like-mindedness rather than direct influence, while the influence of Brecht on the John Osborne of *The Entertainer* and *Luther* or the Robert Bolt of *A Man for All Seasons* resolves itself largely into the superficial imitation of a few obvious tricks of organization. And as for an influence of the American 1930s social drama of Clifford Odets on Wesker, that seems historically so improbable that one can only guess it to derive from a chance resemblance in the situation and attitudes of two working-class Jewish intellectuals at the same period in their respective careers. In any case, the extreme diversity of these influences, real or imaginary, tells its own tale: a 'movement' which can encompass, say, *Roots*, *The Care-taker*, *A Taste of Honey*, *The Sport of My Mad Mother*, *What Shall We Tell Caroline?*, *Progress to the Park*, *One Way Pendulum*, and *Serjeant Musgrave's Dance* can be accused of many things (including being too incoherent to merit the name of movement at all), but hardly of conformity or readiness to follow the easy line of the established popular success.

Even stranger in the context of British dramatic history, however, is the second fact about these writers, their predominantly working-class origin. For many years the West End stage has been a middle-class preserve: middle-class writers, more often than not university educated, have written for mainly middle-class audiences. But now things are different. Few of the new writers have been to university – John Arden and John Mortimer are exceptional in this respect – though whether they could any of them hope to escape the university net were they aged about ten now is another matter. Arnold Wesker is the son of a Jewish tailor in the East End, and Harold Pinter, too, comes from an East End Jewish family; Shelagh Delaney, as all the world knows, comes from Salford and did not even manage to scrape into the local grammar school; Alun Owen is Liverpool-Welsh, an ex-Bevin boy turned straight-man to music-hall comics at the time he wrote his first play; he and several others, John Osborne, Clive Exton, and Harold Pinter among them, have worked their way up from the ranks, as it were, after periods spent with varying degrees of success as humble repertory actors. This reversal of a pattern accepted almost without question for several generations is remarkable enough in itself to set one looking for reasons. Why should these people start writing at all – and why should the theatre, of all things, occur to them as the best, perhaps the only possible, medium for their work?

It is always tempting to try and evolve a cast-iron theory at the outset to account for phenomena of this sort, and then proceed, predictably enough, to find it conclusively borne out by each succeeding case one examines. I am not sure that there is any one answer to cover every instance or even an answer that applies to a majority of the writers studied. What I try to do in this book is to study their finished work as it exists, on the stage and on the printed page, and at the same time to give some account of how it came to birth, what the circumstances of its first staging were, and what reasons, if any, the writers themselves put forward for their choice of medium and their continued cultivation of it. I have resisted the temptation also to group them into schools or even by certain communities of interest: it would be easy to draw up an arbitrary list of realists and oppose it with an equally arbitrary list of non-realists, to postulate a school of Brecht or a school of Ionesco and line up writers behind their supposed leader. But this again is bound to lead sooner or later to at least a slight sacrifice of truth in favour of neatness, a readiness to stress what writers have in common rather than what makes them different, which can only in the end do violence to their integrity as individuals, each with something to offer which no other writer can quite match.

As it happens, however, a natural arrangement presents itself, and that is the one I have followed. For since 1956 each year has brought a new wave of writers, and in each case there has been one thing recognizably in common about their arrival, if nothing else. First there was John Osborne and the whole batch of new dramatists brought forward after his success by the English Stage Company at the Royal Court. Then it was the turn of Joan Littlewood's Theatre Workshop at Stratford, E., to come to prominence with Brendan Behan, Shelagh Delaney, and a number of lesser figures. 1959 was the year which really brought the work going on out of town into the London limelight, with Arnold Wesker's *Roots* from Coventry and all that led to. And before the excitement from that had died down yet another group appeared on the theatrical horizon, loaded with laurels acquired in the more enterprising sections of television drama: Clive Exton built a solid reputation on television alone, Alun Owen began on radio and came to maturity on television before returning to new successes on the stage, and even Harold Pinter had to wait until television had enabled him to reach a mass audience without preconceptions before the more conservative West End audience could be persuaded to take serious note of him. In 1962 it was the turn of an Arts Theatre Club unexpectedly resuscitated under the aegis of the Royal Shakespeare Company to bring forward two interesting new talents, David Rudkin and Fred Watson; subsequently Michael Codron continued a similar policy at the Arts and elsewhere, while the major subsidized companies were to be observed competing for new works by new talents if the commercial theatre did not snap them up first.

So this is the order in which we shall encounter the young playwrights, and incidentally some of the important *éminences grises* of British drama – producers, directors, impresarios, and policy-makers – who have helped to make their achievements possible and brought about the theatrical revolution we are still living through today.

We shall meet them in some surprising places, for nowadays perhaps more than ever before drama is not just a matter of theatre, though there is still the feeling abroad that the dramatist needs a definite West End success before he has truly arrived. Today the dramatist has at his disposal not only the theatre but radio, television, and the cinema, and few of the writers discussed in this book have, in fact, confined themselves entirely to the stage, while several have had experience in all four. Even leaving aside those who have started or up to now made their major impact outside the theatre, the established theatre writers have produced a considerable body of work, particularly on television, which clamours for inclusion, and without which our picture of them would be incomplete and distorted. So for the purpose of our study television plays, radio plays, and even in one or two instances film scripts, will be treated on an equal footing with stage plays, entirely on their merits as constituent parts of the writer's complete dramatic creation.

But before the curtain rises on 8 May 1956 there is some scene-setting to be done and one or two forerunners to be mentioned. If ever a revolution began with one explosion it was this, but in what circumstances did the explosion take place? This I shall try to explain in the first chapter, even if it involves reaching as far back into the mists of antiquity as 1951, the Year of the Festival.

PROLOGUE

The Early Fifties

With practically any 'overnight revolution' it turns out, when one comes to look more closely, that the signs were there to be read by anyone with enough foresight and that the revolution proper was only the final culmination of a whole string of minor skirmishes with whatever party happened to be in control at the time. Was this the case in the British theatre in the years before Osborne? Let us see.

At this distance of time it is difficult to recapture the flavour of that now remote era, but perhaps the best way to begin is to take a look at what was happening in London during the previous year. As usual, most of the big critical successes – those which were felt to add appreciably to the cultural life of the city – were foreign. It was, you will recall, Ugo Betti year, when after a belated discovery by the Third Programme he emerged in the West End with three plays, *The Burnt Flowerbed, The Queen and the Rebels,* and *Summertime.* There were also *The Waltz of the Toreadors* (Anouilh), *The Count of Clerembard* (Aymé), *Hotel Paradiso* (Feydeau), *Nina* (Roussin), *The Strong are Lonely* (Hochwalder), *The Threepenny Opera* (Brecht) – and *Waiting for Godot,* which surprised everyone by going on from the Arts to become a commercial as well as a critical success. (Ionesco also appeared unobtrusively in February 1955, when *The Lesson* was a little-noticed curtain-raiser at the Arts, but his real impact was delayed until the coupling there of *The Bald Prima Donna* and *The New Tenant* in November 1956) America, equally as usual, contributed a sizeable portion of our theatrical fare with musicals (*Plain and Fancy, The Pajama Game*) and straight plays of various sorts (*Anniversary Waltz, Gigi, The Good Sailor, The Rainmaker*).

From British authors, there were an unusual number of artless musicals; in addition to *The Boy Friend* and *Salad Days,* which ran throughout the year, there were another Sandy

B

Wilson *The Buccaneer, A Girl called Jo, Romance in Candlelight, She Smiled at Me, Summer Song, Twenty Minutes South, The Water Gipsies, Wild Grows the Heather,* and *Wild Thyme*; there were also a number of forgotten light comedies and thrillers, one of which, *The House by the Lake,* starring Flora Robson, was one of the year's big hits. But what was there which might be supposed to enhance the reputation of the British theatre? Well, there were a couple of good revivals (Frankie Howerd in *Charley's Aunt,* a glittering *Misalliance* from H. M. Tennent) and three notable seasons: the Gielgud-Ashcroft season at the Palace (*King Lear* and *Much Ado*), John Clements at the Saville (*The Wild Duck, The Rivals,* and a capable new political drama, Norman King's *The Shadow of Doubt*), and the Brook-Scofield season at the Phoenix, which offered memorable productions of *The Family Reunion, Hamlet,* and one new play, *The Power and the Glory,* which turned out to be Pierre Bost's French version of Greene's novel Englished by Denis Cannan. But at least Cannan, since *Captain Carvallo,* had been a name to conjure with; he was 'promising' and certainly a ray of hope on the dim theatrical scene. Otherwise it could hardly be said that new drama had much to offer. Two veterans were seen off form, Coward with *South Sea Bubble* and Priestley with *Mr Kettle and Mrs Moon.* Rattigan, the reigning king of the English stage, had *Separate Tables* still running from the previous year, and another 'veteran', Gerald Savory, scored a mild success with a slightly Chekhovian comedy, *A Likely Tale.* Of the 'post-war' playwrights, few as they were, only one, Peter Ustinov, had a play staged, *Romanoff and Juliet,* which though far from his best proved a big success. Fry, the great reviver of that verse drama which people had been expecting to save the theatre for the previous ten years or so, had been silent since *The Dark is Light Enough* in the previous year, and would remain so, translations apart, until *Curtmantle* in 1962. The same almost exactly was true of John Whiting, centre of controversy since his *Saint's Day* won the Arts Council prize in 1951: his *Marching Song* of 1954 had achieved no great success with the public, although some critics liked it, and apart from a couple of television scripts and an abortive out-of-town tour he eschewed drama until *The*

Devils seven years later. The only decisive success of the year on every level, in fact, was almost the most anachronistic play of them all, the novelist Enid Bagnold's glittering and artificial high comedy *The Chalk Garden*, which could have been written almost unaltered at any time since Wilde.

And was this really all? To all intents and purposes, yes. A new surrealistic revue, *Cranks*, by the choreographer John Cranko, seemed to presage a breakaway from the genre's routine theatrical parish-pumpery. A new manager called Michael Codron put on a comedy called *Send for Catty*, but it would have taken quite abnormal prescience to recognize here the future impresario of Mortimer, Pinter, and Livings. A small and struggling company, Theatre Workshop, which had hitherto concentrated mainly on classical revivals and occasional didactic political pieces, achieved the first West End transfer from their East London home, the Theatre Royal, Stratford, with *The Good Soldier Schweik*, dramatized by Ewan MacColl from Hašek. And in April 1956 a new group, the English Stage Company, took over the Royal Court Theatre with the avowed intention of putting on new plays in repertory. Their first production, *The Mulberry Bush*, by the novelist Angus Wilson, had in fact been previously produced in Bristol, and though it got mixed notices it was generally agreed to be interesting and enterprising. Their second was a superior Broadway hit, Arthur Miller's *The Crucible*. And their third was *Look Back in Anger*, which opened just over a month after the management had been installed.

But before this happened one would have been quite justified in regarding the year as something very much like the end of an era. One by one the theatre clubs and brave little try-out theatres were closing (the New Watergate, the New Lindsey, the Boltons, the Q) and only the Arts remained with sufficient facilities to do justice to a difficult new work, when it could find one (*Waiting for Godot* and *The Waltz of the Toreadors* began at the Arts; the only new native play was a rather precious and high-flown poetic drama, *Darkling Child*, by W. S. Merwin and Dido Milroy). But finding new drama of sufficient interest was the main problem, and though new plays by new playwrights did emerge quite frequently, the main defence offered for British drama when it was compared (unfavourably, of course) with what was being produced in America, France, and elsewhere was that really Rattigan had shown himself in *The Browning Version* and *The Deep Blue Sea* to be a major international dramatist and it was only native British modesty which prevented us from realizing the fact. Even the most enthusiastic defenders of this view, however, could not deny that exciting new dramatists had been rather thin on the ground since Rattigan. There had been the post-war revival of poetic drama, led by Christopher Fry, who after a couple of pre-war religious pieces scored a surprise success with *A Phoenix Too Frequent* in 1946 and especially *The Lady's Not for Burning* (1948), and proceeded with a sequence of seasonal plays (*Venus Observed*, 1950, and *The Dark is Light Enough*, 1954) to show that verse drama could be good box-office as well (naturally, the presence of such luminaries as John Gielgud, Laurence Olivier, and Edith Evans in his casts did not harm the plays' chances at all either). But apart from the unexpected reappearance of T. S. Eliot in the London theatre with *The Cocktail Party* (1949) and *The Confidential Clerk* (1953), Fry's championship of poetry in the theatre went more or less unsupported, the appeal of other verse dramatists proving either merely modish (Ronald Duncan's *This Way to the Tomb*) or too parochial (Norman Nicholson's *Old Man of the Mountains*; Anne Ridler's *The Shadow Factory*) and soon most practitioners of verse drama betook themselves to the radio, where Louis MacNeice in particular had outstanding successes with such plays as *The Dark Tower*, *Christopher Columbus*, and *The Queen of Air and Darkness*.

And since this particular revival had fizzled out there had been very little. There was Peter Ustinov, of course, who had been 'promising' since *House of Regrets* in 1942 (when he was twenty-one) and after a sequence of eccentric and personal half-successes like *Blow Your Own Trumpet*, *The Banbury Nose*, and *The Indifferent Shepherd*, had at last achieved a solid success with his satirical comedy *The Love of Four Colonels* (1951), which confirmed critics in the idea that one of these days he might at last produce an unmistakable masterpiece; unfortunately they hoped for a 'serious' masterpiece, while his more serious pieces – *The Moment of Truth, The Empty Chair* – seemed mainly to confirm that his real talent was for grotesque comedy. But at least *Romanoff and Juliet* revived hopes for him; hopes, alas, which despite *Paris Not So Gay* and *Photo Finish* have not yet been justified.

Then there were a couple of older writers who really came to theatrical prominence only in the fifties: Graham Greene, for instance, whose first play, *The Living Room* (1953), though offering nothing very new to readers of his novels, did prove something of a sensation in a West End theatre starved of ideas (rather as his original film script *The Third Man* had done in the British cinema), and who has continued to demonstrate a satisfactory grasp of the playwright's craft in *The Potting Shed* and *The Complaisant Lover*. Another was N. C. Hunter, whose earliest play had been produced as long before as 1934, but who first became a name to reckon with when his *Waters of the Moon* was taken up as a suitable prestige production for Festival year (1951) and packed with stars, headed by Edith Evans and Sybil Thorndike. The same almost inevitable success attended his second play staged in similar circumstances, *A Day by the Sea*, with John Gielgud, Ralph Richardson, and Sybil Thorndike, and his third, *A Touch of the Sun*, with Michael Redgrave and Diana Wynyard. The unkind said that nothing could fail with such casts (an assertion disproved more recently by Enid Bagnold's *The Last Joke*, which ran barely six weeks despite the presence in its cast of Gielgud and Richardson); the kind said that because of the casts assembled the plays themselves had received too little attention. The truth, as usual, is betwixt and between: Hunter's plays are as well put together as any in the English theatre, with good meaty acting parts, lively, literate dialogue, and a real feeling for atmosphere of a tenuous sub-Chekhovian nature (resembling Chekhov, that is, as usually misunderstood by British actors and directors). They even, particularly *A Touch of the Sun* and his latest, *The Tulip Tree*, have their moments of original observation, but basically they are the work of a solid, academic dramatist, and that, though not a little, is perhaps not quite enough.

Now, who does that leave us? On the stage, at least, no one very much except Denis Cannan and John Whiting (the proviso 'on the stage' is necessary, as we shall see later). Denis Cannan (born 1919) has only once, with *Captain Carvallo* in 1950, obtained a success commensurate with his obvious talents and the reason for this is not too difficult to see: since his first play, *Max*, an uncharacteristic stab at intense drama on the subject of conflicting ideologies, he has concentrated, not on comedy of ideas, which is a recognized if chancy English form, but on intelligent farce, which to most British playgoers sounds like a contradiction in terms. *Captain Carvallo* itself is almost as much comedy as it is farce, and therefore more acceptable than the rest, particularly as it introduces a note of seriousness at the end after its witty variations on the theme of the victor wooing the vanquished in the shape of their prettier women-folk. The theme again is, of course, the conflict of ideologies, and the close thematic relationship between *Max* and *Captain Carvallo*, in fact, serves to underline the principle behind most of Cannan's work – one particularly hard for London playgoers to swallow in practice – that tragedy and farce are merely different sides of the same medal. The theme of conflicting ideologies as material for farce recurs in *Misery Me!*, which is based on one of the principal balances in ordinary life – the balance between two sworn enemies which gives meaning to their lives and would be destroyed if either were removed – and on an inquiry concerning the nature and durability of love. The matter was found too weighty for its framework and the play survived barely three weeks in London.

In his two later plays Cannan appears to have learnt the lesson, since in neither *You and Your Wife* nor *Who's Your Father?* is there much suggestion of a 'message'. The first makes two dissentient married couples (one husband is about to run off with the other's wife) try to sort out their problems while held in captivity by a couple of improbable gangsters, and the second involves a snobbish *nouveau-riche* couple in all sorts of agonizing complications when their daughter's irresponsible fiancé poses as a genealogist and offers them some pretty disreputable antecedents, so that when a bishop turns up to claim the father as his long-lost son he is understandably mistaken for a white-slaver and bribed to leave the country. Neither has any great pretensions to penetration of character (never Cannan's strong point); instead they manœuvre their puppet-characters through a series of intricately devised comic situations more in the manner of a latter-day Feydeau. Consequently their sophisticated agility mystified the sort of audience who might approve of basic farce at the Whitehall, while audiences who might have enjoyed them were put off by never quite knowing whether they were supposed to be taken seriously or not. However, audiences are becoming less and less inclined to demand such unequivocal indications from their playwrights, and Denis Cannan may yet come into his own. Meanwhile, however, his main contribution to the theatre has been his rather vaguely defined part in the writing of the Royal Shakespeare Company's corporately devised Vietnam show *US* (1966).

John Whiting (1915–63) was a more complex case: his arrival was more spectacular and his subsequent withdrawal from the theatre more complete, and while Denis Cannan did not make his initial impact specifically as something new in the theatre, Whiting decidedly did. He began as an actor after a period at R.A.D.A., and continued to act after being demobbed in 1945. His first play, *Conditions of Agreement*, was written shortly after the war, and was put away to be rewritten later for television as *A Walk in the Desert*, of which Whiting subsequently remarked: 'The critics said "What on earth is he doing? He's forty something and he's writing like a twenty-eight-year-old." They were dead right, of course. I changed a good deal, but I couldn't get away from the basic thing.' His next play, *Saint's Day* (1947–9), was also put away unproduced for a while, and then he wrote *A Penny for a Song*, a fantastic poetic comedy (in prose, although one or two critics tried to enrol him among Fry's followers on the strength of it) about two Dorset eccentrics, one a blustering would-be strategist, the other a gentle firefighter, at the time of the Napoleonic Wars. This was actually his first play to be staged, in 1951, and though not particularly successful commercially (it did better when revived in a revised version by the Royal Shakespeare

Company at the Aldwych in 1962) it marked him as certainly a writer to watch. Some six months later the earlier *Saint's Day* was picked as one of the three finalists in the Arts Council's Festival of Britain Play Competition, was produced at the Arts to the general incomprehension of critics and public, and then, amid a storm of protest, awarded the prize.

If one looks again at *Saint's Day* now it is very difficult to understand why it should have caused all this fuss – certainly it is no more exotic or obscure than many of the television plays which are now accepted without demur. But then *The Times* drama critic found it 'of a badness that must be called indescribable' and provoked a correspondence in the course of which Tyrone Guthrie and Peter Brook called it 'remarkable' and found 'its passion and its unbroken tension . . . the products of a new and extraordinary theatrical mind', while Peggy Ashcroft and John Gielgud called it 'moving, beautiful, and fascinating'. Both sides in the dispute seem in retrospect to exaggerate. The play, which takes as its theme one of perennial fascination to Whiting, self-destruction, is visibly immature, overloaded with literary and philosophical reference and playing its plot (which concerns an old writer obsessed with the idea that people are plotting to kill him who, with the other members of his household and a visiting critic, is swept into a series of violent actions skirting if not toppling into melodrama and ending in a number of violent deaths) for considerably more than it is worth. It is rather pretentious in conception, sometimes absurd, and yet at the same time it does generate a powerful theatrical excitement if one allows oneself to be carried away by the momentum of the piece and not ask too many awkward questions.

The third play in this group, *Marching Song* (1954), again takes up the theme of self-destruction: it concerns the dilemma of a general offered the choice of suicide or a trial and public disgrace. Feeling he has nothing to live for, he is about to commit suicide, as the Chancellor wants, when he is distracted by a young girl who restores in him the will to live. Should he choose to live, at any cost? To decide this he must explore his own motives, his own pride, and his discovery of a flaw in that pride (he lost a battle because he refused to plough his tanks through a mass of children to victory, for once putting humanity before his pride in military achievement), before he can choose, quite calmly, to die. This emerged as Whiting's most balanced and artistically successful play to date, eloquently written and creating its dramatic tensions very cunningly, even though almost all the action is internal rather than external. (For this reason Whiting calls it 'an anti-theatrical play'.) It is distinguished, it is formidably intelligent, and yet somehow it is all just a little cold and lifeless, just as *Saint's Day* was over-literary and allusive and *A Penny for a Song*, despite its charm and invention, a little lacking in real impetus and *élan*. Their qualities, in a word, are such as could give great pleasure to a properly conditioned audience, but could never hope to take an unprepared audience by storm.

It is significant, in this connection, to compare the reception of the earlier play with that of *The Devils* in 1961, when Whiting returned to the London theatre after a seven-year silence – a voluntary withdrawal, it seems, during which he worked on film scripts, wrote a bitter comedy, *The Gates of Summer* (1956), which never reached London, and one short and insignificant television thriller, *Eye Witness*. In *The Devils*, which draws its subject from Aldous Huxley's book *The Devils of Loudun*, we find precisely the same qualities as in *Marching Song*: great skill in marshalling the material, great intelligence in its analysis and recreation in dramatic terms, and a remarkable flair for eloquent dialogue which only let the author down (as it let Shaw down at a similar point in *St Joan*) when a great emotional profession of faith beyond the scope of cool, intelligent appraisal is needed. But with all its skill and intelligence the play lacks something. In particular the choice of the rather ordinary libertine priest Grandier rather than the possessed nun, Sœur Jeanne des Anges, his chief tormentor, as the central figure seems a mistake, especially as it involves simplifying the motives of the nuns (who are made conscious deceivers over their supposed diabolical possession instead of self-deluding neurotics) to the point where they become not only tiresomely commonplace but in the historical context totally incredible.

The choice of Grandier as centrepiece is obviously deliberate (again, the theme is self-destruction) and the re-distribution of dramatic emphasis consequent upon it is deliberate, but that does not prevent one thinking it basically wrong, since it makes the material seem that much less interesting than intrinsically it is. But nevertheless *The Devils* has been hailed as a masterpiece, or nearly, by most of the critics, and has achieved a considerable success with the public where Whiting's earlier plays flopped ignominiously. *The Devils* was obviously a happy first choice for commission by the recently established London branch of the Royal Shakespeare Company from Stratford-upon-Avon, and Whiting was commissioned to write them another. He also completed before his death an enigmatic one-acter *No Why*, involving (again) a suicide, this time a child's. The audience is now conditioned, and it is sad that Whiting, honourable precursor of the new drama, did not live longer to ride on the waves of its success.

So that was the London theatre between the Festival and *Look Back in Anger*. Television was still finding its feet, and there is nothing much to be looked for there (indeed, the independent network, from which most of the more exciting television drama has come, did not begin operations, even on a very restricted basis, until September 1955). Radio was rather better, and indeed in general the Third Programme proves the brightest spot in a depressing picture: two dramatists in particular, Henry Reed, known to the stage only for his translations of Betti, and Giles Cooper, who gravitated to radio after having a play, *Never Get Out*, produced at the Gateway in 1950 (and later at the Arts), ventured boldly into new territory which would in those days have yielded very little in the way of possibilities for the commercial stage. Reed's work is often nearer the 'feature' than drama proper, as in programmes like the autobiographical *Return to Naples* and the impressionistic *Streets of Pompeii*; sometimes, indeed, as in his brilliant series on Herbert Reeve, Hilda Tablett, General Gland, and the rest (a saga begun with *A Very Great Man Indeed*), it is inspired spoofing of the feature.

Giles Cooper (1918–66) is more relevant to our purpose, however, since all his best works are very definitely 'plays', even though some of them are so conceived as to be virtually unthinkable in terms of any medium but radio. From *Never Get Out*, an elusive duologue between an army deserter and a disconsolate woman with a death wish set in a house supposedly about to be bombed, Cooper specialized in the exploration of strange emotional states in the margin of human experience, sometimes with strongly macabre overtones and generally on the surface at least in terms of comedy. A whole series of progressively more experimental plays culminated in *Mathry Beacon* (1956), a composite picture of the lives of a group of soldiers looking after a deflector hidden away in the Welsh mountains. His characteristic sinister-comic mode was subsequently seen to advantage in such fantasies as *Unman, Wittering and Zigo*, an obsessive tale of a teacher's persecution by his pupils; *Part of the View*, in which a Nigerian governess takes a roundabout revenge on her English employers for their condescension and ironically thereby saves their marriage; *Before the Monday*, in which an innocent and a would-be suicide gradually change places; *Without the Grail*, about mysterious happenings in a mad planter's private kingdom in the Assam hills, and *The Return of General Forefinger*, in which the desire of a general's widow to recover all the statues of her husband scattered round the world is met by a sculptor who secretly makes them himself (the list of plot-situations is wearisome, but it does give some idea of his range). One or two of these, like *Mathry Beacon*, would not work anywhere but on radio; others, like *Before the Monday* and *Without the Grail*, are quite conceivable in stage terms if properly adapted, as *Without the Grail* was by Cooper himself for television. Cooper's original plays for television, however, suggested even at their most interesting (*The Lonesome Road, The Power of Zero*) that he felt considerably less at his ease when writing for anything but the small, specialized Third Programme audience, and this was confirmed by his first stage play for some years, *Everything in the Garden* (1962). A parable about suburban hypocrisy, depicting a group of suburban housewives who blandly accept spare-time work as highly paid prostitutes and then win over their husbands to the advantages of the situation, it suffered from indecision about the ending (three were tried out during its brief run, and for the Broadway production after Cooper's death it was rewritten by Edward Albee), and some intermittent and ill-advised attempts at modishly sub-Pinter fragmented dialogue. The most successful of his later stage plays was *Happy Family* (1966), a weird comedy-drama about a middle-aged family who at home continue to live in their own private world of childhood in the nursery, which made a surprising West End vehicle for those bastions of solid middlebrow theatre Michael Denison and Dulcie Gray. Cooper had ideas, and considerable technical skill; but apart from *Happy Family* he never quite found a suitable subject on which to apply them in theatre, and his most lastingly satisfactory work is still to be found among his early radio plays.

But even in spite of Whiting, Cannan, and Cooper (most of whose best work dates in any case from after the advent of the 'new drama'), the outlook for the young dramatist must have looked fairly grim around the beginning of 1956. There was hardly a straw in the wind, since it would have been an optimist indeed who relied too strongly on the English Stage Company or Theatre Workshop to save the day. Anyway, managers and critics would ask each other periodically, where was the new dramatic talent to be found? And what sort of reception would the public give it if and when it did emerge? – none too enthusiastic if the experience of Whiting and Cannan was anything to go by. Then, on 8 May 1956 came the revolution. . . .

PRESENTED
AT COURT

Enter the English Stage Company

Though in recent years the legend has grown up that when *Look Back in Anger* opened it was greeted with almost universal incomprehension and dislike until Kenneth Tynan in the *Observer* saved the situation with a glowing recommendation, this is, in fact, far from being the case. Tynan was certainly the most unequivocally enthusiastic, but the reception of the play, or at any rate of the playwright, was almost uniformly favourable, and with a couple of exceptions everyone agreed that Mr Osborne was a dramatist to watch and that this was just the sort of thing required to justify the new company's existence.

T. C. Worsley in the *New Statesman*, for example, caught the prevailing opinion very well when he wrote: 'As a play *Look Back in Anger* hardly exists. The author has written all the soliloquies for his Wolverhampton Hamlet and virtually left out all the other characters and all the action. But in these soliloquies you can hear the authentic new tone of the Nineteen-Fifties, desperate, savage, resentful and, at times, very funny. This is the kind of play which, for all its imperfections, the English Stage Company ought to be doing. . . .' In the *Daily Express* John Barber put the same view rather more briskly: 'It is intense, angry, feverish, undisciplined. It is even crazy. But it is young, young, young.' In the *Financial Times* Derek Granger, describing *Look Back in Anger* as 'this arresting, painful and sometimes astonishing first play', said of it: 'Mr Osborne communicates no sense to us that he has taken even three paces back from the work that has so hotly and tormentedly engaged him. But for all that this is a play of extraordinary importance. Certainly it seems to have given the English Stage Company its first really excited sense of occasion. And its influence should go far beyond such an eccentric and contorted one-man turn as the controversial *Waiting for Godot*.'

Even those who had more serious doubts about the play itself found Osborne an exciting new writer. Cecil Wilson in the *Daily Mail* felt that the English Stage Company 'have not discovered a masterpiece, but they *have* discovered a dramatist of outstanding promise: a man who can write with a searing passion, but happens in this case to have lavished it on the wrong play. . . . The repetitiousness cries out for the knife. But through all the author's overwriting and laborious shock tactics, we can perceive what a brilliant play this young man will write when he has got this one out of his system and let a little sunshine into his soul.' The *Daily Worker* agreed, remarking that the play 'starts rich in promise, but let us down with a sickening melodramatic thud', and concluding that Osborne's 'development as a writer will depend on what he looks forward to'. For Milton Shulman in the *Evening Standard*, *Look Back in Anger* 'aims at being a despairing cry, but achieves only the stature of a self-pitying snivel. . . . But underneath the rasping, negative whine of this play one can distinguish the considerable promise of its author. Mr John Osborne has a dazzling aptitude for provoking and stimulating dialogue, and he draws character with firm convincing strokes. When he stops being angry – or when he lets us in on what he is angry about – he may write a very good play.'

Of the three 'quality' dailies the *Manchester Guardian* (as it then was) and the *Daily Telegraph* were, on the whole, more for than against: Philip Hope-Wallace in the *Guardian* called it 'this strongly felt but rather muddled first drama' and concluded that 'It is by no means a total success artistically, but it has enough tension, feeling and originality of theme to make the [English Stage Company's] choice understandable. . . . I believe that they have got a potential playwright at last. . . .' In the *Telegraph* Patrick Gibbs thought it 'a work of some power, uncertainly directed'. Only *The Times* came out decidedly against ('This first play has passages of good violent writing, but its total gesture is altogether inadequate'), in which opinion it found support only in the *Daily Mirror* ('An angry play by an angry young author . . . neurotic, exaggerated and more than slightly distasteful') and the *Birmingham Post*

1 John Osborne

('We shall be very frank about this. If more plays like tonight's *Look Back in Anger* are produced, the "Writer's Theatre" at the Royal Court must surely sink. I look back in anger upon a night misconceived and misspent.').

Then came Sunday, with a generally favourable review from Harold Hobson in the *Sunday Times* and Kenneth Tynan's great outburst of enthusiasm in the *Observer* which ended: 'I agree that *Look Back in Anger* is likely to remain a minority taste. What matters, however, is the size of the minority. I estimate it at roughly 6,733,000, which is the number of people in this country between twenty and thirty. . . . I doubt if I could love anyone who did not wish to see *Look Back in Anger*. It is the best young play of its decade.'

But if most of the critics felt in a vague way that perhaps some sort of revolution might have been set in motion by *Look Back in Anger*, the public was not at first with them. Not that the English Stage Company did not have the average theatregoer's good wishes; its declared aims of being primarily a writer's theatre where new dramatists and new drama could obtain a hearing were sympathetic, and it had made a sound if unsensational start with Angus Wilson's *The Mulberry Bush* and Arthur Miller's *The Crucible*; *Look Back in Anger* was the third play in their first repertory season, to be followed almost at once by Ronald Duncan's *Don Juan* and *The Death of Satan* in a double bill and, a little later, by Nigel Dennis's *Cards of Identity*. So far, so good: two first plays by novelists in their forties, one distinguished import, one play by an established name in verse drama, and one by a young actor in his twenties. These played turn and turn about until early autumn, when *Look Back in Anger* was allowed, more as an act of faith than anything else, to run continuously for some ten weeks until the advent of the theatre's first 'star attraction', Brecht's *Good Woman of Setzuan* with Peggy Ashcroft. By the time this latter had ended its run (which coincided disastrously with the Hungarian revolution) the company was £13,000 in the red, and only a classical revival, Wycherley's *The Country Wife*, with Joan Plowright and Laurence Harvey, put on as a Christmas attraction, pulled them out of their difficulties by turning the deficit into a £10,000 profit. By now the tide had turned: there was time for another profitable revival of *Look Back in Anger*, and *The Entertainer* was already on the horizon, with a firm undertaking from Sir Laurence Olivier to play the lead. The Royal Court as a home for the new drama was secure.

Before we go on to consider how this came about, however, we should go back to explain how the English Stage Company came into existence in the first place. Basically, it was through the happy conjunction of two groups working hopefully towards the same ends. The initial idea of a dramatic company which would in some measure offer a counterpart to the English Opera Group came to Lord Harewood and the poet Ronald Duncan as a result of some work they did together in connection with the Devon Festival. The plans went through various stages – at one time they envisaged merely a series of Sunday-evening performances along the lines of those given by the Repertory Players – but with the addition of the businessman Neville Blond as in some measure financial guarantor of the group it became clear that it would all have to be organized on a much more professional basis, preferably with a permanent company and a theatre of its own. Casting round for a practical man of the theatre ready to take on such a venture, the planners hit upon George Devine – largely on the suggestion of Oscar Lewenstein, who was at that time managing one of the theatres under consideration, the Royal Court. George Devine had, in fact, been trying, with a young television director called Tony Richardson, to set up precisely such an organization for the last two or three years, first on his own, then with the backing of the Stratford Memorial Theatre, envisaging it as a London branch of that company. Both phases of the negotiations had centred on the Royal Court, but finally the price asked was too high and the owner, who had been losing money on the theatre for some time, lost interest in the deal when the theatre suddenly took on a success, the revue *Airs on a Shoestring*.

When Devine was approached with the plans for the new company, he agreed in principle to take it over, provided only that a permanent home could be found for it. The owner of the Royal Court at that time owned the derelict Kingsway Theatre (since demolished), and suggested that the company should acquire and recondition it, which at first they planned to do. A credit squeeze put an end to that idea, however, and since the Royal Court had meanwhile run into a succession of misfortunes, the owner proved willing in the end to meet the company's terms. So the English Stage Company was officially formed, a lease of thirty-four years taken on the Royal Court, and things started moving. Devine's first idea was that there must be many writers in their forties or thereabouts who would be delighted to write for the theatre if not put off by the prospect of having to battle with commercial managements to keep their plays intact. Here, with the solitary exceptions of Angus Wilson, whose play had in any case already been done at Bristol, and Nigel Dennis, who jumped at the chance of adapting his own novel *Cards of Identity* to the stage, he was disappointed, too, by the meagre response to an advertisement in *The Stage* for new plays: only one play of any interest arrived on his door-mat. But that was *Look Back in Anger*.

In the launching, accidentally or by design, of any new movement, timing is all-important, and there is no doubt that *Look Back in Anger* arrived at just the right moment, even if the public were a little slow to appreciate the fact. As it happens, *Look Back in Anger* is the earliest example of a process which has frequently been crucial in the progress of the new drama: the mediation of television between the playwright and his public. Despite notices that suggested that something exciting was afoot, *Look Back in Anger* had not done notably better than its fellows in the first repertory season; when it took over by itself it coasted along for the first eight weeks just below the takings at which it would break even. Then, at the beginning of the ninth week, an extract was shown on television, and takings jumped at once from about £950 for the week to over £1,300, and in the next week to over £1,700, the progress being cut short only by a previous commitment to open the ill-fated *Good Woman of Setzuan*. The time, obviously, was ripe: 1956 was the year of Suez and Hungary, protest was in the air, and the mood of the country, especially that of young England, veered sharply from the preciosity and dilettantism which had been in vogue at the

universities and elsewhere for the last few years to one of grim
political consciousness. In *Look Back in Anger* and Colin Wilson's
The Outsider (published a couple of months later) as well as in
the extrovert, disenchanted novels of John Wain and Kings-
ley Amis, the under-forties, as well as many of the under-
thirties, found a rallying-point, though as subsequent events
demonstrated this era, in the theatre at least, was to prove
short-lived; when the next bunch of dramatists came forward
they turned out not to be playwrights of protest at all, but
meticulous explorers of a multitude of private worlds, and for a
follow-up to Osborne and Anger the Royal Court could only
find a feeble commercial imitation, Willis Hall's *The Long and
the Short and the Tall*.

Fortunately, however, they did not have to rely on the genre,
nor was it ever their intention to do so. The essence of a writer's
theatre, after all, is that it should be open to all sorts of writers,
not just one sort. The Royal Court has been accused of many
sorts of bias in its time (most persistently of left-wing bias,
though exactly where one is to find good right-wing playwrights these days the critics conveniently omit to say), but
what strikes one most forcibly on looking through a list of
productions is the remarkable catholicity of choice. The range
of the company's foreign productions is extraordinary; in the
normal course of public performances at the Royal Court they
have given British premières to, among others, Carson McCull-
ers's *Member of the Wedding*, Faulkner's *Requiem for a Nun*,
Beckett's *Endgame*, and *Krapp's Last Tape*, Ionesco's *The Chairs*
and *Rhinoceros*, Tennessee Williams's *Orpheus Descending*, Sartre's
Nekrassov and *Altona*, and Genet's *The Blacks*. They have also
staged memorable revivals of *Lysistrata*, *Major Barbara*, *Rosmersholm*, Chekhov's *Platonov* (previously unproduced in this country), and *The Changeling*. But also they have produced some
work by almost every new British writer of any note, taking
over other companies' productions of plays by Pinter, Wesker,
and Delaney, as well as bringing forward on their own account
at least three figures of major interest apart from Osborne:
Ann Jellicoe, N. F. Simpson, and John Arden. And each of
these four principal 'Royal Court dramatists' is entirely indi-

vidual and different from the rest; no simple category can be devised to embrace them all, and there is certainly no question of a clear, consistent Royal Court 'line' – the only visible criterion being applied is that each writer should produce work effective and valuable in its own terms.

The ways that the Royal Court's writers have been acquired vary considerably. Ann Jellicoe and N. F. Simpson were chosen from among the prize-winners in the 1956 *Observer* play competition (the prize carried, finally, no guarantee of production, and these two third-prize winners were selected as the most interesting, though subsequently, owing to an unexpected postponement of *The Long and the Short and the Tall*, place was found also at the Royal Court for the first-prize winner, the West Indian Errol John's *Moon on a Rainbow Shawl*). Arnold Wesker was introduced by Lindsay Anderson, who met him on a film course. John Arden attracted the attention of Oscar Lewenstein with a radio play. Writers from other fields, among them Keith Johnstone, Doris Lessing, and Stuart Holroyd, were encouraged to try their hand at play-writing, and their works were staged, like early efforts of Arden, Wesker, and Alun Owen, at the Sunday-night productions-without-décor which became a regular feature of the Royal Court programmes, giving authors the chance to see their work actually performed and the management the chance to assess their chances in performance as well as to try out new actors and directors on them.

What, finally, has the place of the English Stage Company been in the revival of British drama? Indirectly it has had a considerable influence by helping to make available to British writers and theatregoers the latest and most interesting works from abroad, though its work in this field does not seem to have been systematic; it has also helped writers to meet and exchange ideas in its young writers' group and simply by virtue of their all working in the same theatre. Directly it has brought forward several dramatists of unusual interest, and it is greatly to the company's credit that, having hit by a happy chance on a successful writer, Osborne, and potentially a successful formula, Protest, it did not stick there, but went on to use the profits accumulated from *Look Back in Anger* and *The Entertainer* (including the company's share in film rights, foreign rights, etc., some £50,000 in five years, as compared with £30,000 from the Arts Council in the same period) to put on plays of much less commercial appeal, such as those of Arden, Ann Jellicoe, and the earlier works of Simpson, all of which have incurred sizeable (and predictable) losses. In fact, apart from these two Osborne plays, only eight out of all the plays presented by the company up to the end of 1962 actually made a profit – *The Country Wife, Lysistrata, The Long and the Short and the Tall, Rosmersholm, One Way Pendulum, Rhinoceros, Luther,* and *Chips with Everything* – and only another three, *Platonov,* the Ionesco double bill *The Chairs* and *The Lesson,* and *Requiem for a Nun,* covered their costs.

The record is striking, if not in practical terms very encouraging, and since the death of George Devine and reorganization of the company, policy has been considerably less clear and consistent. The lead in the new drama has certainly passed elsewhere, and indeed did so almost at once, first to Stratford, E., then to the provinces (though, in the case of Wesker, with the Royal Court's active encouragement), then to television. But the respect in which the Royal Court is held, and the almost unfailing distinction of its work, in whatever field, remain unchallenged. Moreover, its disciples are there to spread the word; actors, directors, designers, most of the distinguished young in all departments, have gone through the workshop of the Royal Court before striking out on their own, and the most successful and prestigious British film company today, Woodfall, which has been responsible for the films of *Look Back in Anger, The Entertainer, Saturday Night and Sunday Morning,* and *A Taste of Honey,* is the creation of two alumni, Tony Richardson and John Osborne. Obviously the success, artistic and even, overall, commercial, of the English Stage Company has been largely a matter of the luck involved in the right people happening to be in the right place at the right time, but then without the skill and intelligence of the people, especially George Devine, to exploit the place and the time the new drama might never have emerged, or only in bits and pieces on and off for the next twenty years instead of all in a bang over a mere six. For this, at least, we must be grateful to them.

JOHN OSBORNE

Whatever may be said about John Osborne's subsequent career, at least no one can deny that *Look Back in Anger* started everything off: after a slightly shaky beginning it became the first decisive success in the career of the English Stage Company and established the Royal Court as the London home of young drama. Although the lead in these matters has passed elsewhere in later years, and 'the Osborne generation' proved only the first of several waves, 8 May 1956 still marks the real breakthrough of 'the new drama' into the British theatre, and Osborne himself remains, one way and another, one of its most influential exponents, as well as representing for the general public the new dramatist *par excellence*, the first of the angry young men and arguably the biggest shock to the system of British theatre since the advent of Shaw. And this in spite of the inevitable difficulties of following up a sensational debut with something which guarantees that the first sensation was not merely a freak success or the one work of a one-work writer.

Though *Look Back in Anger* was the first of Osborne's plays to reach the London stage, it was not by any means his first written; he admits to 'several' works unpublished and unperformed as well as *Epitaph for George Dillon*, written in collaboration with Anthony Creighton, which came earlier but was performed later, and an early piece which contributed some material to *The World of Paul Slickey*. He had also already had two plays performed out of town, *The Devil Inside Him* in Huddersfield in 1950 and *Personal Enemy* in Harrogate in 1955. The first, written in collaboration with Stella Linden and revived at the Pembroke, Croydon, in 1962 as '*Cry for Love*, by Robert Owen', is a strange melodrama about a Welsh youth whom the villagers think an idiot and his relations a sex-maniac because he writes poetry; his talents are recognized by a visiting medical student, but meanwhile he is constrained to kill a local girl who attacks his idea of beauty by attempting to pass him off as the father of her child. More characteristic was *Personal Enemy*, written with Anthony Creighton, about the reactions of a soldier's relatives and friends when he refuses to be repatriated from his captivity in Korea; the play apparently suffered at the time from wholesale deletions demanded by the Lord Chamberlain, including a whole homosexual strand in the plot. But *Look Back in Anger* it was which provided the first type-image of the new drama, and which has dogged its author ever since, so it seems inevitably the right place to start. When it was first performed Osborne was twenty-six, an actor with some years' experience in provincial repertory, notably at Ilfracombe and Hayling Island, and familiar to regulars at the Royal Court in small parts, though he says that he never took himself seriously as an actor, and neither did anyone else.

Looking back on *Look Back in Anger*, it is a difficult but necessary exercise to try and see it through the eyes of its first audience. In the last chapter I have sketched the situation in which the play emerged, but that still does not quite explain why it had the effect it did at that time. Osborne himself later characterized it as 'a formal, rather old-fashioned play', and the description is not unfair, though it should, of course, be read in the light of his accompanying statement that he dare not pick up a copy of the play nowadays, as it embarrasses him. Certainly there is nothing much in the form of the piece to justify so much excitement: it is a well-made play, with all its climaxes, its tightenings and slackenings of tension in the right places, and in general layout it belongs clearly enough to the solid realistic tradition represented by, say, *The Deep Blue Sea*.

No, what distinguished it as a decisive break with Rattigan and the older drama was not so much its form as its content: the characters who took part in the drama and the language in which they expressed themselves. Though Jimmy Porter and his milieu seem, even at this short distance of time, as inescapably 'period' as the characters in *The Vortex*, quintessentially 'mid-fifties', it was precisely the quality of immediacy and topicality which makes them so now that had the electrifying effect in 1956: Jimmy was taken to be speaking for a whole generation, of which he and his creator were among the most precocious representatives, since it was essentially the post-war generation they represented, those who had, like Lindsay Anderson, 'nailed a red flag to the roof of the mess at the fort of Annan Parbat' to celebrate the return of a Labour government in 1945 and then gradually became disillusioned when a brave new world failed to materialize. Most of the people who felt this way were inevitably in their middle to late thirties in 1956, but with Osborne as a figurehead they were all cheerfully labelled 'angry young men' and Jimmy Porter was linked in a rather improbable twosome with Amis's Lucky Jim as the cult-figure of the younger generation.

The main usefulness of Jimmy Porter in this guise is that he is the stuff of which perennial rebels are made; though it is more difficult now than it was five years ago to see him as heroic, there is no denying the truth of the picture as a permanent human type – the self-flagellating solitary in self-inflicted exile from his own misery. He is, we gradually learn, a university graduate and an enormous cultural snob (only the safe classics and the most traditional jazz, only good books and 'posh' Sunday papers), but he lives in a tumbledown attic flat in a drab Midland town and makes his living by keeping a sweet stall in the market. Everything in his life dissatisfies him, and the tone of his conversation (which is mainly monologue anyway) is consistently one of railing and complaint. The principal sufferer from all this is his wife Alison, whom he cannot forgive for her upper-middle-class background and whom he constantly torments in order to extract some reaction from her, to bring her to her knees, while she, having discovered that her only defence is imperturbability, refuses as long as she can to react. And so they rend each other, under the sympathetic eye of Cliff, the helpless *tertium quid* in this strange *ménage à trois*, until a fourth, Alison's actress friend Helena, arrives. Helena, with her air of being 'the gracious representative of visiting royalty', soon makes the situation intolerable by her very presence, and packs off Alison, who is expecting a baby and has not told Jimmy, to her home and family before herself falling into Jimmy's arms at the end of the second act.

In the third act Jimmy turns out to be settled fairly happily with Helena, as far as he can be happy with anyone – partly, it seems, because she stands up to him rather more (like most bullies in sexual situations, Jimmy appears basically just to want bullying back) and partly because he is bound to her by nothing more complicated than lust. When Cliff announces that he thinks he should leave, Jimmy more or less admits these two possibilities in the play's most familiar pronouncement:

It's a funny thing. You've been loyal, generous, and a good friend. But I'm quite prepared to see you wander off, find a new home, and make out on your own. All because of something I want from that girl downstairs, something I know in my heart she's incapable of giving. You're worth half a dozen Helenas to me or to anyone. And, if you were in my place, you'd do the same thing. . . . Why, why, why do we let these women bleed us to death? Have you ever had a letter, and on it is franked 'Please Give Your Blood Generously'? Well, the Postmaster-General does that, on behalf of all the women in the world. I suppose people of our generation aren't able to die for good causes any longer. We had all that done for us, in the thirties and forties, when we were still kids. There aren't any good, brave causes left. If the big bang does come, and we all get killed off, it won't be in aid of the old-fashioned, grand design. It'll just be for the Brave New Nothing-very-much-thank-you. About as pointless and inglorious as stepping in front of a bus. No, there's nothing left for it, me boy, but to let yourself be butchered by the women.

It is not, however, Helena who finally reduces him, but Alison, returned after losing her baby. When Helena wants to extract herself from the painful situation Jimmy dismisses her with:

It's no good trying to fool yourself about love. You can't fall into it like a soft job, without dirtying up your hands. It takes muscle and guts. And if you can't bear the thought of messing up your nice, clean soul, you'd better give up the whole idea of life, and become a saint. Because you'll never make it as a human being. It's either this world or the next.

Then he rounds on Alison:

Was I really wrong to believe that there's a – kind of – burning virility of mind and spirit that looks for something as powerful as itself? The heaviest, strongest creatures in this world seem to be the loneliest, like the old bear, following his own breath in the dark forest. There's no warm pack, no herd to comfort him. That voice that cries out doesn't *have* to be a weakling's, does it?

But she for once has an answer:

I was wrong, I was wrong! I don't want to be neutral, I don't want to be a saint. I want to be a lost cause. I want to be corrupt and futile! Don't you understand? It's gone! It's gone! That – that helpless human being inside my body. I thought it was so far, and secure in there. Nothing could take it from me. It was mine, my responsibility. But it's lost. All I wanted was to die. I never knew what it was like. I didn't know it could be like that! I was in pain, and all I could think of was you, and what I'd lost. I thought: if only – if only he could see me now, so stupid, and ugly and ridiculous. This is what he's been longing for me to feel. This is what he wants to splash about in! I'm in the fire, and I'm burning, and all I want is to die! It's cost him his child, and any others I might have had! But what does it matter – this is what he wanted from me! Don't you see! I'm in the mud at last! I'm grovelling! I'm crawling! Oh, God –

Faced at last with a really effective example of his own handiwork, Jimmy quails, and at the last he and Alison are united again in their idyllic dream world of bears and squirrels, content, perhaps, never to make it as human beings in the real world around them.

One of the most fascinating things about *Look Back in Anger* is the divergence between Osborne's conscious intentions, as conveyed in his comments and stage directions in the printed text, and what actually emerges in performance. This applies particularly, of course, to the character of Jimmy, and indeed it is arguable that the force and intensity of the play derive mainly from the author's shifting, ambivalent love-hate relationship with his hero. In the stage directions criticism direct or implied abounds. For example, at the beginning Jimmy is described as 'a disconcerting mixture of sincerity and cheerful malice, of tenderness and freebooting cruelty; restless, importunate, full of pride, a combination which alienates the sensitive and insensitive alike. Blistering honesty, or apparent honesty, like this, makes few friends. To many he seems sensitive to the point of vulgarity. To others, he is simply a loudmouth. To be as vehement as he is is to be almost non-committal.'

That does not sound particularly heroic, and the impression

is fostered by the running commentary of stage directions throughout: 'Jimmy is rather shakily triumphant. He cannot allow himself to look at either of them to catch their response to his rhetoric . . .'; 'He's been cheated of his response, but he's got to draw blood somehow'; 'Jimmy watches her, waiting for her to break'; 'Jimmy enters . . . he is almost giddy with anger, and has to steady himself on the chair . . .' There are constant indications of his neurotic determination to establish and keep his supremacy in any situation, inventing trouble if there is none lying around in order to do so, his hysterical persecution of Alison, his childish petulance. Indeed, the image which constantly emerges is that of the spoilt, difficult child, convinced that any world not run entirely for his convenience must of necessity be out of joint, and in need of nothing more than a good slapping down (which would square with the theory that his misfortune sexually is that he has coupled with a doormat when what he really longs for is a strict disciplinarian nanny-substitute).

And yet somehow this is not quite what comes over in the play on stage. For one thing it is called *Look Back in Anger*, not *Look Back in Petulance*, and both the most familiar interpreters of Jimmy (Kenneth Haigh in the original stage production, Richard Burton in the film) have been stocky, substantial, heroic figures rather than the weedy neurotics one might fairly cast in the role. For another, Osborne has, consciously or unconsciously, provided a complete cover for the heroic interpretation: what by the less ideal view would be merely excuses (everyone is out of step but our Jimmy) become if one looks at it from the other point of view genuine reasons: there are no great causes left, the world is all wrong, and it need not be just the weakling who cries out against it; Jimmy is the saintlike witness to right values in a world gone wrong, the mouthpiece of protest for a dissatisfied generation. And finally, what really makes this interpretation stick in the playgoer's mind is the burning rhetoric of his great tirades: even if their motivation is to be found in petty personal disputes and minor skirmishes in the battle of the sexes, once Jimmy gets going they generate their own force and conviction; those around him put up with him and listen entranced instead of briskly telling him to shut up and not be so silly, and his very real personal dynamism and magnetism come over to the audience as they do to the other characters on the stage. The only mystery is, Why should someone so forceful remain so impotent? And there we come back at once to the answer he himself provides: it is the deficiencies of the modern world which have made him so.

Look Back in Anger is demonstrably a muddled play – muddled, that is, in what it has to say and the way it says it – but this naturally is only a very minor consideration: a play is about people, not necessarily about ideas, and what matters is not that Jimmy is a mass of contradictions (most of us are), but that Osborne has managed to make them into a convincing dramatic representation of a complex human being, and one who offered a rallying-point for a number of people from the post-war generation who felt that the world of today was not treating them according to their deserts. It may be argued, though, that Osborne achieved this partly at the expense of his other characters: to build up Jimmy he has had to a certain extent to scale down the rest, and paradoxically (or perhaps it is not so paradoxical, as we shall see) the only other person in the play who measures up to him in solidity and conviction is Alison's father, the Colonel – partly, no doubt, because he is the only one we never see with Jimmy and subjected to Jimmy's normal barrage.

It is, however, a general trait in Osborne's work that he tends to sympathize with his hero in his writing to such an extent that the other characters are made to capitulate to him almost without a struggle and the scope of genuine dramatic conflict is thereby reduced. The remarkable thing about *Epitaph for George Dillon*, the only earlier work we know in anything like its original form, is that this is not entirely so, since though it has an angry young hero, not only is he given an adversary worthy of him, but in the end doubt is more decisively cast on his probity and worth than is ever permitted in *Look Back in Anger* (despite the stage direction referring to Jimmy's 'apparent honesty'). This may, for all we know, be the influence of Osborne's collaborator on this play, Anthony Creighton (who

later collaborated with Bernard Miller on an unusually compelling piece of psychological nonsense about a dominant
woman, *Tomorrow with Pictures*): certainly the character of
Ruth, though somehow never quite of a piece with the rest of
the play (how, one finds oneself asking, could she possibly have
sprung from the background attributed to her?), is in her own
terms decidedly well drawn, and the head-on collison between
them in the second act, when each digs too close to the other's
soft centre for comfort and harsh truths emerge on both sides,
generates a sort of excitement not found elsewhere in Osborne's
work. That has its excitements, too, of course, but they are the
excitements of the monologue and the tirade, the solitary
orator and his captivated audience, not those engendered by the
clash of two equally powerful personalities on one small stage.

George, the central character of the play, is an actor and
writer; he is sponging off the Elliotts, an easygoing, simple
family living just outside London, and though the father does
not care for him he is adept at getting his own way with the
mother, whom he reminds of her dead son, and Josie, the hard,
stupid daughter. Professionally he is a failure, or, as he prefers
to put it, he is waiting for success; he is a recognizable Osborne
hero, restless and dissatisfied – a rebel who knows what he is
against without being very clear what he is for. He pities himself, situated in a hostile and uncomprehending world, but unlike Jimmy Porter he has, every now and then, enough penetration to doubt whether he is worth pity; is he a real artist
deserving of sympathy in the torments an artist conventionally
undergoes, or is he just a confidence trickster who usually tricks
himself as well? In Ruth, Mrs Elliott's left-wing intellectual
sister, he finds someone oddly like himself in certain respects;
an ex-Communist who has just broken with the party after
seventeen years, soon after casting-off her lover of six years
because she discovered their relationship was built on cheap
lies, she is uncertain of herself, uncertain of her value to herself
and others, dissatisfied with her position, but not ready to make
a change.

In their great confrontation, which might be a love scene but
somehow does not turn out that way, they strip each other bare

of comfortable pretences, and George comes to admit openly and even sincerely (as far as anything he says is not part of his incessant self-dramatizing) that he may be living on an illusion, that he may not have talent after all – 'But do you know what is worse? Far, far, worse? . . . Having the same symptoms as talent, the pain, the ugly swellings, the lot – but never knowing whether or not the diagnosis is correct. Do you think there may be some kind of euthanasia for that? Could you kill it by burying yourself here – for good?' Whether or not this is possible, in the last act he sets out to do it: he rewrites his play so that it rakes in money on tour in the provinces as an adults-only shocker, recites his own epitaph to Ruth (who does not even hear it out) to mark his own spiritual death, and at the end of the play seems all set to marry Josie as soon as he has divorced his wife and live an ordinary suburban life, trying to kill the spark inside him which he can never for a moment confidently accept as the real thing.

By virtue of its balance, its ability to see round the central character and offer him some genuine competition without sacrificing at all the passionate rhetorical drive of the dialogue, *Epitaph for George Dillon* still remains the most wholly satisfactory of the plays Osborne has worked on. This, coupled with the fact that it was staged after *Look Back in Anger*, tended at first to obscure the lines of Osborne's development. But not for long, and Osborne, never at a loss for words to explain himself, was not slow to tell us why his style was changing: it was the first impact of Brecht on his consciousness which made him see the light and begin to find the limitations of realism (against which he was already chafing in *Look Back in Anger*) too impossibly restricting. In *The Entertainer*, his next play, the influence of Brecht is very marked in a number of incidentals, though one would guess that, at that time at least, he had not fully grasped what the epic theatre was about (the totally misconceived film version, scripted by Osborne himself, which tries to transplant all the least realistic sections unchanged into a setting of documentary realism, would tend to support such an opinion).

In effect, the structure of the play presents a series of realistic scenes – more realistic, perhaps, than anything in *Look Back in Anger* – dropped quite arbitrarily into an 'endistancing' epic framework. On the realistic level we have the story of Archie Rice, a corny, fading comedian playing in a holiday show called *Rock'n Roll New'd Look* at a large seaside town. He is, we gradually learn, a hollow man, unable to make real contact with anyone – his father Billy, whom he loves but who maddens him, his wife, whom he pities, or his children, two of whom we meet, the shy, easygoing Frank and Jean, who is intense and rather priggishly left-wing. He uses his comic persona to ward off anyone who may want to look him straight in the face and, cornered as he is, he can be completely unscrupulous – he sets up an affair with a young girl so that her parents will finance his new show, and when that fails because Billy goes and tells them that he is married with three grown-up children he allows Billy, one of the few survivors from the great days of music-hall, to return to the stage to recoup the family fortunes. His son Mick, fighting at Suez, is killed, and for a moment it touches him, but only for a moment; he is dead almost beyond rousing – the portrait, perhaps, of Jimmy Porter twenty years later, or George Dillon in ten years, when the effect of their capitulation is complete and visible.

Encasing these scenes is a framework of supposed music-hall numbers, performed mostly by Archie, which make an oblique but unmistakable comment on the main action, their burden being that the world is rotten, riddled with apathy, and the theatre, as we see it and as it is summed up in the person of Archie, is the symbol of this state of decay: audience and actors are equally inert. As Archie puts it drunkenly to Jean just before the news of Mick's death arrives:

You see this face, you see this face, this face can split open with warmth and humanity. It can sing, and tell the worst, unfunniest stories in the world to a great mob of dead, drab erks and it doesn't matter, it doesn't matter. It doesn't matter because – look at my eyes. I'm dead behind these eyes. I'm dead, just like the whole inert, shoddy lot out there. It doesn't matter because I don't feel a thing, and neither do they. We're just as dead as each other.

'Anger' is, in fact, again the keynote of Osborne's comment

2a 'Look Back in Anger'
2b 'Live Like Pigs'

3a 'One Way Pendulum'

3b 'The Hole'

on the modern world (the label of the 'angry young man', now
fortunately almost dropped from currency but in its time much
overused, still has that grain of truth in it) – Jimmy's statement
that there are no good causes left to die for finds its exact visual
parallel and commentary, for instance, in the staging of Archie's
song 'Thank God I'm Normal', with its pseudo-patriotic verse
('if we all stand By this dear old land The battle will be won')
illustrated by a blowsy nude Britannia wearing only a helmet.
But, of course, if the modern world is to be castigated it must be
by comparison with something else, some other era, and here we
come straight to the central contradiction in Osborne's work:
what is looked back on with nostalgia is precisely the era of
Edwardian settlement and complacency which in other contexts would be looked back on with the fiercest anger. We noted
in *Look Back in Anger* the surprising fact that the only character
apart from Jimmy who is allowed his say and some measure of
genuinely independent existence is Alison's father, towards
whom Jimmy's own reactions are ambiguous: Alison says she
thinks that in spite of everything Jimmy rather likes him,
though he is obviously in many ways the representative of
everything Jimmy is against. And the reason for this is clear
enough, on a moment's consideration: at least in their heyday
Alison's father's generation knew where they were, what standards their lives were ruled by, and where their duty lay (or so,
at least, it now seems); they had causes to die for and even if
they were wrong they had a certain dignity. Their security in
an apparently secure world is eminently to be envied by someone, like Jimmy, who finds no certainty anywhere, outside
himself or within.

Similarly in *The Entertainer* there is at least one point of
reference in a sympathetic member of the older generation,
Billy Rice. With Archie, as with George Dillon, we can never
be sure how far he is really a victim of the world around him
and how far he is the creator of his own situation: basically, it
seems, he never was talented and he could never have done
much better than he is doing now, catering for the decadent
tastes of modern audiences (and not, apparently, doing that
very well, since even on this level he fails to bring them in); his

one moment of realization, when he heard a Negro woman singing in a way which told him, for the moment, that 'it didn't matter how much you kick people, the real people, how much you despise them, if they can stand up and make a pure, just natural noise like that, there's nothing wrong with them, only with everybody else', has served merely as a painful reminder, a glimpse of a lost Eden he could never attain and to which no one holds the key any more ('I don't suppose we'll ever hear it again. There's nobody who can feel like that'). But Billy was great, and is great still, a survivor from the heroic past of popular entertainment's heyday in the Edwardian music-hall, now gone for ever.

In his note to the printed text Osborne says: 'The music-hall is dying, and, with it, a significant part of England. Some of the heart of England has gone: something that once belonged to everyone, for this was truly a folk art.' Significantly, Osborne is here writing of something, like the Edwardian splendours of India, which he cannot possibly remember himself and which becomes therefore, for him, a romantic legend to be longed for as an alternative to the indecisions and false values of modern life. The intelligent political man of left-wing sympathies in Osborne tells him – and us – that it was the faults in this ante-diluvian world which brought our world into existence, but the incorrigible romantic looks back admiringly, and these plays are the battlegrounds (hence much of their excitement) on which the two Osbornes fight it out.

More sympathetic elders occur in Osborne's next work, *The World of Paul Slickey*, where, in fact, they are almost the only people towards whom even a spark of sympathy is permitted. This 'Comedy of Manners with Music' is generally, and not unfairly, regarded as Osborne's most complete failure; critically and commercially it certainly was, and even allowing for an exaggeration of hostility in proportion to the exaggeration of preliminary hopes for it after *The Entertainer*, it is difficult to find anything good to say for it now. It was based, apparently, on an unproduced script from before *Look Back in Anger*, and was Osborne's first attempt at a genre for which he is totally ill-suited, the social satire. The liveliest passages of Osborne's plays may often involve, or appear to involve, social criticism, but if we look closer it is clear that the criticism, such as it is, is never based on a close examination of its object (hence the curious interchangeability, in different contexts, of his objects of detestation and devotion); it is all entirely subjective, a volley of grape-shot flying off in all directions in which the person who discharges it counts for much more than his nominal targets (that is to say, while some hits, most misses, but this is not vitally important to our judgement of the plays, because they are so devised that it is the force rather than the accuracy of the attack which counts for most). But satire calls above all for a degree of objectivity, if only so that the satirist can size up his object's weak points and aim directly at them; the blunderbuss of open anger must be replaced by the pearl-handled automatic of considered irony. But this is the last thing we would expect from Osborne: in *The World of Paul Slickey* anything and everything comes under the same erratic fire, mountains and molehills are greeted with equal fury, and by the time we are through savaging the church, the aristocracy, the gutter Press, those masculine women and feminine men (as well as their more bigoted opponents), the success ethos, the tawdriness of teenage tastes in music, the sentimentality of the woman's magazine, supporters of blood sports and corporal punishment, anti-semites, anti-Negroes, and anti-anti-H-bomb demonstrators, and just about every other imaginable *bête noire* of the discontented intellectual, we are tempted to turn Osborne's own words against him: 'To be as vehement as he is is to be almost non-committal.'

And, in fact, about one or two of his central targets Osborne is ultimately curiously non-committal. 'Paul Slickey' himself, the gossip-columnist hero-villain who personifies the workings of the bitch-goddess success, proves to be dishearteningly soft-centred: he does not really like his job, he has moments of doubt and depression, he sees himself already as much more the victim of the machine than its manipulator; in a word, he is sentimentalized and the blame for him and his like put on an undefined 'them' who have forced him into the rat-race. Similarly Father Evilgreene, the sinister priest with his parody ritual (seldom, incidentally, can satire have been quite so heavy-handed and basically innocuous) turns out after all the to-do not to be a real priest at all, so that what we may have thought daringly directed against religion turns out simply (and safely) to be directed at imitation religion. And, as we have already remarked, the two embodiments of the privileged, aristocratic tradition which seems to be intended as one of the play's main targets, Lord and Lady Mortlake, turn out in fact to be the most amiable and sympathetic of all the characters, figures of sense and dignity who have strangely survived into a mad and frenzied world; Evelyn Waugh himself could hardly have put the case for aristocracy more unequivocally.

As the plot (which is reduced to a minimum anyway) progresses all these characters are introduced against the background of a surprisingly well-kept stately home, owned by Jack Oakham's ('Paul Slickey's', that is) father-in-law Lord Mortlake; Lord Mortlake does not know that Oakham is Slickey, hence one slight line of plot, but most of the story concerns the complicated pattern of adultery woven by Jack, his wife Lesley, his sister-in-law Deirdre Rawley, and her husband Michael, with the aid of Gillian Giltedge-Whyte, a debutante, Terry Maroon, a rock'n'roller, and Jo, Paul Slickey's secretary – all leading to the conclusion that the only escape from marital boredom is a change of sex. There are fourteen songs, confirming what we had already gathered from *The Entertainer*, that lyric-writing is not Osborne's forte: they include 'Bring Back the Axe', 'The Mechanics of Success', 'The Income Tax Man', and 'I Want to Hear About Beautiful Things', the titles of which are all sufficiently self-explanatory.

Considerably more interesting, though treated to a reception almost equally disastrous, is Osborne's first (and to judge from his subsequent comments on the matter his last) television play, *A Subject of Scandal and Concern*. The history of this was long and involved, and it was offered round a number of the independent companies before being finally accepted by the B.B.C., who agreed to perform it as written, while the other companies had required rewriting and adaptation. The reason for their worries about it became clear when the play was performed and published, for, in fact, it turns out to be not so much a play as an illustrated lecture – an effect which the B.B.C. production intensified by substituting for the costumed narrator of the printed text, placed physically in the prison setting in which much of the drama takes place, an extra-smooth John Freeman playing the television uncle for us against an anonymous studio background. The story that the narrator has to tell is interesting enough: the prosecution of George Holyoake, the last man to be imprisoned for blasphemy in this country. Holyoake was a socialist lecturer who was put on trial in 1842 for saying, in response to a question at a public meeting, that he did not believe in God. In the play we see a little of his relationship with his wife, a careful reconstruction of his trial, in which he conducted his own defence despite a speech impediment and an almost total ignorance of the law, and his later experiences in prison, where he remains enigmatically impassive despite the news of his friend's recantation before death, his wife's reproaches over his daughter's death, and the fervent exhortations of the chaplain; he ends, as he began, very much a man of mystery, rising to eloquence only at his trial, when for the moment he loses his impediment in defence of his own convictions.

All this is handled in a straightforward, not particularly imaginative fashion, and the meat of the play comes mainly in the narration. The Narrator is always there at the viewer's elbow, telling him what has just happened and explaining what is about to happen, drawing the moral or pointing out sententiously that no simple moral can be drawn. This is 'endistancement' with a vengeance, since any attempt on the part of the play to stand on its own feet is immediately stamped on by a prompt return to the lecture-room, and while this may prevent one from becoming improperly involved in the action it runs the severe risk of preventing one also from becoming even properly interested in it. Again, one suspects Osborne's Brechtian enthusiasms have contributed to the method employed, but the Narrator's introduction (modified slightly in the version acted) reads like a parody of Brecht's ideas, with a hint of disdain for the audience very personal to Osborne thrown in for good measure:

Good evening. I am a lawyer. My name is not important as I am not directly involved in what you are about to see. What I am introducing for you is an entertainment. There is no reason why you should not go on with what you are doing. What you are about to see is a straightforward account of an obscure event in the history of your – well, my – country. I shall simply fill in with incidental but necessary information, like one of your own television chairmen, in fact. You will not really be troubled with anything unfamiliar. . . .

Similarly with his readings from *The Cheltenham Chronicle* of the day about the part of the meeting we have just witnessed, his imparting of the information that 'Mr Holyoake had finished, his voice notably stronger and his impediment astonishingly improved' when we have just seen and heard this very event, and his pretentiously throwaway conclusion (slightly shortened in performance):

This is a time when people demand from entertainments what they call a 'solution'. They expect to have their little solution rattling away down there in the centre of the play like a motto in a Christmas cracker. For those who seek information it has been put before you. If it is meaning you are looking for, then you must start collecting for yourself. And what would you say is the moral then? If you are waiting for the commercial it is probably this: you cannot live by bread alone. You must have jam – even if it is mixed with another man's blood. That's all. You may retire now. And if a mini-car is your particular mini-dream, then dream it. When your turn comes you will be called. Good night.

(Note, incidentally, the decay of Osborne's earlier angry eloquence into a merely mannered abruptness of delivery applied to words which are more than ever gesture without real meaning.)

What Osborne is after in this use of narration seems clear enough, but the weakness of *A Subject of Scandal and Concern* is still the same as that of *The Entertainer*: that his adoption of Brechtian processes is only half-hearted. What happens in both of them is that the framework of comment – the music-hall songs, the narration – is in one convention and the scenes contained by that framework are in another: the same *verismo* as *Look Back in Anger*. This persistent failure to evolve an integrated new dramatic technique to replace the old lent a particular interest to the appearance of his second historical play,

Luther; would he in this, tackling for the first time a theme right away from contemporary realism in the medium in which he was most at home, the stage, manage at last to find a satisfactory new form for his work?

The answer is still yes and no, but the reasons for this evasion are unexpected. First it must be said that the play as a whole corresponds very closely in dramatic method to the reconstructed scenes in *A Subject of Scandal and Concern*: the historical material is straightforwardly presented on the whole, with Luther's own words used whenever possible (as Osborne and his supporters rapidly pointed out to the tender-minded who quailed at the dramatist's apparent obsession with constipation and defecation). Moreover, it is not 'Brechtian' in the senses conventional to the English theatre, being neither dressed up with songs and dances *à la* Theatre Workshop nor equipped with a ubiquitous audience-representative in the shape of a Common Man (as favoured by such examples of Brecht tamed and commercialized as *A Man for All Seasons*): 'narration', in fact, is reduced to a brusque announcement from the stage of time and place. Here the model seems to be rather the direct chronicle of *Galileo*, in which man as an individual and man in society are held as far as the spectator's interest is concerned in an edgy balance. Brecht manages to preserve the balance very effectively between the inner forces which drive Galileo on and the social forces (Church and State) which hold him back. In Osborne the balance is less satisfactory, since so much time is spent on the 'psychological' material early on – Martin's obsession with his own sinfulness, with the sinfulness of merely being alive, and his relations with his father, whom he loved, and his mother, who beat him – that by the time this all bears fruit in his rebellion and heresy, and he moves out (like Galileo) into the world of repressive social forces (emanating, like those that opposed Galileo, from the Vatican), there is not enough room left to deal with them properly.

From Act 2, Scene 4, at the end of which Luther nails his theses to the church door at Wittenburg, the issues involved are scurried over in unseemly haste, with a rather feeble scene of disputation between Luther and Cajetan, the papal legate (which again demonstrates Osborne's deficiencies when a conflict of equals rather than a tirade to a captive audience is called for, since, though apparently engaging in a discussion, Luther and Cajetan never really interlock so that one answers the other; their 'dialogue' turns out, in fact, to be two monologues skilfully intercut), and another, even weaker, showing Pope Leo about to go hunting, to take care insufficiently of the theological side before we get to the Diet of Worms. Then we jump four years to learn something, but not to the uninitiated enough, about the intervening period of war and Luther's apparent betrayal of the peasants, though what happened and why remains obscure (even with the scene between Luther and the Knight, not in the original text, inserted to clarify matters). The closing scene, in which we see Luther at home two years later with his wife and son, returns unashamedly to the personal with, finally, a note of nostalgia which should by now be familiar to us in Osborne's work; Luther, himself the instigator of a period of unrest and unsettled values, looks back to an earlier, happier day:

A little while, and you *shall* see me. Christ said that, my son. I hope that'll be the way of it again. I hope so. Let's just hope so, eh? Eh? let's just hope so.

Well, what about *Luther*? Does it really represent, as one critic opined, 'the most solid guarantee yet given of Mr John Osborne's dramatic stamina'? Alas, although after the relative failure of *The World of Paul Slickey* and *A Subject of Scandal and Concern* one had hoped that it would provide a reasonably clear answer, there was nothing for it but to hedge again. However, one or two pointers there were. It is noticeable, after the extreme thinness of the material in *The World of Paul Slickey*, that both *A Subject of Scandal and Concern* and *Luther* are historical reconstructions relying closely for their material and even for their dialogue on the documentary sources. This seemed to suggest a drying-up, perhaps temporary, of Osborne's inventive faculties at least in so far as they concerned the creation of new characters and plot-situations; instead he was turning to plots and characters already in existence. The failure of *The World of*

Paul Slickey and *A Subject of Scandal and Concern*, followed by the popular and critical success of *Luther*, suggested also that after some fumbling he had mastered the technique of handling pre-existent material efficiently, to form a play which if not completely satisfactory in detail is at least well enough written and interesting enough in its material to provide a generally satisfactory evening's theatre.

I do not think anyone would deny that *Luther* is that – especially with the magnetic personality of Albert Finney in the title role – but it would surprise me if anyone on mature consideration can find it as intense, as eloquent, as personal, as – to bring out the key word here – as *felt* as *Epitaph for George Dillon, Look Back in Anger*, or *The Entertainer*. It is a good, sensible, commercial piece of work, spiced with enough anger and naughty words to establish it as representative of a later generation than, say, Rattigan's *Adventure Story*, but basically it is not so different from *Adventure Story*, or for that matter *A Man for all Seasons* or Anouilh's *Becket*. It has been popular, as they (the last two, at any rate) were popular, and on the whole it deserves its popularity. But the most positive new discovery about Osborne it offered us was that he was not just the primitive we had feared he might be – inspired or nothing; he could turn his hand to play-writing simply as a craft and turn out something perfectly presentable. But equally, taken in conjunction with the two previous plays, it did make us wonder whether, barring any sudden unforeseen transformation, we would have to say good-bye to Osborne the innovator and greet instead Osborne the careful craftsman. To such wonderings Osborne's subsequent work offers little in the way of definite confirmation or denial. His next work for the theatre was in any case fairly slight after the elaborate and ambitious *The World of Paul Slickey* and *Luther*, a sort of intermezzo in his career produced by the pairing of two contrasted, though both primarily comic, one-act plays, *The Blood of the Bambergs* and *Under Plain Cover*, in a double bill under the general title *Plays for England* (1963). Development in various directions they certainly showed, but neither could be said to provide a startling revelation. *The Blood of the Bambergs* is by general consent the least satisfactory of all Osborne's plays: a clumsy attempt at the sort of satire for which he showed himself signally unfitted in *The World of Paul Slickey*, it concerns the last-minute substitution at a royal wedding of an Australian press photographer for the royal groom, who has just been killed in a road accident and whom the photographer by a curious coincidence happens to resemble like a twin brother (the dead prince's father, it seems, had known the photographer's mother not wisely but too well). The subject-matter caused a certain preliminary fluttering in the dovecots (a satire about a royal marriage with a photographer – how daring!) but in fact the result proved to be perfectly harmless and acceptable; indeed, with its accent on the fact that royalty's life is no bed of roses and its final demonstration that even the interloper is of blood royal and therefore fitted by birth for the life he is to lead, it ends up curiously like a conservative tract, with most of its venom reserved for the press and television journalists who cheapen the image of royalty. Perhaps Osborne himself more than half believes, to quote one of his less happy would-be epigrams, that 'An orb in the minster is better than a monster in orbit'.

The second play in the bill, *Under Plain Cover*, is much more interesting. It is tempting to see it as a sort of fourth act to *Look Back in Anger*, in which Jimmy and Alison have tired of Bears and Squirrels and gone on to a few more sophisticated party games. The married couple this time, Tim and Jenny, lead perfectly ordinary lives except for their odd hobbies, which consist of acting out a variety of sado-masochistic fantasy situations in clothes which they receive 'under plain cover'. Sometimes one dominates, sometimes the other: she may be a strict, nononsense nurse and he a cringing patient, or he a heartless employer and she a down-trodden maid, and so on. They put real enthusiasm and imagination into their charades: when she wonders, for example, why the maid she is playing doesn't leave if she is so badly treated, he decides that it is the 1930s and there is nothing else for her except the bread-line; in the second scene there is a long nonsense-fantasy about knickers (a fetish they share) in which every conceivable description is applied to them, including a number from reviews of Osborne's earlier plays ('the total gesture is altogether inadequate'). And as a result of their fantasies and fetishes they are happy, well-adjusted, efficient parents and, as far as the outside world is concerned, just what the postman calls them, a nice ordinary couple. Indeed, absolutely they are just that: they have a marriage which works; they merely externalize changes in the emotional balance of a power and make positive use of them where others experience them only as a bugbear and a puzzlement.

So far, so good: an interesting point interestingly made, if perhaps at excessive length, in two scenes where one would be enough. But at this point Osborne seems suddenly to be confronted with the need to make his sketch into a play, and the ghost of Paul Slickey enters, slightly disguised as Stanley, a snooping, cynical reporter. When he starts interfering, Osborne's own obsession with the evils of gutter journalism takes over and the play goes to pieces: Stanley unearths evidence that Tim and Jenny are, unknown to themselves, brother and sister, separates them, gets Jenny remarried and even brings Tim in as a loving brother to the wedding reception. But the marriage does not last: sometime later Tim and Jenny are apparently together again in their semi-detached, and Stanley, a broken man, knocks on their door, desperate to talk to them. But there is no answer. . . .

If *The Blood of the Bambergs* is easily the feeblest work Osborne has yet allowed to reach the stage, *Under Plain Cover* does show some signs of a recovery; at least for its first half it finds a new subject, or anyway shows an old subject – the relations of husband and wife – in a new light. It is, in parts, the most interesting thing Osborne has written since parts of *The Entertainer*, but as a whole it just does not work; in the second half he dissipates most of the effect he has spent the first half building up (drawing heavily, by the way, on an actual case related in Harry Proctor's book *Street of Disillusion* for the incest theme and the role of the reporter). Osborne the innovator is present – though the subject is less daring than it would have been some years before, and one cannot help thinking that

Pinter would do it better – and Osborne the careful craftsman conspicuous by his absence.

The year after *Plays for England,* 1964, did much to answer the questions they raised, with two major new plays produced at the Royal Court. The first of them, *Inadmissible Evidence,* at least effectively silenced any doubts left after *Under Plain Cover* that Osborne the personal dramatist might have written himself out. It became at once almost a commonplace of critical judgement that *Inadmissible Evidence* was Osborne's best play; and this is not a verdict I would argue with. It seems to me that in this play Osborne has found, perhaps as a result of thought, perhaps by a lucky chance in the material he has chosen to make his play out of, a solution to most of the problems which previously tended to snarl up his plays. For example, to take the basic one: his constant trouble with dialogue, or perhaps I should say with duologue. Only in the middle act of *George Dillon* is there anything approaching a genuine, unrigged, head-on clash between two equally matched characters who actually connect at several vital points. Elsewhere Osborne's forte has always been impassioned monologue, carried along by the power of its own rhetoric and cheerfully unconcerned with what was going on around. The trouble is that monologue of this sort is always difficult to accommodate in normal dramatic form. In *Look Back in Anger,* Jimmy monologuizes endlessly and, rather unbelievably, everyone else sits round for most of the time and lets him; he is a stunning talker, admittedly, but not that stunning, and the effect is weakened because in the context it is necessary that the other characters should not be quite so infatuated as the dramatist obviously is with the sound of his own protagonist's voice. Osborne's subsequent plays found no very satisfactory way out of this dilemma – think, for instance, of *Luther,* which works best when Luther is permitted to deliver his sermons entirely without interruption.

But in *Inadmissible Evidence* Osborne has at last stumbled on an elementary truth: that his trouble in making characters connect arises primarily from the fact that what really interests him, anguishes him indeed, is the non-connection of people;

it is – oh dear that one should have to come back to that most
hackneyed piece of critical shorthand – failure of communication. It is as though this has always been his subject, but that
up to now he has not fully understood what he was doing or
wanted to do; now that he does, the effect is shattering. For,
critical cliché or no critical cliché, failure of communication,
failure to connect, is still a perfectly viable dramatic subject; a
subject, after all, is as good as the intensity of a writer's reaction
to it allows it to be. In *Inadmissible Evidence* there is no doubt
about the vividness and intensity of Osborne's vision: he achieves
a degree of imaginative identification with his hero (is 'hero'
the *mot juste* here? Yes, in spite of everything I think it is)
unequalled in his work since *Look Back in Anger*.

The agony of the hero concerned, Bill Maitland, comes
from his gradual, inexorable realization that the world and he
are parting company. He is fortyish, apparently well-preserved
and well-off, a solicitor with a slightly unsavoury business
(mainly divorces) which seems to run itself fairly well, with a
weather-eye cocked for the Law Society; he has a wife, a
daughter and a mistress; and he is hovering on the verge of a
complete breakdown. The world, it seems, is conspiring to
ignore his existence: his friends and associates turn away from
him, taxis for hire take no notice of his attempts to hail them,
people he is talking to on the telephone hang up on him in
mid-sentence, or at least he is obsessed with the fear that they
may have, that he may be talking on and on to the unrespon-
sive air. And for the most part, as it happens, he is – not particularly on the phone, but just in general. His employees in
the office throw up their eyes – it's just him, carrying on again –
and don't take a blind bit of notice; his clients burble on about
their own problems, sublimely unaware how beside the point
his responses are; his daughter, when she comes to visit him,
stands wordless and reactionless throughout his great tirade
and leaves without opening her mouth. Osborne has at last
discovered the profound truth that nobody really listens to
anybody, and least of all do they listen to those who most
imperatively require their attention, their imaginative participation – in life, that is; on stage the reverse is the case,

because our imaginative participation, our mere listening, does not immediately involve us in consequences in the world of action; we have only to listen, we don't have to do anything. That is why, when we saw everyone on stage being profoundly affected by Jimmy Porter, we did not quite believe it; the spectacle of nobody at all being affected by Maitland, on the other hand, is all too painfully believable. We all begin to wonder uneasily just how far our lives depend on the goodwill of others.

'*Tu causes, tu causes, c'est tout ce que tu sais faire,*' as Zazie's parrot would no doubt remark. But it is not quite all that Maitland knows how to do. He can suffer, for example, as well as talking about suffering; and he can, maybe, die. Though the old Osborne knack of telling us the worst about a character and yet still somehow leaving us on his side is still clearly in evidence in his treatment of Maitland, it is not unfairly done; we really are told the worst, and yet we are drawn unavoidably into Maitland's own faltering concern for himself, his feeling – which is the feeling of all of us – that for all his faults he has not quite deserved whatever it is that is in the process of befalling him. And technically the play is remarkably adroit. There are still a few weak points. The opening dream sequence, in which Maitland is on trial for exhibiting an unspecified obscene object (presumably himself) and tries fumblingly to defend himself, could with advantage be compressed and concentrated; and it is not at all clear how the episode in which he listens to the story of a homosexual client – well done though it is in itself – fits into the rest of the play. The women seeking divorce are clearly various aspects of Maitland's own unseen wife (which is why they are directed to be played by the same actress) but what does the homosexual represent in this otherwise intensely subjective play? On the other hand, few things are more impressive in Osborne's work than the way in which reality here gradually, almost imperceptibly, slips from Maitland's, and our, grasp as little by little the passage of time blurs, characters fuse and merge into each other. After *Inadmissible Evidence* there could be little doubt any more that whatever his ups and downs – and his is the sort of large undisciplined talent which almost inevitably balances the spectacular ups with equally spectacular downs – it would not be possible to write him off even after a succession of downs.

This comforting judgement was, as it happened, to be severely tested in his next few works. The companion piece to *Inadmissible Evidence*, *A Patriot for Me*, was a case in point. Its 'martyrdom' at the hands of the Lord Chamberlain, which necessitated the temporary transformation of the Royal Court into a club theatre, admittedly clouded the issue at the time, but though some critics found it one of Osborne's finest works, others regarded it as a disappointing return to his *Luther* style, reworking historical material dutifully but with little real flair or feeling of involvement. The occasion this time is the story of Alfred Redl, a self-made officer in the Austrian army (of Jewish origin, a programme note told us, though the play does not remark on the fact) who is a homosexual and therefore can be blackmailed by the Russians into working as a spy for them. The first act of the play shows us Redl the careerist advancing his career in the Austrian army, until at the very end we learn that he is homosexual. The second act elaborates on the homosexuality, mainly in the most famous (if only dubiously relevant) scene of the play, the drag ball, and ends with the Russian spy-chief blackmailing Redl into working for him. The third act leads up to the foregone conclusion of Redl's discovery and disgrace – or, rather, ends with it, but meanwhile switches alarmingly from one subject to another, mostly connected with Redl's emotional situation as a practising homosexual and permitting him a few big monologues in Osborne's best manner defending or explaining his position.

Despite the favourable opinions the play garnered at the time, it is curiously blurred and unmemorable in effect. Again, as in *Luther*, Osborne seems to be reaching out towards a new 'objective' sort of dramatic writing, but to have lost the urgency of his one-man monologue plays without acquiring any compensating gift for varied characterization or cumulative dramatic story-telling which might make up in solid construction for the headier excitements of high rhetoric. The first act is quite well constructed to show us what sort of man Redl is before we learn for sure that he is homosexual. But once the revelation is made the play wanders all over the place, neither building up any sort of suspense nor making the character of Redl himself more vivid for us. The author is not able, it seems, to put himself completely inside Redl's skin, but he cannot either detach himself completely enough to give us a clear rounded picture from the outside. The result is that a lot of the play remains rather dull, despite its moments of eloquence as Redl passionately elaborates on the physical attractions he finds in other men.

Osborne's next work, his adaptation of Lope de Vega's *La Fianza Satisfecha* as *A Bond Honoured*, need not detain us long. It was commissioned by the National Theatre, and presented perhaps a task too immediately congenial to Osborne for us to hope that it might bring out his best. Lope's hero Leonido is a sort of cosmic rebel who devotes his whole life to the destruction of honour, the defilement of his family and the systematic rejection of any and every force in the universe, human or divine, which might stand in his way. Before the start of the action he claims to have tried to rape and to have killed his mother (among various dubious activities), and during the play he also tries to rape his sister on her wedding eve, insults and savages her and her groom at the wedding, and blinds his father after subjecting him to various humiliations. He also forsakes Christianity for Mohammedanism, and finally defies Christ himself, the great creditor who at last arrives to have his bond honoured. Osborne follows this fairly closely, though compressing drastically from three long acts to one and adding a few details, such as making Leonido's sister not only a potential rapee, but a fairly willing accomplice in incest. The end is somewhat modified too, in that Osborne permits Leonido at last to wriggle out of full responsibility for honouring the bond by conveniently blaming God for everything, refusing to repent and demanding judgement instead. Meanwhile, the play is turned almost into a parody of Osborne's monologue drama: Leonido is required to rail endlessly at everyone and everything, and the other characters he encounters are more evidently pasteboard than ever before. In the circumstances, it is difficult to take the play very seriously; perhaps if Osborne had thrown Lope out of the window and started again from scratch he might have made something of the subject, but as it is the play represents merely an unfortunate interlude in Osborne's career as an original creator.

This was taken up again, spectacularly, with a pair of full-length plays produced consecutively at the Royal Court in 1968, *Time Present* and *The Hotel in Amsterdam*. Taken individually and together they seem to represent an attempted new departure in Osborne's work: though each has, unmistakably, a central character, they seem to aim at drama based on a pattern of social and emotional relationships. Neither of them seems to me to achieve this aim with consistent success, though *The Hotel in Amsterdam* is the more satisfactory of the two. *Time Present* is to date unique among Osborne's plays in that it has a female character at the centre, the 'resting' actress Pamela. Nothing much happens in the play. Her father, a famous actor of the old school, dies off-stage (he seems to represent another of Osborne's nostalgias for things he cannot possibly have known at first hand) and Pamela turns out to be having an affair with the lover of her best friend, a blue-stocking M.P. According to a pattern familiar to those who have followed Osborne's work, the action is punctuated by outbursts from Pamela directed against critics, politicians she dislikes, a young and popular actress whose easy success she resents, and other ready-made targets for Osbornian diatribes. But this time they seem a little half-hearted and perfunctory, as though they are there to meet audiences' expectations rather than driven by some real force of feeling in Osborne himself. There are also attempts at the old Osborne technique of presenting an essentially pretty dislikeable character as though he (or in this case she) is likeable and sympathetic. Pamela spends a lot of her time asking – like Leonido, though on a smaller scale – to be judged. 'I'm a bitch, tell me to get out', she said, and everybody, as frustratingly perhaps to herself as to the audience, keeps replying that on the contrary she is beautiful, good, loved.

E

Pre-first-night rumour had it that the play was full of covert references to public figures of the moment, and disguised autobiography. This, plus the fact that the heroine was played by John Osborne's new wife Jill Bennett, possibly helped to lend the play an interest it did not intrinsically possess. Similar rumours were even more rife of *The Hotel in Amsterdam*, which was also helped by the presence of Paul Scofield in the leading role. But anyway, the play is more interesting in itself. It concerns a stolen weekend snatched by three married couples from the pervasive influence of 'K.L.', a film producer who employs several of them and dominates the lives of all. The escape is at best very partial: throughout the weekend they continue obsessively to talk and think of him, and when at the end it transpires that in their absence K.L., the allegedly invincible tyrant, has killed himself, they are all shattered. Meanwhile there are various cross-currents in their relations, notably in the admission of love between Laurie, the ring-leader, and Annie, the wife of one of the others. There is also a lot of cross-talk in the private language of the circle, full of homosexual reference and jokes about 'the Golden Sanitary Towel Award' – the sort of low camp we have previously encountered in Osborne's work in the knickers conversation of the couple in *Under Plain Cover*. None of it, to my ear, rings quite true, but the fact remains that in Laurie, Osborne has created a character who moves beyond the merely vituperative image of the 'typical' Osborne hero to admit involvement in others and even compassion for them, as well as for himself. This may suggest a new maturity in Osborne, both as a writer and as a man. Or it may not. But at least it leaves us waiting for his next play with interest, and indeed with considerable hope.

N. F. SIMPSON

Whether one likes or dislikes N. F. Simpson's work, it seems to me, there is very little to be said about it. It is uniquely all of a piece, all written in pretty well the same style, and all based on one principle, the *non sequitur*. This seems to link it with the Theatre of the Absurd (especially if we take *au grand sérieux* the pronouncement of the author-character in the first version of *A Resounding Tinkle* that 'The retreat from reason means precious little to anyone who has never caught up with reason in the first place; it takes a trained mind to relish a *non sequitur*'), but it also links it with such humbler native prototypes as *Itma* and *The Goon Show*, even without dragging in Lewis Carroll and the English nonsense tradition. And it is with *Itma* that Simpson's plays seem happiest; certainly compared with the works of Ionesco, who appears to have served to a certain extent as Simpson's model, they look very parochial and unresourceful.

Simpson is a schoolmaster by profession, and it is irresistible, though probably quite unfair, to suggest that this may explain a certain academic quality in his writing, a tendency to demonstrate rather than just say something, to explore every possibility of a joke and run it right into the ground by overexplicitness and rigid application of logic instead of letting it get its laugh and then go. Indeed, sometimes one suspects that Simpson is not primarily a funny writer at all, that the laugh is not intended to be the final product of his sallies, since when it comes at all it usually comes half-way through a sequence and not at the bitter end. But if he does this deliberately (not, that is, just by accident, like the comedian who outstays his welcome) and intends us to see beyond the jokes to a deeper truth embodied in them, one cannot help feeling that this truth – that the world is not logical and logic can be turned against itself to prove anything, since it all depends in human terms on a number of premises not open to question – is rather too obvious and too limited to support a complete dramatic *oeuvre*.

Born in London in 1919, Simpson (the N. F. stands for Norman Frederick) worked in a bank for two years before the war, served in the Intelligence Corps, and took up teaching after he was demobbed. His first play, the two-act version of *A Resounding Tinkle*, shared third prize in the *Observer* play competition in 1956 with *The Sport of My Mad Mother* and Richard Beynon's *The Shifting Heart*, was produced in a revised version without décor at the Royal Court and later, shortened to one act, reappeared with another of Simpson's one-act plays, *The Hole*, in a double bill there. It was not a great success commercially, but by December 1959, when *One Way Pendulum*, his second full-length play, was produced at the Royal Court, public taste had become sufficiently acclimatized to this sort of humour (the play is sub-titled 'A Farce in a New Dimension') to give it a run there and justify a transfer to the West End; subsequently, to everyone's surprise, it proved a highly successful repertory play, and even the most conservative reps found themselves doing good business with it. Simpson has also contributed successfully to several West End revues, written television comedy series, and for all practical purposes may be taken as one of the most obviously popular of the new dramatists, despite a certain, probably increasing, amount of resistance from the critics.

The reason for this resistance can be explained quite simply by reference to any of Simpson's plays: it is his complete abandonment of any form of continuity. Not only is there no plot in any normal sense of the term, but there is no attempt at character differentiation; most of the lines could be equally well delivered by any character on the scene and even in *One Way Pendulum*, his most highly developed piece, the only formal device for holding the play together is the attribution to each character of an *idée fixe*, in the humours tradition, so that if travel is the subject we know it must be Aunt Mildred speaking, if it is weighing-machines or funerals Kirby Groomkirby must be concerned, and so on. And in every play the pattern of constant *non sequitur* is rigidly adhered to, so that the participants, as well as being non-existent as individual characters, cannot even communicate with each other at the most elementary level.

All this means that Simpson's plays are quite arbitrary in their overall effect, even though each individual gag may be carefully calculated (William Gaskill in an interview in *Encore* bears witness to the exactitude with which Simpson times his effects); they are strips of varying lengths cut from the same roll, and there is no reason at all why they should not be lengthened or shortened at will. In a note to the one-act version of

A Resounding Tinkle Simpson remarks: 'From time to time parts of the play may seem to become detached from the main body. No attempt, well intentioned or not, should be made from the auditorium to nudge these back into position while the play is in motion. They will eventually drop off and are quite harmless.' And though this is obviously just a squib, it has enough truth in it to be uncomfortable; the fact that *A Resounding Tinkle* could be cut by more than half in its final version and *One Way Pendulum* reduced by nearly an hour for television without any noticeable harm being done is not entirely without significance.

The first version of *A Resounding Tinkle*, though in many ways gauche and awkward – the one-act version improves on it in other respects besides just being shorter – is of particular interest because in it Simpson shows his hand more clearly than elsewhere. Not only is there a character representing the author brought on to comment every so often, but there are a number of other direct acknowledgements from the stage that this is a play being performed, that the audience may have certain expectations and requirements, and that these are not being met. The picture of home life with Bro and Minnie Paradock (all that is left in the final version) is here interrupted by the arrival of two comedians who perform a sketch in the kitchen and are then left by themselves to entertain the audience. The second scene begins with a long speech from the 'author' apologizing for the performance, suggesting that all the actors are drunk, but in any case their sobriety would not help matters, as the play came to him in Portuguese and he doesn't know a word of the language. Then there is a sequence in which the characters discuss Bergson's ideas on comedy, another long speech by a technician about a supposed reaction-index which is being compiled, and in Act 2 there is a scene when we see the actress playing Minnie talking to a couple of cleaners behind the scenes, and a final parody discussion by the critics of the play we have just been watching.

The technique used, it will be seen, is all very self-consciously experimental; the audience is told so several times and its offence at not receiving what it probably feels it has a right to expect in the theatre is carefully smoothed down by letting it into the joke. The author's speech in the first act contains among other material what is probably, even allowing for its context, Simpson's own apology for his technique.

There is no desire, no intention on my part, or on the part of any of us on this side of the footlights, to impose upon you any ready-made idea of our own as to what this play ought to turn out to be. So often the author – we have all known him – moves invisibly among his audience nudging one and distracting another, muttering and mouthing among his betters. Or he leans forward from time to time to make simultaneous overtures of sumptuous impropriety to every Aunt Edna in the house. Such has never been my conception of the relationship that should exist between us. No. It is together that we must shape the experience which is the play we shall all of us have shared. The actors are as much the audience as the audience themselves, in precisely the same way that the audience are as much the actors as the actors themselves. We are all spectators of one another, mutual witnesses of each other's discomfiture. . . .

The implication here, that each audience, indeed each member of each audience, constructs his own play from the materials offered by author and actors, holds good for all Simpson's plays, and perhaps explains why opinion on them is divided sharply between those who find them funny and those who do not (for if one does not they work in such a way that there will be precious little else to appreciate). It is difficult to suggest the flavour of Simpson's humour without quoting a whole scene, but something may emerge just from a description of the sort of action we can expect from his plays. In the final version of *A Resounding Tinkle* (which is taken mainly from Act 2 of the original but with an interpolation from Act 2, Scene 1, a new ending and a character change whereby Don Paradock becomes Uncle Ted) the Paradocks are complaining that the elephant which has just been delivered is too big – it is certainly bigger than the one they usually have. On the other hand, their neighbour's snake is too small, so small it can be fitted in a pencil-box, so they decide to exchange animals. Someone arrives at the door to invite Bro to form a government, but he refuses ('How can I start forming a government at six o'clock in the evening?') and it may all have been a joke;

then Uncle Ted comes in and turns out to have changed sex, though no one seems to feel any surprise at this, or indeed at anything else that happens in the play.

The Hole, the new one-act play Simpson wrote to complete a double bill at the Royal Court with the one-act version of *A Resounding Tinkle*, is a slight piece with even less plot than that, but as far as construction goes it is easily the most finished of Simpson's works; indeed, it is the only one which shows any sign of 'construction' at all. It is built in the form of an elaborate rondo, the recurrent themes being a conversation between two women, one of whose husbands does all he can to be different from everyone else, while the other's does all he can to be the same, and the unchanging vision of the Visionary, who lives in a private world. In between the recurrences of these themes there are interludes in which three widely differing people come along and, having examined a hole in the road, proceed to explore a succession of possible interpretations of it: it is a chaos of jumbled sports, an aquarium, a prison, a voodoo rite – or perhaps even just a hole with an electrical junction-box in it. The strictly logical nature of Simpson's fantasy has never been more clearly demonstrated, nor more lightly carried, since here for once the temptation, ever present in Simpson's work, to work every idea to death by over-elaboration is on the whole mercifully resisted.

With *One Way Pendulum*, Simpson's second full-length play, we do approach, however obliquely, something a little like a plot: Kirby Groomkirby stays constantly in his room upstairs trying to teach a collection of speak-your-weight machines the 'Hallelujah Chorus', despite the obstructions of one who will not say anything but 'Fifteen stone, ten pounds'; Kirby always wears black (plot point). Meanwhile downstairs his mother is always worrying what they would do with the left-over food if they did not pay Myra Gantry to come in and eat it all up; his sister keeps a skull on the mantelpiece to remind her of death, except that it doesn't much; his aunt in her wheelchair is convinced she is touring the Outer Hebrides, and his father, in the spare moments from standing in front of his own parking meters at sixpence a time to scrape together enough money to pay the bills, is building a do-it-yourself Old Bailey in the living-room. When this is complete a judge and jury move in and start trying the father, Arthur Groomkirby, for some unnamed offence, before finally discovering that it is Kirby who should really be on trial: his passion for wearing black has driven him to provide occasions for it by killing numerous people so that he can attend their funerals. Fortunately, however, the judge lets him go, on the grounds that if he were executed now the law would be cheated of exacting due penalty for all the crimes he may subsequently commit.

One Way Pendulum, as it happens, provides a fairly full demonstration of the theories of drama suggested in the first version of *A Resounding Tinkle* as put into practice: there is the classic Bergsonian subject of humour, the human being acting as – and consequently treated like – a machine (Sylvia refers to Aunt Mildred at one point as a 'great old-fashioned thing . . . cluttering up the place'), as well as its inevitable Simpsonian topsy-turvy reversal, the machine (weighing-machine in this case) acting like and treated as a human being. There is the wilful discontinuity of the action, and the ruthlessly logical and in the end joylessly exhaustive exploration of the possibilities inherent in each absurd premise (the cross-examination of Arthur about his meeting with Myra Gantry is a classic instance of this process in its most extreme form). Finally there is the employment of the gag (frequently derived from some sort of pun or double-entendre) as the basic dramatic unit. It replaces plot with a series of interlinked gags, and the action, such as it is, progresses by a number of 'visual puns' like that which turns Arthur's do-it-yourself courtroom into a real court. It also replaces character, since each participant is characterized, if at all, by a running gag like Aunt Mildred's obsession with travel. And though some of the gags are good ones (the notion of the singing weighing-machines, for example) the net result just goes to demonstrate the futility of trying to build a play out of units so small and insubstantial, with nothing firmer to bind it together: even judged by the amount of amusement to be derived from the gags as they occur the procedure is unsatisfactory, since gags without anything else soon pall. (How many comedians can play for longer than fifteen minutes at a time?)

In any case the gags are all of very much the same type; deprived of any possible foundation in character they rapidly reduce themselves to various forms of the same obsessive verbal doodling. Charles Marowitz, reviewing Simpson's subsequent play, *The Form* (a tiresome one-act fantasy about a man who gets through an interview on the principle that if you look after the answers, the questions will look after themselves, and then grows so powerful that his former interrogator becomes a humble amanuensis, recording his slightest pronouncement) in *Encore* remarked unkindly but aptly that 'There is about Simpson the odour of civil service levity; the kind of pun-laden highjinks one associates with banter around the tea trolley and the frolic of Ministry amateur societies'. This seems to me to place him exactly, and covers equally well his more recent works in the same vein, a group of 'Tall Tinkles' for television and *The Cresta Run* (1965), a stage play which intermittently pretends to be a send-up of a spy thriller. His plays, aspiring to be considered illustrations of the Absurd (he once remarked to an interviewer 'Sometimes I'm afraid that form distorts what is essentially amorphous. One's breaking faith with chaos'), end up as a rule with absurdity in a much humbler form, and one which very rapidly loses its charms in a life-and-death struggle with the law of diminishing returns.

ANN JELLICOE

Ann Jellicoe is certainly exotic, and perhaps unique, among the younger dramatists in that her prime ambition initially was to be a director, and her first full-length play, *The Sport of My Mad Mother*, was in fact written first and foremost as a means, she hoped, of strengthening her hand when it came to the practical realization of this ambition. Her experience up to writing this play, which won third prize in the *Observer* drama competition of 1956 (along with *A Resounding Tinkle* and an Australian play), had, in fact, been largely in the field of direction: born in Middlesbrough in 1928, she studied at the Central School of

Speech and Drama, then worked in repertory and travelled before joining the staff in 1952. During her two years as staff producer at the Central School she was responsible for many student productions, and since leaving has frequently returned to direct, mainly productions of plays by modern English writers (her productions of *The Hole* and *Live Like Pigs* in particular were far superior to their original professional productions). In 1952 she founded and ran for two years an open-stage theatre club, the Cockpit Theatre, directing many plays there, including an early one-act indiscretion of her own which she now prefers to forget; in it, according to her own account, she fell prey to the contemporary vogue for the verse-plays of Christopher Fry, with disastrous consequences.

In 1956, wanting if possible to break into the professional theatre as a director, she began work upon *The Sport of My Mad Mother*, not fully understanding then that no one is looked upon more askance in the theatre than an author, particularly a new, young author, who wants to direct his (or even more startlingly *her*) own plays. However, the play won its *Observer* prize, was accepted for production on the strength of this by the English Stage Company, and staged with the help of a grant from Schweppes. Ann Jellicoe and George Devine shared the direction, and the play was a complete commercial disaster; from the critics it received slightly more approval than from playgoers, but on the whole not very much. Even so, one or two critics recognized that Ann Jellicoe was trying, not yet with complete success admittedly, to do something quite new in the English theatre: to make her play primarily something which happened in front of its audience and made its effect as a totality, rather than a piece of neatly carpentered literary craftsmanship which would 'read well' and work largely by way of its dialogue's appeal to the mind.

The script of *The Sport of My Mad Mother*, in fact, makes very little sense just read cold: it is simply the short score from which a full orchestral sound can be conjured by a skilled musician, or the scenario for a ballet waiting for a composer to write the music and a choreographer to stage it; it is, not surprisingly considering the circumstances of its writing, 'director's theatre' to the nth degree, clearly seen by the author mainly as an *aide-mémoire* in the transference of her initial conception from the stage of her own mind to a real, physical stage. Consequently when staged it makes extraordinary demands on the playgoer schooled in the traditional techniques of the English stage: he expects the play he sees to be, in effect, written mainly for the ear, with the eye required to act on its own just once in a while when it may note a bit of business and aid the mind to deduce some logical significance for it. But here is a play which assaults (the word is used advisedly) both eye and ear, and makes very little appeal to the intellect at all.

It is about a group of Teddy-boys, whose behaviour throughout is instinct with a purely arbitrary spirit of violence, one or two outsiders who become involved mysteriously with them (Caldaro, a young American; Dodo, a retarded thirteen-year-old) and Greta, their spiritual leader, a legendary figure of destruction and in the end, when she gives birth to a child, of creation too, who corresponds presumably to Kali, the Indian goddess of creation and destruction who is the 'mad mother' of the title ('All creation is the sport of my mad mother Kali'). Much of the dialogue, most of it in fact, is almost entirely incantatory in effect, with a minimum of analysable sense; just enough to create the atmosphere of menace and violence always on the point of being unleashed, without ever defining the nature and purpose (if any) of either too exactly. Quite a lot of the 'dialogue' indeed, is merely sound – cries and ejaculations, repeated monosyllables shorn of any associative effect and used entirely for their tonal qualities. On the page it looks as intimidating and uncommunicative as the hieroglyphs of some unknown tongue; in the theatre it all surges over and around one, a strange, disturbing pattern of sights and sounds which produces a corresponding series of emotional reactions from which gradually a total picture of a violent, instinctive way of life emerges: it is about people who are for the most part inarticulate and uncommunicative, and instead of trying to externalize their emotions and reactions in necessarily stilted and artificial words, it creates in the theatre a sort of symbolic equivalent of the mental climate in which they live and thrusts us willy-nilly into it.

But it can do this only so long as we abandon ourselves to the experience instead of stopping to question it. As soon as we deliberately extract ourselves from participation in what is happening and ask what any particular line or section *means*, we are lost and the play is lost to us. In an interview in the *New Theatre Magazine*, published by members of the drama faculty of Bristol University, Ann Jellicoe herself put all this very clearly:

I think the word 'meaning' shows exactly what is wrong with people's attitudes. If they were to ask 'What is the play about?' it would be a better approach. This is a new kind of play, which demands a new approach. Most playgoers today are not used to taking anything direct in the theatre. What they do is transform it into words and put it through their brain. For instance, there is a scene in my play where Caldaro is knocked out, and the Teds stand him on his feet, wrap him up in newspaper, cavort round him, chant-ing until they get to a pitch of ecstasy when they tear the newspaper off him. Now in this action there are hardly any words that make sense – there is nothing which your intellect can take in. If you sit watching and say 'What does this mean? What does this mean?' you're not going to get anywhere; but if you allow yourself to be excited by the visual action and the gradual crescendo of noise under-lining this, you may begin to appreciate what it's about. . . .

You see, so many plays tell you what is happening the whole time. People don't act angry; they tell you they're angry. Now, my play is about incoherent people – people who have no power of expression, of analysing their emotions. They don't know why they're afraid; they don't even know that they are afraid. So they have to compen-sate for their fear by attacking someone else; they're insecure and frustrated, and they have to compensate for that by being big, and violent. And all this is directly shown, instead of being explained; if you're content to watch it without thinking all the time 'What is the meaning?' so that you don't even see or hear, you're so busy thinking – then you will get what it's about.

The Sport of My Mad Mother might well appeal to a variety of people for a variety of reasons, but the Girl Guides' Associa-tion is about the last body one would expect to find its attitudes, its tone, or its style palatable. Yet shortly after it was produced Ann Jellicoe was commissioned by them to write a show for staging at the Empire Pool, Wembley, the only conditions being that it should be 'of interest to youth', have a 'positive ending', make room for some foreign Guides, and have a cast of about 800 girls, 100 boys, and possibly some adults. (The most likely explanation of the commission seems to be that they had heard she wrote 'interesting plays about teenagers'.) Her imagination fired by the possibilities inherent in the form of presentation, she decided to accept the commission and produce something personal which at the same time satisfied all these conditions. The result, *The Rising Generation*, was rejected out of hand by the committee, even after complete rewriting and conventionalization, but the original text was later published in *Ark*, the magazine of the Royal College of Art.

From this it emerges as by far the most interesting and imaginative work ever written in the simple but spectacular form of the youth pageant (though that, admittedly, is not saying very much). It is a story about intolerance and totalitarian rule, told in parable form, though a parable, surely, little calculated to appeal to the Girl Guide ideal: it postulates a conspiracy by the monstrous regiment of women, headed by Mother, 'an enormous woman half-masked with a padded headdress and shoes', to dominate the world and exterminate men. Men are banished and expunged from history; girls at school have to repeat religiously 'Shakespeare was a woman. Milton was a woman. The Black Prince was a woman. Robin Hood, she was a woman. King John was a woman. Newton was a woman'; while their teacher firmly indoctrinates them: 'Men are black. Men are thick. Men are tall. Men are strong. Men will tear you, beat you, eat you. When you're older, you will know.' But finally the girls get together with the boys to rebel against the tyrannical domination of Mother, and though she puts into operation her final threat, the Bomb, they survive and as the show ends the whole vast arena is transformed into a flying saucer to carry them all to a new life somewhere in space. Throughout, the piece not only says something, and says it clearly enough to 'appeal to youth', but it also uses the wide open spaces of the Empire Pool and its resources brilliantly: the spotlit pursuit of the boy Stephen, the triumphal progress of Mother, her opponents held at bay by a battalion of charladies with flaming mops, and the great final transformation could hardly fail to make their effect. It was perhaps too much to expect the Girl Guides' Association to see the singular merits of *The Rising Generation*, but by refusing it they rejected the most interesting work they are ever likely to receive in response to a commission, and incidentally deprived the 7,000 Guides who fill the Empire Pool every night when such a show is on of a strikingly effective piece of spectacular entertainment, to put it no higher.

If *The Rising Generation* suggests in some ways a re-handling of themes from *The Sport of My Mad Mother* in a rather different context, Ann Jellicoe's next play, *The Knack*, staged by the English Stage Company at the Arts, Cambridge, in 1961, and the following year at the Royal Court, shows a complete departure in subject-matter, allied with a remarkable consistency in form and style. We might have imagined that the style employed in *The Sport of My Mad Mother* applied only to the completely inarticulate and non-intellectual who could not be got at in dramatic terms any other way, but even from the *New Theatre Magazine* interview we should have known better, for there Ann Jellicoe generalizes her views on dramatic expression like this:

When I write a play I am trying to communicate with the audience. I do this by every means in my power – I try to get at them through their eyes, by providing visual action; I try to get at them through their ears, for instance by noises and rhythm. These are not loose effects; they are introduced to communicate with the audience directly through their senses, to reinforce the total effect of the play, and they are always geared to character and situation. The theatre is a medium which works upon people's imagination and emotion – not merely their intellect. And I am trying to use every possible effect that the theatre can offer to stir up the audience – to get at them through their emotions. . . . I write this way because – the image that everybody has of the rational, intellectual and intelligent man – I don't believe it's true. I think people are driven by their emotions, and by their fears and insecurities.

The Knack might be a direct illustration of this statement: it is a comedy about, as far as can be seen, normally intelligent, articulate people caught at precisely the point where the image of rational, intelligent man breaks down just because they are completely ruled by their emotions, their fears, and insecurities. The subject of these feelings, naturally enough, is sex – where else is the normally civilized man more subject to non-civilized, indeed anti-civilized, influences? The situation is classically simple. Three men, Tolen, Tom, and Colin, live in one house: Tolen has more than enough sex, being a living demonstration of sexual determination, stamina, and resilience; Tom, having one supposes struck a fairly happy balance, is not violently involved; and Colin, their landlord, does not get anything like enough and worries about it. Into their lives comes an innocent – at least she seems to be an innocent – called Nancy, and a tussle for her develops between Tolen, who sees her as yet another scalp for his belt, and Colin (though their conflict only slowly develops, and at one stage Colin is happy to let Tolen seduce Nancy while he takes notes on technique). Colin is to some extent in a one-up position because he is landlord, but Tolen has the advantage of him in the enviable field of sexual experience, and while Nancy is out of the room being sick after a fainting fit Tolen tries to play off his advantage against Colin's, offering to take Colin into a girl-sharing arrangement he is negotiating with a friend if in return Colin will throw out Tom, whose ironic and unpredictable presence he finds irksome, in favour of the other womanizer. Their plans are swept aside, however, by Nancy's vociferous assertions upon recovery that she was raped while unconscious – by Colin. Colin and Tolen have a violent row on the point, Tolen saying Colin couldn't, Colin saying he didn't but he could; finally Tolen leaves and Colin and the girl are left together under the friendly eye of Tom. . . .

That is what happens – what *happens*, not for the most part what is *said*. Whole sections of the text make no noticeable sense in themselves, because it is always what is going on, and what the audience apprehends from participating in what is going on that counts. Often the dialogue is simply a series of disjointed *non sequiturs* or uncomprehending repetitions, and in one key scene, where Colin and Tom gradually draw Nancy into their fantasy that the bed in the room is actually a piano, of 'pings' and 'plongs' variously distributed and extending virtually uninterrupted over some three pages of the script. The most remarkable quality of the play, in fact, is the sheer drive of the action, physical and emotional, right through its three acts in one unbroken movement; in the theatre not only does the play not demand rationalization on the part of its audience but, unlike *The Sport of My Mad Mother*, which is by comparison sometimes uncertain and immature (the last act in particular fails to cap the previous two conclusively), it positively forbids it: the spectator is carried along irresistibly by the verve and ebullience of the play, and at the end, even if he does not know what, stage by stage, it means, he certainly knows vividly what it is about.

In the five years between *The Sport of My Mad Mother* and *The Knack* Ann Jellicoe matured and developed extraordinarily as a dramatist while continuing obstinately to plough her solitary furrow (her translation, during that time, of two Ibsen plays, *Rosmersholm* and *The Lady from the Sea*, had no noticeable effect on her writing).

With her third full-length play, *Shelley, or the Idealist*, staged at the Royal Court in 1965, she continued as independent as ever, though the furrow had spectacularly changed direction. Dramatists more than anyone are liable to find themselves in that maddening quandary critics tend to offer writers: if they continue along the same line they get blamed for repeating themselves; if they do something entirely different they get blamed for not going on doing whatever it was the critics first liked. Ann Jellicoe ran on to the second of these two prongs with *Shelley*: while *The Sport of My Mad Mother* and *The Knack*, for all their differences, were appreciably products of the same mind at work and the same conception of theatre, I doubt whether anyone, however well versed in the work of the newer British dramatists, would be able to assign *Shelley* to the right author from internal evidence alone.

That, of course, is not necessarily a bad thing, but it can be disconcerting. Previously, Ann Jellicoe's theatre had been primarily one of action rather than words. Words tended

to be used in the two earlier plays mainly as sound, as material
for pattern-making while the real drama of the plays went on
behind and beyond. There was never any doubt that Ann
Jellicoe could use words, and use them sharply to the point
when she chose, but before *Shelley* she had not chosen, in her
plays, to make words the centre and the principal vehicle of
communication. *Shelley* changed all that; hence the surprise of
its first audiences. What it is, essentially, is a relatively straightforward account of Shelley's life from the moment when he
embarked at University on pamphleteering against religion to
his death as described by Trelawny. The method used in
dramatizing all this is not markedly different from that of, say,
Laurence Housman's *Palace Plays*: in a series of neat, short
scenes we follow Shelley's dismissal from Oxford, his sentimental
romance with Harriet Westbrook, his progressive detachment
from her and attachment to Mary Godwin, and then the unsatisfactory course of his second marriage, roaming round
Italy in a succession of more or less high-toned relationships
with nit-witted young women until death came by shipwreck.
The portrait seems accurate and unsentimentalized. True,
it does not do justice to the great charm that Shelley must
obviously have had; but then that after all must have been a
strictly personal and decidedly period thing – in the heyday of
Romanticism it must have been easier to admire and find
charming someone who carried on the way Shelley did, and to
render the same sort of appeal now it would be necessary to
alter the facts of the case, as well as making altogether unfair
demands on the leading actor.

It would, in fact, be virtually impossible to show Shelley in
a completely sympathetic light in the 1960s, when even Jimmy
Porter has become a tiresome period piece. Of course, if
Shelley was, to use the cant phrase of a few years back, an
angry young man, he was an angry young man of genius. But
geniuses are notoriously not the easiest people to live with,
especially if their genius is for anything but thinking clearly.
Shelley took himself for an intellectual, but his capacities for
self-deception were infinite; he was one of those peculiarly
tiresome people we all know who believe themselves to be

F

idealists, and are to some extent, except that their ideals become infinitely adaptable to embrace anything they want to do, and curiously contracted when it comes to judging anyone else's actions and desires. Of course, he was a great poet, but a play can concern itself little with that (though the major piece of verse-quotation is very well handled). It has to be about the man in the artist rather than the artist in the man.

That Ann Jellicoe manages very well: we can believe that Shelley was like this, even if we have to throw his poetry into the balance also as a corrective. Her portraits of the other people around are equally believable. She is obviously right about Godwin, who must have been a monster (though, again, a monster with a touch of genius); moreover, she makes it clear that Godwin was exactly the sort of monster Shelley deserved, for if ever a man asked to have his blood sucked by a leech of Godwin's sort it was Shelley. The two principal women in Shelley's life are sharply drawn, and Mary Shelley is given one of the best acting scenes on the play, near the end, in which she expresses her hate of Italy, where the children die and her cooling husband is constantly unfaithful to her, in body maybe and certainly, what is worse, in mind. Few people are likely to come away from seeing or reading the play without having a clearer idea of Shelley and his circle, and nobody should be positively bored by it. It is, for what it is, holding and intelligent entertainment.

But that is not the whole question. Why is it the work of Ann Jellicoe in particular, rather than that of any of a dozen other dramatists who might take it into their heads to write a solid repertory play about Shelley? That, admittedly, is something of a mystery. Sympathy with youth, of course, counts for something. Ann Jellicoe's continuing interest in the role of woman in a generally male-orientated society gives an intriguing and unexpected undertow to some scenes (it is not for nothing that Mary Shelley was the daughter of Mary Wollstonecraft). There is one little scene, that in which Shelley rehearses his high-sounding reasons for abandoning her to a dazed and nearly hysterical Harriet, where Ann Jellicoe's gift for making over words into meaningful patterns of sound without logical sense comes to the fore. And there is the very theatrical idea of writing the play as a composition for a company of actors, designated by type on the programme (2nd Lead, Juvenile Character, Walking Gentleman), though this was not particularly emphasized at the Royal Court, where Ann Jellicoe herself gave the play a predominantly naturalistic production.

But still, for all the good things in the play, a shade of disappointment remains. It has many merits, to be sure, but not really the particular merits which are Ann Jellicoe's and hers alone in the contemporary British theatre. At least her next play, *The Giveaway* (1969) does return in certain respects to more characteristic territory: it looks like an attempt to use some of her earlier techniques, particularly those of *The Knack*, within a framework of popular, fairly conventional farce. The family at the centre of the play have won a ten-year supply of breakfast cereal, present on stage in eight huge crates. Around them a tenuous plot develops, involving the son of the house, the lodger he hankers after, and the neighbour who hankers after him. The play seems to be an unhappy compromise between low farce (which on this showing Ann Jellicoe has little natural feeling for) and a more personal sort of non-verbal comedy which occasionally gets an enlivening look-in. Again, as with *Shelley*, Ann Jellicoe seems to want to demonstrate that she is not limited to writing in just one way. She has proved her point; but perhaps we may hope that in her next play she will not choose to keep the most personal and individual elements of her talent on such a tight rein.

JOHN ARDEN

Perhaps the biggest single thing to stand in the English Stage Company's favour, whenever and wherever these things finally come to be totted up, will be their continued championship of John Arden in the face of a Press dubious to hostile and of almost complete public apathy (his three plays to be performed publicly at the Royal Court achieved in all a mere seventy-three performances). And in this perseverance they have been absolutely right, as more and more people, both among the critics and among the theatregoing public, are coming to recognize. All the same, the hostility and plain indifference manifested by the vast majority of the plays' first spectators is quite easy to understand; one could even understand why many not properly attuned to Arden's work should find it downright boring. The explanation resides in one fact, simple in itself but extremely complex in its implications: Arden permits himself, in his treatment of the characters and situations in his plays, to be less influenced by moral preconceptions than any other writer in the British theatre today.

Hence the difficulty. His work would be perfectly easy for audiences if he attacked morality; that would be shocking (even now, since conventions still rule even where convictions have flagged), it would be 'provocative', and most important of all it would imply by catagorically rejecting certain standards that these standards nevertheless existed – there would still be clear, dramatic blacks and whites, even if they did not always come in the expected places. But instead, and much more puzzlingly, he recognizes an infinitude of moral standards, all with their claims to consideration and all quite distinct from the individuals who hold them and try, more or less imperfectly, to put them into practice. Well, we can stand a little uncertainty about which are our heroes and which are our villains, but where do we stand in a situation which seems to deny the very possibility of heroism or villainy? The question may not be all that worrying on a purely personal level – one could argue that such concepts as heroism and villainy have little meaning in Pinter's work, for example – but Arden brings us face to face with it in its baldest form by writing plays which appear to be about general social, moral, and political issues: colour prejudice and prostitution, social clashes on a housing estate, pacifism, the treatment of old age. Arden the man no doubt feels strongly about all these subjects, or he would hardly choose to write about them, but his dramatist's instinct absolutely prevents him from stacking things in favour of the characters whose opinions most closely resemble his own; in an interview he has expressed 'grave objections to being presented with a character on the stage whom you know to be the author's mouthpiece'.

For behind Arden's work there seems to be brooding one basic principle: not exactly the obvious one that today there are no causes – that would be altogether too facile, and in any case just not true – but that there are too many. There are as many causes as there are people (more, since many are quite capable of espousing two or more mutually exclusive causes at the same time), and only the naïve can suppose that any two people who are, say, pacifists (to choose a nice, convenient label) will believe the same things for the same reasons. In other words, in all Arden's plays the characters we meet are first and foremost just people: not concepts cast into a vaguely human mould, with built-in labels saying 'good' or 'bad', 'hero' or 'villain', to help us into the right grooves. It follows, therefore, that the behaviour of any one person or group does not imply any general judgement. (Arden himself has said that he 'cannot see why a social play should not be so designed that we may find ourselves understanding the person's problems, but not necessarily approving his reactions to them'.) *The Waters of Babylon* is not a play in favour of prostitution and tenant-exploitation (or for that matter the reverse); *Live Like Pigs* tells us nothing about 'The Welfare State'; *Serjeant Musgrave's Dance* is not for or against pacifism *per se*; *The Happy Haven* offers no solution to the problem of old age: they are just plays about individual people affected one way or another by these issues. Hence, perhaps – until one gets used to Arden's way of seeing things at least – the confusion and irritation of his audiences: when 'parity of esteem' for all the characters is pushed so far, identification and taking sides become difficult if not impossible, and though undeniably the characters con- flict – they are conflicting all the time – for many theatre- goers a conflict in which they are not asked themselves to participate is in effect no conflict at all; left rudderless and all at sea, they end up lost and bored.

This happened in its most extreme form, to judge from the notices anyway, with his first professionally staged play, *The Waters of Babylon*, and with *The Happy Haven*. At the time *The*

Waters of Babylon was put on for one Sunday-night production-without-décor at the Royal Court, Arden was still a practising architect (he was born in Barnsley in 1930, educated partly at state, partly at public schools, and studied architecture at Cambridge and Edinburgh); he had written various plays in verse or prose (including a schoolboy effort 'on the death of Hitler written in the style of *Samson Agonistes*' and 'a pseudo-Elizabethan tragedy on the Gunpowder Plot, which was very bad, a sort of academic play in verse'), had a period comedy about the building of a railway called *All Fall Down* (which he compares with Whiting's *Penny for a Song*) performed by fellow students at Edinburgh, and won a B.B.C. Northern Region prize for his radio play *The Life of Man*. This, though Arden now regards it as immature, shows already much of his mature technique: the blend of verse and prose, the ballad songs and snatches and the more general recourse to images from the ballad world. It tells of the last, fated voyage of the packet-boat *Life of Man* as it passes through the muddled mind of the one, half-crazed survivor, and though influences from *The Ancient Mariner* (in the form and some of the details) and *Moby Dick* (in the character of the possessed, fanatical Captain Anthract) are strong, and influences from two of John Masefield's sea novels, *The Bird of Dawning* and *Live and Kicking Ned*, are, Arden tells me, even stronger, the sections dealing with the victim-cum-avenging angel Jones and his life as a shepherd in the Welsh hills already reflect Arden's interest in the roaming life and 'the sturdy beggar', and the overall effect is, even so early in his career, fully characteristic. *The Life of Man* attracted the attention of the Royal Court, and though they rejected the first play he submitted (based on an Arthurian legend), they accepted *The Waters of Babylon* as the first of their low-budget Sunday-night ventures.

In general the critics did not think much of it, and without agreeing with them one can easily see why: it is in many ways the most teasing and apparently perverse of all his plays in what it says (or appears to be saying), even apart from the eccentricity of its form and style. Briefly, its central character, its 'hero' if you like, is a Polish émigré who leads a double life,

working in an architect's office by day while out of office hours
he runs a lodging-house occupied by eighty exploited foreign
tenants and a number of the string of prostitutes he 'manages'.
Worse, he claims to have been in Buchenwald, and so he was,
but as a member of the German army. And yet in spite of all
this he is certainly the most sympathetically delineated character, in most respects amiable, good-natured, and thoroughly
likeable; and so indeed are the prostitutes and ex-prostitutes,
with whom his relations are of the friendliest. If we start lining
up characters and concepts, as many of the play's first audience
did, we shall be forced to some very odd conclusions. But that,
clearly, is not Arden's intention. Instead he gives us a picturesque mixture of comedy and a little drama as Krank (Sigis-
manfred Krankiewicz) tries desperately to raise the money to
pay off a patriotic fellow Pole who is setting up a bomb plot
in his lodging-house; he hopes to raise it by rigging, with the
aid of 'Uncle Charlie' Butterthwaite, erstwhile 'Napoleon of
Local Government', the results of a new municipal lottery (the
play began as a satire on the Premium Bond system). There
are really no heroes and no villains; Krank is quite sympathetic, but too contradictory and elusive to be really heroic,
the girls and the crooks are mostly likeable, while even their
obvious opponents – the straight Negro councillor Joseph
Caligula, the fatuous M.P. Loap, and the shifty chauvinist
Henry Ginger – are too complicated to stand, singly or together,
as villains.

Worse still, for an already sufficiently puzzled audience, the
style in which this mystifying confection is written offers mani-
fold complexities in itself. Some of the dialogue is written in a
springy, colloquial, realistic style, some, particularly the mali-
ciously accurate parodies of the Hyde Park orators' styles, suggests that satire is intended, some, especially Krank's monologues, is written in a fairly highly wrought free verse, and to
make matters worse several of the characters have a disconcerting habit of bursting into song at odd moments. Indeed, were
it not for the life and vigour of the whole thing, its tremendous
theatrical drive and panache, the brisk conclusion of most re-
viewers that 'this young man may have ideas but cannot begin

to put them together into a play' might be comprehensible, if not quite forgivable.

Not quite forgivable because, even apart from the evident and abundant life of the play, Arden does at one point come unusually close to a direct statement of what he is at, and an attentive ear should not have missed it. In the last act Paul, the patriot, is berating Krank for his war record; 'We know what you were', he cries. Krank turns on him:

> But I don't know what *you* are. Or you, Henry Ginger.
> Or all the rest of you, with your pistols and your orations,
> And your bombs in your private house, and your fury,
> And your national pride and honour. This is the lunacy.
> This was the cause, the carrying through of all that insensate war,
> This is the rage and purposed madness of your lives,
> That *I*, Krank, do not know. I *will* not know it,
> Because, if I know it, from that light day forward,
> I am a man of time, place, society and accident;
> Which is what I must not be. Do you understand me . . .?
> The world is running mad in every direction,
> It is quicksilver, shattered, here, here, here, here.
> All over the floor. Go on, hustle after it,
> Chase it, dear Paul. But I choose to follow
> Only such fragments as I can easily catch.
> I catch them, I keep them such time as I choose,
> Then roll them away down and follow another.
> Is that philosophy? It is a reason anyway. . . .

In all his plays Arden has chosen to do just this, to follow only such fragments as he can easily catch, catch them, keep them such time as he chooses, then roll them away and follow others; his world is shattered, like ours, and the plays he has made out of it are comprehensible only if considered as certain fragments selected, isolated, and shaped into a whole; what we must not do is to assume that they are microcosms of a complete, coherent world, and then seek to read its character in their various faces.

This becomes even more evident when Arden's next two plays, *Soldier, Soldier* and *Live Like Pigs* (*Soldier, Soldier* was actually written first, for B.B.C. Television, but not produced until two years later), are taken into consideration. For in

them the style already in the making in *The Waters of Bablyon*
emerges fully fledged, and the affinities of this style as well as the
subject-matter it is used on enforce a more detailed consideration both of Arden's style and of his intentions. The name most
frequently evoked in connection with Arden's work is that of
Brecht, and the affinity is certainly there. Arden, paradoxically,
is at once the most and the least Brechtian of all modern British
dramatists: most, because their views on the proper relationship between the audience and what is happening on stage and
their means of achieving it are almost identical; least, because
one could readily imagine that Arden's plays would have been
written in exactly the same way if Brecht had never existed.
Basic to Arden's drama is something strikingly akin to Brecht's
celebrated A-effect: as we have remarked already, though there
are all sorts of conflicts taking place on stage, the audience is
never invited to participate in them; it is even forcibly prevented on occasion from doing so. Instead it is invited to experience the play as a self-contained totality, and to judge –
though on a human level rather than in terms of general concepts. (Herein lies the vital difference between Arden's practice and Brecht's theory, though, of course, Brecht's practice is
a good deal nearer to Arden than his theory would lead one to
expect.)

This is achieved largely through an unashamed and deliberate resort to 'theatricality', to various formal devices which
keep the viewer constantly aware that he is in a theatre (or in
front of a television screen) watching a *play*. Song plays an important part in Arden's work, and is almost always used quite
nonrealistically: anyone may express him- or herself in song,
usually song closely related in form and style to the English
folksong and ballad. So, too, with passages of heightened
speech in rhyme, or sometimes in free verse which is still appreciably verse rather than prose: indeed, in Arden's later
plays the distinction between verse and prose has become more
marked, and he now finds the parts of the earlier plays in
which such a distinction is not clearly made muzzy and unsatisfactory. He says, for instance, of *The Waters of Babylon*,
where there is a lot of verse:

I feel on re-reading it that many of the scenes would have been better if I had gone about it more naturalistically, and used a more natural prose. I think the use of formal verse and straightforward vernacular prose in juxtaposition is quite a good solution even in a modern play. If people are speaking formal verse with lines that rhyme, the audience does not have to worry whether it sounds natural or not. They are talking poetry. It's with the half-and-half thing that one is in trouble.

And what sort of subject-matter is the critical detachment achieved in this way to be applied to? In both *Soldier, Soldier* and *Live Like Pigs* to evidently 'social' subjects, since in each case we witness an unsettling incursion of uncontrollable outside forces into a hitherto settled community. The only trouble, from a conventional viewpoint, is deciding which side we should be on, that of the intruder or that of the intruded upon. Either, our preconceptions would lead us to suppose, the dramatist must be for order, authority, and all the rest of it and against the forces of anarchy and disorder, or he must be against established complacency and for those who rebel against it. But somehow neither of these neat theorizations seems to work in either case. In the first the Soldier, an obvious bad lot, lies and cheats his way into the household of another soldier missing from his regiment, pretending he knows the boy and that he alone can extract him from some terrible trouble he has fallen into; he proceeds to bleed the family dry, seduce the son's wife, and make off with as much of their savings as he can conveniently extract. So, surely, we should be against him and for his victims. But no, not a bit of it; like Krank, this 'randy chancer' is strangely likeable; there is certainly something fetching about his all-out way of life. But on the other hand the Scuffhams, his victims, are not presented as in any way villains of hypocrisy and complacency who deserve all they get; they are not very bright, admittedly, but they might fairly be described, like the Jacksons in *Live Like Pigs*, as 'undistinguished but not contemptible'.

Their situation, in fact, is in many ways identical with that of the Jacksons, a cosy conventional family happy in their housing-estate semi-detached until the Sawneys, a wild and disreputable family of near-gipsies, are moved protesting into the house next door. But in *Live Like Pigs,* since a political question (for or against the Welfare State?) appears to be involved, the issue of allegiances is even more acute. On this subject one can hardly do better than quote from Arden's own Introductory Note to the printed text:

> On the one hand, I was accused by the Left of attacking the Welfare State: on the other, the play was *hailed* as a defence of anarchy and amorality. So perhaps I had better declare myself. I approve outright neither of the Sawneys nor of the Jacksons. Both groups uphold standards of conduct which are incompatible, but which are both valid in their correct context.
>
> The Sawneys are an anachronism. They are the direct descendants of the 'sturdy beggars' of the sixteenth century, and the apparent chaos of their lives becomes an ordered pattern when seen in terms of a wild empty countryside and a nomadic existence. Put out of their fields by enclosing landlords, they found such an existence possible for four hundred years. Today, quite simply, there are too many buildings in Britain, and there is just no room for nomads. The family in this play fails to understand this, and becomes educated in what is known as the 'hard way', but which might also be called the 'inefficient way'.
>
> The Jacksons are an undistinguished but not contemptible family, whose comparative cosiness is not strong enough to withstand the violent irruption into their affairs that the Sawneys bring. Their natural instincts of decency and kindliness have never been subjected to a very severe test. When they are, they collapse. I do not regard them as being necessarily typical in this. They are the people I have chosen for the play, because they illustrate my theme in a fairly extreme form.

This passage has been worth quoting at length, because it is absolutely central to the full comprehension of Arden's methods and intentions. It makes it clear that his attitude to his creations is so complex it cannot be reduced to simple terms of approval or disapproval. Thus, for instance, he does not defend the standards (or what some might regard as the lack of standards) of the Sawneys, nor, on the other hand, does he condemn them – they are individuals, and there are reasons, valid reasons, why they live as they do, even if they happen not to fit into the modern world. Similarly he does not condemn the very different standards of the Jacksons; they, too, have their reasons. He does not even seek to generalize from them about the behaviour of this *sort* of family; they also are individuals, just the people the dramatist has chosen for this particular play, and in doing so he, too, had his reasons.

Both *Soldier, Soldier* and *Live Like Pigs* achieved, despite and at least partly because of the initial misunderstandings, a modest measure of success (*Soldier, Soldier* even won the Italia Prize, thus laying to rest the B.B.C.'s doubts sufficiently for them to commission another play from Arden on the strength of it). But then both productions stressed the realistic elements at the expense of the others and tended if anything to underplay the comedy; in any case, they made the plays seem considerably more normal than *The Waters of Babylon*. *When is a Door not a Door*, the one-act farce set in a factory office which he wrote at this time as a vehicle for a class of Central School drama students, *was* much more normal. It deals with a bad morning in the factory, a strike threatening, all the office staff at one another's throats, and two carpenters casually repairing a door frame throughout the action, taking no notice of all the excitement.

But with his next play, *Serjeant Musgrave's Dance* (1959), Arden made a break with realism as it is generally understood on the English stage too decisive to be so easily smoothed over. As it happened, this appears to have made his style all the more acceptable (perhaps because playgoers still find it easier to take poetry and song in period drama than in a modern setting) and the play soon became in some intangible way his best known and most successful – 'intangible' because on the stage it did little better than the others (twenty-eight performances to twenty-three of *Live Like Pigs* and twenty-two of *The Happy Haven*), but somehow even before the television production in 1962 it was the one play of his that everyone seemed to have heard of; it continues to be revived from time to time, and the printed text still sells steadily.

The plot concerns the arrival of a group of deserters, led by Serjeant Musgrave, in a northern town in the 1880s, ostensibly recruiting but actually to teach the townfolk a lesson about war. In the town they are mistrusted at first – there are troubles at the mine and everyone equates soldiers with strike-breakers

– but a little free beer gains them the amiability, if not exactly the friendship and confidence, of the miners. The mine-owner and his minions see the bit of colour and excitement offered by an all-out recruiting campaign as a good thing to keep the workers occupied, and though one of the soldiers gets more or less accidentally killed in a struggle, when the day of the meeting comes Musgrave is able to unfold his ideas to an audience initially ready and willing to receive them. But before long he has shocked them by revealing that in one of the boxes he has brought are the bones of a local boy, killed during the occupation of a foreign land; in reprisals five natives were killed for him, so now with the inexorable arithmetic of military logic Musgrave has decided that this five must again be multiplied by five to produce the number of those in authority who must be killed so that the lesson on the horrors of war will be well and truly learnt. Here his supporters start wavering; this is not what they had expected and one at least has believed their mission to be against killing *per se*. In the confusion the dragoons arrive, the soldiers are disarmed, and the sombrely-dressed miners dance to celebrate the re-establishment of law and order, some of them happily forgetful of what is happening around them, others compelled to join in by the looming presence behind them of a solid wall of dragoons in red; red, the colour of the 'blood-red rose flower' which has been the central image of the play and now overtly dominates the black and white of the coal-town under snow. (As Arden once wrote about the world of the ballads: 'The colours are primary. Black is for death, and for the coalmines. Red is for murder, and for the soldier's coat the collier puts on to escape from his black...')

This, even from such a bald summary, is obviously a very complex play, and again one must beware of confusing characters with concepts. At the time it was often found confusing because the liberal spectator saw in it a tract about pacifism which seemed to show that pacifism did not work. For the naïve this was simply because Musgrave and his men are defeated at the end, for the more perceptive it was because the motives and methods of the soldiers are so at odds with each other and often so apparently wrong-headed that it might be interpreted as an attempt to discredit pacifism by discrediting pacifists. Either Arden is for the pacifists, the argument would run, or he is against them, but if he is for them why has he not made them largely creditable and heroic, while if he is against them why has he made their opponents so discreditable and unheroic? Now there seems little doubt from what we know of Arden's personal views and what he has told us of the play's origins (the general concept of the town taken over came from an American film by Hugo Fregonese, *The Raid*; the specific atrocity which inspires Musgrave's crusade from a parallel occurrence in Cyprus) that his sympathies are with the pacifists, yet clearly all his instincts as a dramatist prevent him from siding unequivocally with anyone; though the Parson and the Mayor come perhaps closer to hostile caricatures than any of his other characters, it is evident throughout that this is a play about individual, complicated human beings, and any simple alignment of character and concept is doomed to failure.

Musgrave himself, for instance, is right and sympathetic in his outrage at the atrocities which have been perpetrated abroad, but his decision that they can be expiated and a clean start be made only by a further shedding of blood is clearly much open to doubt; his 'logic' of order and discipline is inhuman and fails to take the natural way of things into account. From any point of view except one he is to blame for his blindness in supposing, as Mrs Hitchcock puts it in the last scene, that at the end of the world he could call a parade, and work everything out like a neat abstract geometrical progression; he is to blame for seeing life and love as a scribble on the neatly drawn, black-and-white plan of duty, rather than as the constants in terms of which any scheme of life must be drawn up. Unless, of course – and this is the one alternative – he is right when he says that God is with him; that he really is the representative of divine and by definition 'inhuman' justice that he believes himself to be. This point of view could be argued, but Arden does not here, any more than elsewhere, take sides; the idea serves simply to give coherence and a context to Musgrave's attitudes and help to explain why he is right in his terms just as Mrs Hitchcock is in hers, Attercliffe, the completely non-violent soldier, in his, and the dragoons no doubt in theirs (in an interview Arden has said himself that at the end 'law and order have been re-established by force; which, if you like, is the natural result of Musgrave trying to establish the opposite by force').

Formally *Serjeant Musgrave's Dance* is one of Arden's most successful pieces, the mature expression of the theme of *Soldier Soldier* and, in a different way, of *Live Like Pigs*: the sudden explosive incursion of the extraordinary and disruptive into the normal and fairly orderly. It has a very slow and elaborate exposition, setting the scene and building up the situation to the climactic burst of violent action, and the songs and passages of heightened speech are integrated more effectively than ever before into the structure as a whole. Already the separation between formal and colloquial in the dialogue is becoming more clear-cut and decisive, though action and dialogue explication are not yet always equally distinct; Arden himself has remarked on the confusing nature of the churchyard plotting scene, and in his television adaptation achieved a clarification which might well be used in further stage productions.

The move towards at once greater formality of presentation and greater clarity and simplicity of expression seen in its initial stages in *Serjeant Musgrave's Dance* was to find a more extreme expression in his next theatrical play, *The Happy Haven* (1960–1), but meanwhile he wrote *The Business of Good Government*, a Christmas play for the church of Brent Knoll, the Somerset village where he was living at the time. Of this there is little to say except that it is of a radiant grace and simplicity which make clear some of the lessons Arden has learnt from a study of the medieval stage and its techniques, and that its depiction of Herod is so sympathetic that one or two critics have been tempted to write about it as a nativity play in which Herod is the hero. This is, of course, a journalistic oversimplification, but it reflects the fact that even here Arden is not ready to paint in unmistakable blacks and whites; Herod may not receive more than his due, but what is due to him he receives in full, and his actions are placed clearly in their historical-political context so that we can see that he was not a monster but just someone acting reasonably and with excellent intentions within the limitations of his own rule of conduct – the extreme case perhaps, of 'understanding the person's problems, but not necessarily approving his reactions to them'?

The Happy Haven, which Arden worked upon during his year as Drama Fellow at Bristol University and first produced there on an open stage, probably created a greater trouble in the breasts of the critics than any of his other plays when it reached the Royal Court in 1961. The things which worried them were (*a*) that all the characters wear masks of some sort at some stage in the production, and most of them do so throughout; (*b*) that this is a comedy (Arden calls it a 'pantomime') about old people in an old folk's home. This meant to most critics that it was (*a*) crankily experimental and (*b*) a joke in bad taste. Both of which conclusions are distinctly curious. As far as the masks are concerned, there are excellent practical reasons for them, which Arden details in the *Encore* interview already quoted, among them mainly the advantages of using young actors so that the play is not slowed down and any too close realism which might incur the charge of cruelty is avoided. This charge has nevertheless been made; indeed, it is the basis of the assertion that the play is a joke in bad taste. But here we are back at the old trouble which has dogged us in any consideration of Arden's work, the confusion of characters with concepts. Certainly the old people are not represented as sweet, amiable, harmless old souls, ever ready with proverbial wisdom and tearful smiles of gratitude for any small attention which is shown them; instead, they are idiosyncratic human beings of distinct and complex temperaments (in itself perhaps a criticism to those who choose to believe that anyone over seventy must automatically become a depersonalized plaster saint). Arden chooses to tell the truth about old age, the unsentimental truth, summed up in Mrs Phineus's great speech in the second act, and sentimentalists do not like it:

> I'm an old old lady
> And I don't have long to live.
> I am only strong enough to take
> Not to give. No time left to give.

I want to drink, I want to eat,
I want my shoes taken off my feet.
I want to talk but not to walk
Because if I walk, I have to know
Where it is I want to go.
I want to sleep but not to dream
I want to play and win every game
To live with love but not to love
The world to move but me not move
I want I want for ever and ever
The world to work, the world to be clever.
Leave me be, but don't leave me alone.
That's what I want. I'm a big round stone
Sitting in the middle of a thunderstorm. . . .

But even supposing that this sort of attitude reflects discredit on the characters in the play – though surely the whole form in which it is cast, not to say its unmistakable humanity, forbids us to suppose so – and admitting that they show themselves in general quite capable of behaving just as badly as anyone else, what then? Does this make it an attack on old age itself? One would have to be pretty obtuse to think so. In fact, the plot of the play makes it, if we may assign any single moral to Arden for a moment, something much more like a plea for the old: an urging that they, too, are human beings and should be treated as such. Of course, such a schematic reading cannot be pushed too far – that is not Arden's way – but it has at least as much truth as the 'bad taste' view of the piece.

If it were the complete explanation, of course, the doctor who treats his patients as so many guinea-pigs would have to be the villain, but though he has been firmly pigeon-holed as such, notably by Mr Tom Milne in the *New Left Review*, this also is oversimplifying. Dr Copperthwaite, too, is acting with the best intentions; he, too, is in the right according to his own standards, and really sees his new youth elixir as a benefit to mankind, even if, carried away by his fanaticism on this subject, he forgets to consider the feelings of the individual men and women in his charge, whom he intends to dose experimentally with the liquid. Indeed, whenever we seem at all in danger of seeing him too completely as the near monster he becomes to the patients, Arden devises a quick change of focus to help us see him in a far other and less intimidating light. For he is a weekend football player, and with his outside friends just an ordinary, undistinguished, rather juvenile young man. One of the patients, Mrs Letouzel, actually points out that this is so:

> He's the undisputed custodian of everything that's good for us. Security. Reliability. Though some people have said he failed to save the score the other Saturday at football. They relied on him to stop the goals, when he came back from the match he was swearing, frustrated – I know because I heard him. He'd let them through, he had to apologize, I tell you I heard him. Apologized – Copperthwaite – in his humility, to the Captain of the Team. . . . But despite that, you silly children, we are all his worms. And he says 'Turn, worms, turn', and he thinks we have got no choice!

But we see and hear it ourselves; just at the moment when he has made his big discovery he has a phone conversation with the captain of the football team, full of fourth-form humour about 'medical goods – plain envelopes' and schoolboy jollity, while later he has an equally revealing conversation with his mother, who is slyly trying to introduce him, rather against his will, to eligible young women. Mr Milne is very hard on the first speech, finding that 'an important point is being made in this apparent digression: at a moment which may radically affect a number of people's lives, the doctor can respond only with prep-school smut and a sense of responsibility which treats people as no more than guinea-pigs. Never *stated*, this point is inescapable if viewed in its proper context'. Now there may well be some truth in this, but it seems to be reading it at once too much and too little into the lines. The moral judgement is too lofty, really, since if the speech does not show the doctor in a particularly flattering light, at least it suggests that by any but a rigidly puritanical standard he is, out of office hours and seen for once through the eyes of someone other than his patients, a fairly normal, not specially bright or mature sort of chap – a point which emerges even more forcefully in the even more apparent digression of his conversation with his mother. In other words, like almost all Arden's other characters he is not a two-dimensional stereotype representing some abstract concept, but a human being with certain standards:

we can understand his problems, too, even if we do not necessarily approve of his reactions to them.

After the extreme formalism of *The Happy Haven* Arden chose
in his next play, the television piece *Wet Fish*, to go to the other
extreme with a closer approach to naturalism than he had yet
attempted, reducing the role of rhymed or appreciably formal
verse to two short songs assigned to an evidently eccentric and
in any case 'un-English' character. This latter turned out to be
none other than our old friend Krank from *The Waters of
Babylon*, complete with double life of architect's office by day
and brothel-organization by night (not to mention Teresa at
the other end of a phone and Alderman Charlie Butterthwaite
rumbling in the distance). This time, however, we are shown
mostly his 'respectable' life at work, since the office and the
various jobs it has on hand – particularly the reconstruction of
a fish shop for a friend of the architect – provide the play's
principal material. Gathered into less than an hour and a half
we have a tragi-comedy about the shop itself, the odd and
intricate business-cum-romantic life of Krank, the initiation
of a new female architect into business practice, some jiggery-
pokery with the local council over new planning in the town,
and quite a bit of semi-documentary stuff about the way an
architect's office works. The result is rather a ragbag, but a
lively one, bursting all over with scenes and strands of good
plays which do not quite, in the end, hold together – mainly,
no doubt, because the circumstances of production did not
allow Arden the chances he had expected to clarify and rewrite
during rehearsals; anyway, this prodigality of material is a
fault on the right side.

After *Wet Fish* Arden turned, unexpectedly, to an early
love, Goethe's first play *Goetz von Berlichingen*, which had fascinated him when he had to study it as an examination set book
at school. *Ironhand*, the play he based on it, is something far
more than a translation, though. What he did, apparently, was
to read each section of the original, using Sir Walter Scott's
stilted translation as a crib, and when then he felt he had got
the point of the scene write a scene in English along the same
lines and conveying the same point. Or, as a matter of fact,

not always quite the same point. Goethe's Goetz is seen almost entirely from his own point of view, a romantic robber-knight whose exploits are uncomplicatedly heroic. Arden's Goetz remains in all essentials the same, but the tenor of the play is altered by the considerably stronger, more positive part Arden makes Goetz's opponent Weislingen play, so that what finally emerges is a critical study of an anachronism, a man who belongs to the Middle Ages, and does not understand that the historical processes at work around him in Germany early in the sixteenth century are making him obsolete. Where Goethe could bring himself to show only one side fairly, Arden again states all sides of the case with equal care and justice. In the process of adaptation Arden has also strengthened the narrative links, concentrated the plot here and there, especially in the second half, which Goethe left rather rambling and disconnected, and boldly identified the 'Brother Martin' of the early scenes as Luther. The result is a lively, action-packed piece of theatre, written in springy, idiomatic prose which in spite of everything corresponds remarkably closely to the spirit of the original.

Arden's next play, *The Workhouse Donkey*, is on the surface very different. Described by the author as 'a vulgar melodrama', it is a melodrama both in the strict sense, a play accompanied by music, and, to a certain extent, in the more popular sense. It is a further episode in the career of Arden's favourite character Alderman Charlie Butterthwaite, though as Arden points out the pieces do not exactly fit together: in *The Waters of Babylon*, which took place 'now', i.e. 1957, Charlie Butterthwaite had just come to London after his downfall and disgrace in the north, but in *Soldier, Soldier* and *Wet Fish* he is understood to be still in power, and in *The Workhouse Donkey*, which equally takes place 'now' (1963) we finally come to the story of how he fell from power. *The Workhouse Donkey* uses much the same sort of technique as *The Happy Haven*: an apparently wild but in fact perfectly calculated mixture of speech and song, highly colloquial prose, blank verse, and highly formal rhymed verse – all on a subject which almost any other modern British dramatist would be inclined to treat, if at all, in a more or less naturalistic fashion. The idiom of the play is related, as Arden himself notes, 'to that of low music-hall comedy and seaside picture-postcards', which is in itself 'a form of "social realism"', but far from the form it usually takes on the English stage.

The play is an intricate tale of political manœuvring in a northern town, with the sympathy (or lack of it) very evenly divided among the various groups. Most of the trouble arises in the first place from the arrival of a new chief constable, Colonel Feng. His job is to clean up the town, but no one knows whether he is in fact strictly impartial politically or whether he is going to concentrate on the sharp practices of one side only, as the Labour council in particular fear he may. There is ample material on both sides, what with the jobbery of Butter-thwaite, formerly mayor and now *éminence grise* to the new mayor, Boocock, on the Labour side, and the financial stake that the local Conservative industrialist Sir Harold Sweetman has in a dubious club nearby, the Copacabana. Caught between the two groups is Butterthwaite's old crony, the disreputable doctor Wellington Blomax, his daughter being involved with Sweetman's son while he himself, in pursuit of his own ends, has married Gloria, manageress of the Copacabana and preg-nant by Police-Superintendent Wiper, who keeps her in-formed of the police's moves. Butterthwaite and his associates decide to discredit the Conservatives and try Feng by laying information against the Copacabana, but their plan backfires when it involves an accusation of police complicity and Sweet-man sets up an opposition story that they were drunk and dis-orderly at the time.

Meanwhile circumstances are conspiring against Blomax, since his wife (encouraged by Lady Sweetman and Wiper) wants him to discredit Butterthwaite and his daughter wants him to reclaim the money the extravagant and now impover-ished Butterthwaite owes him so that she shall have the free-dom to choose whom she shall marry. Cornered, Butterthwaite burgles the council offices to give Blomax his money, and tries to direct suspicion from himself by a trumped-up story of being attacked and robbed of the safe keys. Blomax is forced to go

Queen's Evidence on the matter, but Feng, now in love with Blomax's daughter, deviates from strict impartiality far enough to hush the matter up: nevertheless, the very fact that Butterthwaite has been taken in for questioning in connection with the robbery persuades the local Labour Party to disown him, and a final drunken demonstration at the Copacabana, now prudently turned into the Sweetman Memorial Art Gallery, only completes his downfall; he is an alien in this town, an anachronism like Goetz von Berlichingen, a robber-baron in an age of primly hypercritical respectability. And so he must go. But so must Feng, like him an alien, not so much because his love for Blomax's daughter has made him slightly transgress his own rules, but because such a strict rule of conduct is itself an uncomfortable anachronism in the modern world he inhabits, and makes him a nuisance to too many people (in this way he is curiously like Goetz's arch-enemy Weislingen). Boocock and Sweetman, on the other hand, survive; they are the discreet compromisers, who know how to be moderate, cover their own retreat, and live to fight another day. Blomax, too, survives; he has to, because he knows so much that it is in everybody's interest to look after him and keep him quiet.

Arden's next major play, *Armstrong's Last Goodnight* (1964) was also brought forward for metropolitan audiences by the National Theatre, first at Chichester and then in London, though it had previously been produced at the Glasgow Citizen's Theatre. Though in retrospect it seems to be one of the clearest and most completely achieved of Arden's plays, at the time it was widely received with mystification and resentment even from critics who had previously liked Arden's work. I suppose the first reason for this was the language. The play takes place in mid-sixteenth-century Scotland, and the dialogue is written throughout in a brilliant pastiche, or rather recreation, of Scottish speech at the time. Possibly, therefore, the play's first audiences in Glasgow had a slight advantage over Chichester's sassenachs, but in any case the dialogue requires no special training in Scots, medieval or modern: all that is necessary is to attune one's ear to the way of the language, and after a few minutes one falls readily enough into it.

Otherwise, the play is not particularly difficult. As so often in Arden's work, it turns on the contrast – sometimes, but not necessarily always, the opposition – between two men representing two different codes of behaviour, two different approaches to life. In *The Workhouse Donkey* it is Butterthwaite and Feng; in *Ironhand* it is Goetz and Weislingen; and here it is Armstrong and Sir David Lindsay. And in all cases it is not directly the conflict between the two which results in the defeat of one or both, but the passage of time and the forces of history which finally bring both to their reckoning. In *Armstrong's Last Goodnight* the conflict may be seen simply – no doubt too simply – as that between thought and action. Lindsay is the polished courtier and diplomat, cunning, devious, seeing politics like a game of chess; Armstrong, the border bandit, is the man of action, taking each turn of the game dead seriously and throwing himself into each new role with such gusto and conviction that all question of whether he is sincere, whether he really believes in what he is doing, becomes irrelevant. And this, finally, is why Lindsay cannot manipulate him as he wishes and intends: he does not take the man's violence seriously enough.

But Lindsay is not just a scented popinjay courtier: he is in his own way a man of action too, but it is a different and wholly incompatible way. Equally, Armstrong is no mere unthinking oaf; he has his own brand of cunning policy, and it is just his way of putting it into effect that baffles Lindsay. They live, like the two families in *Live Like Pigs*, in two different worlds according to two different codes, neither better nor worse than the other, but just separate and incompatible. And neither wins in the end: it is the sly, unscrupulous, almost faceless King who at last comes out on top (as in *The Workhouse Donkey*, it is always the small men who survive best). For nothing is ever finally resolved: what might seem a distant skirmish on the fringes of history, quite unimportant to us now, is tied very much to the world we now live in by the play's dedication to Conor Cruise O'Brien. In the Congo, Arden suggests, he was a Lindsay; the same conflicts are ever and ever revived and reshaped; the same questions are always asked, and the complete and satisfactory answer somehow never materializes.

A similar conflict between different codes of behaviour is at the centre of Arden's next play, *Left-Handed Liberty* (1965), commissioned by the Corporation of the City of London to commemorate the 750th anniversary of the signing of Magna Carta. The play is an occasional piece, not of any great importance but subtle, intelligent, interesting. Arden sees the story mainly in terms of the conflict between King John and Pandulph, the big, unpredictable, unclassifiable figure who always seems fated to go down beneath the sheer weight of history and the wily, adaptable survivor. It is characteristic, and not merely perverse on Arden's part, that in many ways John emerges as, if not the hero, at least much the most appealing character in the play; also, that the play is not so much about the signing of Magna Carta as about its failure, the lesson being, in Arden's own words, 'that an agreement on paper is worth nothing to anybody unless it has taken place in their minds as well'.

Since *Left-Handed Liberty* no major play by Arden has been publicly produced. He worked for some time on the book of an elaborate musical about Nelson and Trafalgar before withdrawing from the project (though he has since knocked his book in straight dramatic form as *Trafalgar*). He wrote a full-length children's play, *The Royal Pardon* (1966), in collaboration with his wife Margaretta D'Arcy, as well as a short wordless play, *Friday's Hiding* (1966). He has worked extensively with amateurs, child actors and improvisation-groups, providing a text for Peter Brook's Theatre of Cruelty group, *Ars Longa, Vita Brevis* (1965), a full-length satirical improvisation called *Harrold Muggins is a Martyr* (1968) with a group at the Unity Theatre, and a short parable play, *The True History of Squire Jonathan and his Unfortunate Treasure* (1968) for a lunch-time theatre company. Though this pattern of activities seems to bring him much satisfaction, it is disappointing to those who eagerly await his long-delayed breakthrough to wider acceptance in the everyday professional theatre.

One thing seems certain, though: difficult though Arden's vision may be to accept on first acquaintance, and puzzling his way of expressing it, familiarity makes the approach much easier and breeds nothing but respect and admiration. John Arden is one of our few complete originals, and for the occasional faults in his plays – a desire to force a gallon into a pint pot, a tendency perhaps to overdo the gusty, gutsy side of things just a little from time to time – there are numerous and irreplaceable merits. Sooner or later his definitive success with a wider public is assured.

OTHER ROYAL COURT DRAMATISTS

The consistent championship of Osborne, Simpson, Arden, and Ann Jellicoe has been the main tangible contribution of the English Stage Company to the progress of the new drama. They may also claim some part in the discovery and promotion of Arnold Wesker, since it was they who passed him on to the Belgrade Theatre, Coventry, in the first place, and later it was at the Royal Court that his Trilogy found its London home and *Chips with Everything* began its triumphal career. After these five dramatists, however, there is a considerable diminution of interest among the new dramatists presented for ordinary public performances. The first two discoveries apart from Osborne were both novelists in their forties, Angus Wilson (born 1913) and Nigel Dennis (born 1912), and the dramatic work of both has failed to live up to its initial promise. Angus Wilson's first play, *The Mulberry Bush*, was a subtle and highly literate study of the public benefactor in private life, clearly the work of a novelist rather than a dramatist but effective enough in its own way; three later plays for television, *After the Show, The Stranger,* and *The Invasion,* have mainly emphasized the defects of this approach. Nigel Dennis's first play, *Cards of Identity,* extracted a lot of intelligent knockabout fun from his novel of the same name; his later play *The Making of Moo,* a satirical history of religion, though extremely uneven, also had its moments, particularly in the third act, and aroused a surprising amount of outraged objection. His third work for the theatre, *August for the People,* was an ironic, semi-expressionist parable about publicity and power, badly disserved by a naturalistic production which made the shift of gears in the second act from *The Apple Cart* to *Timon of Athens* seem unnecessarily awkward by trying to cover it up, instead of emphasizing it as a meaningful stage in the central character's obsession. With these two novelist-playwrights should be mentioned a third discovery, Gwyn Thomas (born 1913), whose gusty, erratic Welsh pieces *The Keep* and *Jackie the Jumper* (as well as his musical *Loud Organs* and his television play *The Slip*) show a winning sense of the grotesque and great, perhaps too great, facility in the invention of racy, ebullient, regional dialogue.

The younger dramatists brought forward by the Royal Court have also, apart from the 'big five', lacked any very striking attractions. The theatre has provided a home for two or three wandering productions of some interest from elsewhere (Pinter's double bill *The Dumb Waiter* and *The Room* from the Hampstead Theatre Club, touring companies in Shelagh Delaney's *The Lion in Love* and Errol John's lively *Observer*-prize-winning drama of life among the Caribbean poor, *Moon on a Rainbow Shawl*), but on its own account it has produced very few other plays by new dramatists, two of them, Henry Chapman's *That's Us* and Henry Livings's *Kelly's Eye*, by writers who had already acquired reputations at other theatres, and none of the rest worth more than a passing mention. The most famous of them, though by no means the best, Willis Hall's *The Long and the Short and the Tall* is considered elsewhere in this book (along with a later double bill on which Hall collaborated); it is a variation on the Osborne formula of 'angry' drama concocted by an efficient commercial dramatist, but that is about all. Donald Howarth's *Sugar in the Morning* (which began life as a Sunday-night production-without-décor under the title *Lady on the Barometer*) was really nothing more than a matinée play about a faded-genteel landlady under whose unprepossessing exterior lurks a volcano of frustrated passion, waiting to be unleashed about the head of an interfering young doctor who lives in the house; a certain amount of conscientious outspokenness served to give it a mildly contemporary air. Frederick Bland's *The Naming of Murderer's Rock*, a stop-gap also promoted from Sunday night, was an efficient, dead-pan reconstruction of a nineteenth-century murder trial in New Zealand; Frank Hilton's *Day of the Prince*, more enterprising, was a chaotic farce about the horrors of family life, the abuse of authority, colour prejudice, and all sorts of other things, bundled together with some lively moments but little grasp of stage effect.

More interesting than these, in that at least they aroused some controversy and split audiences into those who liked them very much and those who did not like them at all, were the two productions with which the left-wing poet Christopher Logue (born 1927) was associated, *Trials by Logue*, a double bill of his one-act plays, and *The Lily-White Boys*, a musical with a book by Harry Cookson (who later disclaimed the result) for which he wrote the lyrics. *The Lily-White Boys* was a rather heavy-handed satire about a bunch of crooks who rise to positions of authority by way of trade unions, psychiatry, the call-girl racket, and the beauty contest, and despite Logue's statements about his revolutionary approach to the numbers in a musical as a means of forwarding the story (with Gilbert and Brecht cited as the great originals) it emerged as just another fairly conventional musical about British low-life, at a time when these were quite inescapable on the West End stage. *Trials by Logue* consisted of two trial plays: a very plain and straightforward retelling of the *Antigone* story, and *Cob and Leach*, a rough-and-ready farcical parody of it which to some seemed riotously funny, to others merely tedious, according to taste. *Cob and Leach* began, incidentally, as the second half of a Sunday-evening entertainment, with *Jazzetry*, a programme of Logue's experiments in combining spoken verse with an improvised jazz accompaniment along the lines explored by the American Beat poets. Up to now Logue has proved more effective at attracting publicity than as a genuine creator.

Another Royal Court discovery has been Barry Reckord, a young Jamaican dramatist, born in 1928, whose first play, *Flesh to a Tiger*, was staged at the Royal Court in May 1958. This was a disappointing shanty-town melodrama with too much extraneous local colour and too little working out of loaded situations – a native woman torn between a coloured

religious leader and a white doctor ends by being insulted by
the doctor, smothering her baby, and stabbing the religious
leader – in terms of manageable dramatic dialogue. But with
his second play, *You in Your Small Corner*, which played one
night at the Royal Court and was later revived at the Arts,
he showed a considerable advance in dramatic technique, and
though there were still certain awkwardnesses in the narration,
the story of a group of relatively wealthy West Indians living in
Brixton and looking down on their 'low-class' English neighbours had a number of salutary surprises in store for the conventionally minded, while the dialogue was lively and well-
written and the characterization wholly convincing. The same
characteristics recur in his latest play, *Skyvers*, first produced
at the Royal Court in 1963, which offers a sympathetic and
impeccably accurate account of life in a London secondary
modern school. Young people and teachers alike are observed
with rare fairness and precision, and for once this is not at all
a 'Negro play', but just a play; there is not even a single coloured character or reference to the colour problem. In *Skyvers* Reckord justifies up to the hilt his right to be considered a
British dramatist just like any other, though much more accomplished than most.

Since the change of management and the death of George
Devine the English Stage Company has continued, on and off,
to bring on new writing talent, though during the last few years
it has not been so thick on the ground as in the first years of
the new drama. Probably the most interesting and individual
of the writers they have introduced recently have been Edward
Bond and David Cregan. Edward Bond (born 1935) first came
to notice with a Sunday-night production, *The Pope's Wedding*,
an uncertain but powerfully atmospheric piece about a hermit
in Essex, a young woman who looks after him, and the young
woman's husband, who at first resents him, then takes over
his care and idolizes him, and finally in disillusion kills him.
It was with Bond's second play for the Royal Court, *Saved*
(1965) that he became something of a *cause célèbre*. About two
critics liked it, the rest hated it with quite extraordinary ve-
hemence, and before we knew where we were it had spawned

letters to the papers, television controversy, and even a Sunday-night teach-in presided over by Kenneth Tynan. Despite all of which, it is not really as curious, or radical, or alarming, or good, or bad, as all that. To capsulate, it is by *Infanticide in the House of Fred Ginger* out of *Say Nothing*: a pleasant, ordinary young man goes to bed with an apparently pleasant, ordinary young woman, moves into her home as lodger, and rapidly finds that he has walked into a madhouse. The girl's father and mother hate each other and haven't spoken to each other for years, and the girl herself, it emerges, is a grade-A bitch who, having got what she wanted from the boy, turns on him with utter savagery and pours scorn and derision on his doggily devoted head. She has a baby (by someone else) which she loathes, and before long it is conveniently stoned to death by thugs. Its father (at least, she says he is) is on the fringe of the group, and unaccountably carries the can back for them. The girl stays devoted to him while he is in prison, but when he comes out he doesn't want to know, and repulses her as brutally as she is still repulsing the first young man. The play ends with young man number one deciding, not before time, to move out of his grim home-from-home, but then after all staying on, and the curtain comes down on a picture of emotional deadlock and concerted misery. (Well, the author says it comes down on a gesture of hope, but how he makes that out escapes me.)

The bits of the play that work – rather well, some of them – are those closest to *Say Nothing*: the earlier scenes in which Len drifts into involvement with his pick-up's strange family are quite holding, and the further exploration of his relationships with the parents in the second act throws up a couple of good scenes, notably that in which he nearly seduces the mother, or she nearly seduces him, while he darns a hole in her stocking. The parts which are closer to *Infanticide in the House of Fred Ginger* are a very different matter. The scene which has caused most complaint, of course, is that in which a group of wild young men rub the baby's face in its own excrement and then stone it to death. No doubt the author thinks he has something to say about arbitrary and unmotivated violence in modern society, but there are limits to the arbitrariness permissible in drama – actions may not have, and often don't have, reasonable reasons, but they must surely have some sort of reason, some emotional build-up at least. Perhaps Bond is saying that nowadays teenage tearaways congratulate each other on having run down and killed children just for fun, and simply suggest, in a fairly matter-of-fact sort of way, that they should stone babies to death before casually suiting the action to the word. But I find it difficult to believe, and the way he writes these scenes does not make belief any easier. Quite possibly such things happen from time to time, but in quite this way? And if the answer to that is that the play is not meant to be realistic, then surely it is more than ever up to the author to create a compelling imaginative substitute for life as we think we know it. Perhaps what the play needs, in fact, is not less violence but more, some sort of real sadistic kick which might urge audiences, however shamefacedly, to identify with these characters and share their emotions, instead of coolly watching the actors going through the motions of violence. But anyway, if the play is about anything it is not really about this, and though 'good taste' can hardly be invoked any more as a criterion, relevance I suppose can.

Whether the excitement about the more sensational scenes in *Saved* had anything to do with the shock-content in Bond's next play, *Early Morning* (1968), it is impossible to know. Anyway, its showing was limited by threats of prosecution from the Lord Chamberlain's office if it was staged even in normal club circumstances (this was one of the last major dust-ups over theatrical censorship before it was finally abolished), and critical reactions to it were consequently complicated by irrelevant considerations. Still, in general it was not felt to be very successful, though there was some disagreement about just how profound was its view of cannibalistic Victorian society beneath the surface of outrageous horror-farce, with Queen Victoria involved in a lesbian intrigue with Florence Nightingale and a final feast of human flesh in heaven. Bond's next work, *Narrow Road to the Deep North* (1968), the first of his plays to be staged outside club surroundings (at the Belgrade,

Coventry, in fact) showed a new certainty of touch and purposeful economy in its dialogue. Again its climax is an outbreak of carnage, but the lead-up is cool and controlled, and the resolution pulls the whole thing into shape. In period Japan the poet Basho, on a pilgrimage, leaves an abandoned baby to die. Saved, the baby grows up to be a tyrant, and Basho, to combat him, calls in the even more savage British. A monk who has observed everything kills himself in horror. Remote in time and place, the action is provided with a framework which enables it to carry Bond's complex message with more ease and conviction than in his earlier plays, and confirms that as well as having something to say, Bond is still working hard at acquiring the means to say it to best effect.

David-Cregan (born 1931) is altogether a less spectacular dramatist. His first appearance at the Royal Court was also with a Sunday production, a double-bill consisting of *Dancers* and *Transcending* (1966), the second of which was shortly afterwards taken into the normal repertory. Both are very slight, sophisticated plays on theatrical convention: *Transcending*, the more successful of the two, rips with breathless speed through enough plot to make a five-act tragedy (or farce for that matter) in about half an hour, turning on the progression of a girl who has just failed her A-levels and is desired by more or less everyone around towards (as it finally turns out) taking the veil. The play makes lavish use of direct address to the audience, stylized scene changes and the like and is riotously funny. After it, Cregan's next play, *Three Men for Colverton* (1966) came as something of a surprise. Though it shows some of the same preoccupation with conventions of staging and manipulation of audience reactions by all sorts of sophisticated devices, its subject-matter is far different: it concerns a battle for control (mental and spiritual) of a country village which has been ruled for years by a dying matriarch-figure. She can hand on the succession to whomever she wishes, and a number of people are in the running, most notably the leader of a group of evangelists who have come to the village and are finally undone when his bid for divine recognition by jumping off the local clocktower results merely in his death.

The complications of the play, both in form and in subject, were found daunting by audiences and by critics. Cregan's next work, *The Houses by the Green* (1968), is by comparison simple: an elaborate but uncomplicatedly comic charade in which the four characters each assume a disguise in the course of the action, the three men involved all with the purpose of marrying the girl and gaining control of a fortune and the green where they all live, the girl with the simpler purpose of getting at least one of her ardent suitors actually to make her pregnant. *The Houses by the Green* is recognizably from the same hand as *Transcending*, and is often very funny, if perhaps rather dry and over-mechanical in its detailed working-out. Even so, it confirms that Cregan's talent is fresh and quite unlike anyone else's.

So much for dramatists introduced in the Royal Court's normal repertory system. But a further word should go to the series of Sunday-night productions-without-décor which have already been frequently referred to in this section. These were started in May 1957 as private performances organized by the English Stage Company's social off-shoot, the English Stage Society, with the idea of trying out new plays which might for various reasons be unsuited, or only doubtfully suited, for full-dress productions, but which were nevertheless worth producing so that the playwright could see them on a stage and their possibilities be assessed (as well as the possibilities of actors and directors involved in the performances). A number of plays first staged in this way have, in fact, subsequently been given full-scale productions at the Royal Court or elsewhere: *A Resounding Tinkle*, *Sugar in the Morning*, *Cob and Leach*, *The Naming of Murderer's Rock*, and Alun Owen's *Progress to the Park* have all been staged, and Evelyn Ford's *Love From Margaret* turned up later on television as *Hell Hath No Fury*. But there are also a number of plays, and by no means the least interesting, which have never got any further than these Sunday-night private performances, and these deserve at least some mention.

The two most accomplished and individual dramatists by a

4a John Arden

4b Ann Jellicoe

4c Arnold Wesker

4d N. F. Simpson

long way to appear at these performances are Keith Johnstone and Michael Hastings. Keith Johnstone's first play, *Brixham Regatta*, was commissioned by the English Stage Company and with its companion piece *For Children* appeared for a season at the Aldeburgh Festival as well as at the Royal Court. *Brixham Regatta* is an extraordinary and subtle piece about six characters, three of them normal human beings – a showman, his wife, and his daughter – and three of them in some way freaks: a cripple, a zombie, and a mutilated man. The freaks are in a greater or lesser degree human; they are laboriously pulling themselves up into complete humanity or sliding away from it, rather as in the evolutionary theories elaborated by Macdonald from Novalis, and by their prospective rise and fall we are given in microcosm a picture of what humanity is and what it may be. *For Children* is a two-character play about a boy and girl who discover a skeleton and then use it as a starting-point for their individual flights of imagination (in rather the same way that the passers-by in Simpson's *The Hole* see the hole itself in terms of their own private worlds, though here it is done more searchingly and 'psychologically'), while through what they make of the skeleton we learn what to make of them. A year or so later Keith Johnstone was associated with the director William Gaskill in devising a topical improvisation, *Eleven Men Dead at Hola Camp*, in which a group of actors elaborated without scripts on the official reports of happenings at Hola. This was by general consent a total fiasco, but the interest in improvisation and its possibilities engendered at that time has survived at the Royal Court and in Johnstone's own career, especially in the series of programmes he devised with a group of young Royal Court players under the general title *Clowning*.

At this period he worked much more in direction than in writing, but in 1966 he reappeared as a dramatist with *The Performing Giant*. This is a curious piece, and responses to it, especially from the critics, were complicated by an ill-advised explanatory circular sent out a few days before its opening. The circular explained that the play was meant to be an allegory of the adolescent's battle to master the complexities of the outside world and the mysteries of his own developing body. Prior knowledge of this merely makes it necessary to spend quite a lot of the first half trying to put this knowledge from one's mind, and accept the action simply as an action until such time as internal evidence begins to make everything clear. It is, in fact, quite possible, after the gulp required to swallow the seeming whimsicality of the initial premise (whimsicality is the last quality modern audiences are equipped to accept unflinching), to take the play for some time at its face value as just a story. A giant is approached by a group of pot-holers who want to explore his inside. He protests that he usually gets mountaineers, but agrees and obediently ingests them. Once inside they start busily staking out his vitals as a future tourist playground, and when he tries to resist them and make off with the girl they have brought as bait they blind him. This far the first half. It would surely require impossible percipience on the part of any audience to work out the allegorical side of this, but it doesn't really matter if they don't get it; it is a mistake to alert them, or at any rate the critics among them, and get them looking for clues instead of merely sitting back and observing what is there.

The story, just as a story, has its own strangeness and extravagance, and the inklings which already begin to manifest themselves that there is more to this fantasy than first meets the eye give the whole thing body without wrenching the convention too sharply out of shape. The play, in fact, rapidly shows itself to be in the line of *The Sport of My Mad Mother*: it works on us not through the intellect, asking us to line up characters with concepts and decide that this stands for that, but through the effect of the whole as a theatrical experience on eyes and ears and nerves. The second half, where the giant is finally persuaded to rebel and eject the pot-holers through the love of and with the aid of the pot-holers' woman, is rather more explicit on what the play is ultimately about, and the style of the text becomes correspondingly denser; by the end the underlying subject of the play would probably have emerged even without forewarning. It can most usefully be seen not so much as an allegory, but as what Duke Ellington would call a 'tone-parallel' of adolescence. Even so, the play has a number of sticky passages, touches of sentimentality and moments when the whimsicality of the cover-story is laid on a little thick. It is an easy play to dislike; but not all that easy to dismiss.

Michael Hastings's first play, *Don't Destroy Me*, was written when he was seventeen, in 1955, and was staged at the New Lindsey Club. Though visibly uncertain and immature, its picture of a rackety Jewish household in Brixton, with the various emotional entanglements and disagreements among the adults weighing heavily and finally unbearably on the central character, a teenage boy, did indicate the presence of a genuine dramatic talent, as yet unformed and undisciplined. With his second play, *Yes, and After*, produced a year later at the Royal Court, he came of age: in spite of its occasional *longueurs* (even cut down from its original four and a half hours to a more normal length) this was the work of a mature and accomplished dramatist. The central character is a girl of fourteen who has been raped by a lodger; he has gone, but she is still overwhelmed by the experience to the extent of withdrawing completely from human contact. The resolution, when it comes, is worked out in strictly Freudian terms, with a re-enactment of the rape to break the trauma in which the girl is held, but the development of character along the way, particularly that of the parents, is far from this sort of schematization and the dialogue, for the middle-aged as well as the young, has an astonishing ring of unforced truthfulness.

Yes, and After was followed by a seven-year absence from the theatre, and then a return which although fairly prestigious (Vanessa Redgrave starred in the play) was also extremely brief (it had only a Sunday-night showing). The play in question, *The World's Baby*, carries its heroine through from 1936, when she announces to a gathering of lovers that she is pregnant, but will not say by whom, to 1959. All around her change and develop, but she stays much the same, all-embracing, anarchical, determined to retain her 'innocence' whatever may become of the world. The play is built on a large scale, and has remarkable patches, but suffers from over-elaboration in parts and a certain sentimentalization of the central character. However, it might repay a more detailed, finished production.

Hastings's latest play, *Lee Harvey Oswald* (1966) is completely different: a contribution to the 'Theatre of Fact' briefly fashionable at the time, it reconstructs the story of Oswald's life in the period up to the assassination of President Kennedy and after with documentary sobriety and deliberately heavy dependence on the factual materials of the case. It is holding and informative, and if it does not unlock for us the mystery of Oswald's personality and motivation, that would be asking rather a lot of one writer in one play. It gives evidence, at least, of a real dramatic instinct at work, and leaves us still hoping for something more from its author.

Lastly, there are three women playwrights whose work has been more or less confined to Sunday-night run-throughs: Evelyn Ford, Kathleen Sully, and Kon Fraser. In the work of each there is something of interest, even if none has achieved a total success. Evelyn Ford's *Love from Margaret* looked at first glance like the updated matinée play the title seems to imply, but actually its exploration of the tensions between a middle-aged couple, the wife with a limitless voracity for love and the husband with an emotional need always to be in the wrong with his wife, was unusually acute, and some of the wife's diatribes struck on a happy vein of angry eloquence. Kathleen Sully's *The Waiting of Lester Abbs* had difficulty with the main character – who is constantly put upon by everyone and treated so consistently as a fool that he finally assumes the blame for a murder he did not commit just to escape – but was terrifyingly observant of those around him. And Kon Fraser's *Eleven Plus*, an odd, rather arbitrary piece of stage-craft about a girl who, in compensation for her feelings of depression over her supposed failure of the eleven-plus examination, builds up for herself a fantasy about her aunt as the prospective virgin mother of a new Messiah, also had its telling moments, though these were rather dimmed by too many glaring irrelevancies; her handling of a kindred theme in a later play, *The Sacred Cow*, was rather more ordered but less (intermittently) compelling.

WAY DOWN
EAST

Joan Littlewood and Theatre Workshop

If the Royal Court unmistakably took the lead in the field of new drama with *Look Back in Anger*, it was not long before a rival appeared on the scene; only a fortnight later a new play by a new dramatist was produced at the Theatre Royal, Stratford, which was to create almost as much stir as John Osborne's when it arrived in the West End: *The Quare Fellow*, by Brendan Behan, which opened on 24 May 1956.

At that time Theatre Workshop had not been running so very long in its East London home: after a wandering on-and-off sort of life on tour in Wales, the industrial north and elsewhere since its setting up by Joan Littlewood and a small band of fellow enthusiasts at the end of the war, it had come to rest at Stratford as recently as 1953. Before *The Quare Fellow* it had produced new plays, of course, but nothing very exciting – mostly a series of political journalistic pieces by Ewan MacColl – and it was generally agreed that its best work was done with classical revivals like *Volpone* or *Edward II* and stagings of modern classics like *The Good Soldier Schweik*. In the next five years it managed an almost unbroken series of transfers to the West End and a generally enthusiastic reception from the Press as a nursery for new writers: after *The Quare Fellow* Behan wrote *The Hostage*, another major dramatist seemed to emerge in Shelagh Delaney, whose first play, *A Taste of Honey*, appeared in May 1958, and there were numerous lesser successes, like *You Won't Always Be On Top*, *Fings Ain't Wot They Used T'Be*, *Make Me an Offer*, *Sparrers Can't Sing*, and others.

Then in 1961 Joan Littlewood announced she was leaving the company for a couple of years at least. Consternation. Indignation. And an amount of publicity in the popular Press which would have been unthinkable over anyone in show business except a major Hollywood star five years previously (a comment, no doubt, on the English stage's increasing reputation meanwhile as a place where things happen and news is made). But to understand precisely why Joan Littlewood's departure should set up such a violent reaction, one must look a little more closely at her company and its policy.

The reputation of being a miracle-worker Joan Littlewood acquired during her eight years' tenancy of the Theatre Royal has not been altogether undeserved, though she herself resents it intensely, feeling that people who spoke in such terms were attributing unfairly to her the tonic qualities which actually came from working with the company as a whole and benefiting from its discipline, its dedication and the hard-won ability of its actors to work self-effacingly as a team. But, however this may be – whether these advantages come directly from Joan Littlewood herself or indirectly from working with the company she has created almost single-handed – there is no denying that many actors and writers have seemed much better when working at Stratford than they ever have again. And where this particularly concerns our present study – in the field of writing – the reasons for this are clear enough. Of all the producers and directors intimately connected with the staging of the new dramatists, Joan Littlewood has had the most far-reaching effect on the actual texts we know on the stage and in volume form.

Her own greatest satisfaction has been drawn from her classical revivals, particularly *Volpone,* and of the new plays she has directed the only one in which she sees real achieved literary quality is *They Might Be Giants,* by the young American writer James Goldman, her last production for Theatre Workshop before leaving and, critically and commercially, one of the least successful. By her own testimony what she was reduced to looking for (not, as hostile critics have sometimes suggested, what she chose to look for) in the texts of new plays sent to her was not a finished, tidy, well-written play, but one with at least some spark of life in it from which something, somehow, might be developed. A finished play which possessed also this quality of life would be the ideal, but since she found it only once, with *They Might Be Giants,* for the rest she had to make do with what offered, choosing the rough but lively in preference to the smooth and lifeless.

Consequently almost every new play which was produced by the company under her rule passed through endless transformations in rehearsal – so much so that she compares the work of the actors in them to that of the players in the *commedia dell'arte*, working on a basic text but improvising freely around it, sometimes with the author's aid, sometimes without it. Brendan Behan, we are told, was deposited in the pub opposite the theatre while his plays were being rehearsed, with the words pouring out of him and someone ready to note down anything good to cover that weak spot in the second act or replace the 'chunks of terrible sentimentality' which had to be cut from the original text right away. Shelagh Delaney was in attendance during some of the polishing of *A Taste of Honey* after the first performance, by which time most of the major surgery had been carried out, but how far even that was her own work remains obscure (the trouble with trying to find this sort of thing out is that by now frequently neither author, director, nor actors can remember precisely who contributed what). Frank Norman accepted the system wholeheartedly and worked out *Fings Ain't Wot They Used T'Be* from a 'strange eighteen-page document' (as Lionel Bart describes the original text) with the actors on the stage of the theatre (thereby anticipating by a year or so William Saroyan's more widely publicized experiment in spontaneous drama with *Sam, the Highest Jumper of Them All* at the same theatre). One or two authors objected to the system, of course: Wolf Mankowitz, the most professional and commercial of them all, frequently found himself challenged to defend what he had originally written in *Make Me An Offer*, on the principle that if he could it stayed in, if he couldn't it went; Marvin Kane, author of *We're Just Not Practical*, went so far as to circularize all the London newspapers disclaiming what actually appeared on the stage as a travesty of his original intentions; and when Alun Owen's *Progress to the Park* (admittedly not one of Joan Littlewood's own productions to begin with) arrived in the West End with a different director and a largely different cast all the ill-advised bits of improvised action with which the Stratford production had been diversified were quietly abandoned and a return made to the far superior original text.

All this makes the evaluation of the 'Theatre Workshop dramatists' – Behan, Shelagh Delaney, and the several inventors of material for what Joan Littlewood calls 'our Cockney improvisations' – as independent creators and literary artists extremely difficult. How much is their own work and how much the contribution of actors and director? In the case of *A Taste of Honey* I have been allowed to find out for myself by comparing the original manuscript with the final text, and this at least makes one thing clear; that the (quite considerable) modifications introduced have not violated the spirit of the original or dropped any of the original's good points, while eliminating everything that was undeniably wrong with it to begin with. The only alterations which one might take exception to are the introduction of one or two of those music-hall tricks of presentation – direct addresses to the audience; musical entrances and exits – which have sometimes proved the most tiresome mannerisms of Theatre Workshop directors, Joan Littlewood included. In other words, whoever was most responsible for the revisions has simply arranged things in such a way that the author is shown accurately to the audience, but presented in the best possible light, and, sensibly enough, Shelagh Delaney has found nothing to object to in that. Neither did Brendan Behan, so we may assume that the same was true for him.

Joan Littlewood's hope was that working with the company to remove the crudities and errors of their first attempts would teach them lessons for their later work, but she feels that this has not happened. 'God knows what Brendan's next play will be like if I'm not here to make him write it,' she said shortly before leaving, and we know that *The Lion in Love* was rewritten once by Shelagh Delaney in response to her criticisms ('There's too much in it picked up at smart West End parties'), though even so the result is still badly in need of the sort of tightening and sharpening Joan Littlewood achieved with *A Taste of Honey*. After a year or so in abeyance Theatre Workshop went shakily into action again, without Joan Littlewood, and subsequently brought forward one interesting play, *High Street, China,* a loosely organized but rather fresh and charming picture of life among drifting youth in Northampton by Robin Chapman and Richard Kane, and welcomed Joan Littlewood back to direct one of the company's biggest successes ever, a musical panorama of 1914–18 called *Oh What a Lovely War.* Then Joan Littlewood wandered away to encourage drama in emergent nations and plan Utopian 'fun-palaces' for British workers – do almost anything, indeed, except actually direct. Her actors are dispersed, her theatre taken over by others, and only some uniquely exciting memories and a couple of, after all, rather remarkable plays remain to commemorate the splendours of Stratford E.

BRENDAN BEHAN

An excellent case could be made out, and nearly sustained, for the complete omission of Brendan Behan from a book on the new British drama. He is in almost every respect foreign and irrelevant: an Irishman among the English (who even wrote his plays first in Gaelic), a Catholic among the Protestants, a cat among the pigeons (or perhaps, all things considered, a bull in a china shop is nearer the mark), an historical accident. Had he had his first major stage successes on the English-speaking stage in Dublin instead of at Stratford he would have been hailed, no doubt, as a new Sean O'Casey and we could comfortably have left him out of our London-based calculations; had he even become first of all the talk of Paris (like Beckett) or New York there would have been no difficulty. But no: here in London he had his first, and in many ways his most sympathetic theatrical home, and willy-nilly he must be considered.

Once we have firmly decided on this, however, it is easy enough to invent spurious reasons and adduce little bits of special pleading for his inclusion. He was formed, as much as any other writer to lodge in the same stable, by the taste and theatrical flair of Joan Littlewood and the special circumstances in which the company works? Well, yes, that is certainly so. He contributed to the new British theatrical tradition even if he did not draw anything worth talking about from the old? More difficult to prove, and the nearest thing to a demonstration, *Fings Ain't Wot They Used T'Be*, only goes to show just how far an English brothel comedy is from its evident Irish model. His roughness, his irreverence, his distaste for any establishment, even the establishment of rebellion, linked him with some of the more notable of the new English writers, and made him spiritually, if not technically, an encouragement and a sign to those who came after? That is nearer the mark, and if we look at *The Quare Fellow* and *The Hostage* as products of the new questioning spirit abroad in Britain we shall not be far from gauging their real importance in the revival of the British stage.

Brendan Behan was born in Ireland in 1923, brought up in Dublin and educated by the French Sisters of Charity, joined the I.R.A. in 1937, and was sentenced to three years in Borstal for political offences by a Liverpool Court in 1939. Out of Borstal, he was sentenced again, by a Military Court, in Dublin in 1942, this time for fourteen years, also for political offences, and served nearly six years of his sentence. His first play, *The Quare Fellow*, was written in 1955 and sent finally to Joan Littlewood, who read the first five pages, sent off a telegram at once accepting it, and spent the next few months licking it into shape, tightening, sharpening, eliminating the sentimental passages – all with the help of the author from the safe distance of the pub over the way.

The two most important facts in Behan's life, as far as his work is concerned, are his periods in prison and his involvement with the I.R.A. The prison part of this, the earlier section of which is recounted at length in his autobiographical volume *Borstal Boy*, forms the background also for *The Quare Fellow,* though here the plot is reduced to a minimum and it is the overall impression of prison life which counts. The moment chosen for this study is that at which the prison is most intensely, self-consciously itself: the night of an execution. Of the two men due to be hanged one, 'Silver-top', a mild-mannered wife-killer, has had his sentence reduced to life imprisonment, but the other, who killed his brother with an axe and dismembered the body (or so we are told) is to have no reprieve, and gradually, little by little, the feeling of intense expectancy settles over the prison as each prisoner in his different way awaits the execution. And not the prisoners alone; there are the warders, too, almost as much prisoners as those they watched over, to whose community they belong much more than to that of the outside world. And the hangman himself, an amiable English publican whom the locals assume to be some sort of commercial traveller.

Gradually we get to know the various inhabitants of the prison. There are the old lags Dunlavin and Neighbour, who know their way round all the dodges of prison life, like swigging meths when the warder is giving them their spirit rub against rheumatism, and keeping on the right side of the unctuous visitor Healey, who comes round to collect their complaints and make suitable note of the righteous for assistance by the charitable organization to which he belongs when they come out. There is the shaken lifer, 'Silver-top', who is so profoundly appalled at the thought of life imprisonment that he tries, shortly after his reprieve, to hang himself in his cell. There are the young prisoners, thinking only of the chance to peek through the window at the 'mots' hanging out the washing in the yard of the next-door women's prison. There is the sex criminal whom Dunlavin thinks is more unpleasant to be housed next to than a good straightforward murderer; there is the boy from the Islands whose main comfort is the possibility of talking to a warder from the Islands in Gaelic; there are prisoners hard and soft, young and old, English and Irish, of every conceivable type, for every conceivable offence.

They are not very precisely individualized, for Behan's style is essentially more narrative than strictly dramatic and he could hardly be farther from psychological drama, but all are observed with a rich, all-embracing humanity which reaches, in fact, far enough to embrace the warders as well, particularly Warder Regan, who seems at several points to be the author's own mouthpiece, especially on the subject of capital punishment. The key passage in this connection, and indeed the key to the method of the play as a whole, comes in an exchange in the last act between Regan and the Chief Warder, discussing arrangements for looking after the condemned man during the night:

CHIEF: Is there anything on the practical side we could send down?
REGAN: A bottle of malt.
CHIEF: Do you think he'd drink it?
REGAN: No, but I would.
CHIEF: Regan, I'm surprised at you.
REGAN: I was reared among people that drank at a death or prayed. Some did both. You think the law makes this man's death something different, not like anyone else's. Your own, for instance.
CHIEF: I wasn't found guilty of murder.
REGAN: No, nor no one is going to jump on you in the morning and throttle the life out of you, but it's not him I'm thinking of. It's myself. And you're not going to give me that stuff about just shoving over the lever and bob's your uncle. You forget the times the fellow gets caught and has to be kicked off the edge of the trap hole. You never heard of the warders down below swinging on his legs the better to break his neck, or jumping on his back when the drop was too short.
CHIEF: Mr Regan, I'm surprised at you.
REGAN: That's the second time tonight.

There in a nutshell is the principle on which the piece is built; in prison, even when an execution is imminent, comedy and tragedy are inextricably mixed, as everywhere else in life, and the *memento mori* is seldom without its gruesome humour. Murder is horrible, and legalized murder, in cold blood, with the best of intentions, is even more horrible, but the direct attack is not always the most effective, and Behan invites us not only to pray at this funeral, but to drink as well, to laugh and shout and sing as well as to weep and wail and shudder. His theme, basically, is the inalienable dignity of man – inalienable, that is, in that nobody can take it away from him except himself – and the fact that he chooses his examples from what would normally, with some reason, be regarded as the dregs of humanity makes the lesson all the more potent. A note in the programme said: 'This is not a play about prisons, but a play about people.'

The play, as finally staged, is not only vividly alive from moment to moment (the brimming life of the Irish popular speech is a great help here, especially for an English audience, but everything seems to suggest that it is also selected for its particular dramatic purposes with considerable skill); it also has a finely coherent overall structure, in which the absence of conventional plot development is to a large extent compensated for by the skill in which the various themes are brought to the fore, held in the background, or ingeniously woven together as the play progresses, linking scene with scene and establishing a gradual, orderly progression to the inevitable end, all within the framework provided by the recurrent refrain of a song from an unseen prisoner doing solitary in the basement.

On the whole these qualities do not occur in Behan's second play *The Hostage*, though they are replaced by others which, on first acquaintance at least, may seem almost as satisfactory. In *The Quare Fellow* the tragic undertones are always present, and though they are seldom insisted on we are conscious throughout of a sensation in the comedy akin to that of dancing on a coffin-lid. In *The Hostage*, however, though the underlying tragic theme is still there, there are whole stretches in which it is thrust altogether out of sight and rather wild, uncontrolled, and in some cases essentially irrelevant bouts of farcical humour take its place. Ultimately, in fact, the second play is far less disciplined than the first; at times it looks like going off the rails altogether in its quest for the easy laugh or the rather facile shock effect, and the wholesale introduction of music-hall techniques, direct addresses to the audience, songs with self-conscious cues to the accompanist in the orchestra pit, even a bit of dialogue ribbing the author ('That is, if the bleeding thing has an author'), savours at times of the self-indulgence inherent in all thoroughgoing 'director's theatre'.

Now as this is something, to be fair, that Joan Littlewood has not elsewhere been guilty of, we might assume fairly safely some imperative necessity for these covering-up operations in the original script, and so in fact it proves. *The Hostage* began life as a play in Gaelic (written for the Gaelic League) at about a third the length we know it now, and in its first English version it consisted in effect of three long, barely connected scenes in Behan's most discursive narrative style: Act 1 – a dialogue between Pat and Meg on the subject of 'Monsewer', the old and eccentric rebel-by-conviction, with occasional side references to the recent history of Ireland, almost any line in which could be assigned to either speaker; Act 2 – an extended love scene between the hostage and the maid, very rambling; Act 3 – the raid. Thus while *The Quare Fellow* in rehearsal went mainly through a process of tightening and compression (with a certain amount of redistribution of dialogue to break up the heavier chunks of narrative), in *The Hostage* two potentially contradictory processes were required at the same time: the strengthening throughout of the main narrative line, and the extensive opening-out and diversification of the action with new characters and new sub-plots to fill the play out and give it more dramatic interest. And though on the whole the first aim is achieved (by comparison, at least, with the first draft), the second has also been achieved with a vengeance, so that the minor characters and their business often seem in danger of making us forget the central matter of the play altogether.

The subject of *The Hostage* is drawn from that other side of Behan's life we have referred to, his experience with the I.R.A., and in some respects the play's conclusions are not unlike the despairing final appeal in his brother Dominic's otherwise far less interesting play *Posterity Be Damned*: 'Mother Ireland, get off my back.' The time is now, however many years after the Troubles 'now' may be, and yet still over it all looms the great shadow of national triumphs and disasters in 1916. 'What were you doing in the Troubles?' is the constant refrain, even though by now the answer is generally 'But I wasn't even born then', and officially life is still being lived at a fever-pitch of warlike patriotic fervour. But times have changed; the house that was once the refuge of heroes is now a brothel, the I.R.A. has been taken over by fresh-faced young men, the 'earnest religious-minded ones' who have replaced the 'laughing boys' of the great days, and nobody except the thoroughly indoctrinated quite remembers who was on whose side and why, exactly, the heroes kept on the run for more than twenty years.

6a 'The Lion in Love'

6b 'The Knack'

7 Joan Littlewood and Frank Norman at a rehearsal at The

For a while it seems as if all may at last be made plain when a clear-cut issue is presented: an eighteen-year-old boy is sentenced to die in the morning for killing an Ulster police-man, and while he awaits execution in Belfast jail the I.R.A. take a hostage, an ordinary English soldier kidnapped while leaving a dance, and bring him to lodge in the brothel as the last place anyone would dream of looking. They will kill him, they say, if the Irish boy is executed; the threat may be bluff, as the brothel-keeper and some of the girls (male and female) try comfortingly to tell him, or they may really mean it, as he persists in believing. Finally, after a lot of horseplay and a fair amount of horse-sense, the old man in the fifth-floor back, Mullerdy, appears in his true colours as a secret policeman, there is a raid, and in the confusion the soldier is shot after all. No point has been made, no victory won; the whole thing has been bungled, pointless and futile – like, Behan appears to imply, the general situation of Ireland today, too tied up in considerations of what Queen Victoria did or did not do and who did what forty-five years ago even to move on into the modern world, to realize that the H-bomb makes the I.R.A. out of date, like the R.A.F., the Swiss Guards, the Foreign Legion, the Red Army, and the rest.

All this is clear enough – it is stated more directly than any-thing in *The Quare Fellow* so that there shall be no mistake – and the scenes which contribute to expression of the play's central theme, particularly those in which the rakish old one-legged ex-I.R.A. brothel-keeper Pat explains recent history to his stupid almost-wife Meg or clashes with the priggish young officer ('Have you got your initials mixed up? Is it the I.R.A. or the F.B.I. that you are in?'), and the gentle encounters between the soldier Leslie and the maid Teresa, both orphans who do not really understand what is going on in the world about them, all work very well. But there are other elements, such as those involving the 'girls' and their farcical encounters, the homosexuals Princess Grace and Rio Rita, and the slightly crazed old 'sociable worker' Miss Gilchrist, with her drink and her malapropisms, which seem, once the first entertainment at their antics has passed, to be merely indulgences in raffish and

I

extravagant local colour calculated to *épater les bourgeois*, which tend in the long run to weaken the play by diluting its effect with too many irrelevances.

For this reason *The Hostage*, even if it does, as Kenneth Tynan remarked, 'send language out on a swaggering spree, ribald, flushed, and spoiling for a fight', appears finally, for all its surface pleasures and occasional deeper insights, a far less substantial and effective play than *The Quare Fellow*. And unfortunately there was no real sequel in the theatre. Behan's only subsequently staged works were a group of three one-act plays, *Moving Out, The Garden Party,* and *The Big House*, all first written for radio around 1958. *Moving Out* and *The Garden Party* are merely short, farcical sketches about the removal of a family from the Dublin slums to an allotment on the edge of the city, the first showing their departure and the second their arrival. *The Big House* concerns the looting of an Irish country house just after the Troubles, and is dullish and more than a little incoherent.

His next full-length play, *Richard's Cork Leg*, long-promised, was taken up and put down several times before his death in 1964, but never completed. Maybe *The Quare Fellow* was just a happy accident; we shall never know now. But at least in *The Quare Fellow* we have something very like a masterpiece, and for that, however it came, we should be duly grateful.

SHELAGH DELANEY

Surely no dramatist can ever have got farther on a smaller body of work than Shelagh Delaney. She is one of the three or four names in the new drama that everyone has heard of, she has achieved a considerable reputation with the critics and the theatregoing public, high sales for her published texts, and in one case a prompt film adaptation right on the heels of long and successful runs in the West End and on Broadway – all this by the time she was twenty-two. And yet she has written only two plays, the second a commercial and for the most part a critical flop. Her future career remains the big question-mark in the English theatrical scene; it is quite possible that she will never again live up to the achievement of her first play, *A Taste of Honey*, and after her second, *The Lion in Love*, a number of commentators were quite ready to write this off as a freak success. Too ready, perhaps, for despite its obvious weakness and overall inferiority to *A Taste of Honey*, *The Lion in Love* does show in certain respects an advance on the first, and may well prove to be a transitional work. In any case it is rather early to make any sweeping judgement.

Shelagh Delaney was born and brought up in the industrial town of Salford, Lancashire, in 1939. A late developer, she failed her 11-plus and went to a local secondary modern school. Later, there was talk of transferring her to a grammar school, but by that time she had lost any academic ambitions she might have had and left school at sixteen. With no special qualifications, she took what jobs offered, working for a while in an engineering factory, and at the age of seventeen began to work on *A Taste of Honey*. Why a drama, rather than a novel or poetry? Because, according to her own account, she saw Rattigan's *Variation on a Theme* on tour and thought that if this was drama, she could do better herself. Unlike many other people who have thought the same, however, she set about doing something practical to find out whether she could or not, and the result was *A Taste of Honey*.

Judgement of the play as it originally left its eighteen-year-old author's hands has been complicated, of course, by the fact that it was accepted for production at Theatre Workshop and went through the process of adaptation and elaboration which is usual there. Shelagh Delaney was not present until nearly the final run-through (when, it is recorded, she noticed no differences until they were pointed out to her), and by then most of the major alterations had been made, though further modifications continued to be made right up to the West End opening (including a new, softened conclusion insisted on by the West End manager). Since the play as acted and published is, after all, our prime concern here, I shall write mainly about that version, but I have been able, through the kindness of Joan Littlewood, to read the original script, and I shall give some account of it, for interest's sake and, incidentally, because it helps to clarify the answers to some puzzling questions about Joan Littlewood's production methods and Shelagh Delaney's potential staying-power.

The Stratford production as it finally emerged was in Joan Littlewood's characteristic manner, a sort of magnified realism in which everything is like life but somehow larger than life. This method kept intact the realistic core of the play – the important relationships between mother and daughter and between daughter and homosexual art student – and also helped to carry one over doubts about the two other characters, the Negro sailor and the mother's new husband. The plot is simple enough. Helen, a feckless prostitute (or nearly), and her schoolgirl daughter Josephine move into a comfortless attic flat in a slum, but Helen soon decides to marry her latest friend Peter and leaves; Josephine falls into the arms of a Negro sailor. When we next meet her she is pregnant, and being looked after by Geoffrey, a motherly art student who bustles round keeping the place tidy and making little garments for the baby, but this idyll is interrupted by the return of Helen, whose marriage is not working out, and who has consequently decided that her place is with her daughter. Geoffrey leaves.

Told thus baldly there sounds to be little to the play, and indeed in conventional terms there is little: it has no 'ideas' which can be isolated and considered as such apart from their dramatic context, and if one tries to read the play away from the theatre, without attributing to it characters the *personae* of the actors who originally played them, it is virtually non-existent. One does not even notice the improbabilities of the men, Peter in particular (is he a serious George Sanders-style world-weary charmer or merely a phony with a shaky accent and a shady past?), because all the characters seem equally shadowy. And yet in the theatre the whole thing works, and works almost infallibly – it has the unique power of holding us simply as a tale that is told, and the words the characters are given to speak take on, when spoken, a strange independent life of their own. A lot of it, admittedly, is in any case very funny: one thinks of Helen gazing thoughtfully at her unpromising urchin of a daughter and wondering if she could turn her into 'a mountain of voluptuous temptation', or Jo, remarking wrily of Peter's suggestion that she should give Helen an engagement ring 'I should have thought their courtship had passed the stage of symbolism' (it is humour in the music-hall style, of course, and therefore particularly sympathetic to the Theatre Workshop atmosphere).

But more than that, it has – such of it as concerns Jo and Helen at least – the disturbing ring of truth about it: the two characters individually, and the relationship between them, are completely believable, though their situation must surely be exceptional to the point of uniqueness, even if it is not completely impossible. There is more than first meets the eye in Jo's assertion that she is contemporary – 'I really do live at the same time as myself, don't I?' She accepts life, as it is, without looking for a loophole in time or place: even when she takes an exotic lover it is for here and now, not as a way out (and anyway he proves to come from Cardiff); she makes no attempt to move away from the squalid flat in its squalid area when her mother has gone, and does not even want to go to hospital to have her baby. Her only moments of rebellion, when she announces that she does not want to be a woman, or have the child, are over almost before they have begun. Helen, too, is in her way a realist: she will try various means of escape, but never with any great conviction that they will work, and when things go wrong, as with her marriage, she is not really surprised.

They accept their life and go on living, without making any too serious complaint about their lot; unlike Jimmy Porter and his followers, Jo is not angry, nor does she rail savagely and ineffectually against the others – authority, the Establishment, fate. In practice, she recognizes that her fate is in her own hands, and takes responsibility for the running of her own life without a second's thought – indeed, in almost every way the action might be taking place before the Welfare State was invented. And this is perhaps a clue to the almost dreamlike effect the play has in performance. None of the characters looks outward at life beyond the closed circle of the stage world; they all live for and in each other, and finally the rest, even Helen, seem to exist only as incidentals in Jo's world, entering momentarily into her dream of life and vanishing when they have no further usefulness for it.

(It may be remarked, parenthetically, that this effect, along with much else, is lost in the 1961 film version, scripted by Shelagh Delaney in collaboration with the director, Tony Richardson. Here the treatment is uncompromisingly realistic and exterior, and consequently the script-writers find themselves trapped into devoting an excessive amount of time to useless illustration and explanation. Not only do we see Jo in the real world outside – at school; working, surprisingly efficiently, in the shoe shop – but we have to be present at her first encounter with Peter and see how, exactly, she falls out with him (during a trip to Blackpool), to be shown in detail how she gets involved with the coloured sailor and, later, her first meetings with Geoffrey and the circumstances in which he comes to share her flat. In the process, the special quality the play has of just letting things happen, one after another (like in a dream) disappears and modifications clearly intended to strengthen the material succeed, paradoxically enough, only in making it seem thinner and more contrived.)

The big question which has puzzled critics, of course, is how much of all this was present in the play as originally written by Shelagh Delaney. Well, interestingly enough, the author's original typescript turns out, on inspection, to be not so radically different from the version finally performed as most published comment on the subject would lead one to believe. The dialogue throughout has been pruned and tightened – rather more, evidently, than is usual in rehearsal – but most of the most celebrated lines are already there (except, oddly, Jo's famous definition of contemporaneity) and the character of Jo, the play's *raison d'être*, is already completely created and unmistakably the same. The principal differences there are concern the character of Peter and the ending, though there is some reshuffling of scenes in Act 1 (in which, originally, the second scene between Jo and the coloured sailor came after Helen's departure) and Act 2, where the present single visit of Helen and Peter and Jo and Geof was originally two separate visits, one by Helen alone and the other by Helen and Peter. There are also one or two significant deletions. In the first act Helen tells Peter as well as Jo the story of her brief romance with the idiot who fathered Jo, and he takes it quite seriously (nor does Geof later pour cold water on it). She also has one or two elaborate flights of rhetoric about Life and Death which have subsequently been suppressed, in the interests, presumably, of consistent characterization. Geof, too, has his big speech of self-revelation at the beginning of the second act, explaining how he took to men because he wanted a girl so much but was too unattractive for them to take any notice of him, which has later disappeared in the general toning-down of direct references to his homosexuality.

But the most far-reaching changes are those concerning Peter's character and the end of the play. Peter originally is a complete seventeen-year-old's dream figure of cosmopolitan sophistication, speaking throughout in a style of intricately throwaway cynicism. In the second act, however (in which, incidentally, his marriage to Helen seems to be working out quite satisfactorily), he reveals a child-loving heart of gold beneath the cynical exterior when, in an extraordinary scene just before he and Helen visit Jo, he suggests that they should take on the baby, and Jo, too, if she will come!

And this, ultimately, is what looks like happening. Where in the final version Geof just reminds Jo lightly of his earlier proposal of marriage, in the original he has a long and impassioned declaration and is rejected, after which Helen comes, ready to see to everything and take Jo back to her and Peter's home after the baby is born. Jo is carried off to hospital while Geof is out and when he returns he has a longish exchange with Helen, which ends with his resigning himself to the fact that Jo will go back to her mother once the baby is born, and being left alone in the flat holding the doll, the nearest he will ever get to having a child of his own, as the curtain falls.

The play is obviously much superior in its final version, but it is not *so* different, and the only modifications which one might find out of keeping are very minor: the introduction of a few lines addressed, music-hall style, straight at the audience, and the slight fantastication involved in having the characters dance on and off to music. But essentially the process of communal revision has served (and here the true genius of Joan Littlewood as a director emerges) to bring out the best in the author's work while staying completely true to its spirit.

Even in its final form, the play is still intensely introspective, still very much the acting-out in dramatic terms of a young girl's fantasies, and extraordinary achievement as it remains, the perceptive critic of the day might be pardoned for wondering what would happen when its author, like her own central character, opted for adult life and moved out from her own world of fantasy into the real world about her. In the circumstances *The Lion in Love*, though by no means totally successful, or even as successful as *A Taste of Honey*, is a remarkably encouraging sign. Its scope is much wider than that of the earlier play; it has more characters, a more diffuse action, and the central character is now a mature woman, instead of a girl just emerging from childhood. For though the relationship between Peg and her drunken mother Kit is in some ways similar to that between Jo and Helen, there is no doubt this time that the mother is the centre of interest, and the world outside Peg's own private world breaks in with a vengeance instead of being kept discreetly at a distance. The plot, such as it is, concerns a number of possibilities, some of which are resolved in action while others are left hanging. Peg decides to marry her Glaswegian dress-designer boy friend, her brother Banner decides to go to Australia, their father nearly, but not quite, decides to leave Kit for the prosperous and eager Cross-Lane Nora, but cannot finally resolve himself to it, and Andy, part-time pimp and friend of the family, plans to go into show business again, but gives up the idea.

While in *A Taste of Honey* the essence of the piece lies primarily in what happens to Jo, here the action counts for virtually nothing: rather do the fragments of plot serve as an excuse for us to examine these people, to see how they live together and to try and understand why they are as they are as we follow them through a few inconclusive weeks of their life. For the first time the author tries to offer some explanation: where *A Taste of Honey* really gave us little chance to speculate on the reasons for what we saw, *The Lion in Love* proclaims even by its title that its intentions are more far-reaching and ambitious. For the reference is to the fable of Aesop in which a lion falls in love with a forester's daughter and allows the forester to remove all his defences as a condition of the marriage – after which, of course, he has his brains beaten out for his pains, the moral being 'Nothing can be more fatal to peace than the ill-assorted marriages into which rash love may lead'.

The ill-assorted marriage here is that of Frank and Kit, which is tearing them both apart but keeps them trapped together in a bond of pity and desperation. Kit drinks in her misery and once unsuccessfully attempted suicide, but feels in general 'What good does regretting do? We've just got to make the best of a bad job, haven't we?' Frank, who tells Kit at one point that he has regretted marrying her every day of his life, and believes that if 'it was a pretty poor bargain all round, I got the worst of it, didn't I?' (he married her when they discovered she was pregnant) dreams of escape with Nora, but finds that he cannot make the clean break he wants with Kit whatever he does and returns home at the last.

The relationship between them rings completely true and the character of Frank in particular is perhaps the first really believable man Shelagh Delaney has created. The other principal male, however, the ebullient dress-designer Loll, is not at all convincing, and his romance with the thoroughly real and down-to-earth Peg is consequently one of the weakest elements in the piece. Its chief weakness, however, is not in either the characterization or the plotting, but in the quality of the dialogue the characters are given to speak. One would not question Shelagh Delaney's ear, which seems, as far as a non-Salfordian can judge, impeccable, nor her skill in noting down precisely what she hears, but in this play her critical sense and her ability to select seem at times to have deserted her. A lot of the writing here not only seems like the small change of unintelligent everyday conversation, but actually is just that, virtually untouched by the dramatist's art. It needs thickening in some way – the close-ups of television would help, or the sort of elucidatory narration in which a novel would embed it – but as it stands it makes quite unfair demands on the actors. Take the character of the old grandfather Jesse, with his seemingly endless fund of worn and featureless traditional sayings: if he is meant to be lovable and 'real' the actor must work over-time to make him so, with virtually no aid from the dramatist, who has simply made him as boring as such a person would be in real life to someone with whom he did not share a history of affectionate regard. Or again, take the character of Kit her-self. She is believable, completely believable, and Patricia Burke's playing of her in the Royal Court production was emotionally dead on centre, and yet somehow she failed to come over from the stage as a living character simply because the actress's accent was wrong – a small enough thing in the ordinary way and one which one learns to disregard after an initial adjustment (the television production of Alun Owen's *After the Funeral* afforded a perfect example of the process). But here the accent proved crucial, and it seems reasonable to suppose that a characterization which depends for its success or failure entirely on so tenuous a consideration must have some-thing wrong with it.

What can we expect next from Shelagh Delaney? If she can combine the skill in handling dialogue and the compact con-struction finally achieved in her first play with the wider field of reference and the new penetration of character revealed in her second, the result should be pretty remarkable. But in what mode will it be? There was some talk of a novel, and also a rumour that she was working on a play set in fifteenth-century Derby, which would have made an interesting devia-tion from the modern world and the kitchen sink. In any case, a move away from realism seems on the cards for her. Elements of dream and song were already present in *A Taste of Honey*: there is Jo's dream ('I was standing in a garden and there were some policemen digging and guess what they found planted under a rose-bush – you!'), Helen's dreamlike recollection of Shining Clough, and the strangely moving scene in which Jo and Geof, two children forced to grow up before their time, exchange nursery rhymes. In *The Lion in Love* the elements are even more prominent: Jesse's song 'Winter's coming in, my lass', closely precedes the final curtain, and even more significantly, Peg's long fairy tale brings down the curtain of act two on a totally unexpected note of poetry. This last is an interesting document altogether:

It happened a long time ago. The weather was fine and there was plenty of food and good beer to drink. There was a country and like all good countries it had a King. He wasn't a bad old stick either, as Kings go, and his Queen was a good-looking woman. So, he did his Kinging in the daytime and his Queening in the night and everything passed off very pleasant for everyone concerned. But like all good things it had to come to an end, and soon the King went off to war and the Queen was left on her own for years. And naturally enough she got a bit fed up with it, and one night when she was in bed she heard the West Wind knocking on her bedroom door. Well, she knew what he was after all right, but she let him in all the same, and soon after he'd whispered a few sweet nothings in her ear she succumbed to his passion and one thing led to another and when she woke up next morning she found she was pregnant. So – the West Wind carried her off to his palace and when her husband came back from the wars and found out that she'd buzzed off he was very upset. Anyway, after a bit he got angry and he snatched a thunderbolt out of the sky and threw it and he followed it to the place where it had landed, but his wife wasn't there. So he did the same thing again and again until he arrived at the palace. Well, by this time the West Wind had got a bit fed up with the Queen and he'd left her flat, her and her baby, and when the Queen realized that her husband the King had caught up with her she felt so ashamed of herself that she ran away with her child and jumped off the edge of the world, straight into the sea. And as soon as she touched the water she was changed into a great rock.

The elements of the situation in the play (an illegitimate baby, an ill-matched coupling, a desertion) recur here confused and transformed as though in a dream, and the result is a complete adult fairy story in which, as in life, there is no simple happy ending. The ability to transmute reality into this sort of myth, powerful even if only half-apprehended, is not one we would have necessarily expected to find in the author of *A Taste of Honey*, and apart from this instance it is not enough used in

The Lion in Love. Since then she has written only a book of short stories and sketches, *Sweetly Sings the Donkey*, and the script for an Albert Finney film, *Charlie Bubbles* (1968) a mature and penetrating study of a writer who finds that material success means little to him faced with the empty exhaustion of his emotional life. Perhaps this return (highly characteristic and successful, incidentally) to dramatic writing may portend something more substantial for the stage. At least, we can always hope.

THE ROAD FROM
WIGAN PIER

Productions out of Town

There have been times, notably during the reign of Miss Horniman at Manchester, when the provinces have made a major contribution to the British theatre. At first glance one would expect this not to be so now; the idea that nothing happens in the cultural life of Britain, a festival or two apart, outside London has become deeply ingrained since the last war. And so, in fact, it proves; but when one considers the question this is, after all, still rather surprising. According to Part II of the Arts Council report *Housing the Arts in Great Britain* there were forty-four repertory companies functioning in England at 31 December 1960, not to mention innumerable little theatres and other more or less occasional amateur groups. Here, one might think, if anywhere, there should be at least occasionally room for the new dramatist, and on reflection it is surprising how little contribution they have made rather than how much.

The reason for this state of affairs is to be found mainly in the financial situation of the reps and in the sort of audience they cater for. Most of them, particularly those in the south and west, are in a decidedly shaky position financially, and only just manage to balance their books by the end of the year (supposing they can balance them at all). This obviously inclines them to look as far as possible for works with a proved popular appeal to begin with, in order to keep any losses they may incur to an absolute minimum. Then the type of audiences they rely on for regular support has a lot to do with the choice of play. Many of the reps are situated in towns with a high proportion of retired people (Bath, Bournemouth, Cheltenham, Eastbourne, Folkestone, Harrogate, and so on), or in staid county towns. Even those in industrial areas depend mainly for their regulars on the middle-aged members of the professional classes who pride themselves on being, in a modest way, patrons of the arts, but like to feel they are getting something solid and 'good' for their money.

Consequently, even if they wanted to try something new and revolutionary (and supposing they felt they could master it in the week or fortnight possible for rehearsal), few repertories would be able to take the risk. Of course, most of them do produce new plays from time to time, but with a few noble exceptions the plays chosen are of the most conservative type imaginable: well-made costume plays, drawing-room comedies and the like. At best they will be new translations of foreign classics (as at the Bristol Old Vic) or enterprising importations from America (as at the now defunct Pembroke, Croydon, and its successor the Ashcroft Theatre). The companies which have consistently followed an adventurous policy with the plays they produce could, in fact, be numbered on the fingers of one hand, the leading instances being the Belgrade Theatre, Coventry; Stephen Joseph's peripatetic Studio Theatre (based on Scarborough and later settled also at Stoke-on-Trent); the Playhouse, Oxford, and the Nottingham Playhouse.

The Belgrade, which figures in this book primarily as introducer of Arnold Wesker and more recently of David Turner, is in a rather special position, being an entirely new theatre opened in 1958 and subsidized by the Coventry Corporation as well as the Arts Council. Its record for new productions was excellent during its early days, under the direction of Bryan Bailey, who was killed in a car crash in 1960. Subsequently, however, there seems to have been a move, inspired possibly by those who have to foot the bill, to curb experiment in this direction, and only in 1962 did the theatre show signs of new life with Turner's *Semi-Detached* and *The Bedmakers*. Admittedly, apart from the Wesker Trilogy (which was, in any case, handed on to the Belgrade by the Royal Court) the theatre's first three years brought forth nothing very interesting, though not apparently for want of trying.

Stephen Joseph's company was for years a theatre-in-the-round touring for much of the time, and with a summer home at the Library Theatre, Scarborough; a second company made its home at the Victoria Theatre, Stoke-on-Trent. The Scar-

8a 'The Quare Fellow'
8b 'The Hostage'

9a Harold Pinter

9b John Mortimer

9c Shelagh Delaney

9d Brendan Behan

borough company has an Arts Council grant, carrying with it a strong recommendation that the company should tour widely to bring live theatre to towns which would otherwise go without, and is able to pursue its enterprising policy mainly because of its relatively low overheads – it is a small company, averaging around six actors at a time, and the in-the-round form of presentation reduces props and scenery to a minimum – and the nature of its Scarborough audience, who on the whole drift in to while away a wet seaside afternoon or evening, with few preconceptions about what they are going to see. Stephen Joseph has held on several occasions summer play-writing courses at Scarborough for aspiring dramatists, and, in fact, 'discovered' David Campton, the company's most interesting acquisition, during one of them. Studio Theatre has produced a new play by Campton every year since 1957, and has also given a showing to a number of other young writers, most notably James Saunders, like Campton holder of an Arts Council bursary for play-writing, and 'Ronald Allen', the pen-name of Alan Ayckbourn, a twenty-three-year-old actor with the company, whose *Standing Room Only*, a comedy envisaging the situation when London traffic has become finally im-mobilized in one vast immovable traffic jam, showed more than promise, if still less than complete achievement (the same might be said of his later West End comedy success, *Relatively Speaking*). It is some index of the company's enterprise that of eight productions they staged in 1962, five were completely new plays and the other three were *The Caretaker*, J. P. Don-leavy's *The Ginger Man*, and a triple bill of unfamiliar Shaw one-acters. After Stephen Joseph's death in 1966, David Campton took over management of the Scarborough company; the Stoke company had already separated itself, rather violently, from the parent body.

Oxford Playhouse has encouraged an odd variety of drama-tists (under the aegis of an odd variety of companies) in its time, among them Bernard Kops (*The Hamlet of Stepney Green*), John McGrath (*A Man Has Two Fathers*), Robert Bolt (*The Critic and the Heart*), Doris Lessing (*Mr Dollinger*), and Henry Livings (*Big Soft Nellie*). No clear line of taste is discernible,

K

as at Coventry (left-wing working-class drama preferred) or the Studio Theatre (experimental fantasy), but at least the theatre provides a chance for something new to reach the stage, which is a lot to be thankful for. The Nottingham Playhouse has on the whole steered closer to the prevailing taste than the other three theatres mentioned, and consequently the writers it has chiefly encouraged – Beverley Cross, Willis Hall and Keith Waterhouse – are to be found among the good commercial dramatists in the under-forties group, reviewed briefly in the epilogue to this book, but again the readiness to produce anything even as relatively conventional as *Strip the Willow* or *Celebration* must be accounted by repertory standards unusually daring, and in recent years the company, after reorganization, has shown signs of looking even farther afield.

Otherwise the repertory scene is bleak indeed as far as new drama is concerned, despite the one or two exceptions which can be made to the generalization. The new Flora Robson Playhouse at Newcastle upon Tyne began adventurously in November 1962 with a ragged but lively costume piece about a Tyneside pitmen's strike a century ago, *Aa Went Tae Blaydon Races*, by Cecil Taylor; The Queens Theatre, Hornchurch, has brought us, along with a Sean O'Casey première and one or two interesting new plays by older writers, at least one striking new dramatist, David Perry, and the Guildford Theatre, as well as staging a number of heavily conventional pieces, has introduced us to Terence Frisby, author of *The Suntopians*, and had the sense to persevere with Richard Dellar after his first wildly overambitious play of imminent nuclear destruction, *The Edge*, until rewarded by a quietly strong and capable play of school life, *This Other Eden*. Even so, it seems for the moment that the third wave of new drama from the provinces has broken and receded with disappointing rapidity, and it is as true now as it ever was that even writers with a strong regional flavour in their work (like Alun Owen or Shelagh Delaney) have come to London for production and recognition. But then, after all, the forty-four companies are still there (unless any of them have closed down in the meantime, of course), and one never knows when one of them may find another

Wesker to head another provincial invasion of the West End stage. Let alone the possibility, however remote it may be, that Wesker himself, with his Centre 42 organization, may not carry the battle for vital theatre back successfully into the provinces where, not so long ago, his own work found a first, unexpected hearing.

ARNOLD WESKER

It has always been difficult to judge Arnold Wesker simply as a playwright. He has become in the relatively short time since his first major success (with *Roots* in 1959) not only a writer hailed by at least one critic as 'the most promising and exciting young dramatist to come into the British theatre since the end of the war' (another went further, claiming *Chips With Everything* as 'possibly the greatest post-war play in English'), but a rallying-point and a figurehead. More than with any other dramatist of his generation – more even than with John Osborne – it is virtually impossible to consider the plays apart from the playwright; to separate judgement of the plays as works of art from judgement of the political opinions which are sometimes given effective dramatic expression in his works and sometimes – or so at least the less sympathetically disposed maintain – inartistically crammed in as sermons delivered by the playwright's mouthpiece; to distinguish clearly between his efforts at organizing worker's culture through the body of which he is the principal motive force, Centre 42, and his stage demonstration of what he is about in *Chips With Everything*.

Whatever the practical limitations of Centre 42, it is not the invention of a timid, unadventurous man. And the most striking thing about Wesker the dramatist – even before one looks in more detail at his individual plays – is the boldness of his concepts. The very idea of a trilogy attempting to sum up the situation of the working classes today (and glancing back as far as 1936 for the root causes of their present situation) is extraordinary enough in the modern theatre, but that it should have been carried out, that the plays should have been performed not only singly but together in repertory at a West End theatre, and that the whole thing should have been adjudged a success by most of the country's leading theatre critics is a striking achievement indeed. But when we look beyond the broad picture, and examine in detail the claims to survival of Wesker's work after the fashionable enthusiasm of the moment has died down, a number of doubts intrude, along with the thought that Wesker's work is, after all, particularly apt to appeal on first acquaintance for quite other than strictly dramatic reasons. To see how this may have come about we might first consider the curve his career in the theatre and his general reputation have followed since first he became known.

Wesker is the perfect example of the new working-class dramatist. He was born in the East End in 1932, the son of a Jewish-Hungarian father and a Russian mother, and seemed in the first place a highly unlikely candidate for literary distinction: his father was a tailor and after leaving school his first jobs were as plumber's mate and kitchen porter. From this latter position he set about acquiring a trade, and became a pastrycook: as a pastrycook he worked for four years in Norwich (where he met his wife), London, and Paris, before deciding to take six months off and follow the short course at the London School of Film Technique. While there he wrote his first play, *Chicken Soup With Barley*, and shortly after leaving he sketched out a short-film script, *Pools*, and *The Kitchen*. *Pools* was submitted to the Committee of the British Film Institute of Experimental Film Fund, who approved in principle but found the estimated £3,000 required to film it beyond their resources. *The Kitchen*, a short two-acter written with half an eye on television, was sent, the author relates, to every television company without success (later, when Wesker was a name, they all wanted it and he had the elementary satisfaction of refusing all offers). But fortunately at about this time the Arts Council decided to encourage the repertory movement up and down the country by offering, in addition to the individual grants already being made, a special grant to mark the fiftieth anniversary of the opening of the Gaiety, Manchester, by Miss A. E. F. Horniman. The grants were made available to any rep

producing a new play, and in association with the Arts Council, the Royal Court lent its stage for a month to provincial
repertory companies with suitable new plays to offer. As the
general standard of plays offered was so low, the Royal Court,
wanting at least one play worth seeing in the season, sent
Chicken Soup With Barley, which was then under consideration for
a Sunday-night production-without-décor, to the recently
opened Belgrade Theatre, Coventry, guaranteeing them a
week's showing in London if they would produce it and lending
them a Royal Court director, John Dexter, for the purpose. It
had its first performance in Coventry on 7 July 1958, and
opened for the week at the Royal Court on 14 July.

It is curious, in the light of subsequent events, to look back
on the first reviews it received. By the time the play was revived two years later at the Royal Court as the first panel of
Wesker's working-class triptych, one critic was ready to find it
his best play, and the word 'masterpiece' was freely bandied
about. But on the first showing, the rapture was decidedly
modified. The play was generally found sympathetic but un-
remarkable; its picture of East End Jewish life was distinguished by a sober realism, it was evidently sincere, and though
the expression might be a bit fumbling, the author clearly deserves encouragement. And despite the widespread second
thoughts on the matter, this summary still seems entirely fair.

Chicken Soup With Barley covers twenty years in the lives of
an East End Jewish family, the Kahns, from October 1936 to
December 1956. It works on two levels, which arguably do not
quite correspond, and may even be mutually exclusive in what
the author is trying to convey on each. Personally, the play
seems to be about recurrent patterns of behaviour from generation to generation: socially, it is about the working classes' loss
of sense of purpose with the arrival of a socialist government
and the Welfare State, the disappearance of all the big, clear-
cut issues of the inter-war years. The conflict is obvious: on the
personal level its progression is circular, on the social level it
appears to move in a straight line, and the necessity of reconciling these two contradictory movements in the argument is
no doubt the main reason why one comes out of the theatre

feeling that the play's effect is oddly muddled and out of focus.

The personal argument is simple. When we first meet the Kahns, Sarah is already the dominant figure in the household; she is politically active, for ever helping to organize demonstrations and arranging the lives of those around her according to Marxist–Leninist principles. Harry, her husband, is weak-willed and totally unconcerned in politics; all he wants is a quiet life without worries, but he is constantly having banners thrust into his hand by Sarah and being ordered to demonstrate. He generally runs away and hides till it's all over. Or just sleeps. By the second act, in 1946, he sleeps most of the time, being always out of work, even when the whole country is booming; by the third act he is actually paralysed after his second stroke and virtually senile. Throughout the three acts, Sarah remains firm in her convictions and her determination to do something, but gradually the children begin to follow, so it seems, in their father's footsteps. First Ada, the young firebrand, becomes disillusioned with politics and goes off to start a new life in the country with her equally disillusioned husband, Dave, and then Ronnie, himself eager enough in the second act, becomes by 1956 equally disillusioned: 'I've lost my faith and I've lost my ambition. . . . I don't see things in black and white any more. My thoughts keep going pop, like bubbles. That's my life now – you know? – a lot of little bubbles going pop.' He understands Harry now, and at the end of the play he seems all set to become another Harry, with no sense of purpose to keep him going. He doesn't care any more, and the last words of the play are left with Sarah, on the verge of despair: 'Ronnie, if you don't care you'll die.'

So much for the pattern of personal relationships in the play. But the main point about these characters is the importance in their lives of social relationships, social responsibilities. They are taught to live for others, and the tragedy in their lives comes when they learn through bitter experience that their services are not required and in any case others may well be not worth their trouble. Life is not as simple and clear-cut in its issues as everyone believed when there were barricades in the streets, strikes to be organized for better conditions, and 'all the world was a communist'. First Ada and Dave undergo a personal disillusionment, expressed by Ada:

> I'm tired, mother. I spent eighteen months waiting for Dave to return from Spain and now I've waited six years for him to come home from a war against Fascism and I'm tired. Six years in and out of offices, auditing books and working with young girls who are morons – lip-sticked, giggling morons, and Dave's experience is the same – fighting with men who he says did not know what the war was about. Away from their wives they behave like animals. In fact, they wanted to get away from their wives to behave like animals. Give them another war and they'd run back again. Oh yes! the service killed any illusions Dave may have once had about the splendid and heroic working class.

But then, and even worse, comes the philosophical disillusion. Dave and Ada continue to believe in their ideals, but come to the conclusion that the world is not worth their trouble, and withdraw instead to an ivory tower of arts and crafts in the Cotswolds. But for Ronnie is reserved the harsher awakening, for not only does he come, while working in a kitchen, to the same sort of conclusions about people in general as Ada, but Hungary destroys his faith in the ideals which have previously ruled his life: 'You didn't tell me there were any doubts,' he cried angrily to his mother when she refuses to understand what he is talking about. For Sarah it is simple: her faith is unchanging.

> All my life I worked with a Party that meant glory and freedom and brotherhood. You want me to give it up now? You want me to move to Hendon and forget who I am? If the electrician who comes to mend my fuse blows it instead, so I should stop having electricity? I should cut off my light? Socialism is my light, can you understand that? A way of life. A man *can* be beautiful. I hate ugly people – I can't bear meanness and fighting and jealousy – I've got to have light. I am a simple person, Ronnie, and I've got to have light and love.

But none of it means anything any more, Ronnie answers.

> So what if it all means nothing? When you know that you can start again.

It is all so simple for Sarah, because her faith grew in heroic times and she is indomitable. But what about young Socialists? Can they recapture this single-minded belief if they have nothing to fight for any more? If on the personal level the play ends with a Q.E.D. (like father, like son), on the level of social argument we find only a question mark. How are Ada and Dave making out in the country, and if it is possible to start again, how will Ronnie manage to do so? These are the questions which the second and third plays of the trilogy take up, and so skipping for the moment *The Kitchen* (a parenthesis which might be taken to represent Ronnie's experiences away from home), we must go on to see what answers, if any, they offer.

The answer offered by *Roots* (1959) is a purely personal one. Where *Chicken Soup With Barley* covers a large tract of time and handles a number of changing, developing characters, *Roots* occupies only a fortnight and concentrates almost entirely upon one character, Beatie Bryant. Beatie is a girl Ronnie has met and becomes engaged to in London, but her home is deep in Norfolk and her people are farm-workers. She comes home without him, but he is to follow later, and meanwhile she has time to explain about him and his ideas to her people, and incidentally to realize to the full how far her people fall short of them. But she herself is still in transition. Though she obediently paints abstracts and has learnt to say all the right things about them, though she has picked up all Ronnie's ideas about classical music, popular culture, and human relationships, all she can do is to parrot them; she does not really understand, though she is pathetically willing to learn. Indeed, so far as one can make out, Ronnie has been attracted to her most of all by her potentialities: 'It's going up in flames,' he is quoted as saying, 'but I am going to make bloody sure I save someone from the fire.'

So Beatie arrives home full of half-assimilated ideas and proselytizing zeal, to meet a blank wall of indifference. Her mother has some superficial characteristics in common with the conventional dramatic countrywoman, seen as an Earth-mother figure, unchanging but full of simple wisdom. But this time the illusion is shattered by a cold gust of reality, for she is irremediably stupid: her proverbial philosophy is an easy substitute for thought, her apparent warmth and good nature a shallow cover for the terrifying savagery which lies just below the surface, ready to break out whenever she comes into contact with new ideas or feels that anyone may be looking down on her. In the last act it emerges to devastating effect when the news arrives that Ronnie is not coming and has decided that marriage between him and Beatie would not work. Mrs Bryant does not care that Beatie is suffering; all that concerns her is that she has been proved right and her daughter wrong, that after all 'The apple don't fall far from the tree' and Beatie, though she may give herself airs and think she is better than the rest of them, cannot really escape.

But there she is wrong, for partly in reaction to the news of Ronnie's defection, Beatie does begin to think for herself, to speak for herself: she sees falsity of Ronnie's ideas about country workers, living in mystic communion with nature, but sees, too, that their present abject condition is their own fault: 'The whole stinkin' commercial world insults us and we don't care a damn. Well, Ronnie's right – it's our own bloody fault. We want the third-rate – we got it!' Transported with her own sudden flow of eloquence she cries out as the curtain falls: 'God in heaven, Ronnie! It does work, it's happening to me, I can feel it's happened. I'm beginning, on my own two feet, I'm beginning. . . .' The final stage direction assures us that whatever she will do her family will continue to live as before, but she 'stands alone – articulate at last'.

In other words, *Roots* is a sort of illustration of the ideas expressed by Ada in *Chicken Soup With Barley*: though hardly in the same William Morrisy way (Beatie would be scornful of Ada's ideas about life in the country), Beatie, too, has won through to some sort of personal salvation in her own devious fashion, without recourse to the doubtful panacea of immersion in great causes and the submission of individual interests to hazy ideas of the general good. As an illustration it adds something to the first part of the trilogy: it tells us, for one thing, that even if Ronnie has inherited his father's chronic inertia and indecision he may not be utterly useless – he can help others, or an other, to self-realization, and others can carry on the struggle even if he falls by the wayside.

In a more practical, external fashion also it added something to the first trilogy: critical acclaim. When it opened in Coventry the notices were decidedly mixed, the only point of general agreement being the brilliance of Joan Plowright's performance in the central role. But by the time the play reached London word had somehow got round that it offered a great theatrical experience, and so this time the notices were almost unanimously favourable. It is, admittedly, always difficult to disentangle the merits of a performance from those of the play performed, but in retrospect one cannot help wondering how far the critics were swayed in their judgement by the superb performance of Joan Plowright as Beatie; later productions with other actresses have tended noticeably to cut the play down to size, and the scene at the end of the second act in particular, where Beatie, trying to explain to her mother what she likes about classical music, is carried away in dance of joyous abandon, has proved terribly embarrassing when played by anyone but her.

Certainly *Roots* seems on cool consideration decidedly inferior to *Chicken Soup With Barley* on two major counts: construction and authenticity. Skilled construction is not a notable quality of the first play – it rambles over a number of years in the family's life, and characters are picked up and set down rather arbitrarily – but at least if it is a ragbag it is a full ragbag: every scene and speech is there with a purpose. But *Roots* has every indication of being a one-act play (an excellent one-act play in all probability) blown up to three acts by the exigencies of the modern theatre. The first act is virtually duplicated in the second as far as ideas are concerned, since the main point the dramatist is trying to make is the almost inconceivable limitation of the Bryants' minds: again and again the same clichés recur, the same substitutes for thought, the same pointless stories endlessly, inanely repeated. But whether he needs two whole acts – indeed nearly two and a half, up to the arrival of Ronnie's letter – to make this single point is another matter. For the Bryants are bores. It is necessary to the point Wesker is making that they should be bores, but he does not manage to resolve that perennial dramatic problem, how can one represent bores dramatically without at the same time boring one's audience? The real action of the play does not begin until the third act, and in the meantime the audience would be rather less inclined to boredom if the situation of Beatie in relation to her family and that of her family in relation to her had been sketched in much more economically than the three-act form allows.

As to authenticity, this raises a crucial question about all Wesker's plays. His naturalism, his unvarnished truth has generally been taken as his chief merit, one which excused faults of construction and some carelessness in detail, which even excused occasional patches of boredom, since that was like life and was a risk he had to run if he was to picture the lives of the inarticulate with complete accuracy. Walter Allen summed up the views of many critics when he wrote of *Roots:* 'This is by far the best and most faithful play about British working-class life that has appeared.' But is what Wesker writes 'true' in this elementary sense at all? British working-class life, after all, is a subject about which most critics owe their knowledge to the plays they see much more than to life itself, and the main reasons, it would seem, that Wesker's plays have impressed them as particularly authentic are that (*a*) they differ markedly from the conventional picture, and (*b*) their differences are nearly all in the direction of greater squalor and brutality, especially in *Roots*, which is almost a Zolaesque tract on the degradation of country life.

The argument is then simple: if this account differs from what we are used to and is less what we normally want to hear (no heroic workers for Mr Wesker), then the reason for this deviation from what is standard and acceptable can surely be nothing but a greater concern for truth on the part of the author. Added to this, of course, Wesker's own background – the fact that he comes from an East End Jewish family, he has worked in kitchens, his wife comes from Norfolk and he may be presumed to have first-hand knowledge of East Anglian life – all tells in his favour, since obviously, critics reason, he must know what he is talking about. But if we look more closely at the plays from this point of view, doubts immediately arise. For one thing, one would not deny that in principle the Kahns and their story are possible, but typical, *pace* the critics, they are certainly not. Sarah and Harry, it is made quite clear, are first-generation immigrants, and if one thing has been notable about new arrivals in the Jewish East End for the last hundred years or so, it is their political inactivity. Frequently they have come from states where political activity as understood in Britain has been impossible, and has meant nothing; even when this is not necessarily the case they have usually been fleeing from persecution, and all they have wanted to do is to get on quietly with their lives, make a living and not be noticed. Though, of course, many East End Communists are Jewish, they turn out almost invariably to be second- and third-generation Jews who have been sufficiently established in this country to have had a quite 'suburban' background of grammar-school education, but have chosen to stay in the East End and become involved in local politics, frequently to the consternation of their families, who are only too inclined to judge them as failures because they have done this instead of using their education to better themselves and move away.

This is not perhaps an important reflection on the play – there is no rule which says dramatic characters have to be typical – though it may show the views of some of its critics in a rather different light. With *Roots*, however, the question becomes more important, because if we are to be bored we want to be sure that we are being bored to good purpose. 'Mr Wesker's ear . . . is extraordinarily acute, enabling him to record the speech of his people with immense conviction,' writes Bernard Levin in his introduction to the printed text of *Roots*, but is the notation of Norfolk speech so accurate? It is not, certainly, the standard mummerset that we listen to in the theatre, but neither does it bear more than a very superficial resemblance to the language really spoken by Norfolk natives, and the objections of local audiences to the play on these grounds have been too readily brushed aside. So, too, perhaps, have their objections to the picture of rural life in general which the play presents – ah well, the argument runs, of course they wouldn't like it: it's much too true for comfort. But even in the most backward agricultural areas the Bryants would be exceptional; not, again, impossible, but exceptional in the unremitting grimness of their lives and their apparent isolation from any sort of social life whatever, if only that of the local hop, the Mothers' Union and the village store. They are, like the Kahns, a special case, devised to make a particular dramatic point, and it is as such that they must be judged: if the play bores us from time to time, if what happens in it seems every now and then a little unlikely, it is the author who must bear the blame, not just the life he is reflecting.

All this has particular relevance to the third of the trilogy, *I'm Talking About Jerusalem* (1960), because here the case of its characters is more patently extraordinary than in either of the previous plays. In this play we take up again the story of Ada and Dave, who set off for the Cotswolds in Act 2 of *Chicken Soup With Barley* to live a life of Morrisian devotion to arts and crafts, to individual toil in which a man can be his own master away from the domination of the industrialist and the machine. The idea of a pair of Jewish intellectuals doing this in 1946 is clearly unusual, even improbable, enough to suggest that this time the author's intention cannot possibly be a simple reflection of life as it is normally lived – the very title implies a parable. And so, surely, the play must be judged. By general consent the least satisfactory of the trilogy – there is too much explaining and tying up of loose ends from the other plays to be done before it can begin to stand satisfactorily on its own – *I'm Talking About Jerusalem* begins with the arrival of Ada and Dave at their cottage in Norfolk (not, oddly enough, the Cotswolds, as Ronnie tells us in *Chicken Soup*), where they are helped to unpack by Sarah and Ronnie. This first act is an extreme example of Wesker's casualness about construction: it adds nothing to the play that could not be conveyed by adding a couple of lines somewhere in the second act, just to tell us that Dave is working as a hired man for the time being, until he can set up on his own as a craftsman-joiner with his own workshop.

The play proper begins in the second act, with Dave's dismissal by his employer (a rather improbable squire-figure of the old school) for a bit of petty pilfering and, even more, for lying about it. It is the warning note: Ada taxes Dave with having brought 'the habits of the factory' with him, and the Colonel asks in genuine puzzlement why they came to the country at all. But for the moment they are permitted to continue in the Morris dream of a life in which each workman is a creative craftsman, the family the prime and all-important unit of life. And again a recurrent pattern begins to assert itself: if Ronnie is perhaps a repetition of his father, Ada in the long run turns out to be nearly a repetition of her mother. (She says at one point, after returning from London with the news that Harry has gone mad, 'You say I'm like her (Sarah)? You're right. I shall survive every battle that faces me, too, and because this place means survival to me we-are-staying-put!') But even her determination is not enough to save the situation: the manufacture of furniture on the scale Dave envisages is not an economic proposition, an attempt to turn the place into a guest-house attracts only aunts, and as the Labour government is voted out of office they pack up and return to London. Their experiment has failed and Dave's moment of vision, in which he decided he was a prophet, has faded with it; now he is defeated, he accepts defeat and sadly but not despairingly recognizes that he is not important.

Now, the only things that seem to matter to me are the day-to-day problems of my wife, my kids and my work. Face it – as an essential member of society I don't really count. I'm not saying I'm useless, but machinery and modern techniques have come about to make me the odd man out. Here I've been, comrade citizen, presenting my offerings and the world's rejected them. I don't count, Ronnie, and if I'm not sad about it you mustn't be either. Maybe Sarah's right, maybe you can't build on your own.

Have they gained anything from their experience, apart from some years of happiness? 'Maybe by coming here you've purified yourselves, like Jesus in the Wilderness,' suggests Ronnie, but no answer, confirming or denying, is given by anyone present. But perhaps an answer of sorts is implied by the strange scene at the end of Act 2, in which, as with Beatie's dance at the equivalent point in *Roots*, the play attempts to change register, building the scene in primarily intellectual terms (Beatie has been explaining music to her mother, Ada trying to analyse her relations with her parents), and then attempting a purely emotional resolution. Here the abrupt transition does not work in the theatre, or has not worked up to now, but the acting-out of the creation of man by parents and child which concludes the scene does carry precisely the overtones of a ritual purification, attained by obliteration of the self in a very literal 'return to nature', which would fit in with Ronnie's suggestion. The great millennium has not come, and certainly Ada and Dave have not even done much to bring it nearer, but maybe they were working in the right direction. However, the play leaves us on a question mark by recalling to us the age-old resignation of the Jew, as expressed by Harry, who used to say 'It'll purify itself', but was sure that the millennium would not happen in their lifetime.

I'm Talking About Jerusalem also left us with a question mark in another way: in the consideration of where Arnold Wesker as a playwright would go next. For it is a maddening amalgam of Wesker's best and his worst qualities. The ideas are there all right, but the expression of them tends to be muddled in itself and further obscured by basic technical faults of construction (which are more marked here than in any of the other plays). On the other hand, it does confirm the moving away from the strictly naturalistic which *Roots* to a certain extent foreshadowed: the characters are more obviously and deliberately exceptional than before and what seem to be the play's key scenes, the creation myth, Dave's decking of Ada with flowers and tablecloth when they make up their quarrel, and the argument in which Dave suddenly experiences his moment of vision, are far from the normal conventions of naturalistic or even realistic drama. Indeed, the main reason why the play is far less satisfactory even than the earlier plays is that the author constantly seems here to be reaching for something quite beyond the capabilities of the style he is working in. At this stage a choice was clearly necessary: to go back to naturalism but expand it and deepen it into a broader-based realism which could encompass the sort of comment on life at large towards which *I'm Talking About Jerusalem* constantly strives, or on the other hand to throw over naturalism and even realism altogether in favour of a far more adaptable and adventurous means of dramatic expression. For the moment, however, Wesker paused and took stock, returning instead to his earlier play *The Kitchen* (1958) which, in turn, he revised and expanded for its first full-dress stage production and adapted for a film version.

The Kitchen is a slight piece about a day in the life of those who work in the kitchens of a large restaurant. The day is crowded, what with illicit love among the ladles, a knife fight, a scalding, a miscarriage, and a climactic smash-up, but it all has a purpose: it is to show what happens when people are cooped up, constantly frustrated and limited entirely to the dreariest, least stimulating practicalities. At the end Marengo, the restaurant proprietor, says: 'I don't know what more to give a man. He works, he eats. I give him money. This is life, isn't it? I haven't made a mistake, have I? I live in the right world, don't I? . . . What is there more? What *is* there more?' Well, the author assures us, in one of his slightly embarrassing explanatory stage directions: 'We have seen that there must be more', but the viewer may perhaps be forgiven for wondering precisely what more, judging the question in realistic terms, poor Marengo could be expected to provide; if there is no more in the lives of his employees than that, how can he be expected to put it there? In fact, the tone of the whole play seems designed to support the general disenchantment with modern life *per se* expressed directly by Ada and Dave in *Chicken Soup*, for what is the answer to the rebellion of the kitchen-workers except some woolly Morrisian return of the individual to nature? Certainly this seems to be the corollary of the implied accusation that authority (represented in the play by Marengo) has in some mysterious way robbed the workers of whatever it was, in the days when an individual could take pride in his craft, that made life worth living.

One must, of course, bear in mind that *The Kitchen* is an

10a 'The Kitchen'
10b 'Big Soft Nellie'

11 'Roots'

early play, and that it therefore probably represents an attitude, a nostalgia at least, of which Wesker had seen the
impossibility by the time he came to write *I'm Talking About
Jerusalem*. But the main fault of the play as it stands is not its
'philosophy' (the desire for escape is a reasonable enough
theme for drama, and no rule lays down that the dreams put
forward as an alternative to reality must be practicable), but
in the purely technical matter of the correlation of the play's
two levels, realistic and allegorical, The point is made clearly
on a number of occasions that the kitchen is meant to stand in
our minds for the whole dirty business of modern life: most explicitly in Dimitri's speech in the first act:

> This stinking kitchen is like the world – you know what I mean?
> It's too fast to know what happens. People come and go, big excite-
> ment, big noise. What for? In the end who do you know? You make
> a friend, you are going to be all your life his friend, but when you go
> from here – pshtt! you forget! Why you grumble about this one
> kitchen?

Now, to establish the validity of a parallel like this, it is
necessary that the realistic level should be self-evidently true
and believable; there should be no suspicion that the truth is
being doctored to fit the argument. But if one looks at the set-
up in *The Kitchen* there is far too much evidence, even to the
casual uninformed eye, that this is just what is happening here.
Admittedly the critics tended to be so impressed by their knowledge that Wesker had actually worked for a while in a kitchen
that they supposed he must necessarily know best, but when
one considers it, what restaurant-kitchen could possibly be like
this? The lapses from realism are glaring enough on the stage,
where one makes allowances for the modifications imposed by
convention, but in the film version, made completely under
Wesker's supervision, these lapses are not only not corrected,
but are if anything accentuated. For example, what sort of
London restaurant serves 1,500 lunches in two hours every day,
with waitress service and presumably a seating capacity of
around 500? If such a restaurant did exist, however, and was
not run as a self-service cafeteria, it is obviously inconceivable
that it could have the menu shown here, involving roast

L

pheasant and (in the film) fresh lobster, as well as steaks, chops, and all the paraphernalia of the moderately high-class restaurant (i.e. the sort of restaurant where customers would be likely to complain to the chef that the soup was sour). And as for the suggestion that all the food would be cooked virtually to order during the lunch-hour rush, with cooks frantically trying to keep up with the demand of the waitresses, this is clearly impossible; most of the food would surely have to be cooked some time before and kept warm, according to standard practice in popular restaurants.

Of course, if a kitchen were run as shown here life in it would be hell, but that seems a rather shaky basis for assuming it as an objective reality and then trying to draw conclusions about the world at large from the fact of its existence. The play, admittedly, makes some superficial effect from its neat construction (it is the tightest and best-made of all Wesker's plays) and from the ready appeal of melodrama, especially if a sophisticated audience can be convinced by the exoticism of the setting that this is not just melodrama but life as it is really lived among the other half. But melodrama it obviously is, and melodrama at times so crude that it leans over uncomfortably far into the realm of farce.

Wesker's new work on *The Kitchen*, though apparently a diversion at the crucial stage in his stylistic evolution he had reached on the completion of the Trilogy, is actually not without its significance in his development. The original version of *The Kitchen* is predominantly a naturalistic drama, in intention at least, but there are elements also of dream and fantasy more prominently displayed than anywhere in the Trilogy. In his revisions Wesker brought them even more to the forefront of our attention, and John Dexter's production emphasized the symbolic elements in the play, presumably at Wesker's instigation, by formalizing whole sections of it – the lunchtime rush, the dream interlude – almost into a balletic ritual. In this sense the new version of *The Kitchen* may be seen as the next step towards Wesker's liberation from naturalism as heralded in *I'm Talking About Jerusalem*. When early in 1961, Wesker spoke to the *Twentieth Century* about the direction in which his

work was developing, significantly enough it was the 'Look,
I'm Alive!' game and Dave's bedecking of Ada which he
picked out as indications: he was tired of realism, and was
cutting down sets and props and even dialogue in his new
play, *Chips With Everything*, to conform with his new realization
that 'the theatre is a place where one wants to *see* things happening'. Consequently, in the new play there were 'large
chunks' which were 'very unnaturalistic' and one whole scene
in which nothing was said at all.

Shortly afterwards in an article in the *Transatlantic Review*,
Wesker expressed his reaction from realism at length:

> I have discovered that realistic art is a contradiction in terms. Art
> is the re-creation of experience, not the copying of it. Some writers
> use naturalistic means to re-create experience, others non-natural-
> istic. I happen to use naturalistic means; but all the statements I
> make are made theatrically. Reality is as misleading as truth;
> realistic art makes nonsense. If I develop, it might be away from
> naturalism. I have discovered that this too can be constricting – but
> I will still be trying to re-create the reality of my experience. I would
> no more be non-naturalistic for its own sake than I was naturalistic
> for its own sake; I am concerned with both only in order to com-
> municate what experience has meant to me.

Though the expression is in detail rather confused (is any
distinction intended between 'realistic' and 'naturalistic', and
if so what?) the general drift of the statement was clear enough;
'art is not innocent', style is important even if for Wesker what
he is saying remains the most important thing, and the closest
possible reproduction of actuality is not, after all, the best way
of getting over one's meaning.

All this helped to prepare audiences for a complete break
with Wesker's earlier style in *Chips With Everything*, and this
was to some extent what they got. It does indeed contain 'large
chunks' which are not naturalistic at all in writing or staging,
especially where this is a help in compressing 'real' time into
stage time: the episode in which one of the characters runs
away from the R.A.F. camp where they are in training and
then returns; the final move of the patrician, would-be prole-
tarian hero from the ranks back to the officer class he has tried
to escape. On the other hand, in a number of the most famous

sequences the dictum 'the theatre is a place where one wants to see things happening' is interpreted in the most naturalistic terms: the wordless sequence in which the men steal coke from the store and the passing-out parade in the last scene, for instance, depend quite as much upon the special interest of seeing something one does not expect to see in the theatre done with spectacular verisimilitude and precision as did the horse-races and train-wrecks of Drury Lane melodrama and the air-raid sequences of Lionel Bart's East End musical *Blitz*.

But the retreat from naturalism in *Chips With Everything* is something more subtle and pervasive than is immediately apparent from its manner of staging. In effect, Wesker has set out to close the gap which existed in his earlier work between his style – a detailed and elaborate naturalism – and what he had to say, which was too often extravagantly oversimplified and schematic. Rather than penetrating more deeply into his subject-matter, and allowing his characters to develop into something more than mouthpieces for one view or another manipulated by an all-too-visible puppet-master, he has chosen instead to simplify the form to match the message. The characters here never – or with only one arguable exception, Corporal Hill – attempt to impose on us belief in them as rounded human beings. Instead, they assume the boldly conventionalized characteristics of figures in a political cartoon, and this, indeed, is very much what they are. The play is a neat polemical exercise derived from the basic (highly arguable) assumption that service life is a microcosm of civil life, the class struggle and so on, and using all the resources of the theatre, naturalistic and non-naturalistic, to bludgeon the point home. For this purpose the officers all have to be brutish representatives of the boss-class and the men down-trodden underdogs until they find a leader to crystallize their amorphous dissatisfaction and hostility into a decisive act of revolt. We are not, presumably, meant to accept them primarily as human beings existing in their own right, but rather as quasi-allegorical type-figures of their respective classes.

The trouble with allegory, though, is that unless it works on

at least two levels it is almost certain to be both boring and un-
persuasive. Even if a character has a clear and unambiguous
allegorical significance, like those in *Pilgrim's Progress*, he should
still achieve a measure of credibility in human terms or his
story will not interest us and we shall rebel against whatever
message it is meant to convey simply because common sense
tells us that things aren't like that. In *The Kitchen* already we
have seen Wesker failing to achieve this crucial balance by
making the level intended to correspond to an external reality
of some sort largely incredible. Here again, in *Chips With
Everything*, he tends to fall into the same trap: the immediate reaction is that on the whole officers aren't like that, and neither
are men. When Wesker shows us the officers glaring hostility
at the men during a Christmas party, he is surely not only
failing on the most superficial realistic level – some officers
may behave like this but what we are being offered here must
be a representative bunch of officers – but also badly mistaking
the grounds of his attack on the officer class. If they hate the
men, at least in doing so they are acknowledging their existence as a force worthy of their hate and fear; much more ob-
jectionable, as well as much more believable, is the situation
which actually obtains, more often than not, in which the officers behave with perfect, and perfectly sincere, amiability on
such occasions, simply because they don't take the men seriously as human beings at all – they regard them as they might
children or animals. Equally with the men: one appreciates
the importance to Wesker of the idea that the working-class
will rebel against the ruling classes by refusing to accept any
longer the rubbish of pop 'art' constantly foisted on them by
commerce and returning instead to their folksong heritage
(witness the emphasis in the plans of Centre 42 on a popular
culture of folksong-singing in pubs) but the rebellion stirred
up at this same Christmas party which finds its expression in a
concerted rendering of the old revolutionary song 'The Cutty
Wren' leaves any conceivable reality so far behind that it can
be accepted (damagingly in the context) only as a wish-ful-
filment fantasy – something which ought to happen but we all
know cannot.

So, even after his decisive break with stage naturalism Wesker is not yet finished with the problem which has plagued him throughout his career: the debilitating effect that his inability to see that things may in fact be other than he thinks they ought to be has on his ability to express his ideas in properly dramatic terms. Even in a political cartoon a clear grasp of the real facts is required before they can be adapted to the particular requirements in hand. In *Chips With Everything* one is left with the feeling that Wesker has never taken a good, clear look at service life, and so the initial assumption of his allegory based on it is false and all that follows from it is correspondingly suspect. (Curiously, in *Chicken Soup With Barley* Wesker himself seemed to recognize that war and the services represent to most people an escape from the rat-race of 'real life', precisely because it is not a microcosm of their life outside: was not this why 'the service killed any illusions Dave may have once had about the splendid and heroic working class'?)

Moreover, in this case Wesker adds to his own difficulties by creating a central character who steps right out of the allegorical framework. Pip Thompson is an upper-class young man generally regarded as 'obvious officer material' who chooses, for inscrutable reasons of his own, to reject his class, stay in the ranks, and side with the men. In this capacity he is naturally, as the most articulate of conscripts, the mouthpiece of the author. Though he is shown as being a bit of an outsider – too much of one, perhaps; what hutful of working-class men would in fact listen so docilely to his extravagant accounts of the luxury and power of the home from which he has come? – he is the person who thinks about the working-class situation, as Wesker has thought about it, and comes to much the same conclusions that Wesker has come to: the working class are being exploited and wilfully deprived of the good things in life – good music, good food, even good contraceptives: 'They have babies, and they eat chips with everything.' He it is, also, who decides what is to be done, and here too he agrees with Wesker: pop music must go and folksong come back, chips must be replaced at once by sauté potatoes. So far, so good. But then, in a key scene corresponding somewhat to the breaking-down of T. E. Lawrence in Rattigan's *Ross* by the revelation of his homosexual-masochistic nature, Pip is broken down by the Pilot Officer simply by being told that his only reason for staying in the ranks is the urge to power: 'Among your own people there were too many who were powerful, the competition was too great, but here, among lesser men – here among the yobs, among the good-natured yobs, you could be king.' He is destroyed – 'No man survives whose motive is discovered, no man' – conforms by sticking a dummy at bayonet practice where he had formerly refused to and then inevitably dons the uniform of an officer and goes back to his class.

All of which would be perfectly acceptable in the context of realistic psychological drama, if a trifle naïve, but in a context where everything and everybody has a clear place in a scheme of abstract values, such a character can only cause confusion. Wesker is no Arden; Arden consistently establishes a clear separation in our minds between characters and ideas, but when Wesker suddenly requires us to keep clear in our mind the distinction between the ideas Pip puts forward in the first two thirds of the play and the character himself as he emerges in the last third, the result is merely confusing. Presumably Wesker wants us to approve of the ideas Pip puts forward, but not of Pip himself, but he has not constructed his play in such a way that this is possible without some abrupt and damaging readjustments. Damaging not only because they break up the play, but also because they set us thinking more closely about Wesker's position; they make us wonder whether just as Pip in the play is an outsider imposing his own romantically ideal, outside view of the working class on those who really belong to it. so Arnold Wesker, the self-educated, self-improved working-class writer, is not now in precisely the same way playing the bourgeois game. Is he not attacking the music, the food, the way of life of the working-class just because they are not acceptable to a middle-class point of view? Why shouldn't people eat chips with everything; are *pommes sautés* really preferable, just because to the genteel ear they sound better? Are selections of the tuny bits from Tchaikovsky and *L'Arlésienne* really an indisputable improvement on juke-box music?

Doesn't Wesker's preoccupation with folksong suggest just the sort of patronizing do-gooding approach to the working class (how quaint! how folksy!) which if it came from anyone but a recent graduate from the working class would be regarded as intolerable by the working class themselves? (It is in any case noticeable that up to now Wesker's plays have made their major appeal to the predominantly middle-class London theatre audience.)

The viability of Wesker's position, though admittedly of only peripheral importance to our judgement of *Chips With Everything* as drama, becomes much more important a consideration in relation to Wesker's major preoccupation since he wrote the play, Centre 42. As yet, Centre 42 occupies a rather nebulous position in the cultural life of Britain, and its effectiveness in bringing culture to classes and areas at present unfairly left out of account by the powers-that-be remains to be tested. Centre 42 itself is 'a kind of pool of the best of our artists organized in such a way that they could take their work out to Arts Festivals all over the country'. The basic idea of spreading theatre, music, and the arts wider, of making sure that all sorts of people all over the country have at least the chance to enjoy them if they want to, is obviously excellent; where argument may legitimately arise is over the exact way that Wesker and others in Centre 42 interpret the needs and interests of their audiences. The first festival, at Wellingborough in September 1962, did bring forward one striking new play, Bernard Kops's *Enter Solly Gold*, as well as a slight new work by Wesker, a documentary script for music, *The Nottingham Captain*, about the Luddite riots of 1817, presented in two different settings, one 'classical', one jazz.

After that the Centre went into a state of suspended animation for some time, to re-emerge in 1966, shorn of most of its provincial aspirations, as the moving spirit of the Round House, Chalk Farm, a place where exhibitions could be mounted and happenings happen. By this time, too, the mainly social preoccupations of its organizers seemed to have given place to a more American-influenced interest in the psychedelic and various forms of consciously *avant-garde* art.

Where Wesker himself stands in all this is not clear. Of the two major plays he has written since *Chips With Everything*, one, *Their Very Own and Golden City* (1966) reflects his old interest in society and its improvement; the other, *The Four Seasons*, is almost exclusively personal in its focus. Neither is among Wesker's stronger works, though for rather different reasons. *Their Very Own and Golden City* never seems quite to decide what it is about, triumphant idealism or compromise. Of course, in a way it is about both; its architect hero is gradually led astray from his original purpose of building six cooperatively-owned golden cities, but he does manage to build one. Throughout the play the way that his vision is frittered away in practice through the years forms a constant, bitterly ironical counter-point with his expression of the vision itself, but the end is a sort of triumph, in that the play is not finally one of defeat. The trouble is that the play, by trying to be simultaneously about the failure of socialist ideals and their continuing validity, takes on too much at once: the defeat is real, the triumph only a hopeful dream, and though the play could culminate with either, it really cannot workably culminate with both. Also, it must be said that the play tries to say too much and shows too little: there is not enough of the sort of detailed notation of significant happening which has always been Wesker's strong point (we never really see Andrew functioning as an architect, for instance), and too much heavy verbiage.

This last is also true of *The Four Seasons*; in fact, it is the main thing wrong with this two-character piece. It is, what none of Wesker's other plays are, a completely verbal piece exploring the progress of a marriage through four seasons almost entirely in terms of the words the couple use to each other. And the words, on the whole, are insufficient: oddly, but significantly, all that anyone seems now to remember very clearly about the play is the one scene in which words are left to one side, as we see an apple strudel made on the stage. But for the rest, the play showed Wesker at his weakest, and was by general consent the least successful of all his plays.

There have been signs of development, however, as well as

just change. Wesker's short television play *Menace* (1963) might be seen, hopefully, as a straw in the wind: in it he seemed less determined to preach than ever before, less eager to use two characters as mouthpieces. Instead, he merely presented us with a group of unhappy misfits, only one of whom really has a Weskerian dream (and even he has too much cynicism to give himself over to it wholeheartedly), and left us to draw our own conclusions about them and their relations with the world about them. In *The Four Seasons* he seemed to be continuing and developing this approach; not yet, certainly, with complete success, but with a new consistency and determination. Words are still his stumbling-block. But whatever one may think of Wesker's work so far, it is impossible not to respect his readiness to experiment, to develop, to make his way slowly and painfully towards a style in which he can say to his own satisfaction what he really wants to say. *I'm Talking About Jerusalem* brought him to a point where some important choices had to be made; with *Chips With Everything*, Wesker seemed to have chosen, but his abandonment of his earlier naturalistic style was still tentative and inconsistent. *Menace* seemed to carry him a step further, *Their Very Own and Golden City* was a marking-time, and *The Four Seasons*, for all its faults, still looks like the real beginning of something new in his work. His next play, successful or not, can hardly help being interesting, and one trusts it will not be too long delayed. If in it he can discipline his uneven talents (which is a big if), Arnold Wesker, hitherto by choice and on principle the most prosaic of our young dramatists, may turn out after all to be the poet the committed theatre in this country has so long awaited. It cannot, in any case, be entirely without significance that he concluded his interview in the *Twentieth Century* with the slightly gnomic statement: 'I really would like to write a play which begins "Once upon time . . ."'

BERNARD KOPS

The appearance of a playwright so unmistakably metropolitan as Bernard Kops among writers who have made their mark initially out of town is one of those little oddities in which the progress of the 'new drama' is so fertile. His classification here is almost unavoidable, however, since his first play, *The Hamlet of Stepney Green*, was first staged at the Oxford Playhouse, though later briefly transferred to the Lyric, Hammersmith, and his subsequent plays have turned up in equally improbable places for a dramatist with primarily working-class interests, such as the Edinburgh Festival, Guildford Rep, Cambridge A.D.C., and the Arts Theatre Club, but never yet on the public West End stage.

With the choice of *Enter Solly Gold* as the first production of Centre 42 (still out of town) Kops may have found something like his spiritual home, which hitherto one would have seen as the East End and Theatre Workshop more than anywhere else. Not that he has had any direct connection with the Stratford E. company, except that at one time it announced *The Hamlet of Stepney Green* for production, though the production never materialized. But both Kops's background and style of writing seem to fit in very closely with the Theatre Workshop ideal. He was born in Stepney in 1928, of a working-class Jewish family, left school at the age of thirteen, and drifted from job to job until he decided he wanted to write, producing a number of poems, later collected into two volumes, a novel, and several radio scripts before he settled decisively to writing for the stage. His first play, *The Hamlet of Stepney Green*, was written in 1956, and, like all his other plays to a certain extent, it draws its material from the Jewish life and folklore he knew as a child in the East End. Not only that, but like the majority of Theatre Workshop plays its development is rather free and arbitrary, suggesting often inspired improvisation more than careful literary craftsmanship; the style is basically simple and unsophisticated – in many ways Kops remains even now something of a primitive – and the characters have a habit of speaking in asides to the audience and bursting from time to time into song.

The central character of *The Hamlet of Stepney Green* is David Levy, a dreamy young man with an urge to croon. This character, more or less, recurs in nearly all Kops's plays, along with the Oedipal situation in which he is enmeshed; all Kops's young heroes are tied emotionally to their mothers and all are dreamers obsessed with some fixed idea. In only one case does the dream show signs of winning out (*Change for the Angel*), but elsewhere Kops seems to advocate coming to terms with the realities of normal human life and recognizing that dreams may be delusions which prevent one from seeing the truth instead of insights into the truth denied to more mundane creatures. In this conclusion he avoids one sentimental stereotype, the dreamer-poet-rebel who is an unacknowledged legislator of mankind, only to fall into another: reliance on the good sense and solid values of warm-hearted, simple people to pull us through. Given this tendency, though (which in a primitive is not hard to accept, since one does not expect a sophisticated or subtly reasoned world-picture), it may be felt that Kops's work is at its best when it is most unashamedly simple and sentimental, as in *The Hamlet of Stepney Green*, rather than when, as in one or two later plays, he tries to reason and philosophize.

In *The Hamlet of Stepney Green*, fortunately, there is almost no overt philosophizing at all. In the first act Sam Levy is dying, though as he has been dying so often before and recovered no one takes very much notice. As he looks back over his life he finds it unsatisfactory and realizes that he has been poisoned by his own life (or, in a sense, by his wife, since she was his life). His son David overhears him rambling and, taking only what he wants to hear, assumes that his mother has poisoned his father and revenge must be expected. In the second act, which begins immediately after Sam's funeral, Sam reappears, an amiable ghost, in response, he says, to some unvoiced need of David's; only David can see and hear him. He tries to curb David's enthusiasm for revenge, but David will not listen; when he sees that his mother is likely to remarry a widowed neighbour, Mr Segal, he reaches a state of mania in which he dresses in black, Teddy-boy style, to simulate his model, Hamlet, and is taken for mad by his relatives and the chorus of three salesmen (two start selling tombstones and one insurance, but they keep changing jobs). Sam realizes that, in fact, his wife's remarriage is the best solution, and, persuading David that this is all part of the revenge (as, in a different sense, it may be), he engineers it through a seance. In the last act, after the mother's remarriage, Sam gives David a love potion pretending it is a poison, and everyone who drinks it is suffused with love and good nature. David does not drink it, but suddenly he, too, sees the light, realizes he loves Mr Segal's daughter Hara, and all is set for a happy ending.

The plot is evidently pretty naïve in outline, and the main strength of the play is that it stays naïve and unspoilt all through. Naïvety has its drawbacks, of course – the first act is much too rambling, and the points in which the parallel with *Hamlet* are insisted on, notably a travesty version of the 'To be, or not to be' soliloquy, are sometimes embarrassingly self-conscious, but in the main the whole thing has an unaffected theatrical *élan* which came over even in the not very satisfactory production from Oxford Playhouse (only a Jewish cast could play it naturally; a mainly Gentile cast has to work at it and this, however well they work, weighs the play down and prevents a feeling of real spontaneity). 'What is the purpose of life?' asks David at one point, and Sam replies: 'The purpose of life is to be aware that that question exists'; in those terms, at least, the conclusion is inevitable – the play must end happily with singing and rejoicing, and David can settle down to selling herrings on his father's stall, provided that he stays alive to the world about him and keeps his dreams alive ('Commit arson every day in your imagination, burn down the previous day's lies, have a little revolution now and again in your heart'). The sentimentality is obvious, but at least it is consistent and unashamed.

Much of Kops's work since *Hamlet of Stepney Green* has been uneven and disappointing, mainly, it seems, because the original integrity of his primitive vision has suffered from an admixture of more sophisticated materials which he has not been able to absorb completely into a new and more complex view of the world. *Goodbye, World*, his second play (produced at the Guildford Theatre in 1959) is the least successful of them, being hardly dramatic in any normal sense at all. Its hero,

John, is again the obsessed dreamer we have already encountered, though much more inarticulate than David: he is a habitual criminal at twenty-two, in prison when his mother commits suicide. His obsession is twofold: to find out if she left any message for him (apart from the 'Goodbye, World', scrawled on her dressing-table mirror before she died), and to see that she gets a decent funeral. To this end he escapes from prison and the whole action of the play takes place in a house in the street where his mother died; he has rented a room here from a faded, once-elegant old woman, and awaits his chance to find out more about his mother's death while various eccentric characters – landlady, blind circus clown, drink-sodden Irishman – drift in and out and the police watch and wait in the street outside. Everyone talks interminably, mainly in long autobiographical monologues retailed to a more or less passive listener, and nothing is ever concluded: John never gets out-of-doors because of the police, and finally, after three acts of conversation, he gives himself up.

Here the convention is much more realistic than in *The Hamlet of Stepney Green*, and the result strongly suggests that, as we had suspected, Kops is not a thinker, even if possibly he would like to see himself as one, but just has a natural flair for the theatre which given the right material and the right form can produce a lively piece of theatrical fantasy. *Change for the Angel* (1960) reinforces this belief: it taxes Kops's powers of construction to the utmost, and on the whole they are found badly wanting, but one or two of the fragments into which the play falls have, taken in isolation, considerable theatrical effectiveness, and they are nearly always those farthest from realism. The play is about a family losing its identity and standards in the modern city: the father is a baker who cannot keep his self-respect in a world of mass-produced packaged bread and has taken to drink, the mother is kindly but weak, and their three children are all in various ways dissatisfied and at odds with the world about them: the elder brother has become the leader of a local gang of toughs, the daughter is seduced by an American serviceman, and the young son (the dreamer again) wants to be a writer, though his father wants him to become an engineer, and consequently father and son are savagely at odds.

This son, Paul, is presumably the central character in the play, and it is his final departure after his mother's death in the last act to live his own life and become a writer (the dream, for once, winning out) which concludes the play. But essentially he remains static throughout, complaining constantly about the same things, and staying always on the same emotional level. Consequently, he is virtually useless as a unifying factor in the play, and tends for dramatic purposes to slip into the background, along with his tentative relations with the girl upstairs and the rumble of Oedipal complications with his easygoing mother. Instead, it is the father who is the motive force of the play's action, and he is perhaps the most inconsistent and least believable character of them all, since it is hard to believe that the mild, long-suffering man of the first act could suddenly be galvanized into attempted rape in the second, even allowing for a quality of quiet desperation in all he does. As it happens, though, it is precisely the sections least believable in realistic terms – the passage leading up to the rape, which involves a distant relative recently out of a mental home, and the invocation of the Angel of Death – which come off best in the theatre: once he is away from the tiresome requirements of realistic character development, and able to work in great, simple dramatic symbols or drift off into dream fantasy, Kops comes into his own.

His next play, *The Dream of Peter Mann*, which was written with the aid of an Arts Council bursary while Kops was resident dramatist with the Bristol Old Vic, was something of a return to form; at least, it was a return to Kops's home ground. It starts with children's street songs, like *The Hamlet of Stepney Green*, and a formalized evocation of street-trading life (with some wide-swipes, à la *Change for the Angel*, at the modern passion for synthetic packaged goods), then Peter, who dreams of founding the greatest Superstore ever and winning the flashy and selfish Sylvia, is persuaded by a disreputable old chess-playing tramp that he must go and make his fortune prospecting for uranium, even if it means stealing his mother's savings to do so. He attempts the theft while a wedding is in progress, and Jason, a sinister local shopkeeper, is trying without much success to court his mother. But the safe falls on top of him and most of the play is taken up with his delirious dream. He steals the bride from the wedding, his childhood sweetheart Penny, and away they go with Alex, the tramp, to look for uranium.

Twelve years later they arrive back battered and penniless to find that a new barbarism has overtaken the world they knew; everyone has become obsessed with the search for uranium and Jason has become a sort of war-lord for the district. Neither Peter's mother nor Sylvia recognizes him, and he is on the point of being executed when his mother pretends to recognize him just to save his neck. Subsequently he finds, however, that his old salesman's gift of the gab has not deserted him, and soon he has won over all the downtrodden inhabitants to work for him; his mother and Sylvia recognize him now he looks like being successful, and when we next see him he is the richest man in the world, with his own deep shelter to protect him when the Bomb falls and his own factories manufacturing the vital commodity of the moment, shrouds. As the moment for the Bomb approaches he locks himself in his shelter and everyone else is killed, but he finds that even he is fated; his mother appears as the Angel of Death and sings him to sleep with an old nursery song which told him he would be king – and so he is, but of the kingdom of death, not life. At this point he wakes up, cured of his earlier fantasies, and realizes that it was Penny he loved all the time; she has refused to go through with her marriage to the other man, so he can marry her, and to round things off Alex is revealed as his mother's husband and his long-lost father.

Clearly Kops's imagination has been set free by the unabashed return to fantasy, and the result is much more satisfactory than either of his previous two plays, but unfortunately the 'philosophy' weighs a little heavy on the piece and the author does not seem to have quite the intellectual flexibility necessary to put over such a bald message about human values without making his drama naïve in the least acceptable sense; inevitably the play carries with it reminders of those rather tiresome expressionist dramas of the twenties in which man's life was compared to that of a rockpool or an adding machine, and there is no denying that Kops's play is considerably less successful in this genre than, say, *R.U.R.*, to which in some sections it bears more than a fleeting resemblance.

At least in his two following plays, *Stray Cats and Empty Bottles* and *Enter Solly Gold*, Kops left behind for the moment the hawking of over-simplified social messages which marred *The Dream of Peter Mann*, and to a lesser extent *Change for the Angel*; he even threw overboard his dreamer-hero with a mother-fixation. *Stray Cats and Empty Bottles* is just a ballad-play in one act about a group of derelicts living on a scrapheap in a shack destined for rapid demolition. Jack collects stray cats for skinning and Iris collects empty bottles; the plot of the play, in so far as it has any plot, concerns their attempts to assist Newton, a refined and eccentric tramp, to marry the mad White Lady of Wapping for her money, which turns out in the end to be non-existent after all. The fantasy is worked out in completely theatrical terms, with songs, dances, impro-visatory dialogue, and occasional passages of poetic invention; it appears to have no motive other than simply to entertain, which it does. The amateur production by Cambridge A.D.C. was supervised by the author, who is said to be dissatisfied with all previous productions of his work, and achieved a semi-balletic (or perhaps semi-operatic) drive and precision which suggests that a strong directorial hand (and ideally, perhaps, Joan Littlewood's) is necessary if his essentially artless works are to make their maximum effect.

The fact that such was not, for all sorts of external reasons, forthcoming for his next stage play, *Enter Solly Gold*, made it somewhat difficult to judge from its first performances. *Enter Solly Gold* was chosen as the inaugural production of Centre 42, first of all during Wellingborough's Trades Union Festival in September 1962, then in various places up and down the country where live theatre is not usually to be seen; there were last-minute changes of cast and producer, and conditions of performance were often primitive. It is, too, a very patchy play, but there are enough good patches to make it on the

M

whole one of Kops's most fetching works. The good patches – and most of the weak ones too – are emotionally in the line of *Stray Cats and Empty Bottles*: anarchic, knockabout comedy. But this time it is applied to a world much more familiar to us from Kops's earlier plays: that of neighbourhood Jewish life. Admittedly the Jews in *Enter Solly Gold* are better off than those in *The Hamlet of Stepney Green*, and there is much more room for satire at the expense of their riches and social pretensions, but basically the close-knit world of the large family and the traditional observances is much the same.

The central character, Solly Gold, is a confidence trickster from the East End. In the first act we see him at work in rapid succession on a poor tailor, a tough prostitute, and an old widow from whom he extracts some fat chickens and a rabbi's suit which belonged to her late husband. From there he goes on to take over a prosperous Jewish household in Golders Green or thereabouts; disguised as a rabbi he arrives in the middle of a wedding and has soon wriggled his way, Tartuffe-like, into a secure position in the family, ruling them all from Morrie Swartz, the melancholy millionaire father, down. He announces that Morrie is in fact the long-awaited Messiah, intending that while Morrie is living this part he will unobtrusively take over the shoe business which made Morrie's fortune. Inevitably he overreaches himself and is finally exposed for what he is, but in a burst of sentimentality at the end Kops makes everyone decide that in general they are better for the experience and it doesn't really matter. This is a comedy, and it is to be expected that everyone will live happily ever after, but all the same the resolution does seem a little forced and abrupt; still, before this final stumble the play races on at a tremendous pace, and keeps us laughing at the characters (and in the long run at ourselves, since their weaknesses are weaknesses we all share to a greater or lesser extent) even when the jokes are not quite first-rate. *Enter Solly Gold* shows a more robust side of Kops, less inclined to poetic whimsy, and therefore on the whole more palatable to more people.

If in *Stray Cats and Empty Bottles* and *Enter Solly Gold* we get away from Kops's poet-dreamer hero for a while, in his radio play *Home Sweet Honeycomb* the character is very much with us again. In all other respects, though, the play is far, far different from the earlier plays in which he appeared; it at once fairly resumes Kops's previous work and carries it a significant stage farther. It is an odd, apocalyptic piece, full of dreams and visions. The setting is a nightmare megalopolitan future where everybody lives a zomby-like existence parroting advertising slogans and anyone who does not instantly fit in is handed over to the borough council for 'putting under' at a jolly public execution. In this world lives a new embodiment of Kops's favourite poet-rebel figure, Danny Todd (who is presumably both 'on his tod', i.e. on his own, and already marked by *Tod*, death). Danny understands at once that he must rebel or die, that there is no middle way. Condemned to death in his own life, he escapes through the wall to a succession of other lives, each more horrific than the last, with everywhere the key figure of his first life – mother, father, fiancée – returning in a variety of guises to haunt and betray him until finally his humanity can bear no more: he gives in, marries the girl, makes it up with his family, and settles down to lead the same sort of life as everyone else. Well, of course, that is what has always happened before in Kops's work: his poet-rebel heroes, except in *Change for the Angel*, always conform in the end, or at least reach a satisfactory compromise, if only because the alternative (madness in *The Hamlet of Stepney Green*, total annihilation in *The Dream of Peter Mann*) always turns out to be so much worse than the ordinary life of ordinary people. They realize, in fact – and this seems to be Kops's own comforting message to the rebellious and the misfit – that the 'real life' they are resisting is not so bad after all and their rebellion is just an immature dream. And so it is here, but with how different an effect. For where Kops's earlier work was in the main optimistic, the new play is profoundly pessimistic. Kops no longer believes, apparently, that a satisfactory compromise can be reached in which one may lead an outwardly ordinary life but 'have a little revolution now and again in your heart'. The final return of his new poet-rebel to the world which he initially tries to reject is seen in very much the same terms as Winston Smith's ultimate realization in *1984* that he loves Big Brother. Danny loves, if not Big Brother, at least, in the person of his terrible fiancée, something very like Big Sister, and we leave him condemned to a 'semi-suburban slide' into complete, brainless nonentity.

This horrific vision is conveyed in prose of haunting clarity and precision, which only occasionally slips into the reach-me-down pseudo-folk poetry which weakened some of Kops's earlier writing. A work of intense gloom and despondency, *Home Sweet Honeycomb* still suggests that Kops is, or will be, a more considerable dramatist than we have up to now had cause to take him for. It shows a deeper understanding of human nature (not, of course, just because it is pessimistic) and a firmer discipline in ordering the products of his bounding imagination; perhaps because radio permits a far greater flexibility of locale and removes the necessity, which one sensed as an inhibiting factor in *The Dream of Peter Mann*, to bear the limitations of the theatrical stage in mind, the form seems for once to sit naturally on the material rather than being forced on it arbitrarily and not very efficiently from without. Kops is still in many ways a primitive, but in *Enter Solly Gold* and *Home Sweet Honeycomb* he has proved capable of real development without losing any of his essential qualities. His latest notable work at time of writing, a radio play called *Lemmings*, is a sort of companion piece to *Home Sweet Honeycomb* about a future world in which masses of humans are moved by some instinct to march to the sea, lemming-like, and throw themselves in; but in whatever direction Kops develops in the future, at least the danger which threatened after *The Dream of Peter Mann* that he would be stuck for the rest of his career with one limited style and one limiting conception of form seems now to have been overcome once and for all.

DAVID CAMPTON

David Campton is one of the most interesting and (as far as London is concerned, anyway) one of the least known of the new dramatists. Apart from odd peripheral appearances in theatres like the British Drama League Theatre-in-the-Round in Fitzroy Square, and The Questors, Ealing, his work has been seen in London only in the shape of two revue sketches, 'Service', in *One Over the Eight*, and 'Table Talk' in *On the Brighter Side*, neither of which gives more than the slightest hint of his highly individual qualities, and a short one-acter, *Soldier from the Wars Returning*, which played for a fortnight in an ill-assorted triple bill. For Campton, though not a 'provincial' dramatist in any of the usual senses, has been produced almost entirely in the North, where he has had a close and fruitful connection with Stephen Joseph's Scarborough-based Theatre-in-the-Round since 1955. This fact has placed Campton up to now in a disadvantageous position, since his work has either been totally unknown to the London critics or where known has been too hastily written off as imitation-Pinter, a supposition which, while not completely tenable even on the evidence of his plays themselves, proves to be quite impossible when one checks the dates and discovers that *The Lunatic View*, in which his work most closely approaches Pinter's, was staged in 1957, a year before even the first unsuccessful run of *The Birthday Party*.

But this is to anticipate. Campton was born in Leicester, where he still lives, in 1924, and, three and a half years' war service apart, worked from 1941 to 1949 for Leicester Education Authority, and then from 1949 to 1956 for the East Midlands Gas Board. Having begun writing 'shortly after I was first presented with a stick of chalk and a slate', and after twenty-odd plays 'written while I was first learning how to write', he had a play accepted for publication, *Going Home*, in 1949, and then two others, also one-acters. During his time with the Gas Board he became in a modest way quite a successful writer of one-act plays, one of them, *Sunshine on the Righteous*, winning the Leicestershire finals of the British Drama League Festival in 1954, and another, *The Laboratory*, coming second in the Drama League National One Act Play competition of the same year and winning first prize in the international competition organized by the Tavistock Repertory Company, as well as being televised in 1955. His first full-length play, *The Cactus Garden*, was produced by the Everyman Repertory Company, Reading, in 1955, and in the same year his comedy *Dragons are Dangerous* was produced by Stephen Joseph in Scarborough: the first association between Campton and the Theatre-in-the-Round company. Another play for the company, *Idol in the Sky*, followed in 1956.

All these plays Campton dismisses now as 'rather conventional': the real break in his life came in 1956, when he left the Gas Board and became a professional writer under contract to Associated-Rediffusion, for which he wrote children's programmes, episodes of *The Groves* and *Starr and Company* and comedy scripts for Richard Murdoch. He also wrote for Theatre-in-the-Round *The Lunatic View*, his first decisively original work, and from then on has written something for them each year, joining the company as an actor in 1958.

The remarkable originality of *The Lunatic View* on its appearance in 1957 can perhaps best be gauged by a brief summary of its plot. It takes the form of four playlets, or 'glimpses', as they are called, linked by spoof television announcements. The first, *A Smell of Burning*, tells in a completely deadpan fashion of the incursion of a local government official called Robinson, who appears to be deep in some anarchic plot (gasworks blown up, gunfire in the streets, bodies hung out of the window), into the uncomprehending but quite unruffled ménage of Mr and Mrs Jones (she it is who is finally left hanging). In the second, *Memento Mori*, an old man showing a young man round an empty house gradually allows us to understand that he has murdered his wife and buried her beneath the floorboards; finally he immures the young man, too, to avoid the risk of anyone buying the house again. In the third, *Getting and Spending*, the whole life together of a married couple is telescoped into one brief scene, rather like a piece of stop-motion photography, in which the house is never completed, the husband's applications for key jobs never sent, the baby they are waiting for never arrives, and the one piece of knitting the wife is working on grows little by little to gargantuan proportions. The fourth, *Then . . .*, concerns the only two survivors of the ultimate nuclear explosion, a schoolmaster and a Miss Europe, who have survived because they, and apparently they alone, acted on the official instruction that in case of emergency they should put brown paper bags on their heads. They get to know each other, but the main difficulty is, when will it be safe to take the bags off? They may have to spend their lives without ever seeing each other, but in the end they decide to make together a gesture in favour of life, whatever it may cost, and as the curtain falls they take off the bags.

The oddity of all this, in an England not yet properly habituated to Ionesco, an England in which Pinter and N. F. Simpson would still have to wait two or three years before finding any sort of public, does not need insisting on. Campton calls *The Lunatic View* 'a comedy of menace', which implies perhaps a greater unity than, in fact, the programme has, but four little comedies of menace they certainly are, and only the second, which has a close similarity to a short story by Walter de la Mare, presents menace in any of its traditional forms. Here the *Old Dark House* set-up and the suggestion of bodies in cupboards and beneath the floorboards will come as something fairly familiar to audiences used to being scared into laughter by *The Cat and the Canary, Ghost Breakers*, and other such films. But elsewhere the comedy is all too uncomfortably drawn from the normal situations of modern life or a not-inconceivable near future. The couple in *Getting and Spending*, living out in a few minutes' continuous action the whole of a childless, aimless life together, carry their own comment on the modern world without its ever being made inartistically explicit. The casual anarchy of *A Smell of Burning* has some of the riotous inconsequence of an early *Goon Show*, except that the background of the action has enough reality about it to convince us that these things are actually happening amid the general unconcern of the onlookers. And in *Then . . .*, the most controlled and successful of the four, the image of the paper bags as both protection and impediment to communication is one of those rare dramatic symbols which work perfectly on a realistic level and also gather more and more related meanings the more one thinks about them without ever fuzzing the original effect.

The use of the term 'comedy of menace' makes comparison with Pinter almost inevitable, but on the whole, even apart from the chronological impossibility of Campton being a

Pinter imitator, such a comparison serves only to underline the differences between them. There are similarities in formal organization – Campton, like Pinter, favours a free, rhapsodic treatment of the one-act form, working towards some climactic action – and in the handling of dialogue, which tends in their work to progress along lines laid down by unconscious association (reinforced by liberal doses of mutual incomprehension on the part of the characters) rather than by logic. But Campton distinguishes himself from Pinter and the various other British dramatists who have at one time or another dabbled in the Absurd by the fact that his plays do not only betoken a vague unease with things as they are, but show a social conscience worn unequivocally on their author's sleeve.

Campton defines his intentions in adapting the methods of 'the theatre of the Absurd' to the purposes of social comment very clearly:

> To my mind the Theatre of the Absurd is a weapon against complacency (which spreads like a malignant fungus). The weapon of complacency is the pigeon-hole. Pigeon-hole an idea, and it becomes harmless. (We have a clean bomb.) It is difficult to be complacent when the roots of one's existence are shaken, which is what the Absurd at its best does. Of course, now, having been given a name, the Theatre of the Absurd is in danger of being popped into a pigeon-hole itself. . . .

Thus while in Pinter's comedies of menace the menace is the more pervasive and potent precisely because it is undefined – if it is anything capable of elucidation it is the constant threat of the outside world to the integrity of the individual personality – for Campton the menace is clear enough: it is the Bomb. Not for nothing were three of the playlets from his later sequence *A View from the Brink* performed before an audience of marchers at a stop on the way to Aldermaston in 1960. This overt social concern for the troubles of the modern world, with the mushroom cloud hanging over all, is exceptional enough in modern British drama, but what gives Campton his peculiar distinction is that the concern is something genuinely central to his work as a dramatist, and not merely something which, since he feels it sincerely as a political man, he has conscientiously set about incorporating in his art. None of his plays indulge in direct preaching (the nearest to it comes in the linking commentary to *The Lunatic View*), and consequently their effect, being made in properly dramatic terms, is all the more telling.

Campton's 1958 play, *Ring of Roses*, he describes as 'a throwback . . . a very conventional light comedy, far too thin and horribly facetious', but in 1959 he turned his hand to something much more congenial, an adaptation of *Frankenstein* for in-the-round presentation under the title *The Gift of Fire*, which gave him the chance to explore the possibilities of melodrama, 'a basic dramatic form with popular appeal (not in the long-run sense, but appealing to an unsophisticated audience not accustomed to regular theatregoing)'; in any case the relevance of the subject-matter to that of *The Lunatic View* is self-evident.

In his next work, *A View from the Brink*, Campton returned to something like the form of *The Lunatic View*, presenting again four playlets under the general title 'a comedy of menace'; the weakest of them, *Out of the Flying Pan*, a brief and bitter picture of international conferences written largely in a series of cunning gibberish variations on the routine formulas of diplomacy, was later dropped (though it has been anthologized in *New Directions*, a volume of *avant-garde* one-act plays for schools) and replaced by a longer piece, *Little Brother, Little Sister*, to make up Campton's most mature work to date, *Four Minute Warning*. In this Campton's social preoccupations are perfectly exemplified: we have two pieces explicitly connected with nuclear war, *Little Brother, Little Sister* and *Mutatis Mutandis*, one about war in general, *Soldier from the Wars Returning*, and one, *At Sea*, which seems to be an allegory, and a rather gloomy one at that, on the state of Britain today.

Here the application to such material of the techniques familiarized in post-Ionesco comedy is perfectly managed. In *Mutatis Mutandis*, for example, we have a comedy, and a funny one, of gradual revelations, growing more and more outrageous: a new father has to break the news progressively to his wife that their baby son has green hair, a tail, three eyes, and so on. He is, in fact, a mutant; when he was conceived 'it was late summer, and the early chrysanthemums were already tapping on the window; the swallows were calling to each other and the sky was patterned with rocket trails . . .' The latter point is not insisted on – this is a comedy and everything is suitably absurd (as well as Absurd) – but it is there, colouring everything and making us reflect, with salutary discomfort, that perhaps, after all, it is not so absurd as it seems. Similarly with *Soldier from the Wars Returning*, in which a sinister barman and barmaid compel a strong, healthy soldier just back from the war to re-enact and in some strange way to assume all the injuries he has inflicted on others, until he limps away, old and shattered; and with *At Sea*, in which one man discovers that the pleasure cruiser he is on is sinking and the other passengers will do nothing about it, conspiring to ignore the situation while 'Rule Britannia' blares over the ship's loudspeakers. The central character of both is placed in a position both funny and uncomfortable; no explicit moral is drawn in either, but the playwright's intention emerges clearly in the only legitimate theatrical fashion: from the action itself, not from any extraneous gloss on the action.

The method is shown at its most subtle in the last part of the sequence, *Little Brother, Little Sister*, which is by far the longest of the four plays (too long, in fact, for its context, since it overweights the programme and consequently loses some of its effect, though in itself it is arguably the best section). The situation here could hardly be simpler; two *enfants terribles* (in the Cocteau sense of the term), an adolescent boy called Sir and an adolescent girl called Madam, live with an incredibly ancient and crabbed cook, and have been living for as long as the children can remember, in a deep shelter insulated from a world which probably no longer exists. Behind the forms of respect, Cook rules them both with a rod of iron (or, to be more precise, a shining steel chopper), but she is having more and more trouble keeping them in line as all three of them grow older. The children are discovering sex – Sir finally uses it with devastating effect on Cook – and longing to escape, and from their intricate relations with Cook, her determination to stay where she is, and her garbled reminiscences of the world before the last warning, the play is gradually built up. Nothing is overstressed, nothing is hurried. The action takes its time to develop, and allows Campton room to establish his characters as individuals still, even in their extreme predicament (an ear for speech-rhythms hardly inferior to Pinter's is a great help here).

This playlet, in fact, suggests that Campton will be well able, when he wishes, to break away from the one-act form and write a good original full-length play. In most of his other recent works there has been little chance to build up character, and that has not been any important part of their purpose: more often than not the people in them have been required merely to be comic puppets trapped in terrifying situations, and only occasionally, as with the teacher and Miss Europe in *Then . . .*, have they been permitted to grow beyond these limits. In *Little Brother, Little Sister*, however, the author's touch is sure in dealing with something as difficult and intangible as the dawn of adolescence: the uneasy, semi-incestuous relationship between Sir and Madam is exactly caught and so is the strange, casual routine of their lives, with the needs and desires of an adult world already beginning to break up the uncomplicated patterns of childhood play. Sir's cadenza of sexual experiment, too, is brilliantly accurate at once on a literal and a metaphorical level. He realizes all at once that sex has placed in his hands an unexpectedly potent weapon against the hitherto impregnable Cook and, feeling his way at each step, makes verbal love to her with whatever snatches of half-forgotten love songs and romantic clichés he can summon up from years of her own desultory conversation. Literally it is a totally credible reaction in this specific situation, but it also has the force of a metaphor for that groping discovery of sex, first of all through the experiences of others, as yet beyond one's own, for which one must use the vocabulary of others, which is part of every adolescent's early experience.

Since *Four Minute Warning* Campton has written a number of revue sketches along much the same lines as his plays, most notably 'Table Talk' in *On the Brighter Side*, in which a wife talks to her husband over the dinner-table, inventing wilder and wilder tales about herself and the neighbour while he, oblivious, continues to read his seed catalogue, and 'Yellow in the Autumn Sunlight' from the Nottingham Playhouse revue *Second Post!*, in which an old man is little by little disillusioned about his favourite view when a firm young woman forces him to put on her glasses and recognize that the daffodils he so admires are only brick council houses gleaming distantly in the sun. His more substantial works in the same period include a couple of short radio plays, *A Tinkle of Tiny Bells* and *Don't Wait for Me*, the first a mixture of science fiction and North Country comedy, the second a piece of quiet observation about a couple fated never in their lives to get together, and *Resting Place*, a sketch for a programme of playlets for two performers on 'the Seven Deadly Sins of Marriage', as well as a one-acter commissioned by a Townswomen's Guild drama group, *Funeral Dance* (about a common law wife and a real wife under the same roof after the funeral of the man in their lives), which he describes as 'one of those unfortunate efforts, despised by their authors, which end by being successful in spite of their origins'. His 1962 play for Stephen Joseph was *Usher*, another all-out melodrama along the lines of *The Gift of Fire*, adapted this time, very freely, from Edgar Allan Poe. Since then he has written plays in a variety of styles for television, radio and the stage, the most striking being probably the brief parable about prejudice called *Incident*, written originally for television. Up to now the production of his plays almost exclusively in the North has prevented him from receiving the attention he certainly deserves from the national critics and the more influential members of the theatre-going public, but this omission surely soon must be remedied. His voice is individual and deserves to be heard.

DAVID TURNER

The work of David Turner is far more difficult to place than at first glance it seems. He is of working-class origin, born in Birmingham, where he still lives, in 1927, and writes about working-class and lower-middle-class characters, so the first temptation is to place him in some sort of school of working-class realists. But faced with the plays themselves one soon finds this just will not do. Of all the new British dramatists, with the possible exception of Arden, Turner is the one most steeped in dramatic history – maybe his studies at Birmingham University and his years as a teacher have something to do with it. Other dramatists may stumble on to their characteristic forms without ever, till after the thing is done, understanding precisely and intellectually what they are doing, or work out, like in their very different ways Ann Jellicoe, John Arden, and Henry Livings, their own original approaches to form, but none, I think, can explain so clearly *ab initio* just where their plays fit into the classical genres, what dramatic models they have taken, and how exactly they have set about transforming them. This 'classical' quality about Turner's work probably explains another apparent oddity of his career: that writing the sort of play he does about the sort of characters he chooses, he should exert such an attraction for the established luminaries of the British theatre. His first play to be produced, *Semi-Detached*, caught the attention of Laurence Olivier, who promptly acquired it for West End production with himself in the lead; his second, *The Bedmakers*, offers another classical part for an older actor and has recommended itself strongly to Ralph Richardson. Ten years ago it would almost certainly have been a choice between Rattigan and N. C. Hunter – *o tempora, o mores!*

Turner took to writing quite casually when he was twenty-seven; as he explains it, he was looking round for something to supplement his pay as a teacher, and writing seemed more pleasant than sweeping crossings. So he decided to try his hand at radio script-writing, and had a modest but gratifying success, in that at the end of the year he reckoned he had made about £200 from his efforts. This went on for some time, until winning a prize offered by the B.B.C. for an original television play (£500) decided him to take the plunge as a full-time professional writer, on the principle that he could always go back to teaching if it did not work – he had to once, for just four days. Soon afterwards he was contracted as a regular script writer for the long-running weekday radio series *The Archers*, which he describes as 'at least a fairly honest job of work', and wrote various plays for radio and television, and then finally, around 1960, for the stage.

Before this, however, and his emergence before the public at large as a dramatist worth watching, his television plays had already shown a lot of his individual gifts and a number of their corresponding failings. The very first, for example, *The Train Set* (which won the B.B.C. prize) shows very clearly the grounds for misunderstanding his plays offer and the way they have tended in fact to be misunderstood. Ostensibly – and as produced – it is a slice of working-class life about a working man, Harry, whose marriage to a girl he got into trouble is rather grim but whose son is the chief object of his devotion. He wants to buy the boy a train set, but in the course of the play hopelessly gambles away the money which would have provided a down payment on it and then, facing his foolishness and irresponsibility in the matter, reaches finally a more balanced and satisfactory relationship with his son. The text of the play is very intricately organized, as a progression from images of dark, dank, and gloom – the backyard, the rubbish dump – at the beginning, to images of light, beauty, and dynamic energy – the open high ground, the bird singing, the real trains father and son watch – at the end. And this is what the play is about: Harry passes through an ordeal which ultimately purifies and enriches his life; starting in virtual apathy he makes his way painfully to a position where he can begin really to live again. The main trouble with the play, though, is that in this care for the inner realities some of the outer realities seem to have been neglected. We are given no explanation – except that presumably things have to be like this or there would be no play – why Harry, apparently a skilled worker with chances of overtime, should be so poor that he has to live in the utmost gloom and squalor with half-empty milk bottles on the table and not even a television set in sight, or, indeed, why the train set should be such an almost unattainable luxury to begin with. One suspects that Turner, by his own admission a graduate from the working to the middle class (not least by virtue of being a graduate in the more literal sense) is writing here about the working-class situation of his own childhood in the 1930s rather than the way things are now; certainly his touch seems surer, his ear acuter in dealing with suburban life in the 1960s.

The class divisions created by education are in fact the subject of his next major play for television, *The Final Result* (1961). This is a subtle and uncomfortable study of a family on the borderline between working and middle class. Ed Horner, the father, is a working-class self-improver of the old school, the sort of man who has carefully improved himself into all the worst middle-class habits of mind. He is infatuated with the idea of education, and has a code of standards apparently derived from uncritical study of Kipling and Henley at their most high-tonedly hearty. He has taken a middle-class wife who is conscious of having married beneath her and unthinkingly patronizes him, and the play really turns on the crisis in their relationship when both daughter and son announce their intention of 'betraying' the family by leaving home, he – which is particularly galling – taking off his first-class degree in mining to South Africa. Again the pattern is that of progress from apathy and stagnation through suffering to a new understanding of the situation and a new ability to deal with it, but this time the externals are very acutely observed and the wife's final realization of what precisely her relationship to her husband is consequently becomes considerably more believable and effective than Harry's moment of truth in *The Train Set*.

No doubt a similar pattern attracted Turner to John Hampson's novel *Strip Jack Naked*, which concerns a marriage between virtual strangers contracted when the intended groom dies on the eve of the wedding and his brother, taking pity on the pregnant bride, marries her instead. Again in Turner's free dramatization, *Summer, Autumn, Winter, Spring*, which takes only the bare bones of the novel's plot, we get the same sort of mental Odyssey, and again the expressive progression of images through dark and death to light and rebirth, this time, as the title implies, mirrored in the passage of the seasons.

A subsequent television play, *Choirboys Unite*, marks a complete change of pace from these earlier works, however, and points to the way his talent was to develop in *Semi-Detached*, his best stage play. It is only a slight work, designed as a Christmas romp, about a strike organized by a group of choirboys when the new vicar refuses to endorse their subscription book so that they can go carol-singing, but it showed a hitherto unsuspected gift for the broad comedy which was soon to prove Turner's most interesting and individual register.

When he returned to writing for the stage at the end of 1960, Turner wrote three plays in fairly rapid succession, *Trevor*, *The Bedmakers*, and *Semi-Detached*. The first two he regards as in many ways immature, as belated expressions of 'the moans and whines, the sort of adolescent romanticism I suppose practically any writer starts with'. *Trevor*, which is a play about coming to terms with one's past by transferring the guilt of it to another (the hero, a sexually experienced man of thirty-five, decides to settle down and marries a girl of nineteen, only to discover that she previously had an affair with an unseen man called Trevor, who gradually takes on in the hero's mind all his load of guilt feelings about his own past) has not been staged yet, but *The Bedmakers* was produced at the Belgrade Theatre, Coventry, in October 1962, a few months after his subsequently written *Semi-Detached*. According to Turner, *The Bedmakers* arose from a desire to transpose certain tensions and relationships in *King Lear* to a modern context, but he wonders how far his own understanding of Lear as a predominantly unsympathetic character, carried over into *The Bedmakers*, has damaged the play by puzzling audiences excessively about where their sympathy should lie.

And undeniably Bill Summers, the old man whose tragedy it is, is a very tiresome old man indeed. He is a skilled craftsman in a bed-making firm, and has no patience with, much less understanding of, the development of modern industry. He has been kept on thus far out of sentiment, but the boss's go-ahead son is determined to modernize the works and Bill no longer has a place in the scheme of things. Conventionally our sympathy should be entirely with him, as, for example, Wesker expects us to sympathize completely with the Morrisian aspirations of Ada and Dave in *I'm Talking About Jerusalem*: while enjoying to the full the fruits of automation we are still capable of retaining a largely sentimental nostalgia for individual craftsmanship. But Bill is a proud, pig-headed old man who will not even try to see any point of view but his own, while on the other hand the go-ahead young manager is not at all an evil boss-figure, cynically exploiting all that is worst in the public; he too is in his way an idealist, an old-style Wellsian utopian who looks forward to the day when machines will give men leisure and put the luxuries of today within reach of all.

Whom should we sympathize with? With both, of course; considered in the abstract both their positions make sense, even though in practice they are mutually exclusive. But as a person Bill is much more difficult to sympathize with, and that may well be, in the context of this particular play, a real weakness. Again the story is that of a progression through suffering to a sort of understanding, but even at the crucial moment of misery, when Bill finds the bedstead he has made as the last and most loved example of his craft thrown out on a rubbish dump for the children to play with, he never seems quite to reach the stage of humility and self-realization which Lear reaches at the last in Shakespeare. It is not so much the unlovability of his beginnings that flaws the play as the fact that he does not get far enough beyond them at the end for us to feel that a total dramatic action is complete. But at least along the way Turner does create some real dramatic conflicts, and resolutely resists the temptation Wesker has so often fallen for of rigging the case in favour of his own pet characters. No doubt, like all of us. Turner finds his own attitude to progress ambiguous, but if so he has faced this ambiguity and expressed it in dramatic terms with extraordinary fairness and precision. And if the failure to resolve this ambiguity (not philosophically – that a play can dispense with – but in human terms) ultimately harms the play, before that happens it has given us a couple of strikingly effective hours in the theatre; which is not, perhaps, all one would ask, but a lot.

In *Semi-Detached* Turner overcomes this particular weakness,

and with a vengeance. His attitude to the suburban life it depicts is so consistently ambiguous from first to last that any
general judgement has to be done right outside the context of
the play: one could regard the play either as a scathing, scari-
fying attack on the suburban way of life, as one or two critics
have done, or as a smoothly cynical apologia for it, as others
have disgustedly seen it; one could even, by a stretch of the
imagination, take the play as totally irresponsible, making no
more nor less of a statement about the way of life it depicts than
Sailor Beware or *Dry Rot.* Certainly within the play itself the sort
of life the Midways lead in their semi-detached in the genteel
suburb of Dowlihull is just presented as a fact, a starting-point
for the action: *Semi-Detached* is that great rarity in English
theatre, a play about the lower middle class which does not
patronize or condemn, but simply accepts (the only other I
can think of is Terence Frisby's *The Subtopians*). If the Midways'
way of life is tragic, it is not so in the immediate snob terms
which spring at once to mind at mention of the word suburban;
rather it is tragic in the way that all our lives are tragic, and in
the way that all great farces are tragic – it is the tragedy of
people who want to disguise from themselves the fact that they
are born and that they die. We are not asked to judge whether
the aims of the unscrupulous insurance-salesman hero are good
aims or not, whether his ambitions are 'worthy' or not. We
simply have to accept that whatever we may think of him, he
knows what he is doing.

In a very real sense Fred Midway is a self-made man: he has
decided, he has made a sort of Existentialist choice of what sort
of man he is going to be, and what sort of life he is going to lead.
He is not only a suburban dweller in a semi-detached, he is *the*
suburban dweller in a semi-detached, and what others believe
without admitting to themselves – that religion, for instance,
isn't real, but only a convenient pawn in the game of respectability; that money is the measure of man – he happily knows,
accepts, and acts on. He is a rogue in the great tradition:
Turner himself cites Tartuffe and Mosca in Jonson's *Volpone* as
parallels, and perhaps another Jonson rogue, Face in *The
Alchemist,* provides an even better one, since he, like Fred and

unlike Tartuffe and Mosca, gets away with it all at the end. Indeed, how else could *Semi-Detached* end? What reality would a concept of absolute justice have in this world, where everyone acts equally unscrupulously and victory must go to the cleverest man with the clearest objectives?

Within the space of two hours on a Sunday morning Fred has to deal with a series of crises. His elder daughter, Eileen, comes back with her young man (well, not with, exactly; separate arrivals are more discreet) from a week in Bournemouth which her parents had intended should bring about a definite change in her status and provide her with that long-sought-for engagement ring. It doesn't seem to have done so, though, and while they are puzzling about this and Bob, the intended husband, is tinkering about with Fred's model railway down the garden (membership of the Loco Club is Fred's most important current stepping stone to higher things) the other daughter, Avril, arrives in tears, announcing that she has left her husband because he has confessed to a brief encounter with a prostitute in London and, more important, because his uncle is about to remarry and cut him out of his will. Divorce seems the best plan, but then Avril's mother-in-law arrives and threatens to expose Eileen as the mistress of a married man (hence the absence of engagement ring) if Avril does not return at once to her husband. Fred twists and turns, and discovering that his son Tom was in fact responsible for the interesting condition of the uncle's intended arranges a rapid readjustment whereby Tom takes the girl off the old man's hands in return for a handsome consideration and Avril goes back to her husband now that his prospects are restored. Meanwhile Bob is to move in with them, which will both facilitate things between him and Eileen and scotch any gossip. Unfortunately Eileen, the idealist with, horror of horrors, 'liberal tendencies', will not accept this, and makes Bob choose; he chooses family life with the Midways and self-improvement on Fred Midway's model rather than her, and she prepares to leave, announcing that she will give herself to the first man she meets just to spite and disgrace the family. But Fred is not beaten: he arranges that the first man she meets shall be old Mr Makepiece, Avril's husband's uncle, so that one way or another all the money going stays in the family. A surprising alliance, 'him the Establishment . . . and her the Honest Intellectual?' wonders Fred in a passage unhappily cut from the London production; not at all – 'There's so few in these parts, they're bound to get together, if only to keep each other warm'.

And so this astonishing play reaches its wholly logical conclusion, to the horror of most left-wing opinion, which found its refusal to come down unequivocally against the standards its characters live by deeply disturbing, and to the mystification of the right-wing critics, who equally could not see the world it portrayed in anything but the most unfavourable light. The truth of the matter, of course, is that it is a play about suburbans, by a suburban, for suburbans. Turner himself lives in a semi-detached, and admits that he is the sort of man who, like Fred Midway, would put down a red front drive just to annoy the neighbours:

Perhaps it's a sort of escapism, but I don't really think so. It's just a coming to terms with something which is in me and has made me. I can't reject it all lock stock and barrel and comfort myself with thinking that what I have rejected is wholly deadening and worthless, because I know it isn't. Of course it is absurd, but at the same time it is perfectly serious and worthwhile: it's a matter of what angle you see it from. I see it from both angles at the same time. I accept the paradox and I think I recognize the truth about myself and the world I live in (and even as I say this I see that the assertion is both true and absurd).

This paradox, in fact, lies at the heart of the play, and for this reason it cannot perhaps mean as much to anyone who does not know the semi-detached world intimately as Turner does, as I do, and as, unfortunately, few London theatregoers do (or, worse, will admit to knowing). *Semi-Detached* is – even in the slightly emasculated London version which toned down the absurdity of Eileen, the third-rate messiah, to leave her as a rallying point for liberal sympathy – a challenge to complacent conventional assumptions, of the right and left wings, about the barrenness and contemptibility of lower-middle-class life, that no man's land of 'by-pass variegated' architecture, telly aerials, and G-plan furniture stretching between the 'real' working class and the socially conscious, responsible upper middle class of the average professional intellectual. As such, if taken seriously, it is bound to be rejected by practically all shades of vocal opinion, though significantly at Coventry, where the audience is predominantly suburban anyway, it was one of the biggest commercial successes the Belgrade has ever had.

Even if the point it is making – something which emerges not from any particular lines or scenes but only from the total action of the play – is found unpalatable, however, the skill with which Turner has developed his modern comedy of humours should not go unnoticed: the way that Fred Midway (the significance of the name is obvious) is lovingly built up from a multitude of little details of speech, taste, and habit to become the quintessential suburban is masterly, and so is the skill with which suburban idiom (north Midland variety) is transfigured into the buoyant rhythms and elaborate rhetoric of Turner's high-comic style. The organization of the play too is complex and subtle; it is strictly accordant with classical style, down to minute observance of the unities and the appearance of the *deus ex machina* at the prescribed moment – 'He's here. Deus ex three litre' cries Fred as Makepiece arrives, and Makepiece is so called not only because he makes pieces, i.e. makes money, and makes the peace, but because, as a *deus ex machina* should, he makes the piece, the play, by tying together the loose ends and regulating the action from above.

Heaven knows to what ends this prodigious skill and invention will be turned next. Turner has already collaborated with Edward J. Mason on another play, *Believe It or Not*, a light Christmas diversion based on an Arabian Nights story for the Belgrade, where he feels, reasonably enough, that his real audience lies. At the Belgrade have also been staged *The Antique Shop* (1963), an elaborate allegory of the state of modern Britain, and *Bottomley* (1965), an ambitious episodic dramatization of the financier Horatio Bottomley's wild career. Turner has also written a number of television scripts, including *Way Off Beat* (1966), an exploration of the exotic world of ballroom dancing championships, and *Swizzlewick*, a not very successful attempt at sustaining a regular soap-opera series in a high farcical style. Hard to know what he will do next, but meanwhile *Semi-Detached* at least deserves a place in English theatrical history as the first play which has accepted the telly-bred denizens of the affluent society on their own terms and let them speak for themselves. In a theatre where one thought there was very little left which could shock and outrage us into new thought and understanding, this last frontier remained, and if David Turner has for the time being obtained more odium than praise for crossing it, the praise cannot be indefinitely withheld.

MORE PLAYWRIGHTS IN THE PROVINCES

Of the other dramatists who have first made their mark out of town, easily the most interesting are James Saunders and David Perry. James Saunders has an unexpected background for a new dramatist: born in Islington in 1925, he is a chemistry teacher by profession, and took up dramatic writing as a spare-time hobby while studying for a science degree at Southampton. He has not yet established a consistent style and personality as a dramatist, and this has probably militated up to now against his wide recognition, since critics like above all to know where they are with a dramatist and what they can expect of him. Most of his early works, generally one-acters, are written in an unmistakably post-Ionesco style (in its published text one of his best-known plays, *Alas, Poor Fred*, is actually subtitled 'a duologue in the style of Ionesco', in tacit recognition, no doubt, of the truth in what the critics said about it). But for his first arrival in the West End, with *The Ark*, the style was much clearer and more traditional; whether this will prove in the long run the divagation it seems at present or an influential new development in his style remains to be seen.

Three of Saunders's plays had been broadcast on the Third Programme, *Dog Accident, Barnstable*, and *Alas, Poor Fred*, but it was with *Alas, Poor Fred* as produced in-the-round by Stephen Joseph's Studio Theatre group that he first made a distinct impression. In this the Ionesco influence is, in fact, very marked and the idea of the play is very similar to that of Ionesco's *Amédée*: a husband and wife talk at length, and for much of the time at odds, about Fred, who was apparently cut in half at some time in the past, but on whom otherwise there seems to be little agreement, even to the question of what he actually looked like. Gradually it becomes clear that Fred is their love and life truly together; it is guilt about the emotional dismemberment of their marriage which keeps husband and wife constantly reverting to the subject, she, at least, with more than a little regret. Of the two characters we see (as opposed to the long-absent Fred) she is the more important, and in two of the key episodes we are allowed to see things through her eyes: one in which, her husband asleep, she takes off all her clothes (in mime) and performs a provocative dance in front of him, and the other when she builds up an elaborate semi-masochistic fantasy about her husband while he is out for a walk. The result, though evidently in some ways derivative, has considerable freshness and life on its own account: in particular Saunders's handling, *à la* Ionesco, of flat conversational clichés in such a way that they build up to something far from flat and cliché is masterly.

Much the same sort of qualities, in the same sort of situation, occur in his earlier play *Barnstable*, which was broadcast in 1959 and staged at Ealing in 1960 in a group of three Saunders one-act plays under the title *Ends and Echoes*, the other plays being *Committal* and *Return to the City*. Here again the title character never appears: he is a mysterious entity in the background, shooting thrushes on the lawn of Dr and Mrs Carboy's garden. The dialogue, too, takes up an accepted pattern of clichés, in this case those of pre-war drawing-room comedy, and works a number of ingenious variations on them: the setting is a drawing-room with French windows, and all the characters come from stock: the platitudinous and unhelpful clergyman, the kindly, absent-minded doctor and his worrying, scatter-brained wife, the awkward overgrown schoolgirl daughter, always apologizing for her 'absolutely fatuous and idiotic' behaviour, and the maid, always on the point of giving notice.

But this time these fugitives from Esther McCracken country are placed in a fantastic modern context, with the house falling unnoticed about their ears, Barnstable shooting thrushes from the west wing, and no one able even momentarily to communicate with anyone else. Again there is the consistent development of a dramatic symbol which is never defined and explained, but from which a clear meaning, or group of meanings, gradually emerges: not so much for the title character this time (he may or may not be God, but the point is not insisted on) as for the house, which presumably represents the safeness and solidity of upper-middle-class life in the thirties being gradually eroded and collapsing while those who live inside the system never notice what is happening around them.

In *The Ark* (produced at the Westminster in 1959 and subsequently included in the Studio Theatre's repertory) Saunders turns aside from this sort of oblique comment to tackle directly a major question: that of human responsibility and divine justice (if such a thing exists) in the face of imminent world catastrophe. The play offers a new and disturbing interpretation of the story of Noah, in which the central character becomes Shem, the awkward brother. Noah is rigidly righteous and fiercely inhuman: convinced of his own rectitude, he is not interested in the fate of the rest of humanity. Japhet is just but not entirely blameless; he falls prey to the sensual temptations represented by Shem's wife. Ham is a good-natured simpleton, happy just to do what he is told without question. But Shem cannot so readily dissociate himself from the plight of humanity: God made them as they are, and how can He then so readily condemn and abandon them? Anyway, Shem would rather die with the condemned than survive with his hypocritical family, and in the end he has to be overpowered and carried into the ark by force. (For the in-the-round version Saunders wrote a new last scene showing the brothers leaving the Ark after the Flood and each going his own way.)

All this is argued out directly and logically, without compromise, and the play conclusively demonstrates that Saunders has a talent (though not perhaps so individual a talent) for the neo-Shavian theatre of ideas and not very much action as well as for the more oblique mode of Ionesco. Perhaps the argument does not seem always to sort quite with our emotional reactions to his characters: a modern audience cannot help identifying to a certain extent with Shem, and yet the argument seems to lead finally to the conclusion that Japhet, the unlovable *homme moyen sensuel* who finds it easier to take refuge in action and not ask too many questions, is in some way nearer the right than Shem is. But then, if there is an ambiguity in the values here, that, too, is the prerogative of the modern playwright, for whom there are almost inevitably no constants, no fixed standards of reference against which human actions and aspirations can be measured.

The tone and mood of *The Ark* are taken up again in the third section of *Ends and Echoes, Return to a City* (the first, *Committal*, is a slight and amusing near-monologue by a Civil Servant faced eternally with the problems of a pathetic but determined intruder called Wall, who persistently bounces back however many other departments he is passed on to). In *Return to a City* we are shown the aftermath of a widespread catastrophe instead of, as in *The Ark*, its prelude. Apparently alone amid the ruins, a man and woman are living out a dreary and apathetic life in a city destroyed some fifteen years before – exactly how and by whom we are not told, for the event, whatever it was, seems to have affected their memories. There is another inhabitant, however, an optimist whom the man meets on a hunting expedition, but he is optimistic for much the same reason that the others are pessimistic: he, too, is a fatalist and believes that nothing can be done, but extends this to the belief that nothing matters, whether things get better or worse, or just stay as they are. Finally the son of the old couple comes back, having been preserved somewhere with his faculties intact – both his memory and his ability to feel grief at the state of complete impotence to which his parents and their world have been reduced. If they are the direct sufferers of catastrophe who have undergone at least a spiritual death, he is Shem from the Ark, still concerned, still able to feel for them, and still ready to hope that there must be some way for life to begin again.

In the plays he has written since *Ends and Echoes* Saunders has continued to change style with chameleon-like rapidity. *A Slight Accident* was a brief, inconsequential dialogue for three women arguing over the corpse of a man who had just been shot; written to complete a bill with a revival of *Alas, Poor Fred*, it favoured the Absurd. *Double Double*, on the other hand (called *Gimlet* on the radio and *Just You Wait* on television), was at once a set piece offering two contrasting roles to each of the actors taking part – it was originally written for R.A.D.A. students – and a piece of realistic observation: it concerned the off-duty problems of a group of busmen in a transport canteen, some of them serious and some of them, like the dilemma of an inspector who has lost a double decker bus en route, rather less so. Slight but persuasive, it is one of the best things Saunders has ever done. More recently he has written two brief satires, *Who Was Hilary Maconochie?* and *The Pedagogue*. *Who Was Hilary Maconochie?*, described by the author as 'an English play for foreigners', concerns two old widows who give a weekly tea party primarily as an occasion for displays of elaborately polite malice towards each other. *The Pedagogue* is a monologue for a teacher ten years hence, preaching the need to trust those in authority, while in the background a blinding flash signals the advent of nuclear war. Both plays are relative minor *pièces d'occasion*, quite skilfully done.

Much better, though, is his full-length play *Next Time I'll Sing to You*. In it Saunders returns to the Absurd, but in a far more personal and elusive way than in his earlier plays. The ostensible subject is Alexander James Mason, the hermit of Great Canfield in Essex, whose story was pieced together and told in Raleigh Trevelyan's book *A Hermit Disclosed*. But unlike Henry Livings, who handled the same subject in his television play *Jim All Alone*, and Edward Bond, whose play *The Pope's Wedding* seems to have taken at least the basic idea of the hermit and his locale from Trevelyan's book, Saunders is not really interested in the story *per se* so much as the crucial point of Existentialist philosophy which the story raises: if Mason was really the world forgetting, by the world forgot, if no one was aware of his existence and history, could he in any real sense of the term be said to exist? The first act works its way slowly closer and closer to the centre of the question and the character of the hermit himself, introducing first a joker, Meff, and a cynic, Dust, then a vague but attractive girl, Lizzie, to whom Meff makes advances, and then Rudge, the author-director figure in the piece, and finally the Hermit himself, or rather the actor playing the Hermit, who would have been there earlier if he hadn't lost his beard. Rudge gets everything tied up to his own satisfaction, with hardly a mention of the Hermit except for a wonderfully evocative account of the Hermit's death, but then the actor playing the Hermit intervenes to suggest that more is needed: 'We'll start with the hut, you see, birds singing, and Fanny Bell . . .' Even though all the other characters turn on him or ignore him, the subject has been broached, and only just in time before the end of the act.

The second act should go on from there – somewhere. In the version first performed by the Questors at Ealing in 1962 it didn't at all; in the revised version performed at the Arts in 1963 it does, though with a slight loss of impetus, and the impression remains that the author has somewhat lost interest after the first act. We learn a little more about the hermit, both from the outside, in the narrations of Rudge (interrupted every now and then by the antics of Meff, Dust, and Lizzie) and from the inside in what the Hermit says of himself. Except that the inside view is not really the inside view: as Saunders constantly reminds us, it is merely an actor's view of the part he has to play, and actors' vanity being what it proverbially is, it is only to be expected that he shall see himself as a saint. No, there is only one solution. As Rudge remarks in the first act 'There's only one thing worth understanding, one thing worth thinking about, and that is that I am a mind locked in twelve hundred grams of brain locked in a quarter of an inch of skull, and the only key to this prison is death'. All the Hermit can do is to die; he is cured then of the disease called life, he is free, and no one is any the wiser. Rudge pronounces his epitaph:

On the seventh of June 1857, a man was born; this is a very strange thing. On the seventeenth of January 1942, he died, which is even stranger. And if you go to Essex and root around in the right place, you may, if you're lucky, come across a little pile of bones: and this is the strangest thing of all, because this man thought himself as *real* as we do.

Next Time I'll Sing to You achieves something which few British plays related to the theatre of the Absurd have managed: it remains constantly interesting as an elaborate structure of paradoxes and apparent non-sequiturs which yet finally holds together and makes intellectual sense, but at the same time it is often very moving. The most haunting sections of the play, admittedly, are those – Rudge's description of the Hermit's death, his disquisition on grief – which are nearest to the conventional in their theatrical effect, but at least these passages are integrated with complete conviction; the disparate elements are in some inexplicable fashion fused together, by sheer force of dramatic instinct, into a unified and coherent whole – and a whole which works triumphantly in the theatre. Curiously, while writing a play ostensibly about the impossibility of writing a play, Saunders has written a play which is far more telling in purely theatrical terms than anything he had written before. He is clearly a man with ideas and the dramatic technique to present them; the only doubt in the past has been of his ability to find, among his wide variety of styles, a voice entirely his own to express them in. With *Next Time I'll Sing to You* he seems to have found that voice; it is heard again, more muted perhaps, in his major subsequent work, *A Scent of Flowers*, a fragile, poetic piece about a young suicide who looks back on the pieces of her shattered life from beyond the grave. This play did not achieve, in Britain anyway, the success it deserved. But whatever his subsequent writing may be like, *Next Time I'll Sing to You* remains one of the most accomplished and individual works of the new drama in Britain.

Unlike Saunders, David Perry, whose double bill *Stuff and Nonsense* and *The Trouble with Our Ivy* was staged at Hornchurch in 1960 after *Stuff and Nonsense* had been produced on B.B.C. Television, has much in common with a number of other young writers as far as background is concerned: he is yet another dissatisfied actor turned dramatist. Born in 1928, he spent much of his life in Paris, and had virtually decided to settle there, when circumstances made him return to England in 1954. After a few months doing nothing very much he decided to take his Paris conservatoire training in both hands and embark on an acting career in England; this he did initially by settling with a company which played mainly North Country farce in Leeds. He began writing in 1958–9, when he decided it would be a good idea to occupy the time between telephone calls with something, and the result was *Stuff and Nonsense,* written originally as a stage play, acquired by B.B.C. Television and promptly shelved for nearly two years until the director Brandon Acton-Bond took a fancy to it and decided he must put it on.

Subsequently the play was staged in a double-bill at Hornchurch, acquired for a West End production and also translated into German for production in West Berlin. It is a fantastic comedy with gruesome overtones about a girl called June Pimble who loves her pets (and she can make a pet of anything that moves and breathes) with a suffocating tenderness which pursues them even after death. And if pets can be made as good as new by grandfather's feats of taxidermy, so her harassed family argue, why not other things, other *people* – like the young man who finds the Pimbles a little too much at close quarters and shows signs of backing out of his engagement to June, for instance? It has, after all, happened before, when her previous escort fell down the cellar steps and broke his neck. The strange household of the Pimbles is not without a suggestion of Pinter, but despite the basic 'sickness' of the joke everything is much less sinister than in his work; Perry's personal contribution is the great amiability which irradiates his writing. One senses, indeed, a more than sneaking sympathy on the author's part for the Pimbles, with their conservatism so ingrained that there is among them a feeling almost of relief when anything so unnatural and unpredictable as a living newcomer is reduced to permanent immobility and ranged alongside the innumerable stuffed birds and fish and furry animals which line their walls.

The Trouble with Our Ivy, which was written immediately after *Stuff and Nonsense,* is much more violent in its implications, and indeed in what actually happens on stage. One long crescendo, it is set in motion quietly enough when the Chards, in obscure revenge for the fate of Ivy, who died three years before beneath the wheels of the up-train to Waterloo, plant in their carefully prepared garden a 'vegetable volcano' in the shape of a rare tropical ivy filched from a hothouse at Kew, which will put an end once and for all to the pretensions of their genteel neighbours the Tremblows basking in the sunlight amid their Betty Uprichards. This it does, but it also puts paid to much more, engulfing the whole suburb and slowly crushing the semi-detached houses in which the Chards and the Tremblows live while they, inside, work out their differences in a wild climax of violent action. In the Hornchurch version, which Perry prefers, there are only the four characters, but in an earlier version subsequently televised by A.B.C. 'Armchair Theatre' there is also a fireman to whom the final word goes: as the Chards and the Tremblows literally tear each other to pieces on the floor and the building crumbles about them, he puts forward a wistful appeal: 'Couldn't we just sit down quietly round a table and talk things over?' This gives a certain colour to the idea that there may be a very general political allegory involved, but Perry feels that if it is there it is only an incidental and should not be in any way emphasized.

Perry's next play, *Little Doris*, was written directly for television, and involves the same casual, common-sensical approach to fantastic material, the same rather gruesome sense of humour. Again there are two families whose paths cross, though this time on the whole their meeting is fortunate. The scene is largely a run-down boarding-house at Yarmouth, where Auntie Flo, a terrible relative the wife feels they have to do right by, has systematically taken over. Into the life of this family come another married couple with a mysterious box in which, we have gradually discovered, there is a creature called Little Doris, the monstrous offspring of a sea-lion in the charge of the husband, a keeper at London Zoo. As the wife in the first family feels a responsibility towards their monster, Auntie Flo, so the husband in the other feels responsible for the welfare of Doris, who, like Grandad in *Stuff and Nonsense* and the creeper in

The Trouble with Our Ivy, is never seen but powerfully present throughout. Having preserved her from swift disposal at the zoo, Stanley has kept her at home until she grew too large and now intends to set her loose in the sea. Auntie Flo has other ideas, however; what a nice, profitable sideshow Doris would make in the summer months . . . Doris's protector is ready to fight to the death for her freedom, but in the end it is Doris herself who resolves things in her own way, by swallowing Auntie Flo, and the play ends with Stanley and his wife trundling Doris (and in a sense, presumably, Auntie Flo) along the pier to the sea.

Perhaps even more than Perry's two earlier plays, *Little Doris* is suffused by his very English sympathy for the odd, the anachronistic, and the useless (he is an eager scourer of newspapers and television for cranks and crackpots like the woman who boiled her alarm clocks on *Tonight* to make them go better and the man who had a complete set of railway buffers in his bedroom). In a way, except that they are more sinister, his plays are like dramatic equivalents of Rowland Emmett's stranger cartoons, but more relevantly there is in him much of the spirit of Lear. The names of the Victorian nonsense writers have been bandied about a lot in connection with the more fantastically inclined of the new dramatists, usually without much justification, but if the mathematical exactness of Simpson's fantasy does at times suggest some sort of temperamental affinity with Carroll there is no denying also that the creators of Little Doris and the Pobble Who Had No Toes would recognize each other across the years (not least for their shared sensitivity to words, which in Perry's plays as in Lear's nonsense poems are used with the unerring precision of the born poet).

In the intervals of writing and re-writing *Little Doris* Perry has also completed a full-length stage play, *Daniel Fugue's Pipe Dream*. Daniel's grandmother, another central character who is never seen but whose presence powerfully suffuses the play, is a sort of religion in herself to the villagers, something they look up to with admiration and indeed with awe. One of the chief delights of her life is to hear the church organ, but since she has taken to her bed, for the last time it seems, this pleasure is denied her. Daniel, however, is the village organist, and an idea strikes him: bit by bit, unobtrusively, he dismantles the organ and brings it, pipe by pipe, to the living room immediately below Grandma's bedroom so that she can, after all, hear the organ just once more before she dies. Since her hundredth birthday, Grandma has had two birthdays a year, her real birthday, just for the family, and an official birthday, a solemn occasion for her believers. This year, on her official birthday, the believers bring her a bell, which is erected in the attic; its muffled tones will announce her death – a matter of some importance not only because of her position in the village but because of the presence nearby of a rival, Great-aunt Mildred, who has come back to the village to die after a lifetime of travel. Great-aunt Mildred represents the opposite of all Grandma stands for, and a terrible rivalry exists between them over which shall die first. In the last act, before the organ has finally been assembled and played, Grandma dies; the believers decide that it is only fitting she should be buried in the console of the organ she so loved; meanwhile the relatives phone Great-aunt Mildred to tell her that Grandma has gone ahead, but there is no answer. . . .

With *Daniel Fugue* and *Little Doris* David Perry establishes himself as one of the oddest and most individual talents in British drama today. His plays attack central questions – the relations of the haves and have nots in *The Trouble with Our Ivy* and his later television play, *The Frobisher Game* (about servants who take it in turns to play master); the individual's responsibility for his actions in *Little Doris*; the need to believe in *Daniel Fugue* – by unexpected and devious routes, but they always end directly on target, while his skill as a dramatic architect and his gift for dramatic dialogue are superior to those of all but a handful of writers in the British theatre today. Of all the writers considered in this chapter his achievement to date is the most solid and his potential for future development the least in doubt.

Another actor-turned-writer who has received his first production on the fringes of London, this time at Guildford, is Terence Frisby (born 1932). He has contributed revue material

to the Establishment Club, but his major work to date is a
three-act play *The Subtopians*, written in 1958 and produced in
March 1961. It looks at first like a passionate denunciation of
suburbia and suburban values, and so among other things it is,
but before long it acquires a dramatic complexity which leaves
any such simple doctrinaire formulation far behind.

It concerns a family called the Manns who live an unremark-
able life in an ordinary suburb: 'the house is called Mon Repos
and inside they're all tearing each other to pieces', as the wandering son Tom remarks to his fiancée when nearing the front
door. The reasons for the family arguments are of the sort
which seem petty to outsiders but can make all the difference
between happiness and misery for those in the thick of them.
At the beginning of the play they are 'a happy family' in the
sense that they do not actually scream and kick and come to
blows. But beneath the surface there are tensions. Dad and
Mum get on each other's nerves, in a quiet sort of way. The
elder son and his wife are expecting a child, and he feels he
cannot take a more exciting but less lucrative job; with that
between them all the good intentions on both sides will not put
things quite right. Into this situation comes an avenging angel
with a flaming sword – the younger son's fiancée. She senses
that the family is held together only by self deception, comprompr-
ise, and fear. With the selfishness of someone in love she determines to extricate at least Tom from this web of deceit, and
precipitates the family row to end all family rows. Unforgivable
things are said and then those involved are left to piece their
lives together as best they can. 'We can't all live out in the
open', says the elder brother: 'We should', snaps back the
other without thinking, and there is the dilemma in a nutshell.

The centre of the play is strong, disturbing, and true – if not
as a generalization, at least of these particular, wholly believable characters. There was one short scene in the version
originally produced (between Tom and his fiancée at the
station) which launched into an elaborate lyrical-satirical
evocation of suburban life which made feebly explicit something that was powerful implicit throughout; in a subsequent
revision the scene has been more effectively accommodated into

o

the play's overall texture. But otherwise Frisby's writing is direct, assured, and devastatingly accurate. He even surmounts, with no apparent difficulty, the major problem of the realistic dramatist: that of making the characters give expression to ideas and feelings which they could never really express but which it is necessary for the play that they should, without in the process forfeiting our belief (the scene in which the elder brother explains his situation to the younger in the last act is an excellent case in point).

Since *The Subtopians* Frisby has completed a satirical comedy, tentatively entitled *Don't Forget the Basics*, about the division in the modern world between Christianity and organized religion (specifically C. of E.), and a couple of television plays, and has had an enormous international success with an unashamedly commercial sex-comedy about a middle-aged man and a young girl he gets involved with, *There's a Girl in my Soup*. This is effective enough in its way, but we may be permitted to hope that his subsequent work will have more in common with *The Subtopians*, a highly personal work of a kind which has been all too rare in the British theatre of late.

John McGrath (born 1935) and Forbes Bramble (born 1938) are the only dramatists considered in this book to have emerged by what was, between the wars at least, one of the most normal and respectable routes: activity in university drama. While still an undergraduate at Oxford (and a producer with O.U.D.S. and the Oxford Experimental Theatre Club) McGrath had his first play, *A Man Has Two Fathers*, produced by the O.U.D.S. at Oxford Playhouse. This is an awkward and immature allegory about relationship, involving a man with two father-figures to choose from, a disreputable tramp and an eminently respectable pillar of the community. First one looks like winning and then the other, until finally he manages to free himself from both (presumably the pulls towards complete rejection of society and complete submission to it) and go off on his own, leaving his two would-be fathers to discover that they themselves are in fact father and son.

The parts of the play which work best are those (more or less irrelevant) tending towards comedy, but unfortunately this hint was not taken up in McGrath's next work, a one-acter called *The Tent*, which was done at the Royal Court on a Sunday night and later broadcast on the Third amid a lot of misleading publicity about the actors' freedom to improvise in performance. Again the theme is responsibility: an Army captain has ordered an Egyptian civilian to be shot in very dubious circumstances in the Suez Canal Zone and then has to argue the resentful private who actually did the shooting into covering up the circumstances in which it occurred. This he does mainly by means of a long and intricate daydream concerning places he and the private might go together. Finally the private decides to cover up, but the reasons for his doing so are never made clear either on an intellectual level or, as presumably intended, on an emotional level, since neither of the characters finally comes sufficiently alive for belief in the relationship between them to become a vital issue.

In his third play, *Why the Chicken*, first produced by the Oxford Theatre Group on the Fringe of the Edinburgh Festival in 1959 and subsequently destined (abortively) for the West End, McGrath returned in the first half to moments of the offhand irreverent comedy which he had previously shown some talent for in *A Man Has Two Fathers*, depicting a collection of quite believable restless and dissatisfied teenagers whiling away their time in card-playing, quarrelling, and engaging in intricate games and burlesque in a derelict barn on the edge of a new town. But once plot intrudes (did the earnest social worker or did she not push the gang-leader over a cliff in order to repel an attempt at rape brought on by her own coquetry?) the play goes to pieces, forcing its initially credible characters to take up quite incredible positions in obedience to a preconceived and decidedly artificial system of sociological principles and suppositions. Since then McGrath has worked for both B.B.C. and independent television as a director, and *People's Property*, an episode he wrote and directed for the B.B.C. series *Z Cars*, contained some of his most mature and acute writing in a study of two ungovernable schoolboys' road to reform school.

His principal original work, though, has been the play *Events While Guarding the Bofors Gun* (1966), later filmed, very faithfully, as *The Bofors Gun*. This is a play which has been very highly praised by some critics, but does not really seem to me to live up to its reputation. Basically it has a quite cunningly contrived sensational plot, lively if short on elementary credibility, about a young N.C.O. determined that his last night in Germany shall go off without trouble so that he can return to an officer selection board in England, and a mad (literally insane) Irish soldier who has determined to kill himself during the night and make as much trouble as possible for everyone else meanwhile. The main trouble with the play, apart from whether we believe it all or not, is that too much depends on the intervention of the lunatic, whose actions, being insane, are unaccountable, and therefore not dramatically very interesting. Suggestions that he has been driven mad by the horrors of military life, and that the play is therefore a powerful anti-militarist tract, find little support in the text. But if this is not what the play is about it is difficult to imagine what it is.

Forbes Bramble, an architect by profession, achieved a considerable success with his first stage play, *The Dice* (1959), written in his first year as an undergraduate at London University; an extract of the original student production was televised, it was produced professionally at Cambridge Arts Theatre in 1961, and later revived on the Fringe of the Edinburgh Festival, translated and performed in German, and published. Before this his only writing had been a group of radio scripts, unproduced, and a prizewinning tape-recording, *Three Mood Pieces* (another experimental tape, *Flight*, followed in 1961). *The Dice* is a one-act play slightly suggestive of Genet's *Haute Surveillance*, which also takes place in a prison cell occupied by three male prisoners. A strange, concentrated piece, it offers a sort of brief, tragic counterpart to Nigel Dennis's satirical epitome of religious history in *The Making of Moo*, reflecting man's permanent need for an arbiter, law-giver, and judge outside himself. Three political prisoners in an unspecified state evolve a religion of their own centred upon the two dice with which they settle all arguments. At first it is the abstract and arbitrary nature of this decision-maker which attracts them, then they begin to doubt whether it can really be completely free from taint of personality; they begin to pray to it and require it to take the blame for all their actions and finally, when the fall of the dice seems to lay the blame on them, they reject it. If it were God it would take the blame on itself. But if it is not, what refuge is there left for them? The point is forcefully made, even if there is still rather too patent an air of calculation in some of the plot-manœuvres Bramble calls on to make it.

In his next play, *The Two-Timers*, however, first produced by the University College London Dramatic Society at the Edinburgh Festival in 1961, this fault is corrected. Taking a situation slightly reminiscent of that in Clive Exton's *I'll Have You to Remember*, with two old people, a husband and wife, living in a world of their own fantasy amid a pile of junk in a derelict house, Bramble builds up on this slight framework a subtle and elaborate play. For much of its length it is generally comic in tone, but veers at times into the sinister, as when the couple terrorize an errand boy and confuse a charity collector with drink into admitting the splendour of their (non-existent) shop-window and acquiescing to their *idée fixe*: that they are the proprietors of a prosperous antique shop. The crisis in their situation comes when their daughter and her fiancé, knowing that their house is threatened with demolition, offer them a real antique shop, but by this time they are so inured to illusion that they refuse to make the hazardous transition to the real world and choose instead to remain wrapped in their dreams. Bramble's strength as a dramatist makes itself really felt in the second act: having rejected the offer of help and disposed for the moment of the demolition contractor's man, his chief characters seem to have nothing more to do but face the inevitable. Instead, he makes them go off at what appears to be a complete tangent, with a series of fantasies involving a suit of armour and a group of stuffed animals, and not only keeps an audience fascinated with a long and rambling conversation of a decidedly esoteric cast, but finally demonstrates that none of it is irrelevant and brings the play to a climax of horrifying intensity, when the old people finally reject reality altogether and assume complete responsibility for their own destruction.

Again in *The Two-Timers* there is more than a hint of Genet, which makes one suspect that the similarity in *The Dice* was not altogether coincidental; the scene of the fairy-stories and its outcome have a sort of obsessive ritual quality which may well owe something directly to the author of *Le Balcon*. Bramble's third play, though, a television piece called *When Silver Drinks*, could hardly be more different. It is a relatively realistic comedy-drama, and a very successful one, about the improbable comradeship, edgy and unpredictable, which suddenly springs up between two quite dissimilar characters, Silver, a hard-drinking openhanded Irishman, and Mike, a rather muddled chemistry student. They meet in a pub where they are drawn together by community of purpose – to get drunk as quickly as possible – and a shared motive – woman trouble. Mike has had a quarrel with his girl friend, and Silver has just found out that his wife has a lover. Their exchange of drunken confidences, after a certain amount of preliminary skirmishing and insulting the other occupants of the pub, takes up most of the first act. In the second half the plot thickens as the couple sober up and begin to consider how Silver's marital difficulties can best be sorted out, Mike confidently setting up as an authority on other people's problems in spite of his inability to solve his own. He devises a plot to dispose of the lover without the bloodshed Silver contemplates, and it works almost too well; the lover gone, Silver and his wife make up with an alacrity the young idealist finds rather shocking – but then, this is life, which has a tiresome tendency not to work out like the books from which educated young men learn about it.

When Silver Drinks is hardly a work of great profundity, but it does show a warmer understanding of human nature than either of the earlier plays, a real comedy sense, and some relaxation of the too schematic, patently intellectual construction which had previously seemed Bramble's chief limitation as a dramatist.

IN THE AIR

Recruits from Radio and Television

During the last ten years or so television has become more and more important to drama in general, not only in offering a valuable testing-ground for new dramatists, but also in forming taste and preparing audiences, almost imperceptibly, for new things. The advantage with television in this respect is precisely what has generally been taken as its main disadvantage: the relatively uncritical approach of the mass audience. This is not to say that they are really 'captive', as superior people like to say: one has only to look at a series of TAM ratings, which record the state of the television set in the testing sample's home every thirty seconds, to find out the speed with which a programme will be switched off if viewers don't like it. But though they know what they like and what they don't like when they see it, they do not on the whole have any marked preconceptions before any given programme begins. A play, whoever it is by and in whatever style it is written, is judged by the same simple but reliable rule of thumb as the latest thriller series, western or panel game: if they like it, if it holds their attention, it stays on; if not they switch to the other channel or even, in extreme cases, switch off.

So when we learn that a record viewing figure for a play, rarely surpassed since, was achieved by Harold Pinter's *A Night Out*, with a minimum audience of fifteen million and probably, in fact, nearer eighteen million, that means something. It means, for one thing, that an audience not conditioned in what to expect of a play by the works of Rattigan and Dodie Smith found it by no means esoteric or highbrow, but simply accepted it as gripping entertainment; the new drama could be enjoyed by a vast popular audience without any need for self-conscious assurances that this was a big cultural experience and one must be prepared. There is no doubt that the difference between the general critical and commercial failure of *The*

Birthday Party in 1958 and the critical and commercial triumph of *The Caretaker* in 1960 was almost entirely the work of television, which with *A Night Out* and a new production of *The Birthday Party* familiarized a vast audience with Pinter's style and created the climate of opinion in which his later work could command instant acceptance.

But how did it come about that television, and commercial television at that – after all the horrible predictions about it – could do this sort of thing? Primarily it has been the work, it is not unfair to say, of one man, Sydney Newman, producer of A.B.C.'s Sunday-night series 'Armchair Theatre' until he moved to the B.B.C. as Head of Television Drama in 1962. From time to time interesting things have come from elsewhere in the system. Associated-Rediffusion put on *The Birthday Party* and has commissioned three original television plays from Pinter. Granada brought us the first two Clive Exton plays, as well as *Serjeant Musgrave's Dance*. The B.B.C. adopted John Mortimer from sound radio and took on, rather warily, John Arden and Henry Livings; latterly, during Sydney Newman's rule, it has developed along more experimental lines, but mainly to the benefit of directors; apart from the works of David Mercer and David Rudkin its dramatic productions, as pieces of writing, have mostly been negligible.

But though 'Armchair Theatre' itself was not invariably good during Sydney Newman's era, 1958–1962, it was never less than interesting. Newman is a Canadian, born in Toronto in 1917, and his worst enemy would not call him an intellectual, but he has a shrewd eye for talent, which he believes, justly it seems, will ultimately always turn out to be the most saleable of commodities. Since he set out to make the series as far as possible all-British, with every play specially written for television, he has swept into his net almost every notable talent in television drama, either under contract or for a play at a time, and has commissioned plays from Alun Owen, Clive Exton, and Harold Pinter, to name only a few. 'The advantage with Sydney,' according to one playwright who has worked on the series, 'is that once he has decided you've got something he lets you have your head. He may hate your play, but he just says: "O.K. Go ahead, make a fool of yourself; perhaps you'll learn something from it next time." He doesn't hold it against you if he's proved right, but neither does he hold it against you if he's proved wrong, though he'll probably go on to the bitter end muttering "Just wait till you see the notices" or "All right, but let's wait for the ratings".'

From the numerous writers who have first made some sort of name for themselves on radio or television I have chosen the four most distinguished for detailed consideration: Alun Owen, who began with radio, went on to the stage, but had his first major success in television; Clive Exton, whose work has been up to now nearly all in television; John Mortimer, who found his way to the stage first with a play written for radio and later produced on television as well; and Peter Shaffer, who found a more sympathetic hearing initially in television than in the theatre, his ardent first love. All of them except Shaffer, incidentally, are still active in television, whatever their other current activities; but then by now there are not so many young dramatists of distinction who have not tried their hand at television at least once.

There are, no doubt, other television writers with claims to consideration. I might mention, for example, Ronald Harwood, author of *The Barber of Stamford Hill, Take a Fellow Like Me*, and *Private Potter*, which last, though defective on its realistic level, had moments of unusual intensity as a symbolic drama. Or Rhys Adrian, writer by himself of several interesting radio and television pieces and, in collaboration with Julian Pepper under the collective pseudonym 'J. MacReady', of *Big Time*, the most believable picture yet of delinquent teenagers. Or Alan Simpson and Ray Galton, whose best scripts for *Hancock's Half-Hour* and *Steptoe and Son* are really one-act plays exploiting the dramatic possibilities of the *temps mort* as subtly, one may think in an irreverent moment, as anything from the new French novelists. Or Bill Naughton, an older man who has graduated from manual labour to professional writing for radio and television only in the years of the new drama, with a number of subtly evocative studies of working-class life in London and the North, among them *June Evening, The Long*

Carry, My Flesh, My Blood, and *Alfie Elkins and His Little Life* (later rewritten for the stage as *Alfie*) and gone on from there to the stage with *All in Good Time* and *Spring and Port Wine*. But undeniably Owen, Exton, Mortimer, and Shaffer are for the moment the leaders by a wide margin, and the rest will have to be left at a mention; one or two of them might have it in them to produce a masterpiece some time, but meanwhile we can only watch and hope.

ALUN OWEN

It is perhaps ironic that up to now Alun Owen has been known to the public primarily as a television dramatist, and indeed suffered on the occasion of his first West End production simply because several critics who should have known better were all too ready to suggest that though his play had merits, he was of course 'only' a television playwright and could not really expect to break into the legitimate theatre just like that. Ironic because his dramatic origins have all been in the theatre, his earliest work to receive a measure of attention was a stage play, *The Rough and Ready Lot*, and he denies ever having set out consciously to write television plays, as distinct from stage plays, at all: 'I write plays. If they are in two or three acts they are stage plays: if they are in one act they are television plays, because what else can you do with a one-act play?'

Even so, the result is that he fits, unwillingly but unavoidably, among those of our dramatists who have made their mark initially outside the theatre. He was born in North Wales in 1926, and spoke nothing but Welsh until he went to school. His parents moved to Liverpool when he was eight, and, like Meme Modryb in *Progress to the Park*, he began to live fully in a predominantly English-speaking society by the time he was ten, so that his Welsh, though fluent, is now, he says, 'a child's Welsh', and English decidedly his first language. On leaving school he did his war service as a Bevin Boy, spending two years in the mines before he returned to civilian life. Here he drifted into the theatre very much by chance; after trying unsuccessfully to get a job on a northern newspaper, he was recommended to try the local rep, was taken on, and continued to work on and off as an actor for twelve years or so, with intervals in which he took other jobs (eight months as a waiter in Paris, for instance). His range of acting activities included, as well as playing straight roles on stage, screen, and television, a period as 'feed' to Arthur Askey, a season with the Groves on television, and appearances as a pantomime dame.

When he began working as an actor in London he felt he needed a 'line', something to distinguish him from the host of young actors looking for work, and with his name and his background the choice was more or less forced on him: he became 'a Welsh actor', and, like Teifion in *Progress to the Park*, discovered the saleability of local colour. But as his works suggest, things are not so simple as that: he is neither completely Welsh nor completely not Welsh, but a mixture, and the conflict between the two principal ingredients of the mixture (to complicate matters his mother was Irish) is one of the recurrent themes in his plays: 'Liverpool and Wales,' he has said, 'they're the two things I really know, and yet I'm not completely at home in either', and the question of divided allegiances, of what Welshness really means and how Wales is best served, is the central subject of *After the Funeral*, as well as cropping up incidentally in various other contexts. Similarly, the conflicts between Roman Catholicism and Protestantism, religion and atheism, which also have considerable autobiographical significance, are recurrent in his work, most notably in *Progress to the Park* and *The Rough and Ready Lot*, but hovering in the background of almost everything he has written, particularly *No Trams to Lime Street* and *The Criminal*.

Alun Owen's first impulse to write came when he was thirteen or fourteen, and found expression for some years almost entirely in verse, some of which was published in English and Welsh magazines. His first dramatic work was a serial for children, never produced or even submitted for production, about the French Revolution and the 'Wild Geese' in Ireland, the central character being an unscrupulous Chevalier (later Citoyen) MacDonald. Owen himself has described the circumstances in which his first real play was produced: 'Suddenly I wanted to write just a little episode – one event which came to me – as a drama, so I wrote *Two Sons* and sent it to the B.B.C. They produced it on the Third Programme, and I wrote another and another. It seems silly to say now, but somehow I never thought of anything of mine being rejected while I wrote it: when someone told me after my first four plays had been accepted that I was lucky, I didn't know what he was talking about. . . .'

Two Sons was a significant beginning in several ways. The sons of the title are Taff and Cass, later to become more familiar to us as two of the sailors in *No Trams to Lime Street*, and in outline the story of this play is the same as that of the later one, minus the love story of the third sailor, who does not appear in this at all: Taff and Cass go ashore in Liverpool; Taff asserts himself against his bullying father, the ship's first engineer, and Cass has an inconclusive meeting with his father, which reaffirms their absolute inability to communicate with each other. But the treatment differs considerably, not only in its form (inevitably in radio many things must be explained which on television are simply to be seen), but in its style as well. The poetry of the situations is externalized much more – significantly, the trams, childhood symbols of romance and excitement, are still running – and the lengthy narration is composed, very effectively, in a heightened evocative prose slightly reminiscent of *Under Milk Wood*, with the sort of artful eloquence which Owen will henceforth apparently abandon, but actually integrate more closely into the broadly realistic dialogue of his subsequent work.

After *Two Sons*, which was finished in September 1957, Owen began work on two plays simultaneously, one a costume piece, *The Rough and Ready Lot*, and one set in modern Liverpool, *Progress to the Park*, which began its public life as another radio play (complete with elaborate poetic narration), though in fact originally written with the stage in mind. Both were completed by February 1959, when *Progress to the Park* achieved the first of its three productions, at the Royal Court on Sunday evening, while *The Rough and Ready Lot* reached the stage at the Lyric, Hammersmith, in June.

Both plays deal with the question which, according to the author, was uppermost in his mind at the time: the religious conflict. And neither, hardly surprisingly, offers a 'solution', for there is no solution. Of *The Rough and Ready Lot* Owen says: 'The battle between Catholic and Atheist is one of particular importance to me, and one in which I was very much involved at the time of writing the play. I wanted to work it out for myself in dramatic terms, but of course I couldn't because there's no ready-made answer, so both had to die in the end while the simple and ordinary survived.'

The form the story takes is a variation of the classical formula 'There was an Englishman, an Irishman, and a Welshman . . .'; in this case there are two Irishmen, and they are all mercenary officers in an *ad hoc* revolutionary army advancing towards the capital of a Spanish colony in South America. The period is shortly after the American Civil War, and they have just moved on south from that in search of another war, somewhere else where they will be paid to fight. Only Morgan, the fanatical atheist Welshman, is really involved: ever since a moment of revelation on the North-West Frontier when he decided that God was the arch-enemy, he has determined that 'wherever this enemy was, this God, and wherever a man was in injustice, invaded, put upon, I would be there and be his brother and fight for him'. But if he is in it for his ideals, Kelly and O'Keefe are simply professional soldiers, and the Colonel has his own plans, seeing this country as the last on earth where he can perhaps find a home.

The crucial point in the campaign is reached, however, in a way that rapidly involves them all. The route to the capital is through a pass, but the pass is blocked by a monastery, scene of a visitation by the Virgin, which the Government forces have turned into a fortress. What shall they do about it? For Morgan the answer is simple; even if God were not the arch-enemy it would be the merest common sense to shell the monastery/ fortress out of existence, for if they delay and go round, the government forces will have all the time they want to entrench around the capital. For O'Keefe, equally fanatical in his Roman Catholicism, the answer is equally simple: it would be sinful to touch the shrine in any way, and the fact that the opposition have also sinned by turning it into a fortress in the first place does not alter anything. The Colonel, a Protestant, has no particular feelings one way or the other about the shrine; he recognizes the justice of Morgan's objections, but taking the longer view he sees also that his own chances of winning the love of the natives and being able to make a home for himself at their head as the liberator of the nation hangs in the balance. He may win the war by destroying a shrine the natives venerate, but will they not then always remember him only as its destroyer?

Kelly, the nearest the play offers to a common man, vacillates eternally, wanting to offend nobody, see everything that happens, and stay safely on the outskirts of any decisive action until the decision has been reached. Naturally, therefore, it is he who survives to become Colonel and lead the army on to victory and peace after O'Keefe has spiked the guns to prevent the shelling, Morgan has loaded a rickety old trophy of a brass cannon, and they have both been killed when it rebounds and blows up (the Colonel, meanwhile, being stabbed by an Indian girl under the mistaken impression that he has ordered the shelling). For it is the simple and ordinary who always survive in this world, as they are the only ones unobtrusive enough not to draw the fire of others.

Not that Kelly is altogether negative: he has his own ideas, and he, like O'Keefe, is a Roman Catholic, though unlike O'Keefe he is no fanatic. And fanaticism is precisely the chief target of the play – not any particular set of ideas, but the carrying of any idea to extremes at which humanity itself is disregarded. O'Keefe boasts of the rigidity and inflexibility of his standards; Morgan is clearly the sort of man who loves humanity at large, but loves it only as long as it seems to him worthy of his love, and will brook no opposition to the idea that humanity must accept unconditionally what he considers best for it. The Colonel also has an *idée fixe*: he is obsessed with the idea of finding a home, and refuses to take any decision which may put this in danger – he has chosen the wrong side once before and does not mean to do so again, but it is his indecision about which is the right side that ultimately kills him. However, in a sense he is dead when the play begins, as his long dreamy speech at the end of Act 2 makes clear, proclaiming him already the world's rejected guest (a reflection on Protestantism, perhaps, or is that reading too much into it?). When the decision about shelling the monastery is taken out of his hands he says: 'I seem to be in a world I can no longer understand, so why should I try to control it?' and ironically it is from another displaced person in the world around him that he receives his death: the Indian girl who stabs him not because of the Christian shrine, but because her Indian god lives in the hill underneath.

The Rough and Ready Lot is virtually unique in Alun Owen's work in that it is tightly plotted along conventional lines and at the same time highly characteristic in its preoccupations and thoroughly effective on its own level. The main thing most critics had against *Progress to the Park*, which was written at the same time and treats of the same themes, though in a very different setting, was its absence of formal plot construction in this sense. In it, one can see retrospectively, Owen strikes for the first time on the type of organization which has since proved characteristic of his work, particularly in television. The central situation is essentially static, though it does not appear so: it carries inevitably its own solution, or lack of solution, and though people may battle to change things there is finally no way out. Consequently, atmosphere and character interaction are enormously important, character development through the manipulation of a formal plot almost non-existent.

In this case the reason is obvious: again, the conflict is religious, between Roman Catholic and Protestant, and again there just is no solution. Though individuals may try to fight against the principles of the society they live in, ultimately they come back to the prejudices and inhibitions they started out with. So from the beginning it is clear – though the supposition that every dramatic problem must have its 'solution' might temporarily blind us to the fact – that there is no solution to the dilemma which faces Mag Keegan and Bobby Laughlin, or there is only one, death, but this Liverpudlian Romeo and

P

Juliet are not going to do anything so grand as to die for love. What gives rise to a sufficient glimmering of hope to make the subject dramatically viable is Bobby's background: even though he comes from a family of rabid Irish Protestants and has absorbed from childhood all his father's ravings about the turpitude of the Catholics, he has been at sea and away from parental influence for some time when we first meet him, and he belongs superficially to a more liberated generation in which friendships cut across religious barriers, his three closest friends being a word-intoxicated Welsh writer now settled in London, a stolid Liverpudlian of Welsh origin, and a randy Catholic seaman – one of the opposition and two uninvolved.

Perhaps, after all, then, the long-standing prejudices will be broken down when he and Mag, his childhood sweetheart, meet again after years forbidden each other's company, and for a while it seems so. But Mag, in her love for him, has been running around in his absence with his friends, talking all the time about him and using them to be near him. They understand that, but he will not – for him it just means that she's easy and he is the fool because everyone has had her except him. But then, after all, what could he expect; what had his father always told him about Catholic girls? In the last act he tries to make love to her, as he might to any girl, swallowing down his reproaches until he has got what he wants, but she senses the falsity – for her this is the greatest insult of all, and she leaves him. He is torn between her and his father, and finally she seems to win a victory in his mind against his father, but Teifion leaves us in little doubt that the victory will be only temporary, that soon he will lose his urge to fight and be back toeing the Orangeman line like an obedient son.

Teifion's despairing final speech draws the conclusion forcibly (in a favourable example of Owen's highest rhetorical style, incidentally):

No harm's been done? No, you're right, Charlie, come to think of it, no harm's been done at all. Because if you take the long view of things – Bobby's never going to catch up with Mag. Oh no, boy, I can see Bobby – sliding along the lane back to his dad. He'll fumble in his pocket, get out a clove, chew it a bit and get it round his tongue. After that he'll start to sing 'just to keep up his spirits'. And d'ye know what he'll sing? . . . 'The Orange sash me father wore.' Oh, he's a good boy for his dad our Bob is! Oh, he'll study through tomorrow and all the rest of the hot days that are coming up for a hot July. And – comes August, every week-end he'll be off on the bike and across to Wales and with a bit of luck, and Bobby's the boy for luck, he'll find the girl campers from Bolton, waiting for him, ready to drop their morals specially for a week. Well, it's Wakes Week! And after dissipating his strength all the way through August, he'll be in a suitable frame of mind to buckle down to the exams in September and by the time these exams are over it'll be October and he'll be away and life'll go on and on. Good old Bob! October boy! The seas boy! Back to the free-easy riding sea. Anywhere – just to escape from Mag. Oh – she's a demander is Mag. They're all demanders! And anyway, it'll be all right for Mag, 'cos – no harm's been done there, ye know. No! She can lose herself in plates and spoonfuls of scouse. She can get away from her mother's nagging through the heat of July with the beads of sweat on her upper lip out in the kitchen. But in August, she's got the Holy voyage and her mother's demands will be drowned by the busy gnats of Ireland. The slabs of Soda bread washed down with orange coloured tea. Yes – she'll live through September. Her sex is resilient! . . . And by God, this town is resilient! I'm not worried for Mag. October may be a bad month for her, but Mag's not a suicide girl. Despair is outside our Mag. Despair is outside this town, because this town is like an India-rubber ball and it makes us all India-rubber! Throw us on the ground and we'll bounce back! And, Charlie, with any luck at all, tomorrow I'll get on that train, clutching in my hot sticky hand a second-class ticket and brazen me way past Crewe in a first-class seat and he can drop me off at Sloane Street any time at all, son, any time at all. No harm's been done – Charlie – no harm at all.

(It should be mentioned, incidentally, that this speech was cut and all sorts of other modifications introduced for the play's second production, which was at the Theatre Royal, Stratford, and was made to conform closely with the theatre's normal production policy. In the third production, at the Saville, the original text was largely restored, and it is this final text which I refer to here.)

Nothing has been resolved – the situation is much as it was at the outset, except that Mag has more reason to be hurt and Bobby has more material for his prejudices to work on – but a lot has been elucidated. Well plotted the play is not, in any conventional sense; the real action is all crowded into the last act, leaving Act I as an extended prelude (in the Stratford production it was the first two of three acts). But then, it is the point of the play precisely that we should experience the atmosphere of Liverpool, come to recognize the distinctive quality of its religious and social conflicts, while the plot is of quite secondary importance; partly it helps us to understand Liverpool, but more importantly Liverpool is necessary to the understanding of it. And so atmosphere and the interplay of characters whose situation in relation to each other proves unchanged and unchangeable remain paramount: the atmosphere of a charged Sunday morning in the pub, an aimless evening girl-chasing in the park; the relations of the four childhood friends who have, after all, nothing much in common except having known each other for years, and perhaps do not even like each other very much; their relations individually and collectively with Mag.

In all this, too, the basic pattern of *The Rough and Ready Lot* can be seen, though changed and enriched. O'Keefe finds his obvious ideological counterpart in Mr Keegan and Morgan in Mr Laughlin (though – and perhaps this is a comment on the kinship of all fanaticisms – temperamentally O'Keefe bears a closer resemblance to Mr Laughlin; possibly the fact that O'Keefe was written with the actor Patrick Magee in mind, and Magee actually played Mr Laughlin in the Saville production of *Progress to the Park* may have something to do with it). The Colonel has certain features in common with Bobby, who is also torn between various lines of action and will ultimately be destroyed because of his inability to decide between them, while Mag is in a sense the Indian girl – certainly she is a misfit in this world, being ruled by an antiquated code of her own, the rule of love. And what of Kelly, the representative of ordinary humanity in all the turbulence of *The Rough and Ready Lot*? Where is he to be found in *Progress to the Park*? In Charlie Modryb, surely, who throughout it all keeps his own counsel and looks forward quietly but not unintelligently to the time when he will find the right girl, marry her, and settle down to a normal life without any of the extremes to which religious

fanaticism and personal passion lead the rest. He is our standard of normality, and to judge the other characters aright we
must measure them against him.

Progress to the Park is richer, in comparison with *The Rough
and Ready Lot,* by the addition of two more important figures:
Jameson, who as far as the plot is concerned embodies the
deliberate malice which is the only weapon of the stupid and
unattractive, and Teifion, who acts as a sort of chorus on the
action and whom it is tempting to see, given his character, his
situation, and many of his utterances, as the author's representative in the play. Teifion, in fact, provides an excellent example of the way Owen's dramatic method works: if we were to
judge the play by traditional standards we would have to say
that the central theme, the plot if you like, is the love between
Mag and Bobby, and its frustration by circumstances (in the
broader sense of environment as well as in the more limited
sense of mischance). Teifion does not really, except when he
reasons with Bobby at the end, exert any decisive influence on
this action, and even at the end the point of his intervention is
that he himself already knows it to be hopeless. So why should
his role bulk so large in the play as written? The answer, and
the justification, is to be found in what I was saying earlier
about Owen as an 'atmospheric' dramatist: Teifion is essential
to Owen's picture of Liverpool as an atmosphere, and in so far
as the play is a conversation piece he is undeniably the most
interesting conversationalist on the scene. Whether or not he
contributes to the plot, his presence increases our understanding of the issues before us and adds enormously to our enjoy-
ment – which, if one is ready to put aside any notion of the
well-made play when it patently is not intended to apply,
seems more than enough to justify the important role he
assumes.

In all this, though, we have been considering the ideas
behind Owen's dramatic writing, which are interesting
enough, but do not really give more than a hint of the final
effect his plays have on us. Owen is not primarily a cerebral
dramatist, and his plays present a view of the world more
intuitive than reasoned; they hit one, if at all, in the emotions

rather than the intellect. If his plays are not well made in the sense that a play by Pinero or Galsworthy is well made, they are well made in the deepest sense of the term: they have a compelling inner coherence of characterization, a fine unity of atmosphere, and an overall consistency of texture in writing and realization. Their structures are free and rhapsodic, governed only by rules inherent in the material, and in his best work plot is replaced by incident and atmosphere – instead of a neat structure of action and counteraction, solid set piece and calculated reversal of fortunes, we are given simply a situation and some tiny incident which allows the characters to interact and reveal themselves. Lines seldom follow each other in the normal functional give-and-take of the theatre; instead the characters frequently talk listlessly, at odds with or scarcely conscious of each other, revealing their natures and relationships or creating an emotional climate instead of pushing forward a fully articulated plot.

Hence, the quality of the dialogue assumes tremendous importance, though not, of course, in the same way as in the works of a more cerebral dramatist like Shaw. It is the impression of reality which counts here – which is not necessarily the same thing as reality itself. (Owen says of the Liverpudlian speech in *Progress to the Park* and *No Trams to Lime Street*, widely commended for its verisimilitude: 'In fact, no one in Liverpool ever spoke as I make them speak in these plays: it's just my idea of how, ideally, they should speak, and how I would like them to speak, but far, far away from literal truth.') Of all the new dramatists Owen has nearly the most acute ear for English as it is really spoken, and the greatest skill at re-creating it in properly dramatic terms (he is equalled, perhaps, by Clive Exton and surpassed only by Harold Pinter): his dialogue often sounds completely naturalistic, yet on closer examination it proves to be the product of the subtlest art, each line being precisely calculated in relation to the play as a whole, from the casual, disconnected, apparently irrelevant exchanges of the *temps mort* scenes which Owen, like most of his contemporaries, finds useful for conveying the aimlessness and listlessness which often afflicts his characters, to the quite elaborate eloquence of some of his climactic scenes (particularly where the speaker is Welsh or Irish and therefore more readily acceptable to English audiences as possessing the gift of the gab).

With these subtle and, one cannot doubt, very carefully worked out variations of pace and texture, Owen's plays make special demands on the director. In the theatre this has been evident enough: of *Progress to the Park*'s three productions (by Lindsay Anderson, Harry H. Corbett, and Ted Kotcheff) only the third was really satisfactory, substituting a sort of poetic realism for the social documentary approach of the first and the sub-Brechtian trappings of the second. Even more is direction important in the cinema and on television, however. Owen's most serious tangle with the cinema, *The Criminal*, has not in any case been too happy (except for its enormous commercial success), since he was landed initially with an unsatisfactory story line by Jimmy Sangster, author of numerous horror films, and after the film was completed twenty minutes were removed, including much of what was more characteristically Owen in the original script – the criminal hero's Roman Catholicism, his relations with his previous mistress after he is released from prison (made completely incomprehensible in the film as shown) and the playing-off of the two different levels of sophistication, that of his criminal associates and that of the enigmatic foreign girl with whom he becomes involved. But even more damagingly, what was left – especially the probing study of prison life near the beginning – was mostly thrown away in favour of the director Joseph Losey's own personal brand of cinematic baroque, full of those flashy virtuoso passages of technique which had worked excellently in films like *The Sleeping Tiger* and *Time Without Pity*, where the script had nothing else to offer, but proved all too liable to annihilate anything this script might have to say for itself.

Again, on television the director plays an important part in making or breaking a play. Fortunately five of Owen's plays for television have been directed by Ted Kotcheff, whose intuitive, exploratory style, perfectly under control without ever falling into the stale predictabilities of the academically respectable *mise en scène*, allows the author his head completely and makes everything look so natural and unobtrusively right that one is hardly conscious that the play is being directed at all. This is just right for Owen's work, since the illusion of reality plays an important part in its ultimate effect and anything which tends to break into this illusion is destructive. This is particularly so in the detailed handling of dialogue, as one television production not by Ted Kotcheff, *The Ruffians*, demonstrated. *The Ruffians*, though actually transmitted after the trilogy of plays which made Owen's name, was written quite early on – just before the first, in fact – in response to a B.B.C. commission, and then shelved for nearly two years. It is a thriller about an escaped convict who returns to terrorize a pub run by his brother-in-law while waiting to see his wife and force her, if he can, to come away with him, and was intended by Owen as an 'entertainment' in the Graham Greene sense of the term, not to be taken too seriously. Any effectiveness it might have had on this level, however, was destroyed by the completely uncomprehending production: in the very first scene, for example, which shows the publican opening up his pub, exchanging a few desultory words with the potman, and generally waiting for the evening to begin, the casual exchange of aimless conventional formulas used by the author to suggest the slack, routine feeling of a normally uneventful evening before anything notable happens went for nothing, since all the lines were snapped out in a clear-cut stagy to-and-fro, for all the world as though this were early Somerset Maugham we were seeing. The result was that what was being said became literally incomprehensible, or at best began to sound like N. F. Simpson, as the presentation systematically implied a formal, logical connection between consecutive remarks of the two characters which was evidently not there at all.

In contrast, the three Liverpool plays in Sydney Newman's 'Armchair Theatre' series, all directed by Ted Kotcheff, have managed things so successfully that they have persuaded the unwary to accept the powerful illusion of reality for the real thing and class Owen, rather rashly, as a semi-documentary, slice-of-life dramatist – an idea that will not for a moment stand the test of close examination, which shows exactly how much is the result of simply recording observations and how much is imaginative re-creation of the most artful and highly selective sort. The first of the three, *No Trams to Lime Street*, in fact, provides the perfect example of this, since the one thing one or two critics found hard to swallow, the extraordinary coincidence that the sailor on his way to light a candle for a dead shipmate in his home town (Liverpool) should become involved unwittingly with the same man's widow, was as it happens the only thing in the piece which was 'true' in the most basic, literal sense. The play is a very cunning combination of two stories, that from *Two Sons*, concerning Cass and Taff and their relations with their fathers, and an experience retailed to Owen by a sailor friend to whom it actually happened. Originally this latter was a broadly comic tale of a sailor who liked girls with fat legs, but since there were strong elements of comedy in the other story, particularly in Taff's gesture of defiance towards his father when he drinks a double brandy and smokes a cigar just to show that he doesn't think much of the occupation, the story of Billy Mack and Betty has been shifted in tone from Rabelaisian farce to something much more tender and elusive.

The second of the Liverpool plays, *After the Funeral*, is 'Liverpool' only at a distance, in that two of its principal characters are Liverpool-Welsh. Again it deals with the relations between various generations of a family, though this time most importantly between grandfather and grandsons. The funeral is that of Captain John Roberts's daughter-in-law, and the question which arises is, where will he live and who will look after him from now on? The obvious candidates are his two grandsons, Dave and Morgan. Morgan has special reasons for wanting him, since he is a romantic Welsh nationalist, a professor in South Wales who has learnt Welsh, despises his Liverpool upbringing, and sees in his grandfather a heaven-sent opportunity for establishing beyond doubt his Welsh background in the eyes of his colleagues. Dave, on the other hand, wants him simply from personal affection; even the belated revelation that the Captain is not really his grandfather at all makes no difference. ('If you feel a man is your grandfather, he is. . . .') The material of the play is clearly autobiographical to some extent: Owen admits that Captain Roberts is a portrait of his own grandfather and that Dave is in many ways himself, though people have also found much of him in Morgan and he supposes that this must be so whether he meant it or not. In effect, then, as one might guess even without the author's confirmation, *After the Funeral* shows yet another dramatized working-out of a conflict in Owen's mind: as *The Rough and Ready Lot* and *Progress to the Park* dramatized the religious divisions, so this play dramatizes the pull between the realistic Liverpudlian and the Welsh romantic, though admittedly with the dice loaded in favour of the former.

In the third of the group, *Lena, Oh My Lena,* another theme which clearly has an autobiographical significance is taken up – that of the character whom life carries away from his original class or milieu and the nostalgia he may occasionally feel for things as they were. In *Progress to the Park* this is evidently happening to Teifion by virtue of his new life as a writer in London; already it is making him something of a stranger in Liverpool, among the people he knew as a child, but there are so many other reasons for the separation which have more relevance to this particular play (being Liverpool-Welsh among Liverpool-Irish, and religiously uncommitted in a hotbed of religious contention) that this specific difference is hardly noticeable. In *Lena, Oh My Lena,* though, it becomes central: Tom, a Liverpool student, has been cut off from his childhood and background by education, but feels an enormous longing to belong somewhere, which expresses itself in a determination to get back to 'real life' by taking vacation work in a factory among ordinary working people. (He suggests that his own background is working class, but this is rather doubtful, and in the printed text Owen confirms our suspicions by characterizing him as 'from a lower-middle-class family which he has romanticized into the working class'.) The division in his world is symbolized, neatly but not too obtrusively, by the division between the factory and the 'bohemian' student camp of pea-pickers up the road. Tom resents the fact that he belongs with the pea-pickers, who are not 'real'; he wants to believe that his real place is with the factory workers, but the truth, as he finally discovers, is that he does not understand them. The sheltering effect of education has softened him, leaving him naïve and defenceless in personal relationships, and when he becomes involved with Lena, a factory girl who, on the rebound from a quarrel with her regular boy-friend Glyn, is ready enough for a bit of fun to make Glyn jealous, he at once romanticizes the whole business into a great love, and is then cruelly disillusioned and humiliated by his own inability to deal with the situation. Finally he begins, painfully, to learn his lesson: even if the students up the road are stuck-up and artificial, for better or for worse they are 'his sort' now, and he must come to understand where he belongs.

Knowing where one belongs and coming to terms with the realities of one's own life and nature, living in the present rather than the past: those are the recurrent themes in these three plays. One can hardly do better than to quote Owen's own statement on the point in his introduction to the printed texts:

In *No Trams to Lime Street* the three sailors are searching for themselves. Cass and Taff have to get over their fathers before they can live their own lives, Billy Mack has to find the courage to dismiss his dead friend Ben Hogan [Betty's husband] before he can be himself. In *After the Funeral* this problem is heightened for the Roberts brothers, because the death of someone you love means a time of realization. In *Lena, Oh My Lena* I tried to show that physical attraction is not enough to gain admittance to a world you don't really belong to any more. In the three plays the characters are evading the truth about themselves. This is a common failing — so common I don't condemn it, that would be too easy; but I feel it is important enough to be portrayed, if it helps to bring about more understanding of this sort of problem. When in *No Trams to Lime Street* Cass buys a bottle of whisky for his father, he doesn't solve anything: but he tried, and there's still hope. . . .

This passage taken by itself, though it explains well enough what he is about, might seem to imply a rather sticky and sentimental approach on the part of the playwright, but that would be far from the mark: if there is a danger in Owen's enormous tenderness towards his creations, his longing to show first and foremost their potentialities for tenderness and compassion, it is fully countered by the unswerving truthfulness of his observation. Whatever gentleness and love there may be in life he shows, but no more than that, and he shows it as hard won in a world where insensitivity and cheerful savagery are much more the rule. With his impeccable ear for the cadences of spoken English (especially Liverpool-English or Welsh-English) he can conjure up formidably the illusion of reality, but this would count for little were not his observation of the way real people really behave equally acute. Seldom, for instance, can the true flavour of factory life have been captured so accurately as in *Lena, Oh My Lena*, with the little songs that rise out of nothing and die away, the outbursts of noise and horseplay to break the monotony, the often shallow matiness which does not include genuine affection, but on the other hand permits as well an amount of teasing and cheating severe enough to be cruel were they not on the whole so uncalculating. Nor has any other dramatist writing today a more mature, unsentimental grasp of feminine character, demonstrated most notably in the tough, sensible working girls portrayed by Billie Whitelaw in *No Trams to Lime Street, Lena, Oh My Lena*, and *Progress to the Park*, all of whom are totally believable as self-possessed, fully adult *women*, something in which English drama is otherwise singularly lacking.

And finally, important especially in television, Owen has the gift of intimacy, which is more than just putting two people close together, alone, in front of a camera: his characters are genuinely emotionally involved with each other. Sometimes it is in love, sometimes in resentment, often in the tension set up between the two, but whatever it is that binds them they do really touch, they communicate, because it is part of his poetic vision of the world that they should (whereas for most of our other dramatists it is the essence of their vision that people cannot communicate and do not do so). And herein lies the overriding internal unity of his plays: the relations of his characters with each other have an unmistakable inner emotional force and poetic necessity which provides the rock-hard centre of each play's world and from which follows – almost, it seems, automatically – the outer coherence of structure, mood, dramatic progression, and so on.

After these three plays, which represent, as anyone familiar with *Two Sons* or *The Rough and Ready Lot* would already have realized, only one side of Owen's talent, he obviously felt the need for a change, and in his next television play, *The Ways of Love*, he turned to a much less intimate, interior style; though the same problems as were central to the 'Liverpool trilogy' – finding one's own identity; coming to terms with the present, with reality – recur, it is in a very different context, that of sophisticated literary life in London, and with many additions and modifications, as befits the broader canvas. The characters are not altogether strange, however, and their remote backgrounds are still recognizable. The central character, for instance, the Welsh writer David, might almost be Teifion seen from the London end of his life, a writer fighting for survival in an unfamiliar world. The question at the forefront of his more idealistic friends' minds is: Will success spoil David Enoch? Will the fact that his true, sensitive, sincere first novel has become an overnight best-seller change him from the simple, idealistic Welsh lad he has always been into yet another smooth commercial writer who has sold out to films and television? But before very long it becomes clear that David was spoilt, in their sense of the term, long before he became a success. He is perhaps a great writer – we have no way of knowing, and the question is not important to the play. What is important is that he believes wholeheartedly in his creative abilities and will do anything to make the money which will allow him to go on doing what he must do. 'No matter what I do for money, it won't affect my real work or me. It's a matter of confidence. You see, I have confidence in my creative ability. . . .'

One of the things he has done is to write a novel, a very good novel by all accounts, with the intention that it should be a success, and allowed the idea to get abroad that it is autobiographical to help the sales. ('People don't want works of fiction any more. They hate to think that the writer has a richer imagination than they have.') This is what really upsets his friends, especially the idealistic left-wing Charlie; as long as the book was 'true' for them they were ready to be moved by it, but if it is not true then they have been deceived in some way. ('I thought that the book was a sort of epitaph,' says the more susceptible of the women desolately; 'Well, so it was,' replied David, 'but to poverty, not love.') And if it is true in another sense – in the sense that they and their feelings have gone to its making – well, that is even worse; it is unethical.

Here we come to the central questions: the artist's responsibility to himself; his responsibility to the artist in him before his responsibility to the man. How did it feel, for instance, to figure in a book by Denton Welch? More important, had he the right to put you there? David Enoch is thoroughly unpleasant, in many ways, but he also speaks the truth uncomfortably often: he may be ruthless, but it is the ruthlessness of self-protection; it is himself as much as anyone else that he sacrifices on the altar of his art, but he arises phoenix-like from the ashes while everyone else merely gets burnt. In other words, one problem for which he seems to have sought (and found) a solution is much the same as that in which the characters of the Liverpool trilogy are involved; that of finding his own identity, and having found it, of keeping it intact. His solution may be ruthless; he might claim that as an artist he has special privileges, or he might well not bother to advance any such line of special pleading – he does what he does because he wants to and because he has to.

Though *The Ways of Love* is recognizably from the same pen and on the same sort of theme as Owen's other plays, in certain respects, as we have seen, it represents a deliberate break-away from the constricting mould of the regional playwright producing slice-of-life dramas on working-class themes into which the critics have shown some signs of trying to force him. By temperament, perhaps, Owen is basically a realist, but he can use his realistic style in many ways far removed from that implied by his reputation as a 'working-class dramatist': in *Two Sons* he carried off successfully an essay in slightly Dylan-Thomasy, overtly poetic evocation, in *The Rough and Ready Lot* he achieved a costume play of remarkable authenticity and sobriety, and in *The Ways of Love* he showed that he could deal convincingly with the sophisticated and metropolitan as well as the plain provincial – though the early scene at a press reception rings slightly false, the rest of the play, in which a number of intelligent, articulate people get together and proceed systematically to tear each other apart, comes off to perfection.

His next play, *The Rose Affair*, carries the rebellion (if deliberate rebellion it be) still further, marking his most decisive departure yet from the naturalistic end of the realistic scale. This time the form is an undisguised parable, a modern version of the Beauty and the Beast story. The Beast, Mr Betumain, is a tycoon who lives for most of the time behind masks because he suffers from a psycho-somatic condition which causes his face to swell and distort itself into something hideously grotesque whenever he is emotionally disturbed (generally with feelings of guilt engendered, directly or indirectly, by his money). Beauty is Bella Shane, the daughter of an employee of his who embezzled, almost inadvertently, some funds from a rose nursery he owns, and she wins him over mainly by forcing him into an unwilling admission that he is a man and has needs like a man (her, for example) and lifting the weight of guilt from his shoulders by taking over his money. ('Give it to me, girls understand guilt. Eve passed us on a secret, how to live with guilt and other things, then make them into a feminine mystery to bind men to us.') The drama is conceived on broadly non-realistic lines, full of fantastic touches of slightly surrealist humour, and its dialogue is written in a curiously effective sort of mannered and formal prose, not without a hint here and there of Daisy Ashford, which gives the viewer the odd impression that what he is seeing is at once highly sophisticated and unmistakably basic, like one of those paintings by le Douanier Rousseau in which solid suburban Frenchmen in top hats and frock-coats form a perfectly credible part of exotic landscapes filled with equally solid and literally rendered tropical plants and mythological figures. It is a diversion, perhaps, but a diversion of exceptional charm and skill.

Both *The Ways of Love* and *The Rose Affair* have had, very properly, their admirers, but a slight feeling of resentment still seems to linger among critics, and public. Clearly, with the solid achievement of the Liverpool plays and *The Rough and Ready Lot* to establish him already as one of the most original and accomplished writers of his generation, Owen is determined to convince them that any stereotyped picture of him they may be cherishing is too limited and limiting. In the television plays he has written since *The Rose Affair*, therefore, he has continued to experiment with different forms and different subject-matter.

Each play marks a new departure in some direction. *You Can't Win 'Em All*, written for B.B.C. television, breaks out of the hour-minus-commercials form which had proved rather constricting for *The Rose Affair*, and tackles political drama in an unspecified American country something like Cuba. Its main asset, though, is its central character, Corrigan Blake. He is a Cockney, but not a quaint, perky, pearly-king sort of tradi-ional dramatic Cockney: he is very much a 1962 Cockney, tough, disenchanted, uncommitted, keeping everyone at an ironic distance, making no statement which is not couched as a question, talking about himself as though it is someone else. He refuses to be involved in the battles others are fighting, and yet he always gets 'lumbered' sooner or later, if only because his native efficiency (as well as his native goodness of heart) will not let him stand by while others make a mess of things. The same characteristics have subsequently seen him happily through a series of six half-hour situation comedies by Owen, *Corrigan Blake*, also for B.B.C. Television; here he is set against Wally St John Smith, an upper-class con-man with a highly developed gift of personal fantasy, and the episodes show them variously engaged in chatting up a variety of 'birds', rich, intellectual, artistic, and so on.

Dare to be a Daniel, Owen's next play after *You Can't Win 'Em All*, tells its whole story in a mere half-hour, and is a highly successful example of Owen's ability to write a tightly plotted play when he wants to. Superficially it is little more than an anecdote with a Maupassant-like twist at the end, telling of

12 Sydney Newman and Alun Owen during rehearsals of 'The Rose Affair'

13a 'The Caretaker'
13b 'I'll have you to Remember'

how an expelled schoolboy is able, years later, to engineer the sort of revenge on his headmaster-persecutor which many schoolboys dream of in their more sadistic moments but few ever actually achieve. To judge by Owen's own comments, it is also a classic instance of art as therapy for the artist: he describes it as beginning from his own reactions to a slight at school, with the avenger representing his view of the matter, and then gradually bringing him round, as he wrote, to a sympathy with and understanding of the victim. This is not so irrelevant as it seems to the play's final effect, for the shift in the author's sympathies produces an unusually complex and satisfying balance of sympathies in the audience, and raises the play considerably above the cunning piece of mechanical plotting it first appears to be.

The next play, *The Hard Knock*, is another attempt at the entertainment-thriller in the manner of *The Ruffians*, and is interesting but not in the end very satisfactory. The story is ostensibly that of a quest for the truth about a dead brother hanged for murder, which gradually reveals itself as a quest for the truth about the inquirer. The character of the inquirer is rather underwritten, however, and the play consequently tends rather to fall into episodes as he questions various people who knew the dead Kevin. Some of the episodes are excellent, some less so. But the first major sequence, outlining the family background of the two brothers and creating a sharp, complex, believable character in their embittered sister, is one of the best and most fully thought out things Owen has ever written, and the surface observation is so lively and accurate throughout that the occasional weaknesses in construction can be forgiven.

The Stag, another television play, again concerns the relationship of two brothers, this time from a small village in West Wales where the few get a job, marry, and stay put, the majority move to England or farther afield. The elder, John, has moved away, and gone to America; he comes back for the wedding of his younger brother, Graham, to find himself odd man out, resented by his contemporaries, who now seem years older than he is, and appalled at the situation he escaped from and his brother is now about to be trapped in. Does Graham really love the girl? He supposes he must, because they wrote regularly all through his National Service, but John's presence makes him vaguely discontented. In a touching little scene near the end he wanders out from his bachelor party the night before the wedding and talks casually to an English girl staying at the local inn as though it was all happening to someone else; but circumstances are too strong, and in the end he goes back – the marriage will, after all, take place.

Owen's next full-length stage play, *A Little Winter Love*, is striking above all as a clear demonstration that he is far from being, as even his most sympathetic critics have sometimes suggested, a technical primitive whose plays work more on instinctive flair than on solid constructional groundwork. Admittedly this should have been clear from the start, since after all *The Rough and Ready Lot* is a model of tight and coherent plot-management. In his Liverpool love-stories the rhapsodic side of his talent is more evident, but whenever he is writing more about power than about love, as in *Dare to be a Daniel* and *A Little Winter Love*, his gifts as a constructor immediately come to the fore again. In this last play the story of a ruthless, hypocritical American administrator and his effect on a Welsh college to which he comes for a year is grippingly well told, and the characterization of the central character and those about him – his dissatisfied wife, the Welsh poet lover she acquires, the hysterical spinster millionairess whose money lies at the bottom of most of the plotting – is fresh and vivid, especially in the case of the two lovers, who are given a number of amatory exchanges in Alun Owen's best lyrical vein (surely no contemporary British dramatist writes love scenes as well as he).

In fact the only character about whom some doubt remains is Felix Draper, the principal object of the American newcomer's hostility. People are always telling us that he is insufferable only because he is insecure as a result of his slum upbringing, but he never gives any visible sign of anything but overweening self-confidence, plus a touching faith in the exotic glamour of an obtrusively sported working-class background which makes one wonder whether he may not in fact come, as Owen told us of the hero of *Lena, Oh My Lena*, 'from a lower-middle-class family which he has romanticized into the working class'. Anyway, the fact that he seems so richly to deserve the come-uppance he eventually receives, but at the same time that he receives it at the hands of someone even more unpleasant than himself, gives the play a satisfactory ambiguity and complexity without ever taking it beyond what the ordinary West End theatregoer should be ready to understand and appreciate.

Owen's collaboration with Lionel Bart on the book of the Liverpool musical *Maggie May* (1964) hit precisely the West End mark: a lot of local colour, comedy, drama and romance, and none the worse for that, if hardly extending Owen's talents in any direction. This is, quite deliberately it seems, his 'commercial' side, and one which he displays more or less effectively from time to time in such works as *The Loser*, half of his stage double bill *The Game*, produced at the Dublin Festival in 1965, and various minor television plays. But elsewhere he continues to develop, particularly along two distinct lines: a highly personal style of word-intoxicated farcical comedy exemplified best by the three scripts he wrote for the television *Ronnie Barker Show* in 1968, and an equally inimitable brand of strong, believable duologues for mature men and women. Love scenes particularly, but also hate scenes, quarrel scenes and all the scenes somewhere in between in which real sexual tension of some sort exists. Most British dramatists baulk at this sort of drama, but he revels in it. *The Winner*, for instance, the other half of *The Game*, is vintage Owen: virtually a two-hander between an Irish photographer and his Anglo-Welsh ex-debutante wife, it is an object-lesson in how to get the most out of a complex sexual-cum-social relationship by reducing plot to a minimum and just letting the characters rip – into each other, or in whatever direction takes their fancy. Equally successful in the same sort of style, is Owen's ambitious television play *The Fantasist*: a complicated love story about a young woman who determines to unmask and if possible destroy the influence of a dominating employer who seems to be the chief barrier to the happiness of his employees and hangers-on, but falls in love with him instead and discovers that he is really the only thing that keeps his entourage going, providing them all with the fantasies of rivalry, jealousy, persecution by which they live.

Owen has been in the last few years one of the most prolific of the newer British dramatists: his other works include half a dozen television plays of various lengths, film scripts – of which the most notable was for the first Beatles film, *A Hard Day's Night* – another stage play, *The Goose* (1967), concerning the battle for power between an Irish building contractor and his treacherous partner, a Welsh site engineer. Though evidently he feels free to return to Liverpool and the sort of subject with which critics and public most associate him, he has proved that this is not the limit of his human horizon, any more than the slightly heightened realism of the Liverpool trilogy of television plays is the limit of his style. He writes generously, extrovertly, on a large scale (even within a small compass like that of the television half-hour), and pours out plays good, indifferent, and occasionally quite bad. But among them the good, the individual, those which could be written by nobody else always predominate, and in a drama dominated largely by careful, frugal miniaturists a little romantic expansiveness comes by no means amiss. We can accept the faults as a necessary condition of the virtues, and the virtues are big enough in all conscience.

CLIVE EXTON

If there is one thing which emerges simple, clear cut, and consistent from the study of a number of the new dramatists together, it is that there is nothing simple, clear cut, and consistent about them. Every one is in some way an exception to any generalization one may make; each has his own personal quirks, his own unexpected allegiances. Clive Exton, for example, though not specially conscious of any influences at work in his plays, regards himself as really a very old-fashioned sort of playwright and cites as the only influences he thinks likely 'Ibsen, and specially Strindberg'. As if this were not odd enough in a man still in his thirties, he has another claim to uniqueness. Among all the dramatists we have considered he alone has not only never had a West End success with one of his plays, but has never had a play staged in the West End at all.

The explanation of this second statement is simple: he has distinguished himself up to now entirely as a television playwright, though among the playwrights at present exclusively wedded to television he stands out as by far the most individual and exciting. Since he began writing he has worked as a complete professional in television, turning his hand (in the early days at least) to anything which offered; contributions to situation series like *Knight Errant,* collaboration with Francis Durbridge on a detective serial *The World of Tim Frazer,* adaptations of Edgar Wallace's *On the Spot* and of H. G. Wells's *Kipps* (this last, however, was a labour of love – somewhat spoilt, for Exton at least, in the execution), and so on. But he has also written eight plays, and with these he has built up a reputation to excel that of many of the stage dramatists we have been considering – some measure, incidentally, of the prestige the once-despised medium of television has been acquiring in the last few years, although, on the other hand, that it has done so is largely the work of Exton and others who have been encouraged to try their hand by A.B.C.'s 'Armchair Theatre' or by the drama department of Granada.

Exton was born in 1930, educated at Christ's Hospital, and after an initiation into school drama went on to the Central School of Speech and Drama. He says himself that he was a bad actor and determined to get out of the business as soon as he could; the next few years saw him acting intermittently up and down the country with various reps (not to mention interludes in an advertising agency, a dog-biscuit factory and a coffee bar), though he tended to gravitate as far as possible away from acting and towards stage management. Finally he found employment as stage manager and small-part actor with Donald Albery, and settled reasonably happily to this job, except for a growing dissatisfaction at the sort of play he had to deal with. His first step as a playwright was taken around this time, in the simplest way possible; he was complaining, as usual, about the poor quality of the day's drama when his wife, herself an actress, became sufficiently exasperated to throw at him the stock reply 'Well, if you think it's that bad, why don't you do better yourself?' Which is precisely what he set out to do, sitting down to write something which finally emerged as *No Fixed Abode*.

No Fixed Abode was originally meant for the theatre, though Exton now sees it as 'quite unsuited to stage . . . too intimate and uneventful, not sufficiently heightened'. However, by a series of lucky chances he showed it to an actress friend, who showed it to a producer at Granada, and it eventually appeared, with resounding success, on television. The play is, as the author's description suggests, an essay in minute realism, and it was inspired – the background if not the action – by an experience of his own during a lean time after a disastrous repertory season in the West Country. Its scene is a doss-house dormitory and there are just four characters apart from the Guv'nor: Grandpa, Lofty, Corp, and Tich. The play has virtually no plot in the conventional sense – it simply allows us to watch the interplay of the characters and learn something of them during the casual contacts of one night. There are Grandpa, a tough, uncommunicative old man just out of hospital, Lofty, a non-union building worker, and two jailbirds, of very different sorts: Tich, a stupid and insecure young man obsessed with the idea of getting on, and Corp, who spent a time in military prison for maiming a sergeant who had previously debauched his refugee wife. In the second act there is a brief scuffle between Corp and Tich over a pair of shoes Tich has stolen from Grandpa, and then a long conversation between Corp and Grandpa in which they plan to set up business together as buskers, Grandpa taking it all quite seriously and Corp going along with it half wishfully, but perhaps more to please him than anything else. In the morning the proprietor of the doss-house looks like making trouble over the fight and Grandpa panics, denying all connection with it: Corp then takes all the blame upon himself and leaves. Grandpa's dreams of a companionable future busking are shattered.

The core of the play is to be found in an exchange between Grandpa and Lofty near the end. Lofty has been gently reproaching Grandpa for letting Corp take all the blame:

GRANDPA: I'm an old man, though. I got scared.
LOFTY: I know.
GRANDPA: No, you *don't*. You *don't* know. I tell you I'm an old
man. I'm going to die – and nobody won't care. It'll
be as if I hadn't lived at all. As if I just hadn't lived.
LOFTY: No, it won't. . . .
GRANDPA: That's why I wanted to do this busking. If I'd done this
busking – well – there might be somebody. You know –
somebody might see me and one day, when I was dead,
they might say . . . 'What happened to that funny old
bloke what used to do that dancing with that other
bloke? . . .'
LOFTY: Reckon we're all like that, Grandfer.

Here Exton touches for the first time on a theme which
recurs, in one guise or another, in nearly all his plays, but
especially in the realistic trilogy which first made his name, *No
Fixed Abode, The Silk Purse*, and *Where I Live:* the desperate
need of man in modern society to feel he belongs, the endless
search for a context, a hierarchy, a fixed standard by which he
can see himself set in a clear relationship with other human
beings. In *No Fixed Abode* all four characters are in some way
uprooted: Tich by his determination to establish a new and
superior position for himself, dishonestly if necessary (and, of
course, more immediately by his spell in prison); Lofty by his
mysterious 'principles' about union membership, which keep
him roaming the country in search of work and hardly ever
able to see his wife and children; Corp by his experiences with
the sergeant in Germany and by the subsequent and quite incidental death of his wife; Grandpa simply by the fact of being
old, having outlived his contemporaries and finding himself left
with only one son who does not care whether he lives or dies.

Metaphorically, as well as literally, they have 'no fixed
abode', and their restlessness and malaise is seen by Exton as in
many ways symptomatic of the general predicament of twen-
tieth-century man. In an interview he gave to *The Times*
shortly after the production of *Where I Live* he made the point
explicit in answer to the question, would he agree that his view
of life was basically pessimistic?

I think it must be: certainly it comes out that way in my work, though I must admit that I do not know why it should be – that's something I am still working out for myself. The idea at the back of much that I write, it seems to me, looking at it after the event, is a regret for established values such as one imagines existing before 1914 – that magic number which always seems to mark the border-line between 'then' and 'now'. The breaking down since then of religious and social rules and classifications seems to have left many people uncomfortably adrift, without an established framework even to react against and break out of. Of course, there is a paradox here, since I personally do not regret the break away from religion and class-stratification – I'm an agnostic, or something, or nothing, and I imagine that I am probably happier than I would be in a more rigidly patterned society – and yet I cannot help recognizing that most of the characters I invent in drama are affected by the malaise which comes from this lack of fixed standards.

In so far as this relates to class as well as to personal relation-ships, it offers a valuable guide to his next play, *The Silk Purse*. (Actually, the next play he wrote was *Some Talk of Alexander*, a charming light comedy about a retired sergeant-major's woo-ing of a widowed fruiterer with a difficult son which Exton dismisses as 'not honest . . . an attempt to play safe by giving the public what I supposed they wanted', but this was not produced until some time later.) *The Silk Purse* offers a subtle and significant variation on the traditional drama of parental reactions to a daughter's marriage 'beneath her'. Mummy and daddy are living in a state of faded gentility in a faded London suburb when Anne comes home with Peter, whom she has secretly married and who turns out, horror of horrors, to be an apprentice copy-writer for an advertising firm, son of an engine-driver, and clearly 'unsuitable'. Ann thinks so, too, to a certain extent; though she married Peter because he was a man and a much more interesting one than the products of minor public schools her parents usually thought suitable for her to know, she still wants him to tell her parents, for the time being anyway, that he was at a public school and that his father is a Civil Servant.

Once the truth is out, though, another truth also comes out: that the tensions in the family come from precisely the same thing having happened to the older generation: Doris too mar-ried, she believed, beneath her, and has devoted the last thirty years to changing Robert into a gentleman, a sow's ear into a silk purse. It has been a constant strain, he hates her for it, and she remains grimly aware that she has not quite succeeded. There is no simple resolution; Doris and Robert are beyond help but so, too, possibly, are Anne and Peter. Robert regards Anne, in his heart of hearts, as a 'stuck-up little bitch', the fact that it was his hard-earned money which made her so soothing his feelings not a bit. And he may well be right about her; his warning to Peter that she will want to emasculate him in precisely the same way that Doris has already done to himself may well be all too accurate.

But more important even than the obvious social and personal conflicts among the four participants is the evident fact that the standards which are invoked and by which they judge each other are in any case no more than a polite fiction. There is no 'real' system for them to measure themselves against, and the conviction of Doris and Robert that whatever their actual position in the world they are in some quasi-mystical sense superior by virtue of breeding and upbringing to, say, the upstart engine-driver's son is vitiated by their own uneasy half-realization that they are living in a world of fantasy. They continue to cling to it, however, since it is all they have, their only comfort, and even a fictional system to live by is better than no system at all. As much as any of the drifters in *No Fixed Abode* they have been cast adrift by society and have no way of knowing where they belong except to appeal to the probably imaginary splendours of a vanished age to make their position in a world which really no longer has any use for them at least bearable.

Another character adrift in a world which does not any longer want him is at the centre of *Where I Live*, the third play of this group. His tragedy to begin with is that he has not yet realized the fact: an old man in his seventies, Dad lives with his married daughter, Jessy, and her husband, Bert. He constantly compares Bert unfavourably to his own son, George, whom he worships, though George has never done anything for him. It is not that Bert and Jessy resent the old man so much in himself, though he can be very trying and never understands what a drain he is on their modest resources, but they resent the unfairness of the situation, and Jessy determines that George and Vi must do their share in looking after him. George and Vi are too selfish to agree to this, and in her bitterness Jessy decides that Dad shall find out exactly what sort of person his precious George is. She wants him to go, of course, but more than that she wants him to see the truth about his children and be properly grateful if he stays. What she does not recognize until too late is the hurt she must do her father in bringing this revelation to light, since in the process it must be made clear to him that basically neither of his children wants him, and he is being used, without any consideration of his own feelings, as a pawn in the rivalry between them.

Again we find an insoluble dilemma which really exists only because of the shifting and uncertain codes of behaviour in the modern world. Once, as Exton himself points out, there would have been no question of choice when considering how one should deal with an aged parent, but now, except in such closely knit groups as the Jews and Irish of the East End, there is a choice, and the force of the traditional family duties is purely nominal; they become merely a matter of personal inclination. There is, of course, much more to the play than a simple *pièce à thèse* on this theme; the character of Jessy in particular offers a subtle study of conflicting and in the end mutually exclusive emotions, but the fact that she lives in a world where her personal feelings in the matter can become such a vital factor in the fate of her father is in itself indicative. Naturally, to depict the situation in these terms may well imply too rosy a picture of the past, but whether the pre-1914 era of security and accepted values ever had any objective reality is beside the point; several characters in the plays *believe* that it did – Robert in *The Silk Purse* and the fanatical central character of Exton's unperformed stage play *The Land of My Dreams* (significant title!) specifically say so, while the older characters are always nostalgic for the past – and as far as the author's own beliefs are concerned, Exton has said, reasonably: 'I suspect that if I had what I think I envy in others, I wouldn't like it – even supposing that it really exists. But then, if one is nostalgic for something which exists only in one's mind, that does not diminish the potency of the nostalgia.'

All the plays Exton had written up to this point have a number of things in common both in subject-matter and in technique. They are all minutely realistic in the sense that though what the dramatist is saying is perfectly coherent (these are no shapeless naturalistic slices-of-life) he never raises his voice or employs any of the normal heightening devices of oratory to say it. Whether or not he is right about *No Fixed Abode* being altogether unsuitable for the stage, it is obvious that it and the other plays (all of which, incidentally, would be quite easy to stage as they stand in that they have little variation of locale, small casts, and do not involve any virtuoso attempts to 'make the most of the medium' of television) would require a very special, intimate sort of theatre, like Reinhardt's Kammerspiele in which, it is recorded, the movement of a finger had the same effect that the movement of a whole arm had in a larger theatre. But the Kammerspiele of today is obviously television; the television camera can with the greatest ease invest the slightest flicker of an eyelid with significance, and as well as being able to open a play out and give it mobility it can worm its way into a play, moving among the characters with an almost uncomfortable intimacy. Exton explained this function neatly in the interview previously quoted:

Apart from anything else, television offers one such a wonderful chance to explore individual characters. People are constantly interesting, just in themselves – look at any unscripted television interview. Naturally in a play one has to organize, heighten, and select, but one can approach the same effect in television drama, concentrating on the medium's intimacy and immediacy. The actors can talk almost face to face with their audience, without raising their voices or exaggerating anything, so that realism is 'natural' to television in a way that it isn't for any other medium. On the stage, for example, as soon as one has to 'project' to the back of the theatre this sort of detailed realism is impossible.

At this time, however, he felt that the distinction between stage and television worked the other way, too, that for him television was limited to the realistic ('I cannot conceive of a television play which is not realistic in style'). But with his very next play, *Hold My Hand, Soldier,* he was himself to provide a striking repudiation of this view.

This strange battlefield drama of the dead and the dying, originally and more aptly entitled *The Sainthood Stakes,* has a cast of only three characters: a desperately wounded officer, a private who finds him and tries to save him, and a corporal who joins them, out only for himself and with just one idea – to save his own skin. The drama is entirely one of personal conflicts, or a personal conflict, the officer being effectively out of it and merely a counter in the battle between the private and the corporal. Both of these, in bold contrast with the characters in Exton's previous work, are conceived in thoroughly non-realistic terms, as a classic opposition of good and evil. The corporal is vicious, pointlessly, self-indulgently, and in the end self-destructively vicious, with a streak of sadism which drives him to torment the dying officer and the private far beyond anything which his avowed single concern for number one would explain (in the end, indeed, he has to admit that his behaviour showed weakness, since he indulged his hate of officers by staying to enjoy the spectacle of an officer dying when prudence would have dictated his flight – a life of complete selfishness too requires its sacrifices). The private is also inexplicable in realistic terms, since judging him at that level one would find oneself asking whether in his situation anyone could be so intuitively, uncomplicatedly good: he is not conventionally noble, he does not do things on principle, but he has a slogging goodness of heart, an unquestioning, and possibly mistaken – the matter remains in question – feeling for what is right which makes him virtually unassailable.

The conflict between these two opposites is seen at its clearest and purest in the last act, when the officer is dead and the private, having taken over the now badly wounded corporal as his charge, deposits him, protesting and ungrateful as ever, by the fallen crucifix in a ruined cathedral. As the corporal goes on explaining about the sacrifices involved in a life dedicated ruthlessly and unswervingly to the advancement of self the private suddenly realizes the truth; that the people like the corporal, whom he has vaguely envied all his life for knowing what was best for number one and acting decisively on that knowledge while he just stood aside and watched, have not enjoyed their life any more than he has.

I just stood there and I didn't know anything. I just had a sort of vague feeling that I ought not to leave that officer. That it wasn't right. But you *knew*. You knew what to do. You wanted to leave him – then you decided that you'd enjoy watching him suffer, because you hated him. . . . You've made me realize that you haven't enjoyed life any more than I have. You've been so busy being selfish that you haven't enjoyed it any more than I have.

A moment of understanding exists between them; at last they realize that in them the extreme opposites of human behaviour meet, but it is too late, for the corporal is dying, and when the private leaves at the end we have no clear indication whether full communication has at last been achieved or not.

Exton himself is now unhappy about the play, feeling that though it says a number of things which were and are important to him the expression is gauche and the play really needed further work on it before production. There is an element of truth in this: the balance between the realistic side of the presentation and the deeper symbolism is not always maintained with full conviction, and one remains aware, even if the awareness is not particularly disturbing, of a certain disparity between the characters and the relatively realistic setting into which they are put. The sheer intensity of Exton's vision carries off *Hold My Hand, Soldier* (backed up, of course, by his unfailing technical skill in the invention of lively, believable dialogue and the disposition of his materials to produce the maximum dramatic effect), but sometimes it is a close thing, and a certain amount of concern was felt at the time on the score that he might perhaps be heading eagerly in what would eventually prove to be the wrong direction for his particular talents.

All such fears, however, were dispelled by his next play, *I'll Have You to Remember*, which fused the two modes, symbolic and realistic, into a whole of extraordinary force and power. On the surface George and Milly James are just two derelicts, bypassed by the world, to whom their once resplendent mansion is now little more than a vast and echoing hovel, mouldering and cobweb-filled, in which they must last out the remains of a drab half-life amid the litter of empty milk-bottles and piles of unopened letters. But clearly Exton's plunge into the tangles of overt symbolism in *Hold My Hand, Soldier* has left him with a finer appreciation of the unfathomable depths which are hidden just beneath the fragile surface of civilized life, and as we learn more and more of the two characters' situation they become charged with a quasi-allegorical significance; they are everyone whose present existence is rendered impotent by hopeless brooding on a past beyond remedy.

As the play goes on they grow gradually, these creatures of premature and querulous senility, from colourless pygmies, crouched apathetically in front of the television, to monsters of savage frustration, large enough to fill the whole mansion with the force of their hatred and despair. And the cause of it all is the fate which ten years ago overtook their son John, for which each blames the other. He committed suicide when his wife left him; for George this is because Milly spoiled him and tamed him into a weak, dependent mother's boy; for Milly it is more because George bullied him nearly into a breakdown by forcing him to do everything he considered 'manly' against his inclinations. Consequently they appear to hate each other, but more importantly they hate themselves – the house gradually falling into ruins is the symbol of their own minds tottering on the brink of insanity as they try to forget and wait for death. The only disturbance in this routine is the arrival of a letter from John's widow, saying that she wants to visit them and bring their grandson with her; it is this which brings George and Milly face to face with each other and with themselves, and which ultimately provides a ray – no more – of hope in their dark lives.

I'll Have You to Remember finally established Exton, to anyone who yet had doubts (or still felt that drama on television somehow didn't count) as one of the leading talents of his generation. In the two television plays he wrote next he went on abundantly to confirm this, though in a quite unexpected way. Both *The Big Eat* and *The Trial of Doctor Fancy* are savagely satirical; so much so that both were found excessively strong meat by the company for which they were originally intended. The explanation of this disturbance in the case of *The Big Eat*, refused altogether by A.B.C. for 'Armchair Theatre' and subsequently snapped up by the B.B.C., is not far to seek. It is a scathing attack on materialistic advertising culture, symbolically embodied in an eating competition organized by a major food company. For enormous prizes – a house and furniture, two cars, a lifelong supply of Ffarmyarde-Ffreshe products – entrants are made to eat competitively, under the benign sponsorship of a posturing M.P. who just happens to be the managing director's brother. The play is *comédie noire*, as black as they come, of an all-out bitterness designed to make an audience flinch rather than roar with laughter, the climax of unpleasantness coming with the chef's account of the new 'freezi-squeeze' method of slow slaughter, during which Harold Britten, the more expert and likeable of the contestants, dies to the laughter and applause of a moronic audience, and the feeble ministrations of a young man who has been persuaded to stand in for the firm's unwilling doctor. Still, the dead man's sorrowing family reason, perhaps all is not lost; if competitive eating is a vocation, maybe the son can take up where the father left off; certainly, all things considered, the firm would be well advised to work something out. . . .

One would hardly expect this sort of thing to go down well with advertisers, but the case of *The Trial of Doctor Fancy* is a little more mystifying. The play was directed, like *Where I Live, I'll Have You to Remember*, and *The Big Eat*, by Ted Kotcheff, A.B.C.'s ace director, recorded by A.B.C., and then shelved indefinitely on grounds of taste. The story postulates a fantastic conspiracy between a trouser-manufacturer and a fashionable surgeon to persuade people that they are too tall, suffer terrible neuroses because of it, and can only be cured by amputation of both legs at the knee. The surgeon, of course, makes a profitable business out of the amputations, the trouser-manufacturer supplies the victims with special clothes, and everyone is happy. The amputees have their own clubs, they belong, they are insiders: they even marry each other, and the only odd man out is the idealistic young doctor who has brought the charges against Fancy. But of course the urge to conformity is too great: Fancy is praised as a humanitarian and benefactor, and acquitted on all charges – by a jury who, as they move out of court, prove all to be amputees themselves. The play is a biting parable illustrating – far more effectively than Ionesco's *Rhinoceros* – the lengths to which people will go not to feel odd man out, not to be noticeably different from their fellows. Tell them they are too tall, not stock size, and they will have their legs cut off to fit in; there is no limit to human gullibility and conformism. Like *The Big Eat, The Trial of Doctor Fancy* is a *comédie grinçante* (to use Anouilh's expressive phrase), full of bitter, savage satire which like the carpet-sweeper beats as it sweeps as it cleans: it clears our minds of cant, but the clearance is hardly a comfortable experience.

The two plays show a hitherto unexpected side of Exton's talent, a ruthless Swiftean black humour which approaches the inhuman, though it could hardly be further removed from the modishly 'sick'; it is directed exclusively against those human beings who have deliberately dehumanized themselves to become animals or machines, and what could be more eminently sane and healing than that? They are among the most powerful works this brilliant, disturbing talent has given us, and undoubtedly two of the most astonishing products yet of British television.

Where will Exton go from here? *I'll Have You to Remember* began life in his mind as a possible stage play. After writing it in its present form for television it continue to grow in his mind, and he took time off from his television activities to write a stage play, *The Land of My Dreams*, which, though not by any stretch of imagination the same play, does embody certain aspects of the George-Milly relationship in a completely different plot: a British fascist leader is preparing his little group to welcome back his son from prison, where he has been serving a sentence for killing a Jew; the leader's wife has retired, like Milly, to a state of gloom and apathy, mixed with resentment that her husband can no longer satisfy her physically (a theme which occurs also in *The Silk Purse* as well as in *I'll Have You to Remember*), but stemming chiefly from her know-

14 'A Slight Ache'

15 'No Trams to Lime Street'

ledge that the son killed the Jew not because he was a Jew but because he was her lover. The play is primarily an atmospheric piece, with little plot and not much progression – the wife tries to make her husband face the truth, without much success, and in the process herself comes back a little into the world, but that is all: the whole point of the action is that the son is not coming and never will, so it can hardly be other than inconclusive. Exton himself was not very happy with the result, and finally decided to re-write the play for television. After *The Trial of Doctor Fancy* Exton wrote another stage play, this time in his 'black' manner, about a school for hangmen – 'Just to get it out of my system' he says. His major television works since then are *Are You Ready for the Music?* (1965) and *The Boneyard* (1966). The first is a strange and tenuous atmosphere-piece about an actor playing *Hamlet* on tour and a girl he encounters in his lodgings, who lives in a world of nostalgic fantasy and seems ready-made as a real-life Ophelia. All the characters are dreamers, the girl's family as much as her, and the actor who tries to lure her out into the 'real' world perhaps more than any. In *The Boneyard* we have only one character who is a dreamer, or at any rate in his own estimation a visionary. P.C. Miller believes that he is addressed directly by the figure on a crucifix in the local cemetery, and the play is a black farce in Exton's best manner about the troubles he runs into not only with his own practical superiors but also with the church itself, which, as represented by the vicar, remains determinedly sceptical. More recently still he has at last had a stage play produced, *Have You Any Dirty Washing, Mother Dear?* (1969), a witty satirical fantasy about the deliberations of a Parliamentary committee regulated by an intricate structure of absurd rules and conventions. Clearly he remains as unpredictable as ever, and still has many surprises up his sleeve for us, whether on his original home ground, television, or on radio, the cinema screen, or the West End stage. And in whatever medium he chooses to work we may feel sure that the results will continue to witness the strength and independence of his talents, for 'oldfashioned' or not in his allegiances, he remains clearly one of the true originals in British drama today.

R

JOHN MORTIMER

Like Clive Exton, John Mortimer sees himself as a pretty traditional sort of playwright, in whom traditional influences are at
work (Dickens, Chekhov, the Russian novelists), and feels that
his admiration for the plays of Pinter and Simpson, the ideas of
Osborne and Wesker, does not imply any very close kinship.
Many of his critics, particularly those unequivocally left of
centre, have tended to agree with him, suggesting that though
on a number of occasions he has been bracketed with 'new
dramatists' – in reviews like *One to Another, Pieces of Eight*, and
One Over the Eight, and in Emlyn Williams's triple bill *Three*,
where *Lunch Hour* was presented with one-acters by Pinter and
Simpson – he is really an 'old dramatist' in disguise, writing 'in
almost every respect typical Shaftesburiana', as a reviewer in
Encore put in connection with *The Wrong Side of the Park*.

Now there is something in this: certainly *The Wrong Side of
the Park* in particular is nearer the sort of play which a British
dramatist would be writing now if no real challenge to the
supremacy of Rattigan had been heard in the theatre than
almost any other new play by a writer under forty. But even
here there are important differences, and when one looks more
closely at Mortimer's one-act plays it rapidly becomes clear
that he is after, on a more popular level, the same sort of thing
as many of his contemporaries. His subject, like theirs, is more
often than not the failure of communication, the confinement to
and sometimes the liberation from private dream-worlds; his
approach to language is not so far from that of, say, Alun
Owen, involving the use of a hypersensitive ear for the way
people really talk and a talent for selecting and heightening to
produce a fully theatrical eloquence which yet carries the hall-
mark of reality.

To a large extent the differences between his works and those
of the other new dramatists – almost alone of them (Exton ex-
cepted) he applies his exploratory techniques to the middle
classes in decline rather than the working classes ascendant –
can be traced to his background, which is virtually unique for a
dramatist of this generation. Born in 1923, he was educated at

Harrow and Oxford, spent the war as an assistant director and then scriptwriter with the Crown Film Unit, in 1948 qualified as a barrister and continued during the next eight years to practise at the bar while writing six novels: *Charade, Rumming Park, Answer Yes or No, Like Men Betrayed, The Narrowing Stream,* and *Three Winters,* which also exists in a radio version. It was for radio, too, that he wrote his first play, *The Dock Brief,* which won the Italia Prize and made him realize that in drama 'at last I was writing what I had wanted, all my life, to say'. Since then he has entirely given up the novel and concentrated on drama, producing ten more plays and a number of revue sketches, as well as working on the scripts of several films.

In keeping with all this, his plays take place entirely in a seedy middle-class world of run-down private schools, draughty seaside hotels, nine-to-five offices and the shabbier corners of the courts. *What Shall We Tell Caroline?* and *David and Broccoli* are both set in schools, *The Dock Brief, Two Stars for Comfort,* and at least one of the sketches have law in the background, and so, in a more roundabout way, does *I Spy,* though it is set in a seaside hotel; most of the rest are about office workers at work or at home in faded but 'quite nice' suburbs on the wrong side of the park. The world they present is consistent in its mixture of tragedy and comedy, the mixture being a practical expression at once of Mortimer's views on what the writer should be doing in the modern world and what the dramatist specifically should be offering audiences in the theatre.

The classic statement of Mortimer's attitude to comedy comes in the introduction to his *Three Plays*:

Comedy [is], to my mind, the only thing worth writing in this despairing age, provided the comedy is truly on the side of the lonely, the neglected, the unsuccessful, and plays its part in the war against established rules and against the imposing of an arbitrary code of behaviour upon individual and unpredictable human beings. There may, for all I know, be great and funny plays to be written about successful lawyers, brilliant criminals, wise schoolmasters, or families where children can grow up without silence and without regret. There are many plays that show that the law is always majestic or that family life is simple and easy to endure. Speaking for myself

I am not on the side of such plays and a writer of comedy must choose his side with particular care. He cannot afford to aim at the defenceless, nor can he, like the more serious writer, treat any character with contempt.

In an interview with *The Times* he has amplified this in so far as it concerns the immediate effect of his comedy on its audience:

> I use comedy because it's a better weapon than frontal attack. I want to give audiences the shock of recognition in which they see actors reflecting their own behaviour and laugh at it. I want to open their hearts. Normally they come along expecting to see something funny or something serious. But, as we know, life isn't like that, and I don't force the two things apart. In any case, it makes for surprise when you don't know what to expect next. There's the interaction between reality and illusion, circumstance pulling against fantasy. It gives you that feeling of your stomach turning over.

The implications of these statements (which would, incidentally, fit very well what Chekhov is doing in his plays or, given a slightly more grotesque colouring, what Dickens or Gogol are at in their novels) might lead one to expect something more overtly on the offensive than, in fact, emerges in Mortimer's work. Indeed, Mortimer's championship of 'the lonely, the neglected, the unsuccessful' is the more telling in that it is, strictly, an elevation of them and not a degradation of 'the others' – in Mortimer's plays there are no ready-made villains on whom the blame can be put ('This man would not be lonely and unsuccessful if it were not for . . .'); instead, the seedy and down-trodden are accepted on their own terms, as human beings, mixtures inevitably of good and bad qualities, and then without glossing over or minimizing the bad qualities, Mortimer gradually unfolds the good for our inspection.

The danger in this is obvious enough: that in showing all one's characters in the best possible light one will fall imperceptibly into the sort of sentimental whimsy favoured by Frank Capra and Robert Riskin in such thirties comedies as *Mr Deeds Goes to Town*, *Mr Smith Goes to Washington*, and *You Can't Take it With You*, in which each character tends to be established by some 'quaint', 'lovable' peculiarity (as though for a contemporary comedy of humours), and a fantasy world of good intentions is hopefully substituted for the real world in which, even at its most comic, everybody does not mean well. Up to now Mortimer has managed to avoid falling into this particular trap, though he is often near enough the brink for his audience to be aware of the danger. Partly it is his taste for the grotesque (Dickens is the obvious parallel here) which saves him, and partly his precise ear for the way people really talk, which enables him, by a sort of sleight of hand if nothing else, to give his plays a certain stiffening of reality whenever they look like going too soft on him.

These qualities are evident right from his first play, *The Dock Brief* (1957), originally written for radio but later performed on television and the stage. This is an extended duologue between a simple prisoner who has disposed of his wife and the broken-down but continually hopeful barrister who has been assigned by the Court to defend him. Morgenhall, the barrister, sets rapidly about weaving an elaborate fantasy about the trial, gaily inventing surprise witnesses, rehearsing his appeals to judge, jury, and the public, while Fowle, the accused, amiably plays all the other parts and from time to time introduces, rather apologetically, a note of reality into the proceedings. ('It's a remarkable thing,' says Morgenhall on one occasion when Fowle points out to him that the surprise witness he is banking on is a figment of his own imagination, 'but with no legal training, I think you've put your finger on a fatal weakness in our defence.') In the second scene it transpires that they have lost the case, but that paradoxically Fowle is to be freed, since as Morgenhall never said a word in his defence the trial is null and void. This Fowle kindly attributes to Morgenhall's ingenuity, and they both go with enough illusions left to continue living. The play is perfectly calculated in terms of radio (so perfectly, in fact, that it seems just a tiny bit overwritten in any other medium), and despite its soft core evades sentimentality by the strength of the elements of almost Gogolian grotesquery in it. Morgenhall in particular might well have stepped straight from the pages of Gogol – his seediness and unreliability, his proliferating fantasy life and his impotence in the world of action at once proclaim his kinship with many of the characters in *Dead Souls*.

Much the same sort of imaginative background recurs in Mortimer's second play, *I Spy*, also written for radio, transferred to television, and published in a revised version suitable for the stage. Here the law again figures, by implication, in the activities of the private detective Frute, as he tries to find something discreditable in the behaviour of Mrs Morgan, waitress in a seaside hotel, to explain to her husband why she could possibly have left him. Here, too, we find in full flower a quality which is only hinted at in *The Dock Brief* (mainly in the incidental reminiscences of Fowle) – an almost Betjemanesque nostalgia for the faded, the shabby, and the anachronistic. This applies here not only to the loving depiction of life in a rather down-at-heel seaside town during a wet summer, but also to the character of Frute, the detective, who is placed (as the lawyer his current employer sends to urge him on points out) beyond the pale by virtue of his job. ('What honourable man, I ask you, would invite a private detective to take tea with his wife or play with his children? The absurdity of the idea strikes you at once, does it not?') But then, if he is beyond the pale, so, in a sense, is Mrs Morgan, since she is, as Mortimer himself says, 'completely "good" from a moral point of view' (the only such he has ever enjoyed writing about), and even in a world of good intentions that is enough to place her apart. Inevitably, the two outcasts gravitate towards each other, and we last see them setting off together towards a future in which, the evidence provided for her husband, she can become Mrs Frute and lend a hand with the sleuthing, since after all 'another pair of eyes is often a help'.

With his third play, *What Shall We Tell Caroline?* Mortimer finally approached the theatre directly, and wrote what still remains in many ways his most completely satisfactory play. Caroline is the enigmatic daughter of Arthur and Lily London, who run Highland Close School, Coldsands, a small and dilapidated boys' prep school. It is her eighteenth birthday, but neither of her parents has noticed she is now nearly a woman. They have been too entangled in the curious emotional *ménage à trois* they share with Tony, the assistant master, who carries on a continuous but merely formal flirtation with Lily (or 'Bin' as her husband calls her).

It is the tension between the two men and Lily – Tony all little superficial attentions, Arthur deeply fond of her but able to express his love only through anger – which keeps their lives on an even keel, and when the unexpected maturing of Caroline and later her even more unexpected departure to a job in a London bank sets them questioning the relationship and trying to find some way of resolving it, disaster seems to be near, for it is only by keeping it as it is, and keeping their illusions about it, that they can preserve their *modus vivendi*. Caroline's unspeaking presence unleashes first a long speech by Lily in which she tries to explain to Caroline the dissatisfactions of her own life and do something to ensure that Caroline's will not go the same way, and then a confrontation of the two men, with Arthur finding himself insulted because Tony admits that he is not, in fact, in love with Arthur's wife. Again the solution is that put forward in *The Dock Brief*: man can stand only a very little reality, and after a short exposure to its dangerous radiations the best thing is to go back to the comfortable compromise of illusion.

It should not be taken, however, that this is necessarily Mortimer's solution to all problems; it is just the solution most suited to these characters, the only possible solution for them, in fact. In at least two of his later plays, the television play *Call Me a Liar* and his first full-length stage play *The Wrong Side of the Park*, it is the final encounter with truth, and the characters' coming to terms with the realities of the situation, which at last brings them the possibility of happiness and serenity. In the case of Sammy Noles in *Call Me a Liar* it is his habitual lying which has to be curbed; he is as incorrigible a weaver of fantasies as Morgenhall, but tries to do it in ordinary life, where most of his lies soon catch up with him. He has his reasons though; his first major lie was to pretend that the bomb which wiped out his home and family had nothing to do with him, because he did not want to be pitied, and subsequently he has gone on lying to make up for the lack of incident in his real life.

The only trouble is that when something really does happen to him – he meets and falls in love with a German girl looking for work from the employment agency he works for – he nearly loses the opportunity by continuing to lie; until, that is, the girl knocks some sense into him and persuades him that truth is better than illusion.

In *The Wrong Side of the Park* the lies are not conscious: they arise from the inability of the central character, Elaine Lee, to face the truth about her two marriages. She insists on seeing the present one as one long round of misery and boredom, and her conversation is full of elaborate reminiscences of her first marriage, which was so much fun, and her first husband, Peter, who was in every respect so much superior to Henry, her present husband. The truth of the matter, it turns out in the last act, is precisely the reverse of this: she could not bear Peter, and all the happy times she remembers and attributes to him were, in fact, part of her first acquaintance with Henry. Peter was killed in a road accident on the very night she went to bed with Henry for the first time, and ever since then she has been assuaging her feelings of guilt by systematically, albeit unconsciously, transferring in her mind every happy time she ever had with Henry to her marriage with Peter, leaving Henry, as he puts it, 'the formalities; the flowers we had to buy, the dates we had to remember; the guilt and the middle age'. But a moment of truth comes with a shock, just as before oblivion came with the shock of Peter's death; in a seance they hold to to get into communication with Peter something happens to Elaine, she rushes out to revisit 'home', the home she once shared with Peter, and on the way the truth at last begins to dawn. It will be a slow process, but once the truth has been faced she and her husband can start living again.

Both plays depend rather on a last-minute revelation which explains the actions of the central character; in *Call Me a Liar* it is not really vital that we should know why Sammy lies, but in *The Wrong Side of the Park* it is important that we should understand Elaine (and incidentally Henry), and it is a pity that the revelation is so long delayed and at the same time so completely predictable right from the middle of Act I. But then, *The Wrong Side of the Park*, for all its incidental felicities of character and dialogue, is essentially a one-act play blown up to three by the introduction (very neat and craftsmanlike in itself) of a largely irrelevant sub-plot concerning the machinations of a shady but amusing lodger to get hold of the lease of the house from Henry's crusty and eccentric old father in order to carry out some mysterious plans of his own. In these two plays, in fact, there are some signs that Mortimer's evident facility for writing speakable, lively, entertaining dialogue about almost anything is likely to get the better of him from time to time, at the expense of his plays as a whole: the character with the gift of the gab more or less highly developed (Sammy in *Call Me a Liar*, the lodger Miller in *The Wrong Side of the Park*) is obviously a sore temptation to him, since he can always be relied upon to fill up any gaps in the play with some conversational extravaganza and probably entertain the dazzled audience sufficiently in the process for them not to notice that what he is saying has little or no dramatic necessity and is really just so much makeweight. Also, the explanations, when they come, are rather badly treated and do not seem to have any real organic connection with the action they spring from and supposedly justify: *The Wrong Side of the Park* especially has rather the air of being chunks from a couple of characteristic, easygoing Mortimer one-acters pressed mechanically into the mould of the well-made play *à la* Pinero; such a play must have a revelation in the last act, and dutifully enough this has, but only at the expense of a lot of unnecessary and not particularly successful mystification earlier on.

Indeed, Mortimer is at his happiest when he does not have to explain directly, but can imply as much explanation as we are entitled to expect in the action of the play as it unrolls. For despite himself Mortimer seems to be at one with other dramatists of his generation in the belief that human behaviour cannot really be explained by some simple formula which makes everything clear; you cannot turn every play into a sort of whodunit – a why-did-he-do-it, perhaps – in which the clues are planted and then just before the curtain someone explains which was the one vital clue to explain a whole personality.

Life is seldom if ever as clear-cut as that: all sorts of explanations may fit the facts, and any or all of them may be true; motives are generally so mixed that even the principals in any given event do not know quite why they are acting as they are. When, as in *What Shall We Tell Caroline?* or one or two of his later plays, Mortimer is content just to show us such a situation and leave us to 'explain' it how we will, the result is far more satisfactory than in his cut-and-dried *pièces à thèse*, since then the audience's imagination is quickened instead of deadened, and the dramatist is compelled to integrate cause (what would be explained) and effect (what is actually said and done in the present) into dialogue of a fairly uniform density, instead of letting his play disintegrate into wads of aimless, if for the instant quite entertaining, chatter among which are scattered occasional hard nodules of too clinical explanation.

Several of the later one-act plays offer good examples of this less direct technique, and so do a number of the revue sketches, such as 'Triangle' in *One to Another*, in which a waitress weaves a web of amorous fantasy around two completely unconscious regular customers: 'Night Life' in *One Over the Eight*, in which a rope manufacturer tries first to interest his companion of the evening in his work and then, frantically, to escape the subject, and 'Please Step Down' in *Second Post!*, in which a plain, arty spinster uses all the wiles at her command over the telephone to lure down the man from upstairs. In these, obviously, the discipline of extreme brevity precludes explanation. The situations have to carry such explanation as they need as graphically and succinctly as possible – and the same applies slightly less forcibly in the one-acters for stage and television. In *Lunch Hour*, for example, we have what is in effect an extended sketch about a couple, a fairly respectable business-man and an office-girl, trying to find somewhere where they can make love in the lunch hour. He is not very expert, chooses a respectable boarding-house near a station and spins the landlady a story about having to talk something over quietly with his wife. But the secretary, being a simple unimaginative soul, begins to act as if what he has said is true, wants to know what was the business which was so urgent she should be summoned down from Scarborough to discuss it, and wonder if she ought to have anything to do with a man who can behave so heartlessly towards his (imaginary) loved ones. The joke is prolonged and elaborated much too far, but at least the characters are permitted simply to reveal themselves in what they say and do and the explanation ('Telling the truth is often a great concealment; we are given away by what we pretend to be') is kept for the preface to the published text.

In *The Encyclopaedist*, Mortimer's contribution to the B.B.C. Television series *They Met in a City*, the method is similar: an encyclopaedia salesman has three encounters with the same woman and sees three faces of her in three successive phases of her marriage, phases in which the question of knowledgeability plays an important part, hence the relevance of his encyclopaedias. And in *Collect Your Hand Baggage* we have another comedy of misunderstanding when Crispin, the forties bohemian surviving bravely into the sixties, decides to bestow himself as a favour on the daughter of his landlady, plain and therefore, he believes, loveless, only to find that she does not want him, has hardly noticed him, and is about to go off to Paris with someone else altogether. (This is an odd and none-too-well-balanced piece, since the role of the young people who accompany Crispin is never made clear, though they seem to have more significance than the sort of collective straight-man to him they are here required to be; Mortimer tells us in his introduction that 'It was written with another, larger play in mind; a play in which the youthful characters would play a bigger and more destructive part and the central character more fully represent, than Crispin, the errors of experience'. This is, in fact, a description of his later full-length play, *Two Stars for Comfort*, in which, apparently, he set out to make things rather clearer.) *Too Late for the Mashed Potato* is another television piece about the role of illusion in life, again very schematic in its demonstration of 'Lies for the sake of truth, infidelity for the sake of fidelity'; a husband revitalizes his marriage by pretending to flirt with a girl in a deserted Italian lakeside resort, and thus satisfying his wife's need for drama.

But arguably the most successful of all the later plays is

Mortimer's second foray into the world of school, *David and Broccoli*, written originally for B.B.C. Television. Here the scene alternates between two of Mortimer's pet stalking-grounds, the old-fashioned, slightly disreputable private school in North London and a faded residential hotel cluttered with potted plants and tea-room wickerwork. The story is that of a timid, unathletic boy's fear of and animosity towards 'Broccoli' Smith, the rough, powerful, but slow-witted P.T. coach. He has his chance to get even with Broccoli when he discovers Broccoli's weakness – a passion for the elementary occultism of Everyman's Almanac of future events – and exploits it to such effect that he convinces Broccoli that the end of the world is due the very next Thursday, the day of the prize-giving, and thereby brings about a scene as a result of which Broccoli leaves under a cloud, with no other job open to him. Though the central premise of the plot is rather far-fetched, the play scores by the precision with which the backgrounds are evoked and the unsentimental reality of the boys, particularly David, who is a fascinatingly accurate amalgam of overdeveloped intellect and undeveloped understanding: in his terror he sees no farther than the immediate object of his terror, and sees it as something to be disposed of at all costs. But even when Broccoli is routed and thoroughly cut down to size he feels, apparently, no particular compunction about having removed the one security in his victim's pathetic life: he is a child, yet he has vanquished a man, and that is enough. About children at least Mortimer has no illusions, and the end product, though evidently more fantasticated than *What Shall We Tell Caroline?* is as far away as that minor masterpiece from the sentimentality which always tends to soften unduly the sinister and grotesque elements in Mortimer's work.

As much can hardly be said for *Two Stars for Comfort*, his second full-length play, though it does in some respects show an advance on *The Wrong Side of the Park*: it is concentrated fairly and squarely on one character and the events which lead up to his belated moment of truth, and it resists the temptation to tie everything up too neatly with a cut-and-dried explanation of him and his way of life in the last five minutes. But these improvements are counterbalanced by the recurrence in exaggerated form of other faults from Mortimer's earlier work, notably the shameless reduction of minor characters (and even some major characters) to comedy-of-humours stereotypes, each tirelessly parroting variations on his or her *idée fixe*, and the tendency to play what is basically a rather slight and sentimental plot anecdote for considerably more than it is worth.

The story this time is a sort of minor-key reworking of the *Summer of the Seventeenth Doll* formula. For some years now Sam Turner has been running the Riverside Hotel on the banks of the Thames, happily regardless of bills and hard times and looking forward each year to regatta week, when his wife goes away to relatives at Ruislip, the lively young people come to stay, and he is called in to crown the Regatta Queen (with all the incidental advantages the job can be made to carry). This year things are different, however: when his wife leaves for Ruislip she really means it, and sets about obtaining a legal separation; business is going downhill and the arrangements of the regatta are handed over instead to his despised rival at the Station Hotel; the young people are not so carefree as they used to be; and this time, when he gets involved with one of them he finds himself taking it seriously and trying to hold on to her. In fact, he is getting old. Having given up the law in a moment of revelation and set out to keep a pub 'dedicated to the principle that man is born free and is everywhere not enjoying it', he has had his run of happiness, his succession of wonderful moments. But living in a sentimental dream-world of his own creation, telling people only what they want to hear (each of his regulars has a craving for comfort in constant need of satisfaction), and listening in return only to what he wants to hear, he has been brushing aside reality long enough, and now it is beginning to catch up with him. He is, as his latest Regatta Queen realizes, a hollow man who has gradually degenerated from being the master of his world to being its slave; he is worn out with feeding other people fantasies and incapable of speaking the truth for fear that someone should be upset – until, that is, she chooses to leave his comfortable but insecurely founded world of illusion for the cold world outside, and in consequence he decides as the curtain falls that it is time some changes were made.

The most obvious miscalculation in the play is Mortimer's apparent mistaking of this story, eminently suitable as it would be for one of his more insubstantial one-act *comédies larmoyantes*, for the real stuff of tragedy. Neither of the principal characters develops, they just change: Sam right at the end, when like his namesake in *Call Me a Liar* he is persuaded by the action of the girl he is involved with to forsake illusion and embrace reality; Ann, the girl, twice, first of all when she (predictably) succumbs to Sam's advances and the charms of a twirl of the drum-sticks, and then at the end when an unkind burlesque of her relationship with Sam staged by the other young people snaps her back, rather less explicably, to the realities of the situation. But the progression of their affair and the effect it has on them both is made the central theme of the play, a position it is far too weak to sustain. To support it Mortimer has in effect devised two contrasting choruses: the quartet of young people from *Collect Your Hand Baggage*, who represent presumably iconoclastic youth and vitality (though they appear rather softened and the 'bigger and more destructive part' they were intended to play is confined to their cathartic regatta-night entertainment), and the matching quartet of old regulars (the woman whose one subject of conversation is her vanished husband; the schoolmaster obsessed with local history, and so on). For the most part, in fact, these other characters are present just to fill in any gaps in the action with amusing and characterful conversation – which they do quite efficiently, though by this stage in Mortimer's work the device is becoming rather too mechanical for comfort, an over-glib way of inflating a slight inspiration to superficially imposing proportions.

Mortimer's latest full-length stage play, *The Judge* (1966) is more problematical. A judge at the end of his career comes to hold his last assizes in his home town, which he has never returned to during the previous forty years. Evidently he has come back to deal with some unfinished business; evidently, too, he is quietly going off his rocker. He talks darkly of past crimes he has allowed to go unpunished. He expects some sort of protest in court, some challenge of his fitness to judge, and we gather that the crime must be something he has done himself, or connived at, in his youth: it is himself first and foremost that he wants judged. And little by little, from his devious allusions, we can piece together that it was a guilty liaison with a girl living in the cathedral close, that he agreed to her having an abortion, and has been haunted by this, and the wrong he feels he then did her, ever since. Now he has come to square things, to face the accusation he feels must necessarily come from the girl, now a woman in late middle age keeping a run-down antique shop as a front for a sort of casually organized and perhaps largely amateur brothel. By half-time the judge has got a couple of his old schoolmates, now a doctor and a journalist on the local paper (and both regular visitors at 'Aunt Serena's') into such a tizzy that they are ready to start a witchhunt against Serena, whom they imagine to be the object of the judge's obscure fulminations, in order to take the heat off themselves. From this arise some rather unlikely plot manœuvres, with Serena being not only ostracized by her regulars but set upon in the streets and chased home from the off-licences. And so, finally, to the inevitable confrontation between the judge and his past (Serena), from which, in a slightly unexpected way, he gains nought for his comfort, because not enough for his discomfort.

Basically, there is a good plot here, but in its treatment Mortimer has taken on several liabilities and then loaded things still further against himself by writing the play in the particular style he does. To begin with, it is surely important, for a plot so odd, highly charged and mysterious, that all the people involved should seem at the outset very ordinary and everyday. In particular, the judge, eaten up by a hidden obsession, should seem the model of correctness and sanity, instead of being presented as an evident nutcase from the start. Similarly, it would surely be more effective if his victim were a peaceable, respectable body, keeping, perhaps, lodgings for girls studying at the local teacher-training college, instead of the garrulous old bore she is here, wildly over-characterized with endless requests that others should save her life with a ciggy and chats about the Fitzroy and the Café Flore over glasses of cheap vino. It would also help if the various twists and turns of the plot were better motivated. For example, why are the judge's schoolmates so terrorized by him? What can a judge do to clean up local morals in a town where he is holding assize if the police are not playing along with him, as here they patently are not? To remove things even further from familiar reality, the play is written for much of the time in Mortimer's most flowery and picturesque vein, with a number of long addresses straight to the audience which rely on telling us (very eloquently, to be sure) about the town and its atmosphere instead of showing us in the course of the dramatic action. Clearly at long last Mortimer has hit in this play on a plot capable of going the necessary length for a whole evening's entertainment; what a pity, then, that he has not hit on the right style to make it work.

Mortimer remains in many ways an unknown quantity among the new dramatists, if only because he appears too completely knowable. There is no noticeable development between *The Dock Brief* and *The Judge*: each successive work has shown the general expertise, the amazing skill and facility with dialogue, and the thorough practical grasp of the medium for which it was originally intended which marked the first play of all, and the most we can proffer, tentatively, by way of a subsequent discovery is that the full-length play may not be his *forte* and that he should eschew the temptation to point his moral too plainly. Mortimer's world is consistent and instantly recognizable, and he knows his way round it with complete certainty: the question now is will he find it in subsequent works the trap it looks now like becoming, or see it rather as a launching-pad to the discovery of fresh worlds elsewhere? His most recent work does not begin to provide the answer.

PETER SHAFFER

Whereas with practically all the other dramatists considered in the body of this book it is the personal quality as much as anything in their writing which fascinates, the feeling it gives one of being allowed glimpses of a private world – more or less like our own, more or less recognizable in terms of the reality we see about us, depending on the writer – with Peter Shaffer the most interesting quality of his work is its impersonality. His work has all the classic qualities of the traditional dramatist – cast-iron construction, a coherent and well-plotted story to tell, solid, realistic characterization, extreme fluency in the composition of lively, speakable, exactly placed dialogue – but ultimately he emerges in it as mysterious and impalpable as Walter, the central character of *Five Finger Exercise*, who, if he is the hero, must be one of the most chilly and enigmatic heroes on record.

Shaffer fits in this section, evidently, more by accident than by design; if ever there was a dramatist whose works were meant for the stage it is he. But the fact remains that after a long apprenticeship spent writing and tearing up plays in the intervals of working in a New York library and a London music publishers (Shaffer was born in London in 1926, took a degree at Cambridge, and started play-writing almost immediately upon coming down) he had his first two productions on television before achieving a major West End success with *Five Finger Exercise*. And to be honest, it is unlikely that anyone would have predicted great things for him on the strength of these first two plays; the earlier, *Balance of Terror*, was a thriller about spies and counterspies tussling over an intercontinental ballistic missile, cunningly put together along conventional lines but nothing very out of the ordinary, and the later, *The Salt Lands*, was a patchily worked-out though serious and well-constructed attempt to present a classical tragedy situation in terms of modern Israel.

All the more surprising, then, that his first performed stage play, *Five Finger Exercise*, should be so outstandingly successful on every level. For one thing, in it Shaffer invades that most dangerous of all territories for an English dramatist, the prosperous upper-middle-class drawing-room of a house in the Home Counties. Not only that, but his play is put together with the theatrical aplomb of a Pinero, well provided with

s

dialogue of remarkable crispness and articulacy, and technically very much part of the mainstream tradition of British drama; it would have been written in much the same way (though perhaps it would not have found such ready backing) if John Osborne and the rest had never lived.

What is it doing, then, in a book about new drama? Not every writer under forty is a 'new dramatist' and not every first play produced since 1956 has a necessary claim to admittance, after all. Well, it claims our attention not only for its traditional virtues, which are considerable, but because if we look at it more closely it turns out to be an unusually skilful and unexpected foray of new ideas and new perceptions into the fustiest stronghold of convention; having convinced the old-fashioned West End playgoer that it is 'all right' – not sordidly concerned with the kitchen sink, and certainly not in any way experimental, but just an ordinary play about people like you and me – it proceeds bit by bit to strip its characters and their way of life bare with as much ruthlessness as Ionesco sets about rather the same business in *The Bald Prima Donna*. Only here the weapon is psychological penetration: Shaffer takes the typical Dodie Smith-Esther McCracken family – fussy, scatterbrained mother, stolid, inarticulate father, bossy tomboy daughter, arty varsity-bound son – and instead of accepting them as the self-evident, indisputable *données* upon which a light comedy or drama can be based, he asks us to look at them, consider why they are as they are, and what would happen if suddenly something unexpected, from outside their normal experience, should intrude on the settled picture of complacent mediocrity.

The intruder in this instance is Walter, a strange, charming, mysteriously reserved young German tutor who acts as a catalyst for all sorts of violent and unexpected emotional reactions. Each member of the household sees him as a potential ally or lover: the mother dreams perhaps of a discreet affair with him or more probably of amorous proposals flatteringly pressed upon her and skilfully parried; the father finds he can talk to him in a way which is unthinkable with his own son; the level-headed daughter finds his lack of involvement disconcerting, and the son discovers in him at last the congenial companion he has been seeking (his mother in a bout of bitter fury at the end, when Walter has revealed that his feelings for her are infuriatingly filial, suggests that Clive's feelings for him are tinged with homosexuality, but there seems no real reason for us to believe her).

The originality of the observation, all the more potent for being disguised beneath an apparently conventional surface, is paralleled by the veiled originality of the form of expression used. Taken line by line there is nothing at all surprising or upsetting about Shaffer's style: it is just the usual pruned, heightened realism of traditional stage parlance. But if we look at the play as a whole it at once becomes apparent that the action does not progress, as one would expect, by way of conversations leading purposefully towards clear stages in the dramatic argument; instead, the play organizes itself into a series of splendid self-revealing tirades, usually directed at the passive, uninvolved head of Walter, who remains so mysterious (necessarily to his function in the play) precisely because he alone of the characters is not permitted to reveal himself in this way – the other characters reveal themselves to him just because he does not react sufficiently to spoil the imaginary pictures of him they are building up in their minds or step outside the role each has assigned him in his or her personal drama.

Five Finger Exercise is immensely clever, extremely well written, and completely theatrical in the best possible sense of the term. It is also quite impersonal, almost as though the author has felt it his duty to keep himself entirely out of the picture. This is not necessarily a bad thing – most authors err in the other direction, by not detaching themselves sufficiently from the object of their labours – but it is disconcerting. Even more disconcerting, on the face of it, were the details released of the play Shaffer wrote next, *The Royal Hunt of the Sun*, a spectacle-cum-religious drama about the Spanish conquest of Peru. The complexities of its staging delayed its appearance for some time, and the next works of Shaffer we saw were two one-act plays, *The Private Ear* and *The Public Eye*, presented as a double bill in the West End in 1962.

The first shows Shaffer rather out of his depth with a lower-middle-class milieu. A tentative romance between a shy young clerk and a girl he met at a concert is rapidly destroyed when a smart-alec friend he has asked to advise him on the conduct of the affair first of all monopolizes the conversation and then helps him to see the girl as she really is – ordinary, non-intellectual, frivolous – rather than the paragon of Botticelli beauty and spirituality he has idealized her into. The story is predictable and the dialogue, particularly that of the flashy Ted, not very credible or precisely placed, though the play is put together with great technical aplomb. *The Public Eye* is much better: it concerns the remote-control affair of a young wife unjustly suspected of infidelity by her staid, older husband and the exotic, improbable detective whom the agency the husband patronizes has sent to track her. The agent is a part perfectly tailored to the eccentric personality of Kenneth Williams, who first played the role and for whom it may well have been written; he is the perfect detective mainly because he is the unlikeliest person one could conceive of for the job, and he has all the best lines, even at the end when he develops enough of a heart to bring wife and husband back together again. *The Public Eye* is the sort of play which is taken as being both witty and wise; in this case the wisdom is rather phoney but the wit is genuine enough, and that is a lot. Whether the bill supports Shaffer's claim to be a 'new dramatist' in any but the strictly chronological sense is another matter: the plays are the work of a good, solid, workmanlike talent and have no pretensions to be anything more.

The Royal Hunt of the Sun, when it finally emerged – produced by the National Theatre Company with great lavishness – seemed to remove Shaffer even further from 'new drama'. It was at once a spectacular drama and a think-piece written in rather elaborate literary terms. As Shaffer himself summarized its theme, it is 'a play about two men: one of them is an atheist, and the other is a god'. The atheist is Pissaro, Spanish conqueror of Peru, and the god is the Inca Atahualpa. The play, again to quote Shaffer, 'is about the relationship, intense, involved and obscure, between these two men, one of whom is the other's prisoner: they are so different, and yet in many ways – they are both bastards, both usurpers, both unscrupulous men of action, both illiterate – they are mirror-images of each other. And the theme which lies behind their relationship is the search for God, the search for a definition of the idea of God. In fact, the play is an attempt to define the concept of God'. Which is all well and good in theory, but seems to me to make for a rather heavy, self-conscious script in practice, highly respectable, intelligent, well-written (to use the great dismissive term of praise) but rather lifeless and unexciting. Fortunately the play is constructed with all Shaffer's cunning to give ample opportunity for two big performances in the central roles and for spectacular staging, with glittering golden sets and eye-catching Inca costumes. On this – admittedly less exalted – level of theatre it works very well, and achieved a big popular as well as critical success.

Shaffer's particular personal gifts were more happily displayed in his next, considerably less pretentious effort, *Black Comedy*. This glorious farce, written for the National Theatre, is based on one strikingly simple idea: the action takes place almost entirely in the dark, during a power failure, but the light-values are inverted, so that when the characters can see we are in darkness, and vice versa. The task of conveying that the action is all governed by the complete darkness in which it takes place called for virtuoso comedy playing, a challenge to which the National Theatre Company rose superbly; the complications arising from the hero's desire to impress his idiot deb fiancée's peppery father by borrowing, without permission, his queeny neighbour's most treasured possessions and then coping with the unexpected arrival (in the dark) of the neighbour and of his own former girl-friend, bent on mischief, followed one another with seeming inevitability and art-concealing art. When the play was staged in New York and in London's West End it was equipped with a curtain-raiser called, finally, *The White Liars*. Much rewritten between New York and London, it never came out very satisfactorily, but again it was nearly saved by Shaffer's gift for writing big acting parts: in this case the role of an apparently illiterate pop-singer who is able spectacularly to turn the tables on a fraudulent seaside clairvoyante who enters into an alliance with the singer's unscrupulous and parasitic manager. None of which, of course, has anything remotely to do with new drama as defined by the work, say, of Arden, Pinter, Ann Jellicoe or even John Osborne. But as long as it results in something as enjoyable as *Black Comedy*, who is likely to complain?

BY WAY OF
EXPERIMENT

The Arts through Thick and Thin

New year 1962 would reasonably be taken as the lowest ebb in the fortunes of that stalwart, long-standing London theatrical institution, the club theatre. At the beginning of 1956, had anyone been optimistic enough to predict a revival in British drama, he would certainly have picked the club theatres as the most likely place for it to start; by the beginning of 1962, if he were wondering – by this time fairly complacently – where the next batch of interesting new dramatists would emerge, the club theatres (or theatre, since the Arts was the only one left worth a moment's consideration) would have seemed just about the least likely place. And yet, as it happened, the Arts was the very place where the next batch did find a hearing. But before we go on to consider them it may be useful to go back a bit and consider exactly why in the meantime club theatres had fallen on such evil days – especially as it throws light also on the general effect the new drama in general and the English Stage Company in particular had been having on the theatrical scene into which they had so spectacularly intruded.

The idea of the theatre club first became current between the wars. Members would pay an annual subscription, often nominal, which would entitle them at least to buy tickets for performances and use the bar; where the facilities were more elaborate there might be a separation between theatre membership, for those who merely wanted to attend performances, and full club membership for those who wanted to eat at the restaurant, use the club for poste restante and so on. The advantages of this arrangement were two-fold. First of all, the registered membership provided a pool of interested people who could be relied on as a potential audience for plays a little out of the ordinary, could easily be kept in touch with club activities and if necessary jollied along a little, and were probably willing to accept rather less comfort in their surroundings and elaboration in the productions set before them than the ordinary paying customer in a West End theatre. Then, equally important, the club performances were not subject to the Lord Chamberlain's approval, being bounded in what they did only by the general obscenity laws; this meant that they could stage plays which were denied public performance altogether, and could present uncut plays which would be passed for public performances only after some cutting and rewriting.

Consequently, club theatres could risk producing plays which ordinary producers would consider wildly uncommercial, and were free to produce plays which might well be commercial but were not at that time permissible: anything referring directly to homosexuality, for instance; anything showing God on the stage; anything using a variety of fairly mild expletions such as even the most tender-minded theatregoer might hear any day on the pavement without blushing at but was supposed to find intolerable if delivered from a public stage. In short, as far as anyone seriously interested in the theatre was concerned, or even anyone interested in seeing something just a little off the beaten track, the club theatres had all the advantages. And so it was still, just, at the beginning of 1956. Even though rising costs, rebuilding schemes, and other external troubles had taken their toll, the club theatres that remained had virtually their pick of the best contemporary drama from the Continent and America, and were the best hope for any new dramatist to get a foothold on the London stage: Christopher Fry, for example, had first achieved a big success at the Arts with *The Lady's Not for Burning*, and moved on to better things; John Whiting had the relatively uncontroversial *Penny for a Song* presented publicly, but it was the Arts which staged *Saint's Day*.

What this meant in practical terms may be gauged by a quick look at the record of the Arts in the two years or so before the arrival of the English Stage Company. Since Campbell Williams took over the management of the theatre in December 1953 it had presented, *inter alia, Crime and Punishment,* Lorca's *Blood Wedding,* Pirandello's *Six Characters in*

Search of an Author (which subsequently transferred to the West End), Siobhan McKenna in *St Joan, The Immoralist* (after Gide), Pirandello's *The Rules of the Game,* André Obey's *Sacrifice to the Wind* supported by Ionesco's *The Lesson* (Ionesco's first appearance in London), Julien Green's *South,* O'Neill's *Mourning Becomes Electra* complete, Beckett's *Waiting for Godot* (another first appearance in London, later transferred to a public theatre), Betti's *The Burnt Flowerbed* (also a London first) and Anouilh's *Waltz of the Toreadors* (another transfer). A striking record by any standards. But already things were on the move. To begin with, the Royal Court immediately announced itself as in the market for interesting new drama from any source, and proceeded to snap up Brecht, Beckett, Ionesco, Sartre, and even Tennessee Williams; obviously a public theatre and a full-scale production would be preferable to a club theatre presentation, however good. Moreover, public taste was so far catching up that even not particularly adventurous managers had begun to see the commercial possibilities of Anouilh; *Waltz of the Toreadors* was to be the last major Anouilh play to begin its career in a club theatre. The reputation of the Royal Court and soon afterwards of Theatre Workshop was built on new British drama, and naturally a young hopeful would look to them rather than to the Arts for an opening. And, perhaps, worst of all, the Arts was scooped on three of the most famous and potentially profitable plays banned by the Lord Chamberlain, Arthur Miller's *A View from the Bridge,* Robert Anderson's *Tea and Sympathy,* and Tennessee Williams's *Cat on a Hot Tin Roof,* by another theatre club, The New Watergate, which had been temporarily resuscitated with a large West End home and a nominal subscription entirely as a means of evading the control of the Lord Chamberlain. This manœuvre led in its turn to a relaxation of the Lord Chamberlain's ruling on homosexuality in drama which promptly diverted most of the interesting plays which might otherwise have come the way of the club theatre to commercial managements.

For the time being the Arts continued respectably, with every now and then something exceptional: in 1957 Salacrou's *No*

Laughing Matter, Genet's *The Balcony* (*Les Bonnes* had been done the year before by a club since defunct, the New Lindsey), Lorca's *Yerma*, and a quirky gothick comedy by Mervyn Peake, *The Wit to Woo*; in 1958 O'Neill's *The Iceman Cometh*, Gabriel Marcel's *Ariadne*, and Tennessee Williams's *Garden District*; in 1959 Anouilh's *Traveller without Luggage*, Zero Mostel in *Ulysses in Nighttown*, and Dürrenmatt's *The Marriage of Mr Mississippi* (a London first); and at the beginning of 1960 O'Neill's *A Moon for the Misbegotten*. They also found one or two plays by new writers worth looking at: Roger Gellert's *Quaint Honour*, which handled a difficult subject – *amitiés particulières* at a public school – frankly, realistically, and without sanctimoniousness or sentimentality; Kenneth Jupp's *The Buskers*, an elaborate Pirandellian exercise which some thought promising, but which has been followed only by *My Representative*, *Strangers in the Room*, and *Blue and White*, television plays of unrelieved banality; Bernard Kops's *Change for the Angel*; and a double bill of undergraduate plays, one of which, *Deutsches Haus*, a very capable drama of service life in Germany by Richard Cottrell, subsequently turned up on television as *Marking Time*. But anyone who feared that standards were slipping when faced also with horrors like the pretentiously pseudo-poetical *Less than Kind*, the drivellingly problematical *A Lonesome Road* and, incredibly, *Something's Burning*, 'a cooking comedy by Bon Viveur', was soon to have ample confirmation of his fears. From early in 1960 the Arts more or less gave up as an independent management, and instead the house was for most of the time made available to any management or individual who chose to hire it. This seemed like the end. At best it might be used as a tryout theatre for the West End proper by an enterprising manager – Michael Codron, for example, opened Pinter's *The Caretaker* and the Pinter-Mortimer-Simpson triple bill *Three* there before taking them on to the public stage; three of his other plays, Henry Livings's *Stop It, Whoever You Are*, Barry Reckord's *You in Your Small Corner*, and Murray Schisgal's *Ducks and Lovers*, were not so lucky and consequently were seen only at the Arts. At worst it might be – and apparently was – hired by authors with more money than sense to put on plays the badness of which was almost beyond belief. A sad come-down for the first London home of Ionesco, Beckett, and Betti.

So things stood at the beginning of 1962. The Arts seemed about to go the way of practically all the other professional club theatres; it had apparently outlived its usefulness in the world the Royal Court had made. But then things started happening. First an independent management put on a play, Johnny Speight's *The Knacker's Yard*, which was new, exciting, and undeniably, even given the Lord Chamberlain's current fairly liberal disposition, suitable for club consumption only. Then, almost simultaneously, the Royal Shakespeare Company took over the theatre for an experimental season of plays unsuited, for one reason or another, to their main London home, the Aldwych, and the building was taken over by a new management bent on combining ordinary drama with morning or afternoon film shows and late-night revue. Under this new dispensation the theatre brought us two neglected classics, Middleton's *Women Beware Women* and Gorki's *The Lower Depths*; one play by a French writer virtually unknown in this country, Boris Vian's *The Empire Builders*, two plays by known but by no means 'safe' dramatists, Giles Cooper's *Everything in the Garden* and Henry Livings's *Nil Carborundum*, and two by totally new British writers, David Rudkin's *Afore Night Come* and Fred Watson's *Infanticide in the House of Fred Ginger* – both of the latter plays which could not yet be done as they stood in a public theatre. After this financial difficulties forced the Royal Shakespeare Company to withdraw, and look for suitable premises for experiment elsewhere, preferably not in a ready-made theatre at all. In their place our two most enterprising commercial managements, Michael Codron and Oscar Lewenstein, took over to present a season of out-of-the-ordinary drama, in the course of which Codron brought forward three plays of some interest: *Doctors of Philosophy*, a first play by the novelist Muriel Spark in which she transferred the characteristic comic tone of her books, at once crisply intellectual and sinisterly elusive, with remarkable success to the stage; *A Cheap Bunch of Nice Flowers*, another first play by the novelist

Edna O'Brien; and James Saunders's *Next Time I'll Sing to You.*

For the time being the Arts seemed to have found again a useful function in the London theatre, though its intimacy and relative cheapness to run were in general more important than its qualities specifically as a club theatre. Since then, however, it has undergone several changes of ownership and management, and has become so inconsistent in its policy that even longtime supporters have tended to drift away. Still, it undoubtedly played its part in the progress of the new British drama by giving managements with a taste for experiment a practicable frame for it at a time when no real alternative offered. The subsequent commercial success of *The Caretaker* could hardly have been foreseen when it opened for a six-week season at the Arts; neither of the Livings plays first presented there, *Stop It, Whoever You Are* and *Nil Carborundum,* has achieved even a brief transfer to the normal West End theatre; and *The Knacker's Yard, Afore Night Come,* and *Infanticide in the House of Fred Ginger* could hardly have been staged in any other context without undergoing severe emasculation. All these may reasonably be regarded as direct results of the Arts's club theatre policy, while the indirect results of the Royal Shakespeare Company's adventure in experimental theatre at the Arts still remain to be seen. The 1962 wave in the new drama, is, inescapably, the Arts Theatre wave.

HENRY LIVINGS

Although *Stop It, Whoever You Are* was first produced at the Arts as long ago as February 1961, Henry Livings is still the most controversial of the new dramatists – as far as the critics are concerned anyway; some find it and his subsequent work both profound and riotously funny, others determinedly find it neither. The reason, basically, would seem to be that Livings is a working-class dramatist in a far more important sense than any other treated here: not only does he come from the working class, but he writes principally for the working class. He uses one of the lightest and most popular forms, farce, to convey serious truths to his audience, but the first intention of his plays, as of any farce worthy the name, is to make people laugh. A Whitehall Theatre audience would have little difficulty in taking his plays at their face value and enjoying them on those terms; the more severe playgoer who likes to know at once where he is and be sure that he is not wasting his time on something which may turn out, after all, not to be really 'serious' at all, is in a less happy situation. Livings is essentially the sort of dramatist who should come to critical approval by way of popular success rather than the other way round. This he has not yet really had a chance to do, except for a production of *Stop It, Whoever You Are* at Manchester Library Theatre in 1962 which he says was the most satisfactory he has yet achieved in terms of audience response.

Livings was born in 1929, and like many dramatists of his generation has done a variety of other things besides writing; he is, in particular, an expert cook, sure of getting a job in one of London's most expensive restaurants whenever money gets short – a guarantee many another struggling writer would welcome. He left Liverpool University at the end of his second year, and after two years National Service in the R.A.F. he wandered in and out of a number of jobs apart from cooking, including quite a bit of acting up and down the country. Around 1956 he settled at Theatre Workshop, where he appeared in, among other plays, *The Quare Fellow*. There is evidence in his work that he learned a thing or two from the experience, and the influence of Behan, though the Behan of *The Hostage* rather than *The Quare Fellow*, is to be seen in his first play, *Jack's Horrible Luck*, written in 1958 but not produced on television until 1961 (he sold it to the B.B.C. after some eighteen months hawking it around, and in fact it was the encouragement gained from this sale which set him off on a full-time career as a dramatist).

In form, *Jack's Horrible Luck* is a picaresque adventure story on the Elizabethan model, retailing the encounters of Jack, a naïve young sailor ashore for the night in Liverpool. The tone is largely that of broad farcical comedy, with elements bordering on complete fantasy: the central sequences, in which Jack takes up with a bunch of buskers and meths drinkers, goes home with Fred, an odd and crochety busker who has invited him to share a supper of pig's trotters and peas, and becomes involved in a wild and rowdy celebration at Fred's lodgings, suggest something like Joyce's Nighttown seen in the distorting mirror provided by the 'brockel' in *The Hostage*. Despite these apparent influences, the play remains richly personal, notably in the early scenes with the buskers when Jack amicably encourages Fred to do his dance in the alley and thereby indirectly causes him to trip up and spoil his entrance.

There is also a framework suggestion of the parable-in-farce-technique Livings was later to develop in *Stop It, Whoever You Are*: Jack's quest for a semi-mythical café, Uncle Joe's, which he expects to offer him an evening of complete contentment, though when he finds it, of course, it has turned into a rexine-and-formica coffee-bar and 'Uncle Joe' himself has dwindled to a timid employee with a police whistle always at the ready. The theme of the search for Uncle Joe's is perhaps the least satisfactory part of the play, however (indeed, it is completely lost sight of for most of the time), and though we know that his longing for the external dispenser of happiness represented by Uncle Joe is doomed to disappointment it seems rather too unsubtle to establish this right at the beginning by making his mate remark, in an attempt to keep his expectations within bounds, 'Uncle Joe's not God, you know, he's just a man. . . .' (As a matter of fact, the whole framework of the quest for Uncle Joe's – all the play has in the way of 'plot', that is – was not in the original script at all, but was added at the suggestion of the B.B.C.; this may explain why it does not seem always quite to fit in with the rest). Even so, bearing in mind, as its first critics could not do, that *Jack's Horrible Luck* is Livings's very first play, its originality and promise are clear and unmistakable, though naturally, coming apparently after *Stop It, Whoever You Are*, it seemed in some ways to represent a disappointing regression.

The principal point of interest in relation to Livings's subsequent work is in its construction. Though the framework obscures the effect to some extent, the play is constructed in blocks or episodes laid to end, with virtually no 'story' in the conventional sense to bind them together. In this still unsure, immature instance the effect might merely be absence of construction, but in *Stop It, Whoever You Are*, Livings's first work to be produced, the significance of what Livings is at becomes obvious. The progression of *Stop It* is still rather erratic, and Livings does not seem yet to have his method altogether under control, but at least the play suggests a powerful individuality at work, and as it builds up sequence it gradually gathers a wealth of subsidiary meanings without ever (and herein lies the author's artfulness) departing from the farcical tone in which it began, so that by the time we reach its extraordinary final scene we suddenly discover that the apparently simple artless North Country farce has taken on the force and intensity of a parable. The story concerns one William Parkin Warbeck, lavatory attendant in a big northern factory. Trying to keep order in the wash-rooms he is beaten up by two young apprentices he takes for homosexuals, then is virtually raped by a local Lolita, caught *in flagrante delicto* by the police and put on a charge. A little revenge he plans to spoil the moment of triumph of his detested landlord, Alderman Oglethorpe, at the opening of a library he has built goes astray when instead he accidentally soaks his employer and one-time military commander, Captain Bootle, whom he regards highly. He collapses, has a breakdown in which he imagines himself to be a clock, and dies. In the last scene, a séance, he is allowed to get his own back by telling his dreadful wife, from a safe distance beyond the grave, that he enjoyed the attentions of the precocious Marilyn, and in a grand finale the whole place is blown up when a leaky gas-pipe explodes.

The great pleasure to be derived from this cycle of disasters is basically that of seeing the meek at last inherit the earth, but meanwhile Warbeck's many misfortunes are told with a robustness and gusto which command amused attention and at the same time do not work counter to the author's serious intentions, though they may occasionally disguise them from the unwary. The comparison which suggests itself is again with Behan, though this time there is no suggestion of a direct

T

influence. Rather, it is a kinship between Livings and Behan in their implied attitude to the relationship of the wildly comic and the deadly earnest; just as Behan can joke even as the Quare Fellow goes to his execution, so Livings can keep us laughing even while we fully recognize that Perkin is potentially a tragic figure. In this Livings is still true to his Theatre Workshop heritage, and he has described how Joan Littlewood, whom he regards as the greatest single influence in his work, not only made him read Stanislavski but, more importantly, made him understand what Stanislavski was getting at, so that when he took up playwriting again after a period of discouragement

> I had entirely theatrical tools to use. I chose simple stories and corny situations because I didn't want to be wasting time going forward along a single track when I could see a way of covering St Pancras station. And I broke down the story into 'units' of about ten minutes each – about as long, I reckoned, as you can hold a new situation clearly and totally in mind. Each unit I then tried to lay against what went before and what followed, so that the audience would be fresh each time and yet carry an accumulating imaginative world along towards the end and completion of the play.
>
> And each unit I analysed into objectives. What did the people want to *do* or not to *do*, never what they were; no states, only action. And where those objectives met was the through-line of the play. Perkin wants to cut the hedge and so placate his wife and present a respectable front and not be affected by the vividness of Marilyn's presence and curiosity. Marilyn wants to know things and make contact with a man. Mrs Warbeck wants to humiliate Perkin and be thought good enough for Oglethorpe's dazzling world, etc. And inside Warbeck the blood goes round, an individual human animal forges on, sabotaging all attempts to cover it up. Marilyn senses it, Mrs Warbeck attacks it head on, Oglethorpe tries to ignore and is pierced by it, the reporter gets one glimpse and all his anarchic impulses rear like prickles on a gooseberry.
>
> None of this is supposed to have anything to do with appreciation of the show: it's what I have to explain sometimes to actors and directors, so that they can hold on to the line.

As far as 'appreciating the show' is concerned, of course, such explanations should not be necessary and are not necessary, as the reception of the play by a totally unsophisticated audience at Manchester shows. They accepted the play at its face value – they took the business of Perkin and the clock as a joke and laughed, instead of worrying about what it means. Audiences at the Arts were more self-conscious, and so less fortunate. To the sophisticated, therefore, what Livings was getting at emerged more clearly in his television play *The Arson Squad*, produced later, but written earlier, than *Stop It, Whoever You Are*, when the disguise behind which the parable lurks is instead that of sober documentary. Chris, the floor manager, is persuaded to cover up the cause of a fire which has nearly burnt down the factory in which he works because the perpetrator, Norman, is simple-minded and if he gets the sack from this job will be virtually unemployable. It is easy for Norman's fellow-workers to cover up for him – they don't stand to lose much anyway, provided they stick together – but for Chris it means that he must lose his reputation and his position of responsibility, since he will inevitably be blamed and unless he speaks he cannot clear himself. Then Norman leaves to go to a better job elsewhere, and Chris can speak, but by now no one is likely to believe him, and even his workmates, for whom in a sense he has sacrificed himself, do not want to be involved and will not lift a finger to help him. But is he so innocent after all? At the last it emerges that one reason the fire was not more quickly dealt with was that he was wasting the odd few minutes flirting with a stupid typist whom he despises even as he finds her attractive, and having come face to face with his pride (the pride, basically, which shrinks at having to admit a transgression so slight and childish) he is able to become truly humble and live again.

There is no escaping the force and conviction of Livings's writing here, even though its form is considerably less adventurous than in *Stop It, Whoever You Are*; the play was in fact, Livings tells us, written in the face of criticism that his plays were all plotless, to prove to himself that he could write a play with an ordinary plot if he wanted to, and did not write as he usually did simply from incapacity in that direction. Thus in many ways *The Arson Squad* stands aside from the main line of Livings's development, unlike *Jack's Horrible Luck*, which emerged after it in B.B.C. Television's backwards exploration of his work. The methods of construction *Jack's Horrible Luck* had initiated in Livings's work were taken up again, however, and far more effectively, in *Big Soft Nellie* (originally titled *Thacred Nit*), Livings's next play to reach the stage, but before we come on to that there are three plays which should be mentioned, for the record at least: *The Rise and Fall of a Nignog*, an as yet unproduced television play written just before *Stop It, Whoever You Are*, which concerns a character whose weakness compels him to accept any challenge offered to him and finally involves him, almost fatally, in a fantastic scheme to break a prisoner out of gaol; another television play, *Jim All Alone*, which concentrates the crucial action of Raleigh Trevelyan's book *A Hermit Disclosed*, when the 'hermit' finally reaches the point of total withdrawal from the world, into a close-knit poetic drama foreshadowing *Kelly's Eye*; and *The Quick and the Dead Quick*, a highly unconventional historical drama about Villon, whom Livings sees as a strikingly modern figure living in an age which offers many parallels with our own (this last was given a private production-without-décor by younger members of the Royal Shakespeare Company in 1961, and may yet reach full-dress production somewhere).

Big Soft Nellie carries Livings's characteristic disregard of normal plotting much further than *Stop It, Whoever You Are*; indeed in it there is virtually no plot at all, only a series of incidents in the background of an electrical appliances shop. The 'Big Soft Nellie' is Stanley, a mother's boy who is the butt of the staff (with the exception of the dreamy Benny, who is so stupid he hardly counts) and resents it. During the course of the first act Benny and then Stanley practise judo, a police sergeant is called in by Stanley's mother for no good reason, and the other members of the staff persuade Stanley to tell a story while they laugh at him. He decides to do something to make them take notice, and so carries off the vast cabinet of the boss's television set and then (after a long and farcical investigation of its disappearance at the beginning of the second act) returns to give himself up and proclaim himself the thief, hoping optimistically for five years imprisonment (for all the world like the hero in *The Rise and Fall of a Nignog*, who ends, after his ludicrous attempt at prison-breaking has failed, contentedly asking how long a sentence he will get, secure in the knowledge that at last someone has had to take notice). Unfortunately his best efforts are all in vain: he is given a conditional discharge, but his workmates conspire to say nothing of this misfortune in front of him, treating him instead with the deference due to a real prisoner, 'coming-out party' and all, and so finally, even if he remains basically just as 'soft', he can at least stand on his own feet as a self-respecting man.

In this play, plot being reduced to the absolute minimum, we can study Livings's individual techniques in their purest state. Basically, like so many of the new dramatists, he seeks just to show people together, interacting, existing. He carries his interest in this – at the expense of normal dramatic construction – far further than most, however, and in this play comes perhaps closest to an otherwise very different dramatist, Ann Jellicoe. Like her, he writes in terms of a total stage action rather than simply in words; much of what his characters say is merely a gloss on what is happening, and often an apparently completely random exchange in a sequence of *non sequiturs* makes sense only when we see the actors together and understand the relationship between them at that particular point. A conversation between the sergeant and Marris, the owner of the ship, in the second act is an excellent example. The sergeant is felicitating himself on a satisfactory conclusion, the culprit discovered, and the charges dropped:

MARRIS: Do you ever get those anxieties coming on unexpectedly? No, I don't suppose you do.

SERGEANT: Don't you be surprised.

MARRIS: So we can expect you to grace the British Legion very shortly?

SERGEANT: Thank you. I think I'd better just talk to the staff to wind this business up. Don't want to leave them with the idea that they've got away with everything.
           [*He turns to the door where Benny and Stanley stand pale and resigned.*]
           Ouf!

MARRIS: Yes, they gave me a bit of a start I'll admit.

SERGEANT: They'd gone clean out of my mind. Why don't they go and do something?

MARRIS: I don't know. Perhaps they can't think of anything suitable.
SERGEANT: Eerie, aren't they? That's how I imagine condemned men look, on the morning.
MARRIS: Funny how these anxieties come on unexpectedly, isn't it?

On the page it means almost nothing, but when the actors in front of us speak the lines and at the same time we see them together and understand what they are feeling, the shared tension, the sudden intuitive points of contact which lead Marris first to ask about the anxieties and then, out of the blue, to see when the Sergeant is experiencing one, it all makes perfect sense. Similarly, when Benny flings himself at Stanley in the first act with a frenzied cry of 'Tomoe Nage' it is because he has been stoking up his imagination on Stanley's reluctant sex-instruction and has to do *something*; it is not the complete irrelevancy inserted just for a laugh that it might seem from a reading of the text, but a logical continuation in action of an idea already established in words. On a larger scale, if the play seems bit by bit to be just knockabout comedy with no particular point beyond entertainment, the total action nevertheless says something clearly: that what the ignored want more than anything else is attention, and even a very little, not particularly deserved, will do to set things right.

The method is carried even further in Livings's next play, *Nil Carborundum*, a comedy of life in the peacetime services – specifically, in the R.A.F. On the surface this is simply a collection of farcical incidents, with a slight thread of plot, such as has passed for 'service comedy' in the British cinema for the last twenty years or so. A new cook, Harrison, comes to a unit replacing one who has been put on a charge for theft, and Meakin, the camp's other cook, fears that the combination of a newcomer in the kitchen and a stricter watch on kitchen supplies will spoil the profitable relationship he has had for some time with a blind and apparently sweet-tempered but really rather menacing local fence. He decides, however, to risk just one more job, but unfortunately his attempt gets disastrously mixed up with some manœuvres, the unit is taken in a surprise attack, and in the final reckoning Meakin is marched off under escort while Harrison, who has remained cheerfully uninvolved, stays on in charge of the kitchen.

But while again the incidents, taken one by one, are just funny, setting a collection of sharply sketched service types in collision for our entertainment, the total action in this case too conveys a very subtle picture of and attitude to service life in peacetime. In effect, Livings sees it as a game which hardly any of the people taking part realize is a game. In the play there are only two characters who, though from totally different angles, see it for what it is. One is the C.O., a survivor of the great old Battle of Britain days, whose point of view is conditioned entirely by the function of the service: in war it has its use, it is 'real life', but in peacetime it is impossible to take seriously: 'It's the sheer bloody fantasy of the thing that gives me heartburn', he remarks to his eager, pink-cheeked Adjutant, who of course doesn't have the slightest idea what he is talking about. The other sane man is the new cook, Harrison, a national serviceman who didn't want to come into the service, and while he is waiting out the two years before he can return to the real world outside simply wants as quiet a life as he can manage, interfering with no one and being interfered with by no one. He knows, 100 per cent civilian as he is, that it is all nonsense, not to be taken seriously for a moment; he will join in with the fun and games the others are taking desperately seriously only so far as it does not actually incommode him to do so, but if 'they' get really tiresome – if the other side in the manœuvres want to take him prisoner for instance, instead of leaving him happily brewing tea – he reacts with a threat of real violence which soon puts them back in their place.

In between these two meeting extremes, the wholly military and the wholly non-military, the characters arrange themselves according to their various degrees of involvement in their fantasy world. They are all involved to some extent, whether, like the Adjutant, they accept it all with guileless enthusiasm, or, like Meakin, they think they are being very wise and wide in playing the service for a sucker to show they don't take it seriously: calculated rebellion with sizeable risks and fairly negligible gains implies, in fact, an acceptance of the fantasy at its face value quite as complete as the Adjutant's uncomplicated reverence for forms and conventions. Oddly enough, *Nil Carborundum* was produced at the Arts by the Royal Shakespeare Company just after the appearance of Wesker's *Chips with Everything*, which presents a diametrically opposed view of peacetime service life; to Wesker it is a microcosm of the outside world, to Livings it is an escape from reality into fantasy. Livings's play, though far less pretentious than Wesker's, seems in retrospect not only far better as a piece of dramatic writing – making its effect, that is, in truly dramatic terms without recourse to the sort of direct preaching favoured by Wesker – but a far more subtle and intelligent approach to its subject. Though a subsequent television production brought it to a much wider audience than the Arts could offer, *Nil Carborundum* has still not received its just deserts.

After *Nil Carborundum* came three slight, characteristic pieces, a television play called *There's No Room Here for You for a Start* about a lackadaisical household who grow a nine-foot hedge round their housing-estate semi-detached, and then get into further difficulties when a mysterious lodger with a hook instead of a hand who has forced himself on them undertakes to keep official interference at bay; a half-hour radio play, *After the Last Lamp*, which is mainly the interior monologue of a man who sets out boldly to walk home across some waste land where someone has recently been attacked, and then finds his courage ebbing little by little away; and another television play, *A Right Crusader*, about some rather intricate hanky-panky in fish marketing, during which the crook and the moralist find themselves little by little changing places.

But Livings's next stage play, *Kelly's Eye*, shows a complete change of style; at any rate the change of subject-matter and tone is so complete that the style seems very different, though in fact when one examines the play in detail its construction shows the unmistakable hand of Livings at work. And, in fact, the idea that *Kelly's Eye* is a startling new departure for Livings comes largely from the chance that we are familiar almost exclusively with his farces: if *The Quick and the Dead Quick* and particularly *Jim All Alone* had been produced in the proper sequence of his work the 'new Livings' of *Kelly's Eye* would not seem so new at all, but only a logical extension of certain interests already clearly present in his earlier writing. *Kelly's Eye* is the tragic story of a stupid man and an inexperienced girl caught in circumstances too complex for them to understand, too overwhelming for them to come to terms with. One of the things determining the course of their relationship has already happened three years before the play begins: for no particular reason – for no reason anyway which seems very clear to him – Kelly three years earlier shot a Jewish friend and burned his own wood-yard around the body to cover up the crime before disappearing. So much we are told by the blind commentator before the action proper starts; 'Inside, for good or ill, we are on fire', he remarks. 'It is the purpose and the results of the fire in one man that is the purpose of this play.' The curtain goes up on a bare dune with a small hut occupied by Kelly, who has finally taken refuge here. A girl, Anna, comes with a young man, or rather running away from him, and takes refuge with Kelly, who represents to her freedom and animal vitality – this, she decides on the spur of the moment, is the life she wants. They do not for a moment understand each other, but some sort of bond is formed, some sort of need in her cries out to him, and when in the morning the young man comes back with Anna's father Kelly prevents them from taking her away against her will. Kelly and Anna then decide to move up coast, to escape interference.

In the second act they arrive together at a run-down seaside boarding-house, and settle in together, though their relationship remains tenuous and elusive, with Kelly more of a father to Anna than a lover. They play games together, but have not yet made love, and even at this stage Kelly, little as he understands, understands at least that 'When you come down to it, we've got about as much to do with each other as a pair of railway lines.' Obscurely, he feels that he is fated by his move to the town, but it is something he has to do for her, to show that he can be good to somebody, that he can bring life as well as death. He knows that it will not last; she does not want to think of it.

When she gives herself to him he is outraged to discover that she is a virgin – this, to his mind, makes his responsibility for her all the more binding. Inevitably, life catches up with them. They are spotted by a snooping reporter, and both the reporter and Anna's father try to get her to leave quietly. She will not, but Kelly is already prepared to face death and falls, almost knowingly it seems, into a little trap the reporter sets for him. In the end he is cornered, disabled, and takes poison, happy at least in the thought that he has done something for Anna: he must die, but she will go on living:

KELLY: Now I can love you, Anna. Now I can. You will feel free to go on, won't you? Don't listen to old herrenvolk here any more. You couldn't could you? Not any more.

ANNA: No, Kelly. And I shan't forget our little time.

Kelly, the violent man, the man who lives through his fists, dies, but ironically the fact isn't even news any more, for the date is 3 September 1939; the small horror is swallowed up in the greater, and what is one death beside the prospect of so many? Only that Kelly was human; he wanted to do some good in life, and perhaps managed to do so. 'The only thing that can recommend him to us is his humanity, which we share and so must love. But that he has in common with the woman, with her father, with all the others. Think. Kelly was not the only one who needed to love his own, and therefore others' humanity.'

Kelly's Eye is in a very curious way a counterpart to *Jim All Alone*. Kelly, like Jim, is stupid, though his stupidity makes him violent and cruel, good only as a killer, while Jim's carries him to the other extreme, to excessive tenderness for all living things. Both might be regarded as mad and both become hermits, withdrawing from the world. But withdrawal is not enough: Kelly responds, muddledly and unhelpfully perhaps, but responds to a human need, an unspoken cry for help. Cut off from the world he could probably survive, but going to help another, as he soon realizes for himself, can only end one way. For a life bestowed, a life must be taken. Is his gesture even necessary? Perhaps not: as he asks Anna when he suddenly sees clearly the prospect of his own death:

Do you think because there's a box hedge round your father's garden it's some kind of padded cell? Couldn't you just walk out of the gate, or in again if that was your fancy, without rattling half a ton of non-existent locks and bolts? That's right, skrike; it's my bloody life you've been serving up on toast for the Sunday papers.

The revulsion is only temporary, though; necessary or unnecessary, Kelly's actions could not have been different – he did what he had to and he is satisfied.

In Livings's drama the tag-line of *Death of a Salesman* works both ways: 'Attention must be paid', both for the sake of those to whom it is paid – the Nig-nog, Perkin in *Stop It, Whoever You Are*, the Big Soft Nellie – and for the sake of those who pay it. Sarah Kahn in *Chicken Soup With Barley* says 'If you don't care you'll die', and that might be the motto of *Kelly's Eye*. If you do care you will die too, of course, and perhaps sooner for the sake of caring, but if Kelly instinctively prefers this to the mental death of isolation, surely he is right. *Kelly's Eye*, like all Livings's other plays, is a parable, but at last the parable is out in the open and he can be recognized definitely for what he has always been: even at his funniest a serious writer whom serious people can enjoy without supposing that in some way they are letting down the side.

It was unfortunate, in the circumstances, that his next major play, *Eh?* (1964) was produced by the Royal Shakespeare Company at the Aldwych, since again this set up in an acute form the problem of how it should be taken. Especially, one might add, since it was given an unsympathetic production including at least one radical piece of miscasting. Like Livings's earlier plays, it is an apparently loose-jointed farce about an eccentric misfit and his relations with the world about him. In this case Valentine Brose manages to get work minding the boiler in a factory, but the main purpose of his doing so, as it proves, is to continue his own private experiments in the growth of hallucigenic mushrooms. The play is partly his battle with the boiler, which takes on a major role in the action, and partly a demonstration of how the obsessed individual can throw a spanner in the works of the largest, most efficient organization. The message, if one cares to look for one, is happily anarchic, but the play works on audiences largely as a very funny farce, dependent for its effects on the interrelations of a group of characters each following, at his own pace, the working out of his or her own private purposes and obsessions – a farce of character, that is, rather than a farce of external action. This the Aldwych production failed to demonstrate, and the film its director, Peter Hall, made of it under the title *Work is a Four-Letter Word* departed even further from the spirit of the original, in effect throwing the play away and retaining only the central metaphor as the basis of a knock-about physical farce.

Since *Eh?* Livings has written mainly in the shorter forms, his work including an eccentric play-revue called *The Little Mrs Foster Show* (1968), about (vaguely) imperialism in black Africa, and an 'entertainment' called *Good Grief* (1967) made up of playlets and sketches on such weird subjects as a pie-eating contest, a man whose limbs get longer and shorter while he talks and a ventriloquist and his dummy who change places. These two later works have been staged in the North, where at the moment it seems Livings's own highly individual dramatic style seems more readily acceptable than in London: there, it seems more and more of his audience are willing to take the first step on trust, being content for a start to laugh heartily without worrying their heads too much about what it all means.

JOHNNY SPEIGHT

In the course of this book I have had occasion every now and again to mention the influence exerted on public taste and directly on the work of individual writers by popular radio and, latterly, television entertainments. There is a whole underground tradition – underground, that is, as far as 'respectable' criticism is concerned – of crazy, knockabout, verbal humour running through from the intricate punning and cheery brutality of Gilbert's *Bab Ballads*, Harry Graham's *Ruthless Rhymes for Heartless Homes*, and Hilaire Belloc's *Cautionary Tales*, with healthy transatlantic infusions from Perelman's early scripts for the Marx Brothers and the later films of W. C. Fields, to *Itma* in the war years and the more calculated surrealism of

The Goon Show, and thence back into the main stream in the plays of N. F. Simpson, David Campton, and even Harold Pinter. This tradition, in fact, has contributed quite as much to the theatre of the Absurd in Britain as has the more immediate and intellectually respectable influence of such continental proponents of the movement as Eugene Ionesco and Samuel Beckett.

On the whole, however, the influence of the popular humorists has most satisfactorily made itself felt in the work of writers who themselves were far removed from this sort of writing (the popular script-writing of David Campton on *The Groves* and David Turner on *The Archers* hardly counts as an exception to this rule, since it was not primarily humorous and anyway regarded by the authors only as an exercise in the craft of writing for money). In general the humorists themselves have steered clear of anything more extended than the half-hour radio or television segment, and where they have tried their hands at anything else the results have been less satisfactory: the Simpson and Galton film scripts (*The Rebel, The Wrong Arm of the Law*) do not equal their work in the shorter forms; Spike Milligan, main writer of the original *Goon Show*, has written a stage play, *The Bed Sitting Room* (a post-nuclear comedy in which one of the characters turns into a bed-sitting room and his psychiatrist, the psychiatrist's fiancée and her father, once Prime Minister and now a parrot, immediately move in), which runs to a lot of good jokes but fails to support the weight of a whole evening's entertainment; and Milligan's collaborator on *The Bed Sitting Room*, John Antrobus, has himself written a full-length television comedy, *The Missing Links*, which showed mainly that it takes a Pinter to write a Pinter play, and a couple of full-length stage plays, *You'll Come to Love Your Sperm Test* (1964) and *Trixie and Babs* (1968), both shapeless knockabout pieces of verbal farce, but intermittently entertaining.

One popular humorist, however, has successfully broken through into straight drama, Johnny Speight. Johnny Speight was born in 1922 in the East End of London, and has worked as a factory labourer and a jazz musician; almost all his career as a professional writer has been bound up with writing television comedy shows, particularly *The Arthur Haynes Show*, which he wrote from 1956 until its star's death in 1966. *The Arthur Haynes Show* was never a prestige show, or rated much attention from the more intellectual critics (unlike Milligan's *A Show Called Fred* and *The Idiot Weekly*, or Simpson and Galton's Hancock shows); it has coasted along very nicely as good popular entertainment, based closely and profitably on the personality of its star, whose principal trademark within the context of the series was a sturdy working-class obstructiveness, not unmixed with slyness, in dealing with toffs and snobs. Sometimes the ideas of the sketches were gleefully brutal, with a weakness for the dentist's or barber's chair as a location for funny business; sometimes, when they concerned the sufferings of a postman locked in his own letterbox and other similar oddities, the comedy of discomfort was liberally laced with fantasy. But seldom was there any indication that the writer might have something original to offer in other forms; and so his stage play *The Knacker's Yard*, produced at the Arts early in 1962, came as a very agreeable surprise.

Not a complete surprise, as it happens, since his half-hour television play *The Compartment*, a two-character piece about a strange young man who, for no particular reason that we are told, terrorizes an older man with whom he finds himself closeted on a boring train journey, had already shown that Speight had a distinct gift for dramatizing this sort of funny-sinister situation. But *The Compartment* is short and slight, like his later television piece *The Playmates* (another half-hour play, this time about a man who comes to the door of a private house in the West of England, insists that it is a boarding house, and gradually forces the woman living there to accept his view of the situation); *The Knacker's Yard* is something very different, a full-length stage play in three acts with a fully articulated plot.

And yet, despite many and obvious weaknesses, it has a curiously bitter and individual flavour, and it does display an ability, which apparently even Speight's most expert colleagues in television comedy lack, to construct successfully on a large scale. The theme is the same as that of *The Compartment* and *The Playmates* (indeed, once alerted one can find it again and again in sketches in *The Arthur Haynes Show* as well):

the power of individual obsession to defeat external reality. In each play a mysterious intruder breaks into a clear, ordered, everyday situation, and by intimidation, ingratiation, or sheer force of personality takes it over and reshapes it according to his own interests and requirements, browbeating all those around him and unsettling them to such an extent that they lose all sense of what is and what is not real and true.

The Knacker's Yard shows this happening in a squalid boarding house which is, it is suggested, the end of the road (the 'knacker's yard', in fact) for its inhabitants. To it comes Ryder, a mysterious and sinister young man with an obsessive urge to privacy; he fixes a collection of bolts on to the door of his room, nearly gouges out the eye of a shambling derelict from next door whom he suspects, rightly, of spying on him by jabbing a cane sharply through the keyhole, and once convinced that he has complete privacy he settles down to his evening occupation, ritually slashing a series of voluptuous nude pin-ups with a razor on a little patriotic altar of Union Jacks he has erected. All of which, plus his large collection of handbags, seems to suggest that he must be the Jack the Ripper-like killer in the neighbourhood whose trademark is that he always steals his victims' handbags. In the second act this supposition appears to be confirmed when he turns on the blowsy blonde who runs the boarding house for an unseen landlord (who spends his time collecting stray dogs and shutting them up in rabbit hutches in the basement), brandishing a razor at her as the curtain falls. A similar fate would seem to be in store also for the old tramp from next door, but instead Ryder gets friendly with him and starts telling him his recurrent dreams (about a man who keeps molesting him), then invites him to become a business partner in a firm selling ladies' handbags. To seal the bargain they have an elaborately formal dinner, observing the utmost nicety in spite of the shabbiness of their surroundings and the unfortunate fact that the tramp is not quite dressed for the occasion, having alas no suit of tails to hand. It finally breaks up, though, when Ryder tells his guest that the pie the latter has been so eagerly consuming was made with cat's meat. So the tramp turns against him, and the police are finally brought in, but too late: Ryder has already gassed himself. And he was not even the local sex-murderer, who proves to have been arrested already; the blowsy blonde is alive after all, gagged and tied up in a wardrobe with all her hair shaved off; Ryder's motives and the nature of his obsessions remain unexplained.

In the play there is obviously a lot that Speight has learnt from Pinter, both in his way with dialogue and his approach to character: in particular the characters of Ryder and the tramp Martin recall Mick and Davies in *The Caretaker*, and the relationship between them is very similar to that between the characters in the Pinter play. But unlike almost every other play strongly influenced by Pinter, *The Knacker's Yard* is not just imitation; subtract everything which comes from Pinter and there is still a considerable residue which derives from nobody. The long scene in which Ryder describes his dream is one such section; the slashing of the pin-ups and the dinner party, even if they have parallels in Pinter's work, end up as something far different – the writing is coarser and more knockabout, inclining to a bitterly misanthropic black humour unlike anything in Pinter or indeed elsewhere in modern British drama. There is a real savagery in Speight's writing which has little to do with the conscientious naughtiness of most would-be 'sick' jokes; it seems to be felt, coming over with the force of genuine obsession. One must stress, though, that the result is above all very funny, unlikely as that may sound from a summary of the plot. *The Knacker's Yard* is arguably the nastiest comedy yet to have reached the stage in this country; it is strange enough, personal enough, and, after all has been said against it, successful enough to make one eagerly await Johnny Speight's next stage play. This has not as yet been forthcoming, since he has subsequently got involved in writing the long-running television series *Till Death Do Us Part*, a splendidly anarchic image of working-class family life in which, as in *The Arthur Haynes Show*, no one showed any sign of the gratitude and submissiveness to the welfare state generally considered suitable for those in their station by left-wing theorists as well as by right-wing die-hards. A section of Speight's next major work, the television play, *If There Weren't Any Blacks You'd Have to Invent Them*, was done on stage in the Royal Shakespeare Company's miscellany 'Expeditions Two' in 1965, but it had to wait till 1968 for a complete showing on television; then it proved to be a wild and savage review of prejudice in modern life, with everybody jockeying for a position of psychological superiority to everyone else, and the perennial victim-figure, having established himself as a Jew and a homosexual, finally finding himself being executed in black-face makeup before his trial can begin. It had, into the bargain, all Speight's splendid old knack of offending everyone equally; which in a period of almost obsessive concern with good taste, especially in the mass media, is a gift to be gleefully cherished by audiences and exercised whenever possible by its possessor.

DAVID RUDKIN

The first of the Royal Shakespeare Company's second group of experimental productions at the Arts was in many ways its most surprising and successful. It was David Rudkin's *Afore Night Come*, a first stage play by a virtually unknown author who immediately established himself with it as one of the most exciting new arrivals in the theatre since the early days of the 'new drama'. The surprise was initially that the Royal Shakespeare Company should embark at all on anything so hazardous as a play set 'in an orchard in a rural pocket on the crust of the Black Country' and written at times in almost impenetrable dialect; much more likely as the type of play to catch their eye, one had thought, would be something like Henry Livings's Villon play *The Quick and the Dead Quick* (costume makes respectable) or the play with which the season actually opened, Giles Cooper's *Everything in the Garden*, a satirical parable attacking suburbia and using the conventions of drawing-room comedy to do so. But even more surprising than the choice of play was what happened on stage once the play got under way.

The setting could be relied on to give us a clear picture from stock, and the opening scene confirmed our notions: a little rough country humour, chaffing among a variety of regional

u

types, the abrupt introduction of a leather-jacketed teddy boy and a self-conscious undergraduate into the group, the hurry of routine fruit-picking to be done before the piece-workers can inherit the earth. Clearly, if this is not going to be a Zolaesque study of country squalor after the manner of *Roots* it will at least be a piece of vigorous lyrical realism like *Lena, Oh My Lena*, which also concerned a student picker involved with tough working people. But the author, it soon transpires, is up to something very different: the slice-of-life introduction and the carefully documentary setting are only the bait which leads audiences cheerfully into his trap. Gradually the chaffing, particularly of an odd, relatively inoffensive Irish tramp who wanders in, takes on a decidedly sinister tinge, dark hints are dropped about what must happen 'afore night come', and before we know where we are the apparently random jottings on country life build up to a gruesomely compulsive climax involving a ritual murder beneath the poison sprays of a pest-control helicopter.

The strength of the play lies in two things: the inexorable theatrical logic with which it carries us from its simple realistic opening to the weird, primitive ritual of its climax; and the efficacy of the play on a literal as well as a metaphorical level. Though such happenings seem on the face of it improbable in the English countryside in 1962, one would hesitate to say they were impossible, and in fact during the last few years one or two unexplained crimes with all the hallmarks of ritual murder have been reported (Rudkin cannot remember having read about them, but thinks it probable that he did and that some impression remained). Accepting, then, that such things might happen and sometimes do, *Afore Night Come* builds up a minutely credible picture of how one such case might come about. In this countryside the dark gods still walk (Rudkin's first favourite adult reading – after *Just William* and Arthur Ransome – was Hardy, which may have something to do with his view of rural life) and superstitions die hard. Strangers are mistrusted, the weak go to the wall and anything out of the ordinary (barrenness, insanity) is as like as not the fault of something unnatural, someone with the evil eye.

The Irish tramp 'Shakespeare' fulfils all the conditions of a scapegoat: he is foreign, different (not least by being literate), weak and nearly blind, wearing dark glasses which at once suggest to the superstitious that he has something to hide about his eyes. Everything tends towards the inevitable conclusion in which the intruder is sacrificed and the childless man reinforces his potency by drinking the victim's blood. The crime cannot be prevented because everyone in the orchard is either involved, or totally unaware of what is happening until it is too late (the student; the town-bred teddy boy) or doesn't want to know (the orchard's owner; the workers from elsewhere; the foreman, whose degree of complicity remains ambiguous). The only exception is 'Hobnails', a harmless lunatic on leave from the asylum to help in the picking. He is the only character who really feels that something is wrong; ironically the religious background which has given the particular shape of religious mania to his madness – the madness which makes him practically speaking ineffectual in this situation – is also the thing that equips him with the moral sense to appreciate to the full the enormity of what is happening. He idolizes the student, and tries to take him away from the horrors which are to come, to keep him pure – though at the same time, by another irony, he has sexual designs on the student and wants to corrupt him; when this comes to the surface the student recoils and consequently is subjected after all to the full horror of the killing.

So, on the level of actuality it all works perfectly in terms of a drama of human relationships; a play about people who believe in the supernatural rather than a play directly about the supernatural. But if it can be read and must be played in this way (Rudkin is the first to recognize this, and to insist that its basic coherence is on the 'documentary' level), it can also be seen in very different terms. The name of Jean Genet was much bandied about by critics at the time of the play's first appearance, and may or may not be relevant; certainly *Afore Night Come* suggests a view of the theatre somewhat akin to Genet's ritual theatre in *The Balcony*. But again the fashionable, intellectually respectable parallel seems finally less revealing than the unfashionable native one. Hardy, clearly, has contributed something, but Rudkin's view of life seems most closely akin to that of, say, Algernon Blackwood or Arthur Machen, with their quirky interest in folk survivals and the occult underworld. In specifically theatrical terms, indeed, it suggests the sort of play Arthur Machen might have written after an intensive course of Antonin Artaud's ideas on the 'theatre of cruelty'; like the French theorist, Rudkin sees dramatic performance primarily as something which acts subliminally, releasing from the subconscious mind forces of which the conscious, civilized mind is virtually unaware.

Perhaps it releases also forces in the dramatist, forces of which he is virtually unaware; certainly though Rudkin denies that any symbolism was intended, various symbolic overtones return constantly – the tramp 'Shakespeare' as a Wandering Jew, Johnny Hobnails as a Christ-figure – though they never give the impression of being worked out in detail to any consistent intellectual end; they merely help to establish the emotional climate in which the action takes place and which, indeed, makes the action conceivable in the first place. So too with the pen which the student gives Johnny; phallic, evidently, though Rudkin insists that it is simply a pen and no more. 'I know it looks phallic', he says, 'but then what doesn't?' – to which the answer is that a lot of things look considerably less so than a fountain pen. It is a pen and it is more, just as the crop-spraying helicopter is a helicopter, literally (derived from a real experience of Rudkin's when he was caught under just such a spray picking fruit in just such an orchard) and also a brooding evil presence surveying the murder with grim impersonal satisfaction. Hence, finally, the power of these things as theatrical symbols: they remain symbols in the proper sense of the term, never fully defined and conveying more than the dramatist is consciously aware of, and never degenerate into mere emblematic equivalences. As Rudkin admits, in the play 'Things may emerge, things I'm not conscious of – but then can you put in a symbol consciously?'.

The theatrical mastery of *Afore Night Come* is especially remarkable when one considers that it is the first full-length play and first produced stage play of an author who had hardly seen a play or considered the theatre at all until nearly twenty. Rudkin was born in 1936 into a family of very strict evangelical Christians who considered all theatre – except Shakespeare – the Scarlet Woman; even his few visits to the cinema as a child were clandestine. He began writing stories for himself in early childhood, but from fourteen to nineteen was obsessed with music (which he now teaches) and composed music to the total exclusion of composition with words. When he returned to words during his national service – the materials of music being too hard to come by – he wrote a Joycean autobiographical volume about a holiday he had spent hiking in Ireland, and then tore it up. A similar fate overtook his next work, a one-act play written at university: in an attempt to overcome the basic problem of writing a play in which he could experiment with words and still maintain credibility he took as subject a group of displaced persons doing menial work in a camp in Germany, with no common language except what they worked out for themselves. But he was not satisfied that he had found a workable solution, and Pinter's *The Birthday Party* came as a revelation. Under this influence he wrote another play which turned out as a 'blatant imitation of Pinter', then decided to give drama up and concentrated for the rest of his time at university on film-making. Soon after leaving university the urge to write plays came on him again, and he wrote a short radio play, *No Accounting for Taste*, which was produced by the B.B.C. This was a fantasy based on a brief experience working in an accountant's office, where the Dickensian jargon everybody used quite unselfconsciously fascinated him; the result was a macabre, rather Kafkaesque piece about a firm run by three unseen partners, who turn out to be the same man, and the unexplained disappearance of secretaries who are asked to stay on and work after hours. After *Afore Night Come* Rudkin went on teaching music in Birmingham for a couple of years, produced plays for an amateur parish group (first production *Hay Fever*; second *The Birthday Party!*) and did a variety of writing, including translations of Aeschylus, Vitrac and Schoenberg (the libretto of *Moses and Aaron*), work on a number of film scripts, the book of a ballet (*Sun into Darkness*, 1963) and four television plays. The first one, *The Stone Dance* (1963) was a further visit to *Afore Night Come* country – not literally, but the dark forces are much in evidence during the strange goings on in Cornwall when the young son of a bigotted itinerant preacher comes into contact for the first time with natural, life-loving people and has to fight for his own soul and sanity in the midst of a larger battle between humanity and fanaticism which surrounds him. In *Children Playing* (1967) the subject was an enclosed world (in this case that of a group of children on holiday) under threat from hostile outsiders – a couple of sinister young men in the youth hostel. The characterization of the children was particularly lively, their natural Black Country speech being tellingly and teasingly elaborated with biblical and literary echoes. In *House of Character* (1968) the latest to be seen at time of writing, the central character is a man who believes he is renting a flat but proves as the play progresses to be mad, so that what we have seen is merely his own insane interpretation of the asylum where he is confined.

In all of these works Rudkin has continued to assert his ability to create with maximum vividness a private world overshadowed by the irrational, edging into fantasy or madness. As yet he has shown little ability, or desire, to break out of this particular dramatic territory, though the tough humour of the children in *Children Playing* suggests that he might if so inclined. But as long as his writing remains so taut and haunting as it has been up to now, no one is likely to complain too much about the voluntary limitation.

FIRST IMPRESSIONS

Apart from Johnny Speight and David Rudkin, the Arts, or New Arts as it is now called, introduced in 1962 at least one other dramatist of real interest if not yet complete achievement. Fred Watson's *Infanticide in the House of Fred Ginger* was the last of the Royal Shakespeare Company's experimental season and as a play almost certainly the least successful. It is really the beginning of one play and the end of another tackled plausibly, but in the last analysis unsatisfactorily, together. The first act lays the foundations of a subtle and perceptive play about an ill-assorted marriage in the later stages of dissolution and then in the second act the author seems to walk away from them and start building on another site, with a dramatized documentary about teenage gang life on the fringes of delinquency. Both parts work well enough in isolation; they just do not fit together.

The more interesting and promising is the first part, in which we are introduced to a sort of Jimmy Porter-Alison relationship turned inside out. The social side of the relationship is the same – the wife, Catrine, a snooty ex-nurse who runs to daddy every so often for advice, the husband, Jerry, a misfit workman drifting from one job to another and clearly hardly the sort of husband daddy would have chosen had Catrine been in any condition for him to set high standards. But the emotional side is the exact opposite: Catrine is the dominant one, always ready with conditions (at least one bath a week and separate beds) while Jerry asks nothing better than to cringe and abase himself. The relations of this couple are sketched in acutely and with unusual frankness (it must be the first time premature ejaculation has been not only discussed on the English stage but also vividly demonstrated), and Watson succeeds remarkably well in conveying that Jerry is rather a drip but that even drips are human and as such worthy of our sympathy and even, perhaps, in an odd way our respect.

Then, in the second act, the couple disappear, having left their baby in the care of a mildly maniac local government clerk turned amateur baby-sitter, and dramatized documentary takes over. Before long the baby-sitter is turned out by a group of three rowdies, one of them the son of the Fred Ginger who owns the house. There follows a long, scene leading up to the 'infanticide', which holds our attention not so much by advancing the play as by telling us 'young people today (or some of them) are like this', and then going on to show us. Aided no doubt by the freedom a club theatre allows the dramatist in employing four-letter words, Watson produces a formidable impression of veracity in the dialogue he gives his young people to speak, and though one suspects a strong element of anti-romantic romanticization in some of the action (and the rather too pat 'psychological' explanation of it) he does manage to capture some facets of the truth more accurately than any dramatist has done before. But at the end, after bringing back the couple only to dismiss their story with hardly a hint of the effect their child's death has on them, Watson rounds off the play instead with Fred Ginger's reactions to his son's crime (presented, incidentally, in a comparatively sympathetic light by being attributed to a period of mental blackout), as though this has really been a play about Fred – which, up to then, it just has not.

Clearly Watson has ideas, and has set out to put them in a unifying frame: the play's title, after all, makes a point of the fact that the action takes place 'in the house of Fred Ginger', and Fred Ginger does appear from time to time, advising Jerry unwillingly on his marital difficulties, talking to his friends and so on, but until the end he is never anything but a bystander, and does not play a positive enough role to provide any real continuity and bind together the disparate elements of the piece. But the various parts, even if they never coalesce into a satisfactory whole, do show considerable grasp of theatrical effect and of the expression of character in action. Watson's main problem at the moment would seem to be disciplining his talents (according to the director, William Gaskill, the produced version of *Infanticide* was a scissors-and-paste job put together from an original twice as long). He has written some television plays on equally bizarre subjects. At best he may develop the subtle and compassionate views of human problems shown in the first act of *Infanticide in the House of Fred Ginger*; otherwise he may extend the nascent talent for intelligent grand-guignol shown in the second, which could also be interesting.

On the whole the Arts has not produced anything quite so interesting since the Royal Shakespeare Company left and began looking for new (preferably non-theatrical) premises to continue their experiments. I liked Muriel Spark's elegant intellectual comedy *Doctors of Philosophy*, which I did not see until the affected non-realistic play with sets and props which alienated most critics had been eliminated, but it hardly counts as 'new drama'. Nor, I would have thought, *pace* most of the critics, does Michael Codron's contemporary success in the public theatre, Charles Dyer's comedy about a forty-year-old male virgin and a prostitute with a burgeoning imagination *Rattle of a Simple Man*. This was written, according to the author (already a prolific producer of whodunits and repertory farces), after seeing *A Taste of Honey* and thinking that if that was all there was to this new drama stuff he could do better himself (it is an interesting reflection that just five years earlier Shelagh Delaney thought the same about Terence Rattigan's 'old drama' *Variation on a Theme* and wrote *A Taste of Honey*); though quite expert in its way, *Rattle of a Simple Man* seems to me a perfect example of the sort of play which, as John Arden once said of something else, 'knows how to talk about sex so as to make Aunt Edna feel In Touch'. Even more is this so of Dyer's later play *Staircase*, produced by the Royal Shakespeare Company, an adroit but decidedly muddled commercial piece exploiting the Lord Chamberlain's newly liberal attitude towards homosexuality on stage. More to the point are two of Michael Codron's subsequent productions at the Arts, James Saunders's *Next Time I'll Sing to You*, discussed elsewhere in this book, and the novelist Edna O'Brien's first play *A Cheap Bunch of Nice Flowers*. This was a strange, muddled play about a battle between mother and daughter over the same man which developed into a battle for the limelight when the mother discovers she has cancer and the daughter retaliates with the news of her own pregnancy. It might have worked as a sort of ruthless black farce, but appears to have been directed as a vague Irish jumble and pleased hardly anyone; the feeling remains, though, that it never really had a fair chance. Certainly Edna O'Brien's second play, *The Wedding Dress*, a short, intense piece written for television about a man who is gradually driving his wife mad by systematically giving away all her clothes, suggests that she has real gifts for drama.

After its days of renewed glory in 1962–63 the Arts has fallen again on hard times, and the latest generation of British dramatists to emerge have had to look all over for openings. Charles Wood, with *Cockade*, came in at the tail-end of Michael

Codron's days at the Arts: later plays have been produced at the Royal Court and by other West End managements, and meanwhile he has written for television and, quite extensively, for films. David Mercer made his name on television before breaking into the West End theatre with the help of Peter O'Toole, who starred in his *Ride A Cock Horse*, and then going on to the Royal Shakespeare Company. David Halliwell's *Little Malcolm and his Struggle against the Eunuchs* made its London bow improbably, and as it turned out disastrously, in the middle of the West End, like any commercial play. Peter Terson has made his name mainly as resident dramatist of the Victoria Theatre company, Stoke-on-Trent, his plays seen in London being by comparison negligible. Cecil P. Taylor has been produced on the fringes – at the Jeanetta Cochrane Theatre in Holborn for instance – while Tom Stoppard began his career, for all most of his audience knew, at the top as far as prestige was concerned when *Rosencrantz and Guildenstern are Dead* was produced by the National Theatre, and his subse‐quent career has been entirely West End.

So, there is no really coherent grouping for these writers; they are just there. The most palpably there of them, perhaps, are Charles Wood and David Mercer. Both of them have suc‐ceeded, certainly, in creating coherent and striking private worlds of drama. The territory favoured by Charles Wood (b. 1932) is military life, with occasional excursions into the tatty provincial theatre which was, it seems, his childhood background. The army provides the material for the three plays of *Cockade* (1963), which vary in style from the vivid naturalism of *Prisoner and Escort*, about a helpless victim-figure being taken to military prison by a leeringly sadistic corporal and his idiotic sidekick, to the home-grown Theatre of Cruelty approach of *Spare*, a mysterious poetic evocation of the military way of life set in a military museum which becomes a sort of metaphor for the army itself. These plays established Wood's reputation; his later works have been more muffled in their impact. *Meals on Wheels* (1965) was a hopelessly muddled farcical drama about a man in his thirties in search of a wife or a girl or something, and his weird family, including a sister given to imaginary pregnancies and an aged father and older half-brother who have to be waited on hand and foot with meals on wheels; nobody seemed to like that very much. *The Drill Pig*, a television play, showed the institutional and private lives of a couple of soldiers with a lot of sharp observation and off-beat humour. *Fill the Stage with Happy Hours* (1966) is a sympathetic, nostalgic picture of life in a small and run-down provincial theatre where father plays the shady manager, always dreaming ineffectually of Ibsen and Shakespeare next week, mother is (allegedly) a born actress reduced to serving behind the bar and staging elaborate (and quite possibly real) death bed scenes, while the son is happily seduced by visiting theatrical celebrity. *Dingo* (1967) brings Wood back to the army, this time with a vigorously anti-heroic view of the North African campaign in which the soldiers are shown as foul-mouthed, sex-obsessed and totally desensitized by the horrors of war. In all these plays Wood's style is concentrated, highly stylized, full of esoteric references and army-cum-theatrical argot: his obsessions sometimes make vivid drama, though his sense of construction seems weak and most of them are more satisfactory piece by piece than taken as a whole.

David Mercer (b. 1928) also has powerful obsessions informing nearly all his work. He began with an ambitious trilogy of television plays, *The Generations*, which moved from straightforward working-class realism in the first, *Where the Difference Begins* (1961) through anti-nuclear polemic in *A Climate of Fear* (1962), to a bolder and more non-realistic style in the last, *The Birth of a Private Man* (1963), which broaches what was to become Mercer's central subject, social alienation expressed in terms of psychological alienation. Most of Mercer's later television plays, such as *A Suitable Case for Treatment* (1962, filmed as *Morgan*), *For Tea on Sunday*, (1963), *And Did Those Feet* (1965) and *In Two Minds* (1967), deal with aspects of the same subject. So does Mercer's first stage play, *Ride a Cock Horse*, which shows the gradual break-up of the hero and his regression into infantilism. The subject even crops up in the two plays of Mercer which have been staged by the Royal Shakespeare Company, *The Governor's Lady* (written for radio in 1960, but never produced) and *Belcher's Luck*. *The Governor's Lady* is a one-act fantasy about an elderly governor and his wife, and how the governor gradually turns into a gorilla (thereby presumably embodying the wife's unavowed desires and instincts). *Belcher's Luck* is a wild tragi-comedy full of Lawrentian symbolism about fertility and impotence (represented respectively by servants and masters) and the ultimate defeat of basic virility by desiccated intellect: it was extraordinary and did not begin to hold together as a coherent piece of play-writing. In general up to now Mercer has done his most convincing work on television, where he has been able to explore his typical subjects with considerable freedom and variety. His two latest television plays at time of writing, *The Parachute* (1968) which relates a young Luftwaffe airman's present anguish to his past, being bullied and corrupted by his masterful aristocratic father, and *Let's Murder Vivaldi* (1968), a sardonic comedy about the incursion of violence into everyday civilized life, show him still developing.

David Halliwell (born 1937) has as yet made his mark with only one play, *Little Malcolm and his Struggle against the Eunuchs* — that is, if one discounts his participation with David Calderisi in a weird, largely improvised entertainment called *The Experiment* (1966) which poked intelligent fun at various theatrical fads of the moment. *Little Malcolm* is a large, sprawling work. Its story, so far as it has any noticeable story, concerns one Malcolm Scrawdyke, who as of the day before the play starts is an ex-art student at Huddersfield Tech. He has been turned out because of his corrupting influence on the others, and during the course of the play we see this at work on a group of his old pals. He starts a totalitarian party of four, in order to stage a fantastic putsch in which the principal who kicked him out will be blackmailed into destroying a painting pinched from the local art gallery, and thus exposed to public ridicule and obloquy. Two of the three disciples go along with this, and the third would, were he not, as a born victim, expelled from the party on equally fantastic grounds of conspiring with the enemy. The main achievement of the three remaining is, egged on by Malcolm, to beat up fairly effectively a girl he is drawn to but too shy to get anywhere with and who commits the additional crime of seeing through him. When the time for the planned putsch comes, though, Malcolm cannot go through with it; he is deserted by his followers and as the curtain falls is seen leaving his gloomy attic studio to phone the girl, apologize if he can, and maybe start over again. The play is gripping and effective whenever Malcolm is talking to himself, or carried away by his own eloquence while talking to others. But when the whole thing is moved from subjectivity, when Malcolm is seen in relation to other people, acting and reacting, the play at once falters and loses direction: scenes like the imaginary enactment of the theft of the painting and kidnapping of the principal rapidly become tiresome because they tell us nothing about the characters and lead nowhere in the plot; they are decoration applied to no sufficient base, time-fillers which only pad out a play already too long for its material. However, Halliwell has a decided gift for theatrical rhetoric, which may yet find a more coherent vehicle.

Peter Terson (b. 1932) is something of a problem. He is extremely prolific, and there can be few even among the most mobile of playgoers who have seen all his plays. The best-known of them is *Zigger-Zagger* (1967), a musical he wrote for the National Youth about football enthusiasts whose frenzy sometimes goes over into hooliganism, and particularly about one boy, torn between the wild influence of Zigger-Zagger, the ultimate fan, and a quiet relative who encourages him to listen to good music. *Zigger-Zagger* is lively spectacle, but not much more, and hardly gives any idea of Terson's real gifts, any more than does his later play for the National Youth Theatre, *The Apprentices* (1968), in which he finds a similar emotional pattern in the rise and fall of the young men's natural, anarchic leader as one by one his cronies drift away. More powerful and altogether more individual are Terson's cycle of plays set in the Vale of Evesham, several of them written for the Victoria Theatre, Stoke. In the earliest, *A Night to Make the Angels Weep* (1964) the locals try to put the clock back by restoring the authority of the lord of the manor, and this sort of simple contrast between the good old days and the nasty present, between urban and rural, hill and valley, recurs at the centre of them all. *I'm In Charge of These Ruins* (1966) is built on the contrast between castle and power station; *All Honour Mr. Todd* (1966) shows villagers breaking ranks and joining the mechanized sewermen who take over the land; *The Mighty Reservoy* (1967), a little like Ermanno Olmi's film *Il Tempo si e fermato*, concerns the relationship between a white-collar worker and a reservoir-keeper both of whom are really a prey to the elemental forces about them, the reservoir itself; *Mooney and His Caravans* (1968) is about town-dwellers who move to the country, as they suppose, but really only to a rural caravan-site slum completely dominated by the profiteer Mooney. All of these plays are conceived in simple, black-and-white terms, and run the risk of deteriorating from the elemental to the elementary. However, they do have a certain crude force and vigour, and if Terson suffers from the obvious comparison between him and David Rudkin, he does still have a quality which is all his own.

Cecil P. Taylor (b. 1929) has done his most characteristic work when working on his own Glasgow-Jewish background, as in *Bread and Butter* (1966) which starts as a rather stodgy picture of two contrasted men, one a perennial political enthusiast for one thing or another, the other a constant passive believer of what other people say, and their respective women. But the second half of the play gains added complexity from the development of the characters and their relationship during twenty years, and the end is surprisingly satisfactory. Other plays by Taylor are less successful: among them is a rather ragged one-acter about a Glasgow journalist torn between socialist ideals and his desire for a quiet life, *Allergy* (1966), and a very loosely-organized and aimless musical, *Who's Pinkus, Where's Chelm?* (1967).

Of the newest generation in the British theatre none has received more acclaim than Top Stoppard (b. 1932), mainly on the strength of *Rosencrantz and Guildenstern are Dead* (1967), the production which, more than any other, introduced the National Theatre audience to modern styles of drama. The idea is simple. In *Hamlet* Rosencrantz and Guildenstern are a couple of characters so unimportant that Olivier could remove them from his film without any noticeable difficulty and with almost no one regretting their departure. They are the perennial 'attendant lords', 'friends to the duke' and what-have-you who lurk on the sidelines of drama ready to receive confidences from the principals, carry out commissions and do any minor dirty work that happens to be going. But what are their private lives like? Do they have any? Stoppard thinks not. They live, suspended in existential doubt, on the fringes of life. They never know what's happening, who is who and what is what. Occasionally they witness puzzling snatches of big events going on around them, but their attempts to interpret them are limited and half-hearted. They recognize, in spite of themselves, that life, like laughter, is always in the next room. In the end they go so far as to make a choice, or at least acquiesce in the choice of another, but it is only death that they choose, a death which will at least define and give shape to their pointless, shapeless lives.

This would seem to provide a fine subject for a gnomic one-acter, but a longish three-act play is something different. There is no denying the ingenuity with which Stoppard spins out his material, or the skill with which he works in such fragments of *Hamlet* as concern his own non-heroes. His play is written in brisk, informal prose, suitable for those waiting in the wings, while Shakespeare's verse marks off the brief incursions of a larger life into the colourless, mystifying existence of Rosencrantz and Guildenstern. A lot of the dialogue is agile and funny. But as soon as the lights go up on the solitary couple playing some interminable coin-tossing game in which every coin, in defiance of all the laws of probability, comes up heads, we know immediately that we are in that pale region of Theatre of the Absurd where knockabout and arid philosophical speculation mix or alternate while the awaited never comes, the characters hover on the point of action without ever actually acting, and our little stage is bounded by the dread unknown world of happenings. And the play suffers, like so much Theatre of the Absurd, from the law of diminishing returns: more and more energy is devoted to saying less and less, until finally the observation on the characters and, more broadly, on life which the play offers seems a very small mouse to emerge from such an imposing mountain.

Stoppard's other plays seem to confirm him as a clever but rather bloodless playwright. *Enter a Free Man* was written in 1964, but not staged in London till 1968: it is a fairly conventional piece about an unworldly dreamer and his unfortunate family, enlivened by neat craftsmanship and some bright lines. *The Real Inspector Hound* (1968) is an intricate joke about drama critics and the play, and at the same time a parody of the commercial thriller, slight but quite amusing. There are also several radio and television plays, all confirming Stoppard's technical gifts but showing no very marked individuality either of subject or of treatment.

Of various other dramatists who have appeared recently I should mention especially Barry Bermange (born 1933). His *Nathan and Tabileth* was originally written for radio and is a delicate, Marguerite Duras-like study of two old people whose memories, especially the man's, are failing and who are growing increasingly afraid of the world outside their own front door. *No Quarter* (1962) was originally written for the stage but broadcast first. It takes place almost entirely in the dark, and concerns the plight of a group of people, three guests forced to share a room in a mysterious hotel where nothing works and which proceeds to fall to pieces about their ears, until two of them are left alone on a landing suspended in space. Does the hotel signify life, in which one never knows one's way for more than short stretches at a time, or who one is with, or when and how it will end? Perhaps, perhaps not, but in this short play Bermange manages at least to play some expressive and highly personal variations on a theme from the Theatre of the Absurd. Less can be said for *Oldenburg*, a slightly Simpsonish fantasy about prejudice, first produced in 1967 in a double bill with *Nathan and Tabileth*, or Bermange's first full-length play, *The Cloud* (1964), a tenuous, Beckettish piece about a group of people in a mysterious deserted tower, menaced by a mysterious cloud which gradually gets closer and closer. But *Nathan and Tabileth* and *No Quarter* have real individual quality.

A ROOM AND
SOME VIEWS

Harold Pinter

'But what would you say your plays were *about*, Mr Pinter?'
'The weasel under the cocktail cabinet.'
                          – exchange at a new writers' brains trust

The assignment of writers to various sections of this book has
been at best a rather arbitrary business: though they have
usually belonged unmistakably to one section rather than another, there are very few who fit completely into the place
allotted to them, without overlapping. But with Harold Pinter
the system just breaks down. He began by writing stage plays,
got his first hearing on radio, had his first full-length stage play
put on in the ordinary commercial theatre, achieved his first
popular success on television and in revue, and finally achieved
a big theatrical success without having recourse to the English
Stage Company (though they briefly housed a transfer of a
double bill by him), Theatre Workshop, or any enterprising
provincial company. Where should he be placed? The only
answer is by himself, a position to which his unique eminence
among the writers we have been considering would in any case
surely entitle him.

Harold Pinter, like several of the other writers we have encountered, is an East End Jew (he was born in 1930) and also,
like two or three others, he was for some time a professional
actor, under the name of David Baron. He still acts from time
to time; he played a minor role in *A Night Out* on television, was
seen as Goldberg in a revival of *The Birthday Party* at Cheltenham, and took over the part of Mick in *The Caretaker* for a
while during its London run. But since he began writing plays
in 1957 his time has become more and more occupied with
writing, and the results are to be seen in, to date, three full-
length stage plays, three one-act plays, six television plays,
two radio plays, several revue sketches, and four film

adaptations of novels by other writers (not to mention adaptations from stage to television, radio to stage, etc.).

Though he began writing while acting, his earliest works were not plays at all. He records that he saw very few plays before he was twenty and then during the next nine years played Ireland in one-night stands (for eighteen months) and in repertory all over. All this time he was writing hundreds of poems, short prose pieces, often in monologue or dialogue form, and a semi-autobiographical novel, *The Dwarfs*, from which some material was drawn later for the radio play of the same name. His first play was a one-acter, *The Room*, written early in 1957, and he subsequently described how he came to write it thus: 'I went into a room one day and saw a couple of people in it. This stuck with me for some time afterwards, and I felt the only way I could give it expression and get it off my mind was dramatically. I started off with this picture of two people and let them carry on from there. It wasn't a deliberate switch from one kind of writing to another. It was quite a natural movement.'

What happens when they carry on from there is very strange indeed. The two people are husband and wife, Mr and Mrs Hudd, and the play starts with a long monologue by the wife from which we gather that the husband is a truck-driver and is about to take his truck out on the icy roads. This is interrupted by the arrival of the landlord, who seems to live in the house and talks about his mother, who may or may not have been Jewish, and his sister. After he and the husband leave another married couple, the Sands, arrive in search of a room and say they were told by someone in the basement that this room is vacant. After they have gone the landlord returns, saying that the man in the basement has been plaguing him all week-end to tell Mrs Hudd he wants to see her as soon as her husband has gone out, and after some argument she agrees. When he arrives he turns out to be a blind negro, who apparently knows her, in spite of her denials, and begs her to come home with him. Mr Hudd returns, talks casually about his trip, then knocks the negro down and beats him savagely. Mrs Hudd is struck blind as the curtain falls.

Even from this account it should be evident that the play is not what one would normally expect from the first work of a new dramatist (particularly, perhaps, an actor turned dramatist). It is not autobiographical, as are many first works, nor, clearly, is it imitative of any model, popular or esoteric. In performance it has an obsessive, dreamlike quality which forbids any questioning on the exact significance of what is happening before our eyes, but even if on reflection we begin to wonder what it all means we soon find that Pinter has covered his tracks pretty effectively. Often this is done in matters of detail: many statements, unimportant enough in themselves and acceptable without question, are suddenly brought to prominence by having doubt thrown at them by another character. After Mr Kidd, the landlord, has been talking at random about his mother and sister, Mrs Hudd says, quite matter-of-factly: 'I don't believe he had a sister, ever.' When the Sands arrive they are looking for the landlord, but firmly deny his name is Kidd – could there, possibly, be two landlords? And why should they be convinced that this room is vacant when we can see perfectly well that it is occupied? Are they going up or coming down? Have the Hudds been living there for some time, as is first implied, or just moved in, as Mrs Hudd says later? Does Mrs Hudd know Riley, the blind negro, or not? Is he perhaps, as some have thought, her father?

The technique of casting doubt upon everything by matching each apparently clear and unequivocal statement with an equally clear and unequivocal statement of its contrary – used rather crudely in some parts of this play, as when Rose Hudd actually comments on the discrepancy between the Sands's initial statement that they were on their way up and their later statement that they were on their way down when they called on her – is one which we shall find used constantly in Pinter's plays to create an air of mystery and uncertainty. The situations involved are always very simple and basic, the language which the characters use is an almost uncannily accurate reproduction of everyday speech (indeed, in this respect Pinter, far from being the least realistic dramatist of his generation, is arguably the most realistic), and yet in these ordinary surroundings lurk mysterious terrors and uncertainties – and by extension, the whole external world of everyday realities is thrown into question. Can we ever know the truth about anybody or anything? Is there any absolute truth to be known?

However, this is to anticipate. In *The Room* the hand is not yet entirely sure and the mystifications are often too calculated, too heavily underlined. The suppression of motives, for example, which in later plays comes to seem inevitable, because no one, not even the man who acts, can know precisely what impels him to act, here often looks merely an arbitrary device: it is not that the motives are unknowable, but simply that the author will not permit *us* to know them. So, too, the melodramatic finale with its trappings of blindness and violent death (the blind negro is so like a parody of a Prévert embodiment of fate that one suspects some lingering influence from those gloomy Carné–Prévert films on which Pinter says he doted in his early twenties) appears in retrospect particularly out of place, since it makes the terrors which beset Rose all too actual and immediate. For essentially Rose, the Rose of the earlier scenes anyway, belongs to that group of characteristic Pinter figures from his first phase (that in which he wrote 'comedies of menace'), those who simply fear the world outside. The plays of this group – *The Room*, *The Dumb Waiter*, *The Birthday Party*, and *A Slight Ache* – all take place in confined surroundings, in one room in fact, which represents for their protagonists at least a temporary refuge from the others (it is tempting, but not really necessary, to see it in terms of Freudian symbolism as a womb-substitute), something they have shored up against their ruins. The menace comes from outside, from the intruder whose arrival unsettles the warm, comfortable world bounded by four walls, and any intrusion can be menacing, because the element of uncertainty and unpredictability the intruder brings with him is in itself menacing. And the menace is effective almost in inverse proportion to its degree of particularization, the extent to which it involves overt physical violence or direct threats. We can all fear an unexpected knock at the door, a summons away from our safe, known world of normal domesticities on unspecified business (it is surely not entirely without significance that Pinter, himself a Jew, grew up during the war, precisely the time when the menace inherent in such a situation would have been, through the medium of the cinema or of radio, most imaginatively present to any child, and particularly perhaps a Jewish child). But the more particularized the threat is, the less it is likely to apply to our own case and the less we are able to read our own semi-conscious fears into it.

This lesson is learnt in Pinter's first full-length play, *The Birthday Party*, which followed almost immediately upon *The Room*. Here the room is precisely situated: it is in a run-down boarding house in a seaside town, inhabited by a mild, self-indulgent man called Stanley, who seems once to have been a pianist and is now content to do nothing and be pampered by Meg, his stupid, doting, suffocatingly motherly landlady, who clearly gets on his nerves, but is equally clearly useful to him. This shabby idyll is interrupted by the arrival of two men, supposedly looking for rooms, a sinister, withdrawn Irishman named McCann, and a talkative, amiable Jew called Goldberg. They have obviously come for Stanley, for what reason we cannot guess, and they seem to be hired killers of some sort. Playing on his fears in the second act they put him through a gruelling cross-examination, throwing at him endless accusations which never add up to anything the audience can grasp as a single comprehensible charge against him, and then proceed to a sort of ritual humiliation of him at his birthday party, at the end of which he is carried off in a state of hysterical collapse. When we see him next morning he is spruce and respectable in striped trousers, black jacket and white collar, carrying a bowler hat. As he is taken by McCann and Goldberg to the waiting car he says nothing.

Clearly, the element of external violence has not altogether disappeared, but the heavy (if cloudy) symbolism of *The Room* has vanished, and instead we get a real comedy of menace which is funny and menacing primarily in relation to the unrelieved ordinariness of its background. The very fact that Stanley, Meg, and her husband Peter are believable figures living in a believable real world intensifies the horror of

Stanley's situation when the intruders come to break into his comfortable humdrum life and take him away. But, it might be said, the arrival of McCann and Goldberg takes it out of the realm of everyday reality: whatever we may have done in our lives, it is unlikely to be anything so terrible and extraordinary that two professional killers would be hired to deal with us. The answer to that is that this might well be so if Stanley's offence were ever named, or the source of his punishment explained. But this is not the case: the menace of McCann and Goldberg is exactly the nameless menace with which Stanley cruelly teases Meg before they arrive – the two men with a wheelbarrow in the back of their van who are looking for *a certain person.* . . . Just as she can be terrified by this nameless threat of retribution for unknown crimes, so we can be terrified when the same fate actually overtakes Stanley. With his habitual dexterity in such matters Pinter manages to rig the scene of Stanley's breakdown in such a way that we never know what the guilt to which he finally succumbs may be: every conceivable accusation is thrown at him, one way and another, McCann, in accord with his Irishness and brooding ferocity, seeming mainly concerned with politics and religion, treachery to 'the organization' and matters of heresy, while Goldberg, clearly a travelling salesman by natural disposition, is more interested in sex and property (Stanley murdered his wife, ran out on his fiancée and so on). Something for everyone, in fact: somewhere, the author seems to be telling his audience, you have done something – think hard and you may remember what it is – which will one day catch you out. The next time you answer a door to an innocent-looking stranger. . . .

The ambiguity, then, not only creates an unnerving atmosphere of doubt and uncertainty, but also helps to generalize and universalize the fears and tensions to which Pinter's characters are subject. The more doubt there is about the exact nature of the menace, the exact provocation which has brought it into being, the less chance there is of anyone in the audience feeling that anyway it could not happen to him. The kinship with Kafka, particularly *The Trial*, is obvious; we do not know what K. is accused of any more than we know what Stanley is accused of, and we do not know who has sent Goldberg and McCann to carry out sentence (if there is a judge and a sentence) any more than we know who sent the two men in black one day to slit K.'s throat. Not only that, but the farther we explore this world the farther we seem to be from an answer. However far K. inquiries into his mysterious judiciary, there are always further, higher levels to be explored, and in the same way Pinter has not omitted to provide a footnote to *The Birthday Party* in a one-act play he wrote immediately afterwards, *The Dumb Waiter*. In *The Birthday Party* the hired killers (if they are hired killers) appear as all-powerful and inscrutable: where Stanley is the menaced, they are menace personified, invulnerable beings, one might suppose, from another world, emissaries of death. But no, *The Dumb Waiter* assures us, hired killers are just men like anyone else; they only obey orders, and while menacing others they themselves can also be menaced.

The Dumb Waiter, even more than *The Birthday Party*, is properly a 'comedy of menace': whereas *The Birthday Party* is really funny only in the opening scenes, with their obsessive repetitions and misunderstanding, *The Dumb Waiter* is consistently funny almost all through (though a friend who saw its first production, in German at the Frankfurt Municipal Theatre, assures me that then it was played as a completely serious horror piece without a flicker of amusement). It concerns two men passing a dull Friday morning in their basement bedroom, reading the papers, talking about football, discussing the grammatical propriety of saying 'light the kettle' when one really means 'light the gas'. Little by little it emerges that they are hired killers in Birmingham on a job and waiting for their final instructions; then the 'dumb waiter' at the back (this basement must have been a restaurant kitchen once) begins to work. An order comes down: 'Two braised steak and chips. Two sago puddings. Two teas without sugar.' Eagerly they try to do what it says, sending up whatever they have to offer, while the demands of whoever is at the other end of the contraption get wilder and wilder: Macaronni Pastisio; Ormitha Macaronnada; One Bamboo Shoots, Water Chestnuts, and Chicken;

One Char Sin and Bean Sprouts. Finally they have nothing left, and go over the instructions they have already been given again; Gus goes out to the lavatory and while he is gone Ben receives an order over the speaking-tube which turns out to be that he must kill Gus. They confront each other as the curtain slowly falls.

Here the elements of the situation in *The Room* and *The Birthday Party* are repeated in a different guise; the room, the inhabitants at their ease inside it, and the disembodied threat of intrusion, in this case the intrusion of the unseen order-giver at the top of the dumb waiter. The fact that the people being menaced here are precisely those whose business it is usually to menace others, hired killers, offers an extra twist of irony, but does not make any essential difference to their situation. It does, however, reflect back on our previous knowledge of Pinter's world, not only, as already mentioned, by raising doubts in our minds as to the possibility of ever meeting our judges face to face (if McCann might be ordered to kill Goldberg, or vice versa, who is to say that someone, somewhere, might not order the destruction of the man who ordered their destruction? – is he not in all probability, like them, just an instrument?), but also by casting doubts on the safety and integrity of the room itself. Without any physical intrusion whatever, the menace may be lurking already inside the room, ready to strike through the disunion of its inhabitants – or, to put it another way, the threat may not come only from outside; it is no good simply keeping our minds closed to outside influence, for even inside there the seeds of destruction may already be planted.

This implication is worked out fully in the last of this group of plays, *A Slight Ache*, originally written for the radio and later given a rather inept West End production. Here for the first time something happens outside the room; here for the first time the menace is invited in and plays a completely passive role – he is not so much a menace in himself as the tool of the room's inhabitants against each other. The two in the room are a husband and wife, and the outsider a match-seller on the deserted country road outside their house. He has been there for two or three months, but what is he doing? He never sells any matches, and never seems to go away; he is there last thing at night and first thing in the morning. He worries Edward and Flora, and Edward insists on inviting him in; once in, he serves as an object in relation to which they act out their own insecurities and dissatisfactions. For Edward he is an impostor; he may be someone returned from the past; he is cunning, he is after something which he will get if Edward makes one false move (he is, perhaps, the personification of all the personal inadequacies Edward feels in himself?). For Flora he is the husband she has wanted, the pet she can fuss over, the child she can mother. And so gradually Edward breaks himself down, faced with this monumentally non-committal figure (a contemporary Pinter short story, *The Examination*, is a useful gloss here, treating of almost exactly the same mental process from the inside), and Flora gathers strength from his presence, until finally Edward and the match-seller change positions, Flora herself hanging the match-seller's tray around Edward's neck before she takes the new object of her devotion out for lunch in the garden, by the pool.

A Slight Ache brings us to the threshold of a new phase in Pinter's career, introducing a number of changes both internal and external. For one thing, it marks the end of a period of relative obscurity. Up to mid-1959 his plays had made very little impact on the public at large. *The Room* was first produced by Bristol University Department of Drama and later by Bristol Old Vic Drama School for the *Sunday Times* Drama Festival; *The Birthday Party* ran a bare week at the Lyric, Hammersmith, to almost total critical incomprehension: *The Dumb Waiter* was produced first in German at Frankfurt; and *A Slight Ache* was commissioned for the Third Programme. Pinter was a name to conjure with, just about, for some intellectual theatre-goers, but that was all.

A Slight Ache also marks the end of the 'comedy of menace' phase in Pinter's work, though ironically just when he was moving out of it the phrase was coined and has become almost unavoidable in discussion of Pinter, though generally applied to work which does nothing to merit the title. For these early plays, however, the description is admirably exact. Menace is unmistakably present: the central characters – Rose, Stanley, Gus and Ben, Edward – are all prey to unknown dangers, unspoken threats, and finally an unpleasant fate (all the more sinister for remaining undefined) overtakes them all. But comedy is present, too, usually in the earlier scenes, but nearly all through in *The Dumb Waiter*. Evidently, on one level at least, Pinter has learnt a lot from the master of controlled horror, Hitchcock, many of whose bravura effects are achieved in precisely this way, from making some horrible reality emerge out of a piece of light and apparently irrelevant comedy. But Pinter's comedy rarely even seems irrelevant: it is 'about' the same things as his scenes of terror, the inability or, he has implied, the unwillingness of human beings to communicate, to make contact with each other. If it is terrifying to open the door to a strange knock, it is equally terrifying to open your mind to someone else, for once he is in you never know what he may do (Edward's trouble, for instance, is almost entirely that he talks too much, that, to parody a phrase of Arthur Miller, he allows himself to be wholly known). Consequently, in ordinary conversation Pinter's characters twist and turn, profoundly distrustful of any direct communication, and even when they attempt it are generally constitutionally incapable of achieving it: hardly ever in his work does one encounter two people of the same level of intelligence in conversation – there is nearly always one leaping ahead in the exchange while another stumbles confusedly along behind – except at the lowest end of the scale, where both are so stupid that communication is virtually impossible anyway. And out of these confusions and conversational impasses Pinter creates his characteristic forms of comedy, which may be examined at their purest in some of the revue sketches which were his next work after *A Slight Ache* and which constitute his first unmistakable success with a wider public.

These sketches are, of course, very slight and of quite minor importance in Pinter's work, but unlike many 'popular' works of 'serious' writers they contain no hint of writing down and are most of them completely characteristic of their author. They came about more or less by accident; Disley Jones, who had worked on *The Birthday Party*, found himself involved in planning a new revue, *One to Another*, and asked Pinter if he would care to contribute. Pinter thought about it and then turned one of his early monologues into a dialogue, 'The Black and White', which he followed with 'Trouble in the Works' for the same show, 'Special Offer', 'Getting Acquainted', 'Last to Go', and 'Request Stop' for *Pieces of Eight*, an even more popular revue, and a seventh, 'Applicant', which first appeared in his volume *A Slight Ache and other plays*. .

The sketches vary in their form of humour: 'Special Offer', which concerns a B.B.C. lady disturbed by an offer of 'Men for Sale' in Swan & Edgars, and 'Getting Acquainted', a farcical episode built around a Civil Defence practice, are slight pieces which Pinter himself does not wish to preserve. 'Trouble in the Works' and 'Applicant' are both interview scenes: in the first a factory manager receives the complaints of the workmen's representative about some of the products they have taken a dislike to (such as the high-speed taper shank spiral flute reamers and the fundamental side outlet relief with handwheel); in the second an unfortunate applicant for a job is fitted with electrodes and bombarded with impossible questions until he suffers a complete collapse. 'Applicant' takes us back to 'comedy of menace' country, being in effect a variation on the interrogation scene in *The Birthday Party*; 'Trouble in the Works' is primarily a linguistic fantasy on themes taken from the terminology of heavy engineering. Neither is typical Pinter, though neither could be written by anyone else. But the other three sketches show to perfection his way with dialogue and also a new relaxation and warmth in handling human beings which suggests more than anything which has gone before the way he will develop.

They are, in fact, as the author himself has remarked, plays in miniature. Of 'The Black and White' he explained: 'I had never done anything with the tramp women because they fitted naturally into a complete play which just happened to be four minutes long: it couldn't be expanded or worked into a more general framework, but on the other hand what can you do with a one-act play which lasts only four minutes? The only thing, of course, though I would never have considered it a possibility unprompted, is to fit it into a revue as a sketch.'

But if they are plays in miniature, they are plays with many differences from what has gone before. There is no menace, no battle between the light and warmth of the room and the invading forces of darkness and disruption from outside. Instead we have two old tramp women in an all-night café comparing notes on the way they spend their nights, watching the last night buses go past; a newspaper-seller and the proprietor of a coffee-stall talking about which evening paper is the last to be sold; a slightly mad woman making a scene at a bus stop by maintaining loudly that a very mild-looking man next to her has made an improper proposal. They are just tiny cameos in which two or more characters are put into relation with each other and allowed simply to interact; they are all, in a sense, about failures of communication, or more properly perhaps the unwillingness to communicate (the two tramp women do perhaps communicate at a very low level, but the woman at the bus stop is completely solitary and neither the newsvendor nor the man at the coffee-stall ever really understands a word the other is saying). Pinter himself stresses the unwillingness: he has been quoted as saying, 'I feel that instead of any inability to communicate there is a deliberate evasion of communication. Communication itself between people is so frightening that rather than do that there is continual cross-talk, a continual talking about other things rather than what is at the root of their relationship.'

This much is true (in varying degrees) of all his work, right from *The Room* to *The Homecoming*, and describes one aspect of his dramatic writing very well. But from these latter three sketches on, the emphasis in his work comes to be placed much more squarely on the relationships between characters, their attempts to live together without giving up too much of themselves. (It might be remarked, parenthetically, that if no character really wants to communicate with the others in Pinter's plays he nearly always wants the others to communicate with him, and much of the tension in the dialogue comes from the constant evasions, the slight revelations and drawings back involved in this endless skirmishing on the threshold of communication, with each character determined to find out more than he tells.) The same shift of emphasis is suggested by something Pinter said just after writing the sketches: 'As far as I am concerned there is no real difference between my sketches and my plays. In both I am interested primarily in people: I want to present living people to the audience, worthy of their interest primarily because they *are*, they exist, not because of any moral the author may draw from them.' For though the earlier plays are certainly not tied to a moral of any sort, they are slightly impeded in the presentation of people just being, existing, by the exigencies of plot, which require them to be menaced and to succumb. But the statement, only partially true of Pinter's plays up to *A Slight Ache*, becomes completely true in the best of the sketches ('The Black and White' and 'Last to Go') and in the plays which followed them, *A Night Out* and *The Caretaker*, where the characters, the one mysterious external menace removed, can get on with precisely the job this statement envisages for them: just existing.

It is, in fact, tempting to see Pinter's progression from the earlier plays to the later in terms of a closer and closer approach to realism. In the early plays the quiet, often wryly comic tone of the opening scenes is gradually replaced by something much more intense and horrific, and something considerably farther away from mundane considerations of likelihood. The probability of what happens, indeed, is never at issue: it is clear from the outset that this is a private world we have been permitted to enter, and as such, whatever relations with any outside world of objective reality we may imagine we perceive, it has its own consistency and carries its own conviction. In *The Room* neither the consistency nor the conviction is altogether unimpaired. The play was written in four days and sent off straight away with only minimum corrections to a friend at Bristol University. Unexpectedly, he offered to stage it, and so the text has become fixed in a form which Pinter now finds unsatisfactory. About the blind negro, the most evidently non-realistic character in his whole *œuvre*, he now says: 'Well, it's very peculiar, when I got to that point in the play the man from the basement had to be introduced, and he just *was* a blind negro. I don't think there's anything radically wrong with the character in himself, but he behaves too differently from the other characters: if I were writing the play now I'd make him sit down, have a cup of tea . . .' So in *The Birthday Party* the characters who embody the menace already behave much more normally – realistically, we might say – in their relations with Meg, with Lulu, the buxom blonde from down the road, and even with Stanley. Menace, the play implies, is a matter of situation: it does not come from extraordinary, sinister people, but from ordinary people like you and me; it is all a matter of circumstances whether at some point I suddenly become the menace in your life or you the menace in mine, and not anything inherent in either of us. Already Pinter is closer to reality than he was in dealing with the blind negro, and in *The Dumb Waiter* he comes closer still by elaborating the point about the normality of those who menace when they are outside the context in which their menace is exerted, and by leaving the violence implied in the final tableau instead of having it directly enacted on the stage. From here it is a short step to *A Slight Ache*, in which the nominal menace is completely passive and the real disruptive force exists in the mind of the menaced. There is no violence here at all, because no violence is needed.

The point at which this gradual change seems to crystallize in a single decision is in *The Caretaker*, where again we have the room, but no outside menace, simply a clash of personalities on the inside, and again we have to have one of the inhabitants displaced by another. Pinter has described his decision on how this should be done as follows:

> At the end . . . there are two people alone in a room, and one of them must go in such a way as to produce a sense of complete separation and finality. I thought originally that the play must end with the violent death of one at the hands of the other. But then I realized, when I got to the point, that the characters as they had grown could never act in this way. . . .

In other words, here for the first time psychological realism overtly won out; these, as much as the inhabitants of 'The Black and White', are people existing, making their own decisions, creating the circumstances of their own lives, and not in any sense the puppets of fate, as were in many respects the characters of *The Room*, *The Birthday Party*, and *The Dumb Waiter*. *The Caretaker* still works completely in terms of a private myth, as they did, but it gains in richness and complexity by also working completely, as they did not, on the quite different level at which comprehensible motivation comes into play: for the first time we can sensibly consider (if we want to) why the characters do what they do as well as, more obscurely, why what happens has the effect it does on us.

There are three characters: two brothers, Mick and Aston, and an old tramp, Davies, whom Aston has invited back to his room. Aston is strangely laconic and withdrawn, and it eventually emerges that he was in a mental home two years before and received electrical shock treatment which has left him as he is. His brother is trying to get through to him, to arouse his interest in something, and Aston had been collecting materials for some time with the intention of building a shed, but shows little sign of getting down to it. Davies, in fact, is the first thing in which he has shown positive interest since the mental home; he likes him and likes his company. Mick's jealousy is instantly aroused, and his one thought is to get the old man out, but he can do this satisfactorily from his own point of view only if Aston voluntarily rejects Davies. So, hiding his dislike behind a mask of flippancy Davies takes for good humour, Mick confides his plans to Davies and leads him on to suppose that he is quite amiably disposed and will hire him as caretaker for the the house when it is fitted up. Davies falls into the trap by trying to play one brother against the other, rejecting Aston, his real friend, and throwing in his lot with Mick. He even goes so far as to curry favour with Mick by saying that Aston is mad, and then Mick has him where he wants him:

What a strange man you are. Aren't you? You're really strange. Ever since you come into this house there's been nothing but trouble. Honest, I can take nothing you say at face value. Every word you speak is open to any number of different interpretations. Most of what you say is lies. You're violent, you're erratic, you're just

Y

completely unpredictable. You're nothing else but a wild animal, when you come down to it, you're a barbarian. And to put the old tin lid on it, you stink from arse-hole to breakfast-time. Look at it. You come here recommending yourself as an interior decorator, whereupon I take you on, and what happens? You make a long speech about all the references you've got down at Sidcup, and what happens? I haven't noticed you go down to Sidcup to obtain them. It's all most regrettable, but it looks as though I'm compelled to pay you off your caretaking work. Here's half a dollar.

Rejected by Mick, Davies tries desperately to make it up with Aston, but it is too late, and he has gone too far: Aston has determined to start work on his shed ('If I don't get it up now it'll never go up. Until it's up I can't get started.'), and there is no place in his life for Davies, who has no alternative before him as the curtain falls but to leave.

As the speech just quoted suggests, the style of *The Caretaker* is much more direct than that of Pinter's earlier plays. Everything that Aston says – suitably enough, considering his mental condition – is perfectly clear and unequivocal. And though Mick's mental processes are devious the intention behind everything he says is clear, even when he is talking apparently at random just to unsettle the old man (there are several examples of this in the second act – the long irrelevant comparisons with his uncle and the bloke he knew in Shoreditch, the fantastic excursion in which he pretends to be letting the flat to Davies). Only Davies is subject in his conversation to the characteristic Pinter ambiguity, and this is here symptomatic not of the general unknowability of things, but of a specific intention on the character's part to cover his tracks and keep people guessing about himself. Not that there isn't a certain forlorn conviction in his assertions that everything would be right if only he could get down to Sidcup and collect his papers, but evidently this is a story he has told so often to excuse himself that now he himself half believes it – whether there is any truth in it at all we have no way of knowing. Whenever he is asked a direct question he either evades answering it directly (when asked if he is Welsh he replies, after a pause, 'Well, I been around, you know') or by offering an apparently unequivocal answer which ten minutes later he will contradict with another equally unequivocal statement.

Shortly before *The Caretaker* was produced Pinter provided a gloss on his use of this sort of contradiction and ambiguity in a programme note to the Royal Court production of *The Room* and *The Dumb Waiter*.

The desire for verification is understandable, but cannot always be satisfied. There are no hard distinctions between what is real and what is unreal, nor between what is true and what false. The thing is not necessarily either true or false; it can be both true and false. The assumption that to verify what has happened and what is happening presents few problems, I take to be inaccurate. A character on the stage who can present no convincing argument or information as to his past experiences, his present behaviour or his aspirations, nor give a comprehensive analysis of his motives is as legitimate and as worthy of attention as one who, alarmingly, can do all these things. The more acute the experience the less articulate its expression.

But as a moment's consideration shows, this applies much more readily to Pinter's earlier works than to those he was at that time writing. In *The Caretaker* verification is seldom a problem. If we want to know why Aston is as he is, he tells us in detail at the end of the second act, and no doubt is ever cast on what he says. If we want to know exactly what Mick's game is, there is enough clear indication throughout, and even though his way of reaching his goal is rather indirect – necessarily if he is to edge the cunning old tramp out and at the same time make sure that Aston also wants him to leave – by the last act the intention underlying all he does becomes unmistakable. Only with Davies is there any difficulty about verification: we have no way of knowing whether he has really left any papers at Sidcup, what really happened at the monastery where he hoped to be given a pair of shoes (if it existed and if he ever went there), or which of the other recollections which scatter his conversation are true or false. But even here the desire for verification is nowhere near the forefront of our minds, because none of this, even by normal standards of play-making, is vital to our understanding (in the way that, for instance, we would normally require to know precisely what Stanley had done to bring judgement on him in *The Birthday Party*, who the blind negro in *The Room* was, who Edward in *A Slight Ache* thinks the match-seller might be). All we need to understand about Davies for the purposes of the play is that he is shifty, unreliable, and probably incapable of telling the truth even if he wanted: his evasions and contradictions imply a judgement on him, but not necessarily on the world around him.

In fact, the play seems to be built upon a proposition new in Pinter's work, one which he has expressed as 'simple truth can often be something much more terrifying than ambiguity and doubt'. The classic instance of this is Aston's speech at the end of Act 2, when he explains about his experiences before, during, and after his treatment at the mental home. As first performed, this seemed quite out of context, being made into a direct, self-pitying appeal for sentimental sympathy, a thin patch representing a weak point in the intricately woven texture of the whole work. But when one studies the play in print it becomes obvious that it is, in fact, no such radical departure from the style of the rest of the play; Aston, indeed, never speaks – could never speak – in any other style, and there is no basic ambiguity in the play in relation to which this single major deviation into unequivocal sense would be artistically impossible. If the monologue were played, as the rest of the text demands it be played, impersonally, almost entirely without expression, as though the speaker were under hypnosis or describing something which happened to someone else, it would become legitimately the climax of horror in the play, the inevitable moment of reckoning with the past – Stanley's ordeal, in effect, but this time self-inflicted, and therefore something from which Aston can begin to recover in the third act by resolving anew really to get started on his shed.

This new directness and simplicity is to be found also in the television-cum-radio play Pinter was writing immediately before, *A Night Out*, and his next television play *Night School*. In *A Night Out* the protagonist, Albert, suffers from the attentions of a clinging, possessive mother, and the play chronicles his attempts to escape from her for one evening. First there is a firm's party he has to go to and which his mother blandly refuses to take into account by disregarding everything he says on the subject. When he finally shakes her off and goes everything goes wrong, the whole thing culminating in a 'liberty' taken by the old employee in whose honour the party is given with a young woman, for which Albert is blamed. He leaves, and on his return has to suffer a long, self-pitying monologue from his mother embodying a series of variations on her favourite theme, that if he wants to go out and leave her he must be leading an unclean life, 'mucking about with girls' or frequenting low pubs.

The end of the second act leaves him, the worm turned at last, poised with a clock above his head as though about to attack her, and exactly what has happened remains in doubt until the end of the third. When we next encounter Albert he is succumbing to the advances of a terribly genteel prostitute, with whom he exchanges fantasies: he is an assistant director in films, she a respectable mother with a daughter at a select boarding-school near Hereford. But finally, the suppressed violence in his mind coming to the surface, he threatens her, too, with a clock, obviously substituting her for his mother. ('Who do you think you are? You talk too much, you know that? You never stop talking. Just because you're a woman you can get away with it. . . . You're all the same, you see, you're all the same, you're just a dead weight around my neck.') He shatters her dream about a daughter by demonstrating that the photograph is actually of her as a child, and then having exercised his power over her by making her put on and do up his shoes he leaves and returns home to a tearful, forgiving, and quite unharmed mother, ready to stifle him as much as ever with her neurotic solicitude. The night out is over.

Here again the question of verification and its problems does not arise; the motivation of all the characters is made quite clear, and even the one or two points on which some doubt exists are rapidly cleared up: the photograph in the prostitute's room is proved to be of herself by an inscription on the back, and the perpetrator of the 'liberty', left in doubt in the radio version of the play, is unequivocally identified in the television version. (The script direction reads: 'The camera closes on Mr

Ryan's hand, resting comfortably on his knee, and then to his face which, smiling vaguely, is inclined to the ceiling. It must be quite clear from the expression that it was his hand which strayed.') Instead, the play concerns itself with the working out of the relationship between Albert and his mother, and the impossibility of their communicating with one another, or at least the impossibility of his communicating with her. Albert is more intelligent than his mother, but he is weak, and so her stupidity makes her impregnable: she just cannot, or will not, understand anything which does not suit her, and when he goes against her wishes she regards this not as evidence that he is an adult with a mind of his own, but simply as the wilfulness of a child, to be rebuked but not taken too seriously. It is the Stanley-Meg situation over again, except that this time Albert has not chosen it and resents it; he has not discovered, as Stanley has, the way of turning his mother's stupidity to his own purpose, and all his gestures of rebellion are impotent. Though he insists on going to the party, once he has his way guilt overtakes him and he tries to get out of it by feigning illness; the party itself is bound to be disastrous for him because he has insisted on going against his mother's wishes. And even when he resorts to physical violence he cannot win: he has to be content with a substitute victory against a substitute victim, the prostitute to whom he pours out the reproaches about her endless talking and the matter of the light in Grandma's bedroom which should by rights be directed at his mother. The final insult, perhaps, his mother's willingness, after all this has happened, to forget everything and let things be just as they were before, since it is the final demonstration that Albert does not count and nothing he can do really matters.

A Night Out offers convincing proof, if proof were needed, that Pinter does not rely in his plays entirely on his ingenuity in thinking up situations of horror and mystery and then giving them a superficial reality by exploiting his undeniable skill at capturing in his dialogue the precise nuances of everyday speech. As in *The Caretaker*, the people in it make their situations rather than being created by them, and in so far as the situations in *A Night Out* are nearer the world in which most of us live than those in *The Caretaker*, we are better able to appreciate at once Pinter's success in the mode of psychological realism. And this, even though the integrity of his dramatic private world remains unimpaired: the myopically detailed, obsessive quality of his observation is just as much in evidence here as before and the effect is to charge a story which could be treated in a simple, conventionally 'realistic' fashion (something one could hardly say of any of the earlier plays) with the sort of feverish intensity which Alain Robbe-Grillet at his best some-times achieves. In fact, the play demonstrates again a basic fact in Pinter's work – that it often seems least realistic when it is closest to actuality. For the form of the dialogue, with its constant leap-frogging and casting-back in sense, its verbal mis-understandings, anticipations which prove to be mistaken, mishearings and all the other characteristics of everyday speech which most dramatists iron out into a logical, grammatical *lingua franca* which passes on the stage for realistic speech, recalls rather the sort of photopuzzles *Lilliput* used to publish in its heyday, in which details of familiar objects would be vastly enlarged so that the grains and textures stood out with hallu-cinary precision and all the normal associative connotations were stripped from them. In effect this is reality turned against itself, for showing something so closely, with such fanatical accuracy, makes it seem far less real and familiar than the conventional simplifications of our normal dilatory middle view.

Pinter's next television play, *Night School*, takes up again and develops certain themes from *A Night Out*, but their handling is rather arbitrary and Pinter later revised it for radio before publishing it, saying that it contains 'characteristics that implied I was slipping into a formula. It so happens this was the worst thing I have written. The words and ideas had become auto-matic, redundant.' Certainly the main thing to strike one about it in performance was the low level of intensity at which it worked: obviously intended to be a light comedy exploiting the new realistic vein in Pinter's work, it failed mainly because it seemed that the author had deliberately reduced the mechan-ical interest of his plot (all the ambiguities are resolved completely in a way which offers no surprises) in order to let his characters act and interact very much as they do in *The Caretaker* and *A Night Out*, but then failed to create characters interesting enough to hold our attention on this level.

A number of the old themes are recapitulated in various ways: the basic conflict of the play, for instance, is a battle for the possession of a room which represents for the protagonist, Walter, an unsuccessful forger just home from prison, quiet and security. ('If only I could get my room back! I could get settled in, I could think, about things.') Unfortunately in his absence his aunts have let it to an apparently genteel, respectable young woman who claims that she teaches in a night school. Again the minor ambiguities and contradictions are significant in terms of character rather than as implied comments on reality: Walter is a liar, but he lies to achieve his various purposes and the discrepancies between his various statements seem only to tell us more about him; the old scrap-dealer Solto is an inveterate boaster, but the truth or otherwise of his boasts never comes into question. In fact, the problem of verification resolves itself into one single question: is Sally, the supposed night-school teacher, what she seems, or is she really the night-club entertainer to whom she bears a quite inexplicable resemblance? And this question is answered for us, unsurprisingly, before the end; the two Sallys are, in fact, one, and when Walter seems to be getting too warm in his attempts to establish their identity she leaves.

The connection of all this with the last act of *A Night Out* is obvious: it might almost be a portrait of the girl there as seen through the eyes of the other occupants of the house where she lives (apparently respectable enough for her visitors to have to creep round in stockinged feet). A number of details are also carried over: the play with the photograph of Sally in a gym slip recalls the other girl's deception with a photograph of herself when young, and Walter's strange bout of obsessive order-giving, when he makes Sally repeatedly cross and uncross her legs, recalls Albert's orders to the other girl – except that there the scene had its dramatic *raison d'être*, while here it seems merely arbitrary, arising from nothing we know of in Walter's character and serving no apparent purpose in the play as a whole except to give it a sensational highlight. The main point of interest about *Night School*, in fact, is its demonstration that Pinter can, like anyone else, make his mistakes, but that (*a*) he is the first to acknowledge them, and (*b*) even when his imagination is working at decidedly less than full throttle he still remains true to his world and produces something which, though markedly inferior to his best work, could still have been written by no one else.

If *Night School* implied that Pinter was 'slipping into a formula', his next work, the radio play *The Dwarfs*, shows him triumphantly escaping the danger. It carried him off on a new line of inquiry which was to prove highly significant in his further development; it has certainly been his most difficult play yet and the most daunting to popular taste. As a matter of fact, its genesis dates back a number of years, to the long, unpublished novel of the same title Pinter wrote between 1953 and 1957. In that there were four main characters, three men and a girl, but in the play only the three men appear, Pete, Mark, and Len. Pete and Mark as we encounter them are 'typical Pinter characters'; they indulge in dilatory, inconsequential conversations with each other and with Len, avoiding real communication as far as possible. Our clearest picture of them comes from Len, with his images of them: Pete, walking by the river, cruel and predatory like a gull, digging under a stone in the mud; Mark, sitting smooth and complacent by his fireside, like a spider in his web. But they are for us almost entirely projections of Len's consciousness; each is convinced that the other is bad for Len, that not Len but only he can manage the other, and this is almost all we know of them objectively: this, and that vanity is the dominant force in Mark's character – otherwise completely negative, he is stirred to action only when he learns from Len that Pete thinks he is a fool.

But Len is a very different case; we learn a lot more about him, and in a way that is completely new in Pinter's writing – we are actually allowed to enter his mind. We have never really known what went on in the minds of Pinter characters before, and the mystery of what they could possibly be thinking, the tension between the known and the unknown, was a large part of the earlier plays' fascination. In the later plays the characters become noticeably more scrutable; we can guess quite often what is in their minds but, except for Aston's speech in *The Caretaker*, we are never told. The freedom of radio has allowed Pinter in this play, however, to switch at will from ordinary conversation to a stream-of-consciousness monologue, and monologue, moreover, from a stream of consciousness far wider and deeper and more turbulent than Aston's, for while Aston is numbed as a result of his shock treatment at the mental home, Len still has that desperate remedy to come; he is hovering on the brink of insanity, and when we leave him is perhaps already in a mental home. (Or is he? It depends whether Pete is being evasive when he says that Len is in hospital suffering from 'kidney trouble', or simply stating a fact.)

The creatures which bedevil Len's mind are the dwarfs, who are ever busy gobbling up garbage, organizing and arranging, observing Len, Pete, and Mark, until finally, mysteriously, they leave. Who are they? What are they? Well, who is anyone, come to that? This is the central theme of the play, summed up in Len's climactic speech to Mark:

The point is, who are you? Not why or how, not even what. I can see what, perhaps, clearly enough. But who are you? It's no use saying you know who you are just because you tell me you can fit your particular key into a particular slot which will duly receive your particular key because that's not foolproof and certainly not conclusive. Just because you're inclined to make these statements of faith has nothing to do with me. It's not my business. Occasionally I believe I perceive a little of what you are, but that's pure accident. Pure accident on both our parts, the perceived and the perceiver. It's nothing like an accident, it's deliberate, it's a joint pretence. We depend on these accidents, on these contrived accidents, to continue. It's not important then that it's conspiracy or hallucination. What you are, or appear to be to me, or appear to be to you, changes so quickly, so horrifyingly, I certainly can't keep up with it and I'm damn sure you can't either. But who you are I can't even begin to recognize, and sometimes I recognize it so wholly, so forcibly, I can't look, and how can I be certain of what I see? You have no number. Where am I to look, where am I to look, what is there to locate, so as to have some surety, to have some rest from this whole bloody racket? You're the sum of so many reflections. How many reflections? Is that what you consist of? What scum does the tide leave? What happens to the scum? When does it happen? I've seen what happens. But I can't speak when I see it. I can only point a finger. I can't even do that. The scum is broken and sucked back. I don't see where it goes, I don't see when, what do I see, what have I seen? What have I seen, the scum or the essence? What about it? Does all this give you the right to stand there and tell me you know who you are? It's a bloody impertinence. . . .

Here a number of themes implicit in Pinter's previous works come to the surface and are defined in terms which show clearly the way his work is leading. Little by little the desire for verification has shifted from the audience into the play they are watching; instead of watching with a degree of mystification the manœuvres of a group of characters who seem perfectly to understand what they are doing but simply offer us no means of sharing that understanding, we are now required to watch understandingly the manœuvres of people who do not understand their situation but are trying laboriously to establish the truth about it. And this truth goes beyond the mere verification of single facts (except, perhaps, in the comedies) to a quest for the how and the why, the who and the what, at a deeper level than demonstrable fact. This involves a new preoccupation with the means of communication, since the question comes back, will people tell the truth about themselves, and if they will, can they? Everyone wants to know the truth about others without letting them know the truth about him – the feeling that once someone is called by his true name he is in the power of the caller lies deep. Pinter has said that his characters are 'at the extreme edge of their living, where they are living pretty much alone'. Even if the disposition to communicate at this level exists at all, it is a possibility? Reality itself is so complex, and changes so quickly, that our only hope is an unspoken conspiracy whereby we tacitly agree to accept certain formulas as true, some constant patterns beneath the constantly changing surface of things. A man may change alarmingly from moment to moment, but for the sake of argument we presume that there is one coherent being underneath; the tide may come and go, the scum be broken and sucked back, but behind the superficial restlessness and change lies the monumental consistency of the unchanging sea.

But is this so? In his next two plays, *The Collection* and *The Lover* (both originally written for television) Pinter sets out to explore the question further, within the context of relations between husband and wife. No longer is there any question of *failure* of communication; in both plays the characters are educated and articulate, they are capable of expressing to each other whatever they want to express. If they want to tell the truth about themselves they have at their disposal the means of doing so, but of course they don't want to, and it remains highly doubtful whether even if they did they could. What each wants to know about the other, and what we want to know about them, is essentially unknowable, perhaps does not even exist – it is the one face behind the faces. They want to break through 'the joint pretence' upon which 'we depend to continue', and discover the truth, even though 'The thing is not necessarily either true or false; it can be both true and false'. In other words, we are back with verification, but at a deeper level at which the desire to achieve it is inevitably and inescapably doomed to failure, since it is not a matter, even conceivably, of verifiable fact (as, say, the reasons for Stanley's persecution by Goldberg and McCann in *The Birthday Party* might be). In *The Collection* this does not immediately appear to be so: ostensibly the matter at issue is whether Stella and Bill, two young fashion designers at the same out-of-town show, did or did not sleep with each other. But when Stella's husband James sets out to meet and question Bill he does not seem to be looking for the truth about that. She has told him it happened, and apparently he believes her. No, the truth he wants to find is the truth about her; he will know more about her if he gets to know the man she has found attractive enough to go to bed with at first meeting. He doesn't, of course: the more contradictory accounts emerge, the more lies, equivocations, and half-truths pile up, the less anyone knows about anyone. The defensive mechanisms of human beings are too well-ordered for them to do anything else but go smoothly into action at the mere hint from an outsider that given half a chance he will find out the whole truth, pin one down, and categorize one forever.

When James sets out with sinister amiability to terrorize Bill (the menace of the earlier plays given background: to Bill, James is at first a nameless and inexplicable terror from outside, but we know why he is doing what he is doing), Bill begins by denying anything happened, then agrees and starts to elaborate. But there is another party interested, Harry, a suave, middle-aged art fancier, who as he tells us found Bill in the gutter and with whom Bill lives on terms of suspicious intimacy. While James is persuading Bill to corroborate Stella's story, Harry is persuading Stella to retract it and say that nothing really happened at Leeds at all. Harry arrives back just as James is getting threatening and indulging in a little knife-throwing (none too successfully; again, the menace is humanized) and when faced with Stella's new version of the incident Bill breaks down and agrees that in fact all that happened was that they sat in the hall for two hours talking about what they would do if they went to her room. It sounds like the truth, but when the play ends James has returned to the attack with Stella and is getting no satisfactory answer from her. . . .

The business of verification, of finding out 'the truth', has become an elaborate manœuvre, a highly serious game like something in *Les Liaisons Dangereuses* (here, for instance, every possible combination of the principals is permitted except that of the two people, Bill and Stella, who were actually present on the occasion in question – if they *were* there, of course – and who alone could perhaps tell us what really happened), but in which what is to be decided may well be a matter of life and death. It is vitally important to James that he should find out what sort of woman Stella is, faced suddenly with the picture of an unknown woman who yet lives in the same body with his wife. Which is the real Stella? If he knows 'the facts' for certain, will he be any nearer a solution? Can the game be played through to a decisive conclusion, or is it doomed to end in deadlock?

For James at any rate it is unlikely to bring satisfaction, because he is naïve enough to demand the truth, but the couple in

The Lover expect nothing so simple. They are, apparently, happily married, with the husband complacently asking his wife as he leaves the house for work if her lover is coming this afternoon and solicitously inquiring afterwards how it was. But when we finally see the lover we discover that he is the husband, differently dressed: it is some sort of elaborate game they play by which they separate the staid husband-wife relationship and the passionate lover-mistress relationship which together make up their marriage. Indeed, so well do they separate them that they begin to act as though they are in fact being unfaithful to each other, telling half-truths about their relationships and becoming jealous of their own *alter egos*. It is in a sense the situation of Osborne's *Under Plain Cover* again, only explored far more deeply: it is not just a game for keeping the marriage fresh and exciting, but an acceptance of the inescapable fact that each person is 'the sum of so many reflections' – husband and lover, rapist and protector (within the lover-mistress situation there are further refinements in which they pretend to be first of all a woman in a park and a sinister stranger who makes menacing advances, then the same woman, prepared now to be provocative, and an apparently kindly park-keeper who intervenes on her behalf and then becomes the willing accomplice in her coquetry); sober, responsible wife, intelligent mistress, whore. . . . And it all amounts to a successfully working marriage of ten years' standing, with children (at boarding school) and no outside involvements. Any menace to the status quo comes entirely from within; if the arrangement looks like breaking down, it is only because the desire to have things clear and unequivocal is part of basic human nature and almost impossible to vanquish. However, Richard and Sarah appreciate the necessity of vanquishing it, the impossibility indeed of living together on any other terms except the acceptance of an infinitude of reflections in lieu of the unknowable, perhaps non-existent, essence. So perhaps if Max, Richard's lover-persona, can visit in the evening as well as the afternoon. . . .

The Lover represents to date Pinter's further exploration of human nature in its irrevocably fragmented form; his most wholehearted acceptance of the idea first clearly formulated in *The Dwarfs* that the Fall of man is more like Humpty-Dumpty's than Adam's and Eve's, resulting in a situation where nobody, oneself or another, can hope to put all the pieces together again into a perfect and coherent whole. Significantly, the only people in Pinter's plays who appear to tell the whole truth, into whose minds indeed we are permitted to look, are madmen – one permanently mutilated in the course of his 'cure', the other clearly tottering, when we meet him, on the brink of a complete breakdown. If Aston in *The Caretaker* allows himself to be wholly known it is only because, as he is now, there is little to know; and though Len in *The Dwarfs* speaks directly to us, as far as possible, by way of an internal monologue, the more we learn about him the less we really know him. Between *The Room* and *The Lover* we have in effect run the complete dramatic gamut from total objectivity to total subjectivity, and discovered in the process that there are no clear-cut explanations of anything. At one end of the scale no motives are explained and everything remains mysterious; at the other as many motives as possible are expounded for us, and if anything the result is more mystifying than before. It is only from a middle distance, as in *The Caretaker* and *A Night Out*, that we can see a picture simple enough to hold out the possibility that we may understand it, that we are given enough in the way of motive to reach some provisional conclusions on the characters and their actions. It is a perfect demonstration of the conspiracy on which normal human intercourse relies, and incidentally of the knife-edge on which dramatic 'realism' rests: if we were told a little less about what is going on it would be incomprehensible, but if we were told a little more the difficulty of establishing any single coherent truth would be just as great.

Clearly, for all sorts of reasons, Pinter's drama could not stick at this comfortable middle distance: ever the most meticulously logical and consistent of dramatists in his development from one play to the next, he was impelled progressively to explore what Len in *The Dwarfs* called the 'contrived accidents' of character-perception on which we depend to continue. But in the process it might seem that he was working himself into a logical and dramatic impasse. In a world where everybody is the sum of so many reflections, where nobody is the same even to himself (supposing that means anything) for two seconds together, and where nobody can be sure even of accurately perceiving what anyone else may be at any given moment, we depend on the joint pretence that people have some sort of underlying consistency, and that perceptions can at least to some extent be relied on, in order to continue living at all. And writing plays, for if the joint pretence is shattered, how shall the dramatist hope to shape or make sense of his material? Both *The Collection* and *The Lover* grapple with this problem, but in them any recognizable reality seems to be dissolving before our eyes. Even more was this the case with his next work, the television play *The Basement* (produced in 1967 but actually written three years earlier as a film script). This is a relatively slight work, the core of which – a man invites an old friend into his flat out of the rain, the guest brings in a girl and then proceeds to take over the flat and all the owner's possessions – is to be found in a short snatch of dramatic dialogue, *Kullus,* which Pinter wrote as long ago as 1949. The development of the situation, with its shifting of power and changing of role between the two men, is new, and the main interest of the piece is that it extends Pinter's preoccupation with the fragmented nature of experience beyond character to include physical surroundings as well, with the décor of the basement flat changing completely and unpredictably from shot to shot.

With the 'joint pretence' so completely rejected, all coherent, consistent vision reduced to so many shattered reflections, one could not help wondering what could logically come next for Pinter the dramatist but silence? What did come next was the television play *Tea Party*, in which withdrawal from the extreme position of the plays which preceded it is actually dramatized. In *Tea Party*, Disson, the central character, an apparently very successful businessman, suffers anguish from perceiving the frailty of the joint pretence. Is his wife's brother in fact her lover, or both, or neither? Were they brought up where and how they say they were, or not, or both yes and no?

We start with him, and up to a certain point in the play we see things through his eyes. But then we come gradually to appreciate that he is in fact going mad. If, in a game of ping-pong, he goes to hit two balls it is not necessarily because two, or an infinite number of balls are or may be coming at him, but simply that for more or less complex reasons connected with his own mental situation he sees two balls when in fact, 'really', there is only one. That is, what we are seeing is not to be taken as an image of the world as it is, but simply as one man's increasingly demented view of it. The two viewpoints fight it out during the climactic teaparty, when Disson's view of it and our 'objective' view are intercut, until finally the objective wins out and we are left decisively outside the character, in objective reality, looking on while he remains in a state of complete trance, unseeing, unhearing, paralysed (literally) by his own inability to make sense of the world around him. His situation at the end of the play might almost be symbolic of a dramatists's situation when he sees so many mutually exclusive possibilities co-existent in any character or situation that he has to stop even trying to fit them into one coherent dramatic pattern. This might well have been Pinter's situation after *The Basement*, but the end of *Tea Party*, significantly, takes us (and him) a stage further: the battle between objective and subjective viewpoints has been resolved in favour of the objective, and reality is reintegrated, leaving the unfortunate Disson as odd man out because he has contracted out of reality.

So, with a bit of hindsight, it was to be expected that *The Homecoming* (1965), Pinter's next play, full length and written for the theatre, would mark the real beginning of a new, 'objective' phase in Pinter's work, and that in fact is just what it does. Compared with what went immediately before it is a work of dazzling directness and simplicity. It is a play about six people in a room, just as *The Caretaker* was, in Pinter's own words, 'about three people in a room'. True, it may not be as simple as it seems. A number of critics at its first performance, for example, wondered whether, when Teddy, the bright boy of the family, comes home allegedly from America with a woman he alleges to be his wife and talking about three

z

children and a good job teaching philosophy at a university, he is in fact telling the truth, or whether it is just a convenient fantasy in which he may even believe himself. He shows, for example, a general unwillingness to engage in philosophical chit-chat with his fast-talking brother, on the grounds that the question posed is outside his own field – a reaction which might be thought suspicious, though actually this sort of niggling intellectual demarcation-dispute seems to me more suggestive of a real academic than an impostor. His wife drifts off into reverie whenever she might be embarking on some precise details of her life in America, and so on. So maybe it is all fantasy. But this is not a question which the play goes out of its way to raise – in fact I can see no real hint in the text that we should take what is said on the matter at anything but its face value – and even if there is a mystery here it is certain that the secret of the play does not lie in any neat crossword-puzzle solution.

No, the point is that Teddy and his wife come home, and by doing so intensify conflicts which already exist in the household and add one or two of their own. The homecoming is a test of strength for Teddy: having got away from his terrible family and built up his own life, his own family, he comes back to meet his past on its own ground, hoping to win this time in his own terms, and finds that nothing has changed. For all his education, his prosperity, his other, settled life, within the charmed circle of the family he is still unable to act. His civilized irony has no effect on anyone; he is a liberal humanist preparing to sit down in protest while the storm-troopers move in and kick him out of the way or, worse still, regard him as too insignificant even to be worth moving.

If the play is about anything other than the interplay of six characters it seems to me that it is about the battle between intellect and instinct, between thought and action. Teddy is the thinker of the family. Max, his ex-butcher father, is a tremendously lively, active, vicious old bastard, consumed with love and hate, but particularly hate. Teddy's older brother, Lenny, is brutal, fast-talking, a coarser, more savage version of Mick in *The Caretaker* without Mick's saving grace of not seeming to believe more than half of what he says. His younger brother, Joey, is an unsuccessful boxer, all brawn, very little brain, and hardly a vestige of amiability to go with his stupidity.

Teddy's Uncle Sam is the only one who might occasionally think before he speaks or acts, but this seems to be the principal reason why he says little and does less – and is disregarded by everyone. And as for Teddy's wife, Ruth, well, she is a quintessential Pinter woman, one who thinks with her body and manages better that way than most men do with their brains. She was, we gather, a 'model' (no doubt in the shadier sense of the term) before she married Teddy; she has allowed herself to be made over by him for so long – just as a cat will attach itself, or apparently attach itself, to a new owner – but now she is ready without a second thought to do what her body tells her and go back on the game, managed by and in her spare moments supplying the needs of her husband's family, and thinking with cool confidence only of what conditions she can impose to make the contract best suit her.

Around Ruth and her fate the action of the play crystallizes. In many ways, the 'homecoming' is much more hers than Teddy's, since she knows intuitively the rules of the tribe, and how to manipulate them, while Teddy, for all his education, has never managed to acquire the basic survival-kit. The action is a straight struggle for power without appeal to any authority outside the wills of those involved. There is no moral framework by which what happens can be judged, morality being invoked hardly at all by anyone, and where it is only according to the speaker's whim of the moment – the dead mother of the family may be referred to as a whore or an angel from one breath to the next, but it is all a manner of speaking, and does not pre-suppose subscription to any hierarchy in which whores are inferior to angels, or indeed noticeably different. In the battle for power naturally the body wins over the mind: the weapons of Teddy and Sam are too feeble to wound Max, Lenny or Joey. But then men, even when ruled entirely by their body, by instinct, are no match for the woman who makes no practical distinction between body and mind: it is Ruth finally who dominates Max, Lenny and Joey just as they have dominated Teddy and Sam.

The logic of the struggle is impeccable, the theatrical force of Pinter's dialogue as unarguable as ever. The play is entirely self-defining: an immaculate demonstration of Pinter's own expressed ideal, the play which has nothing to do with the becauses of drama, but unrolls imperturbably in terms of the simple 'and then ... and then ... and then' of a children's tale. In it he seems to have attained a new certainty, a new directness in his expression which appears to tell us all and yet in the end tells us nothing except the play itself, the unparaphrasable, irreducible artistic whole. The same is true of his next play, *Landscape* a brief and gnomic duologue written for the stage but first played on radio, in which two old people seem to exchange recollections, but actually do not impinge in each other's consciousness at all. The surface realism is perfect, and yet the mystery remains entire.

In fact, Pinter's work brings us up against one of the great paradoxes of the theatre – that 'realism' on the stage can be achieved only by a sacrifice of reality – in its most acute form. With most dramatists the sort of compromise by selection which permits us to feel we have a sufficient understanding of the characters and motives in *The Caretaker* and *A Night Out* is the nearest they get to reality; it seems like reality because in life we often assume much the same (generally on quite insufficient evidence) and anyway the idea that we can safely make such assumptions is reassuring. But in his other works Pinter has, to our great discomfort, stripped these illusions from us: we cannot understand other people; we cannot even understand ourselves; and the truth of any situation is almost always beyond our grasp. If this is true in life, why should it not be true in the theatre? 'A character on stage who can present no convincing argument or information as to his past experience, his present behaviour or his aspirations, nor give a comprehensive analysis as legitimate and as worthy of attention as one who, alarmingly, can do all these things.'

Or in other words, instead of regarding Pinter as the purveyor of dramatic fantasy he is usually taken for, we might equally regard him as the stage's most ruthless and uncompromising naturalist. The structure of his characters' conversations, and even the very forms of expression they use, are meticulously exact in their notation of the way people really speak (and this is as true of his best-educated characters as of his least; compare *The Collection* with 'Last to Go'), while in his minutely detailed study there is seldom room for the easy generalization, even in his most explicit plays, *The Caretaker* and *A Night Out*. But to label him simply as a naturalist so truthful that his audiences have refused to recognize themselves in the mirror leaves several important elements in his drama out of account.

First, there is his mastery of construction, which is anything but naturalistic – life never shapes itself so neatly. Not only can he handle to perfection the one-act form, working up little by little to one decisive climax, but he can also sustain a three-act drama with complete mastery. (He himself says: 'I am very concerned with the shape and consistency of mood in my plays. I cannot write anything which appears to me to be loose and unfinished. I like a feeling of order in what I write.') Of course, this is not to say that he writes what we usually mean by the 'well-made play', with its formal expositions, confrontations, and last-act revelations; for him much of the point of life is that we usually do come in half-way through a story and never quite catch up, that the two vitally concerned parties never do meet, that the letter which will explain all and round things off neatly is probably never opened. And so instead his plays are usually built on lines easier to explain in musical terms. They are, one might say, rhapsodic rather than symphonic, being held together by a series of internal tensions, one of the most frequent being the tension between two opposing tonalities (notably the comic versus the horrific, the light or known versus the dark or unknown) or two contrasted tempi (in duologue there is usually one character considerably quicker than the other in understanding, so that he is several steps ahead while the other lags painfully behind). The resolution of these tensions used to be in a bout of violence, when one key would at last establish an unmistakable ascendancy (usually the horrific would vanquish the comic, the forces of disruption establish a new order in place of the old), but in the later works Pinter has shown new skill and resourcefulness in reconciling the warring elements or ending more subtly and equally convincingly on a teasingly unresolved discord.

This musical analogy points also to the other element in his drama which effectively removes it from the naturalistic norm; what, for want of a better word, we might call his orchestration. Studying the unsupported line of the dialogue bit by bit we might well conclude that it is an exact reproduction of everyday speech, and so, bit by bit, it is. But it is 'orchestrated' with overtones and reminiscences, with unexpected resonances from what has gone before, so that the result is a tightly knit and intricate texture of which the 'naturalistic' words being spoken at any given moment are only the top line, supported by elusive and intricate harmonies, or appearing sometimes in counterpoint with another theme from earlier in the play. It is this which gives Pinter's work its unusual and at first glance inexplicable weight and density; until we understand the process we are unable to account reasonably for the obsessive fascination the most apparently banal exchanges exert in his plays.

If Pinter's plays are the most 'musical' of the new British drama, however, it follows that they are the most poetic, because what else is music in words but poetry? Far more than the fantasticated verse plays of Christopher Fry and his followers, or the verse-in-disguise plays of T. S. Eliot, his works are the true poetic drama of our time, for he alone has fully understood that poetry in the theatre is not achieved merely by couching ordinary sentiments in an elaborately artificial poetic diction, like Fry, or writing what is formally verse but not appreciable to the unwarned ear as anything but prose, like Eliot. Instead he has looked at life so closely that, seeing it through his eyes, we discover the strange sublunary poetry which lies in the most ordinary object at the other end of a microscope. At this stage all question of realism or fantasy, naturalism or artifice becomes irrelevant, and indeed completely meaningless: whatever we think of his plays, whether we accept or reject them, they are monumentally and inescapably there, the artifact triumphantly separated from the artist, self-contained and self-supporting. Because he has achieved this, and he alone among British dramatists of our day, the conclusion seems inescapable that even if others may be more likeable, more approachable, more sympathetic to one's own personal tastes and convictions, in the long run he is likely to turn out the greatest of them all.

EPILOGUE

Art and Commerce: With a Few Tentative Conclusions

Though, as we have seen in the foregoing pages, a considerable number of plays by dramatists under forty have been produced, one way or another, since 1956, their position as part of the ordinary life of the commercial theatre remains unsettled. These have been the big successes – *Look Back in Anger, The Entertainer, The Caretaker* – and many of the productions have at least covered their costs, if not a little more. On the other hand, a number of dramatists, Arden being the most obvious example, have not yet won through to any sort of success with the public at all, and when an example of the new drama fails, it is all too easy to blame the failure on its newness. Not, of course, that the old drama has shown itself much more reliable: when even Rattigan can produce a disaster taken off after four performances we might fairly suppose that nothing in this world is certain, and Michael Codron, the most enterprising of our commercial managers, ruefully admits that he has had his biggest hits with those he least expected, while on the whole he has lost most money on the obviously 'safe' commercial ventures. But, be that as it may, 'the new drama' is a label which can easily be called in evidence against its (probably unwilling) owner; if his play does not do well, there must be some reason, and those nearest to hand will certainly be 'The public isn't ready for it', 'The public doesn't like all this gloom and mystification', 'The public just wants a good traditional laugh or cry with no complications'.

It must be mentioned, however, that the mere fact of being under forty does not inevitably condemn the writer to suffering this sort of complaint; there are several dramatists under forty who are hardly tarred with the 'new drama' brush at all, and who can float comfortably on the margin of any controversy which may arise, ready to be called in misleadingly to bolster either side's case at a moment's notice. ('There now, you liked that and yet the writer's one of these new young men', or alternatively 'Well, if — can write a good straightforward play with a plot and characters and something to hold your interest, I don't see why the rest of these young fellows should consider it beneath them.') They are, on the whole, the sort of capable, workmanlike professional writer who would have made his way at any time, writing in whatever style happened to be most pleasing to audiences at the moment and making a good, sound job of it, but any connection with the new drama which might be implied by their emergence since 1956 is purely coincidental.

The principal exception to this rule, since he has at certain stages very deliberately linked himself with the new drama and been accepted by unwary critics as one of its most adventurous exponents, is Willis Hall, author of *The Long and the Short and the Tall* (anthologized in the Penguin *New English Dramatists* series) and several profitable collaborations with the novelist Keith Waterhouse. Hall (born 1929) is the complete professional, author of over eighty radio and television scripts by himself and any number of adaptations and collaborations – at present he and Waterhouse between them seem to be working on the scripts of every second British film – among which there are only two or three which really give him even the faintest claim to membership of the dramatic new wave.

The best known and most highly praised of these are *The Long and the Short and the Tall*, commissioned by Oxford Theatre Group and first performed by them at the Edinburgh Festival in 1958 under the title *Disciplines of War*, and *Last Day in Dreamland*, a one-acter originally written for television and later staged in a double bill at the Lyric, Hammersmith. These both have all the marks of post-Osborne drama (indeed, Hall is probably the writer in whom direct influence from Osborne, *Look Back in Anger* especially, is most unmistakable): in each there is a Jimmy Porter-like central character with a fund of angry rhetoric which he directs indiscriminately and almost unopposed at anyone within reach, and in each only one side of the typical Osborne ambivalence towards the neurotic and in general insufferable protagonist is allowed to show through; if Jimmy emerges as heroic almost in spite of Osborne's apparent intentions, Bamforth and Fentrill, though equally neurotic, equally insufferable, are clearly the objects of the playwright's sympathy right from the beginning. In so far, that is, as anyone has the playwright's sympathy, since despite the fashionable displays of hysteria and liberal principle (about war in one play, unemployment in the other) both plays have, on reflection, very much the air of being constructed to satisfy a certain taste in the audience rather than to express anything very close to the author's heart (it is noticeable that the only passage in either of them which comes over as genuinely felt, Sergeant Mitcham's diatribe against women in Act 2 of *The Long and the Short and the Tall,* is quite out of character and seems to have no organic connection with the rest of the play at all).

Each has a situation patently rigged for anger (how J. W. Lambert can say in his introduction to *New English Dramatists 3* that 'anger has no place in [Hall's] work' mystifies me): in *The Long and the Short and the Tall* it is the predicament of a group of soldiers lost in the Malayan jungle during the Japanese advance on Singapore in 1942, lumbered with a Japanese prisoner who is first a pet, then a source of danger, and finally, indirectly (when a sentry shoots him in a fit of panic) the cause of their discovery and extermination; in *Last Day in Dreamland* a seaside amusement arcade (representing the commercial degradation of popular taste) on the last day of the season, with the employees about to lose their £8-a-week jobs (surely it could never be so little?) and facing the rigours of six months' unemployment ahead. The central characters, Bamforth and Fentrill, are almost identical: the hectoring angry young man who knows it all and stands for most of the time in the centre of the stage, aquiver as a rule (whether the situation warrants it or not) with almost hysterical intensity, berating the other characters, who in each case, rather mysteriously, accept him as a natural leader and the life and soul of the party. The indebtedness to *Look Back in Anger* is unmistakable: the central character – and docile reaction to him which is the least credible part of Osborne's play – is just transferred lock, stock, and barrel to another context and given a few new twists with some professional adroitness but no genuine originality.

The doubts one experiences in direct contact with either play, the feeling that after all the author may be just jumping for the moment on the angry band-wagon because it is the thing to do, find a measure of confirmation if we look at his other work. *Last Day in Dreamland* was originally part of a trilogy for television, and was staged at Hammersmith with another section, *A Glimpse of the Sea*, a comedy-drama about seaside infidelity in a quite different style nearer to that of Tad Mosel perhaps than any other; the third section, *A Ride on the Donkeys*, to confuse matters still further, is a broad North Country comedy about a young donkeyman with in-law troubles (the horrific wedding reception seems to be the prototype for the similar scene in the Hall-Waterhouse *Celebration*) which disconcertingly turns into a drama halfway through and is even more disconcertingly tricked out with whimsical prologue and interludes at a bureaucratic version of the Pearly Gates. Among Hall's other television plays are a sequel to the seaside trilogy, *Return to the Sea*; a pretentious and implausible Northern variation on the Antigone theme, *Afternoon for Antigone*; a conventional problem play about a girl's battle to keep the secret of her brother's cowardice from their mother (*Air Mail from Cyprus*); an exotic children's serial later turned into a stage play (*The Royal Astrologer*), and another trilogy, this time tending to the farcical, about life in a North Country brass band. All of them are capably put together, but it would be very difficult indeed to find in them evidences of any single creative personality at work; they might easily have been written by a committee.

Apart from *Chin-Chin*, an adaptation from the French of François Billetdoux, most of Hall's recent work for stage and screen has been in collaboration with Keith Waterhouse, and this on the whole is more lively and original, though one suspects that the virtues of their first and best play, *Billy Liar* (adapted from Waterhouse's novel), have been rather overestimated by critics unfamiliar with the norm of traditional

North Country comedy from which it deviates significantly but not too far. The connection is even closer in the team's subsequent full-length plays, *Celebration* and *All Things Bright and Beautiful*, which are indeed strongest when closest to the ordinary vernacular comedy and weakest where they lay rather half-hearted claim to social significance. With *Say Who You Are* they left social significance quite aside and wrote instead a successful West End comedy in the time-honoured middle-brow style. In general Waterhouse and Hall have been best employed in the smaller forms – their revue *England, Our England* and contributions to the B.B.C.'s satirical television programme *That Was the Week That Was*, their double bill *The Sponge Room* and *Squat Betty*, performed at the Royal Court – where their gift for vivid mimicry of everyday speech and their malicious eye for the telling detail of social behaviour can be applied without the extra headache of spinning a plot to occupy a whole evening in the theatre. Their names have also become virtually inescapable on the credits of British films, and two at least of their adaptations, *Whistle Down the Wind* and *A Kind of Loving*, have been among the freshest and most idiomatic in the hopefully-named British 'New Wave'.

At least the second of our old-style professionals to emerge in the middle of the new drama, Robert Bolt, has never sought to be allied with his more enterprising contemporaries in the public mind. He is, basically, a good, traditional playwright whose approach to his craft (and the products of it) is not so different from that of, say, Terence Rattigan. He admits that the breakthrough effected by Osborne no doubt made it easier for his plays to be put on (presumably since the fact that he was born in 1924 was no longer in itself such a strong argument against production), but one can hardly suppose that his commercial and critical success would have been long delayed had he come to drama any time in the last thirty years. The extreme limits of his style are marked at one end by the complete realism of *The Critic and the Heart* and at the other by the discreet adventure into impressionistic staging, half-Brecht, half B.B.C. historical documentary, of *A Man for All Seasons* (the device of a common-man figure, half in, half out of the action may owe something to Brecht's heroic theatre, but surely owes a lot more to Bolt's apprenticeship in radio, for which the play was originally written). The best-known of his other plays, *Flowering Cherry* and *The Tiger and the Horse*, are somewhere in between, 'uneasily straddled', as Bolt himself puts it, 'between naturalism and non-naturalism': on the whole they are realistic in technique, but at their climaxes they both try, not altogether happily, to comprehend something beyond realism (Jim Cherry's vision, Gwendoline Dean's mad scene). In this at least they are experimental, but only very discreetly, with nothing to put off the most conservative playgoer or disconcert H. M. Tennent, who have wisely chosen Bolt as the object of their principal flirtation with the younger dramatist. In *Gentle Jack*, the last of his plays apart from a children's fantasy *The Thwarting of Baron Bolligrew*, to reach the West End (a rewrite of the *Critic and the Heart* called *Brother and Sister* closed on tour) lent further over into the fantastic, in a pseudo-Barrie vein, and was liked by neither the critics nor the public. In all his works (the others worth noting are his first stage play, *The Last of the Wine*, an ambitious radio play *The Drunken Sailor*, and the screenplay of David Lean's films *Lawrence of Arabia* and *Doctor Zhivago*). Bolt offers substantial acting parts for substantial actors (hence his success in attracting such luminaries as Sir Ralph Richardson, Sir Michael Redgrave, and Paul Scofield) and well-made, reliable entertainment for intelligent people, but there are not many theatregoers who could claim to look forward to his next play with any real quickening of excitement.

The third of our 'commercial' dramatists, Beverley Cross (born 1931), has up to now had his major successes out of town: his two most notable plays began their lives at Liverpool and Nottingham respectively. He shares with Bolt an academic concern for form, but carries it to extremes, with the result that *One More River* in particular must be one of the most neurotically well-made plays on record, with every 'dramatic' revelation, every ironic reversal of fortune in its involved tale of a merchant ship mutiny coming in just where most expected with a clockwork precision that ultimately proves not only faintly unnerving but destructive of any real dramatic effect. *Strip the Willow*, which foundered at Golders Green on its way to the West End, is in a quite different convention, aiming, it seems, at being a neo-Shavian comedy of ideas about an ill-assorted group of survivors from a nuclear disaster. The quotation from which the title is adapted implies that 'Strip the Willow' – a country dance – is, in fact, a sort of *totentanz*, and the conclusion suggests that it has all been meant very seriously, but if this is so what comes in between – a sort of atom-age *Admirable Crichton* – allows us too often to lose sight of the underlying theme in a plethora of farcical incident, and suggests that Cross has not yet mastered the distinction between comedy with ideas and comedy of ideas.

A number of other new dramatists have emerged in the 1960s who seemed from the outset perfectly at ease in the commercial West End theatre. The two most interesting of them have been Frank Marcus (b. 1928) and Joe Orton (1933–1967), who have in common the fact that the biggest success of each is a comedy prominently involving homosexuality, a subject only quite recently allowed by the Lord Chamberlain into the enclosed garden of public theatre. Frank Marcus's first West End play, *The Formation Dancers* (1964) was a brisk, neat, superficial comedy of sexual manners. *The Killing of Sister George* (1965) cut rather deeper: though still essentially a comedy, it dealt sympathetically and perceptively with a lesbian relationship between an aging radio actress ('Sister George' in an endless soap-opera series, who now finds herself on the point of being written out) and a rather juvenile young woman who is finally revealed as considerably older and more experienced than she seems. None of Marcus's later plays, among them *Studies in the Nude* (1967) and *Mrs. Mouse, Are You Within?* (1968) has achieved a comparable success, though they show flashes of the same talent.

Joe Orton's big success was *Entertaining Mr. Sloane* (1964), which was preceded only by a short radio 'comedy of menace', *The Ruffian on the Stair*. *Entertaining Mr. Sloane* is a very neat, well-made piece of comic writing about a young man who comes into an apparently ordinary, vulnerable suburban

AA

household as a lodger, having, as we subsequently learn, already committed at least one murder. We therefore assume that he will terrorize his silly, motherly landlady and her businessman brother, with his rather suspicious ideals of masculine friendship. But in the event the tables are turned and they end up terrorizing him, and quite calmly arranging things so that they shall alternate six-month bouts of being entertained by Mr Sloane – until, that is, they tire of him or one uses him to dispose of the other. All of which is written in deceptively proper, formal dialogue which achieves something of the surrealistic dissociation of *The Young Visiters*. Orton's next exercise in the style, *Loot* (1966), a farce about death and inheritance, was equally successful commercially, but showed the style hardening into a mannerism. The other works Orton completed before his premature death, including the television plays, *The Erpington Camp*, about a holiday camp presented as a sort of voluntary concentration camp (later staged in a double bill with *The Ruffian on the Stair* as *Crimes of Passion*) and *Funeral Games*, another farce about death and religion, are too slight and undeveloped to permit any certain guess at how his talent would have developed had he survived. So is his last stage play, *What the Butler Saw*, and avid farce on the same lines as *Loot*. Though no one would think of bracketing them with the new drama, it is perhaps just worth reminding ourselves that several of our most reliable purveyors of light entertainment belong to the same generation, among them the four actor-writers of the phenomenally successful satirical revue *Beyond the Fringe* (one of whom, Peter Cook, has also contributed to such other revues as *Pieces of Eight* and *One Over the Eight*); Anthony Newley and Leslie Bricusse, authors of the hit musical *Stop the World, I Want to Get Off*; John Chapman, author of *Dry Rot, Simple Spyman*, and other farces for the Whitehall theatre company on screen and television; Julian Slade, creator of *Salad Days* and several less agreeable musical fantasies, and Sandy Wilson, unclassifiable and sophisticated deviser of *The Boy Friend, The Buccaneer*, and *Valmouth* (the last at any rate eccentric and in its chi-chi fashion experimental enough to deserve honourable mention). And mention must also be made, if only parenthetically, of *Say Nothing*, a first stage play by James Hanley, a veteran by the standards of this book (he was born in 1901) who as a working-class writer in the 1930s took inevitably to the novel and when he finally found an opening in the theatre proved, with no knowledge of Pinter, Beckett et al., to have reached almost the same conclusions as many of our young contemporaries about dramatic style and form. The Theatre Royal, Stratford E., where *Say Nothing* was staged during Theatre Workshop's period of suspended animation, also housed for a while another unusually interesting play, *A Whistle in the Dark*, Thomas Murphy's savage picture of the descent of a family of Irish thugs on a peace-loving brother who has settled in Coventry. The actor Robert Shaw began writing with an ambitious, uneven play, *Off the Mainland*, staged at the Arts in 1956, then went on to write several distinguished novels, from one of which, *The Hiding Place*, he later drew a powerful television play, and from another, *The Man in the Glass Booth*, an outstandingly true, mysterious stage play. Other novelists have made odd, interesting sallies into the theatre. David Caute wrote one political play, *Songs for an Autumn Rifle*, set in Hungary and London during the 1956 rising, which showed a remarkably sure hand at dramatizing rather unmanageable material when staged on the Edinburgh Festival Fringe in 1961. David Storey wrote a powerful and extraordinarily confident first play in *The Restoration of Arnold Middleton* (1966), which managed to treat with humour and real understanding the situation of a teacher who is, beneath a façade of schoolboy japes, slowly but surely going mad, until at the last he manages to pass the crisis and pull himself back to sanity again. Elsewhere there was *The Tinker*, a spirited bit of Jimmy-Porterage from the provinces by Lawrence Dobie and Robert Sloman (subsequently travestied in a film version called *The Wild and the Willing*).

There are probably others, but it is time to stop splashing among the shallows and try to produce some sort of conclusion. Who are the real hopes of the British theatre? For that matter, to ask the question which has grown more and more popular as *Look Back in Anger* ages into an object of academic study and the 'new drama' has been with us for more than a decade, is the new drama itself dying or dead? Certainly its earlier plays are now coming up for revival: *The Birthday Party, Serjeant Musgrave's Dance,* and *Look Back* itself (with the big question should it or should it not be revived in period costume?). And why not, after all? But it does make one think; all this, which was brave and new and defiant only yesterday, is already retreating into history; not 'new drama' any more, but just drama like any other. Or is it? How far do dramatists who have been labelled new find themselves fitting into the normal theatre scene, and how far will managers, critics and the public let them?

Well, let us consider what has been happening to the principal figures in the new drama since *Look Back in Anger* and the English Stage Company set it all off back in May 1956. Two of the most interesting writers of the movement – let us accept briefly, for the sake of argument, that it was a movement – John Whiting and Brendan Behan, are prematurely dead: Whiting, the movement's principal forerunner, was forty-eight when he died and had had four plays staged in London; Behan was forty-one and had written only two full-length stage plays. Both evidently, whatever one may think of their completed work, had a lot to give the theatre and both seemed to have found a niche and an audience. How far either could have adapted to and maintained his success is anyone's guess; Behan, indeed, fairly evidently could not, hence at least in part his tragedy.

Next, we have those who for some reason seem to have stopped writing, or have turned their literary energies in other directions. The most prominent of these is Shelagh Delaney, who as well as writing a couple of film scripts, has turned recently to prose fiction instead of drama, a development which seemed to be prefigured in her second play, *The Lion in Love,* which was in some places so under-dramatized that it cried out for an enfolding narrative to bring out what the dialogue left scarcely hinted at. N. F. Simpson also seemed for some time to be one of the lost, and when, after several years silence, he re-emerged with *The Cresta Run* and several short television comedy scripts, the routine seemed tiresomely familiar. Clive Exton, though he has written two or three characteristic television plays in the last few years, has chosen to work more on film script writing (often uncredited) and adaptation, and has made little real attempt to break into the theatre. Arnold Wesker's involvement with Centre 42 has kept him away from the theatre too much since 1962, and the two stage plays by him produced since then have been disappointing.

But most of the new dramatists are still in some real sense with us, in the theatre now. They have arrived, they have made their mark, and they have settled in, more or less. The question now, of course, is how far they have managed to settle down, to become reasonably permanent fixtures of our everyday theatrical scene rather than exotics cultivated in the hot-house atmosphere of small, relatively non-commercial theatres and unable to stand the cruel gales of West End exposure. Well, first of all, we have to remind ourselves that youth alone does not make a new dramatist; as I have just pointed out, we do not think of such writers as Sandy Wilson, or Julian Slade, or John Chapman, or Anthony Newley and Leslie Bricusse, as 'new dramatists', and yet they belong to the same generations as the rest; nor for that matter, despite his connections at one time with Theatre Workshop, would we count in Lionel Bart. The reason is simple: they have all achieved the sort of general audience acceptance which marks them instantly as part of the normal commercial world of the theatre. The others have also had their commercial successes, of course – think of *The Hostage, A Taste of Honey, The Caretaker, Chips With Everything, One Way Pendulum, Luther* – and yet somehow one senses a feeling abroad in the theatre that these are all, somehow, freak successes; that you couldn't rely on other plays for the same dramatists doing as well, or even doing well at all.

This is not true of everyone, of course. Peter Shaffer and John Mortimer, having always been formally pretty traditional dramatists, have been accepted fairly readily into the fold, while Robert Bolt's experimental flurries have always been so discreet that he did not seem out of place with H.M. Tennent. John Osborne, though he has stayed faithful to the Royal

Court, has had a number of successful West End transfers, and in 1968 had two plays running at adjacent West End theatres, with a third, the revival of *Look Back in Anger*, already on the horizon. But for the rest their acclimatization to the West End, or one hopes rather the West End's acclimatization to them, is likely to be a slow business, dependent on a gradual establishment of mutual confidence. Presumably it is likely to be easier in the case of a writer like Alun Owen, whose dramatic gift of the gab and mastery of an easy-to-take, slightly heightened naturalistic style should cause no one too much trouble: his musical with Lionel Bart, *Maggie May*, showed the way, and in *A Little Winter* he demonstrated that he can write an excellent West End play, even if in that case the West End never had a chance to see it.

And if the plays of Bill Naughton can achieve some West End success, there seems to be no reason why the work of other dramatists who in their various ways hit something of the same level, like Bernard Kops (even though in his more recent radio plays he has been getting increasingly experimental) and David Turner, should not also find an audience. Henry Livings goes one better: apart from the admittedly difficult and obscure *Kelly's Eye* he seems to have been made to be a popular dramatist first and a critic's darling only in retrospect: his misfortune has been to be put in the position of having to reverse the process, and thereby finding himself puzzling audiences his plays are not primarily meant for and never getting to those they are. Perhaps the best thing one could wish him is a quick move from the Aldwych to the Whitehall, where he would be able to laugh at the critics until they finally came round to laughing at him.

This still leaves us, though, with the 'difficult' dramatists, notably Harold Pinter, John Arden and Ann Jellicoe. Ann Jellicoe, being a sparing and fastidious writer, might never be likely to make a regular West End box-office champion, but it is curious that no imaginative manager came along to take over *The Knack* and sell it in the right way; once it got established in a theatre like the Duchess or, if you will pardon the historical note, the Ambassadors, it might have run for a year. Still, it is encouraging to note that her latest play has been given its start in the West End rather than on the fringe. Pinter remains in a very special position. Again writing relatively little (though more than Ann Jellicoe), he can pick and choose where and how his plays will be presented – with *The Homecoming*, for example, which could easily have found a home in the commercial West End theatre, he deliberately chose to give it to the Royal Shakespeare Company instead. His film scripts, notably for Joseph Losey's films *The Servant* and *Accident*, have reinforced his position commercially, in that they have combined Pinter's characteristic, highly personal qualities with popular success for a mass public. And in them, as well as in his plays for stage and television, he has continued to explore and extend his own private world with the unswerving logic and unquestioning dedication that make him still the most exciting, coherent and at the same time unpredictable figure in the British theatre today. And then Arden . . . Well, Arden is a puzzlement; as spectacularly, prodigally gifted as any of our new generation, he has somehow not yet, in spite of his reputation in enlightened quarters, managed quite to hit the taste of the public. Either they are puzzled because the plot is tenuous and obscure, or, as in *The Workhouse Donkey*, because there is too much plot too directly presented. He has as yet offered no reason why a West End management should trust him except sheer talent, and that, unless the talent is running along reasonably familiar channels, is not quite enough for them.

A recent American book on *avant-garde* drama launches a rather bitter attack on Arden (of all people!) as the overpraised, under-talented darling of a precious clique, and goes on to remark the 'once one of [the new English dramatists] has had a first play produced in one of the 'clique' theatres, such as the Royal Court, the Belgrade Theatre, Coventry, or the Theatre Royal, Stratford, the production of his future work is virtually assured.' That is certainly overstating matters, but even if to some extent it is true, is it enough if the dramatists concerned are fated by their beginnings never really to break out of the original charmed circle? That is the problem which

most of our by now not-quite-so-new dramatists are having to
face at the moment, and on their success in solving it – if the
solving of it is primarily up to them – is likely to depend the
fate of vital British theatre in the next few years.

Index